# Advanced Sciences and Technologies for Security Applications

Indexed by SCOPUS

The series Advanced Sciences and Technologies for Security Applications comprises interdisciplinary research covering the theory, foundations and domain-specific topics pertaining to security. Publications within the series are peer-reviewed monographs and edited works in the areas of:

- biological and chemical threat recognition and detection (e.g., biosensors, aerosols, forensics)
- crisis and disaster management
- terrorism
- cyber security and secure information systems (e.g., encryption, optical and photonic systems)
- traditional and non-traditional security
- energy, food and resource security
- economic security and securitization (including associated infrastructures)
- transnational crime
- human security and health security
- social, political and psychological aspects of security
- recognition and identification (e.g., optical imaging, biometrics, authentication and verification)
- smart surveillance systems
- applications of theoretical frameworks and methodologies (e.g., grounded theory, complexity, network sciences, modelling and simulation)

Together, the high-quality contributions to this series provide a cross-disciplinary overview of forefront research endeavours aiming to make the world a safer place.

The editors encourage prospective authors to correspond with them in advance of submitting a manuscript. Submission of manuscripts should be made to the Editor-in-Chief or one of the Editors.

More information about this series at http://www.springer.com/series/5540

Hamid Jahankhani · Babak Akhgar ·
Peter Cochrane · Mohammad Dastbaz
Editors

# Policing in the Era of AI and Smart Societies

Springer

*Editors*
Hamid Jahankhani
International Journal of Electronic Security and Digital Forensics, London Campus
Northumbria University
London, UK

Peter Cochrane
Cochrane Associates Limited
University of Suffolk
Ipswich, Suffolk, UK

Babak Akhgar
Centre of Excellence in Terrorism, Resilience, Intelligence and Organised Crime Research
Sheffield Hallam University, CENTRIC
Sheffield, South Yorkshire, UK

Mohammad Dastbaz
Waterfront Building
University of Suffolk
Ipswich, Suffolk, UK

ISSN 1613-5113 ISSN 2363-9466 (electronic)
Advanced Sciences and Technologies for Security Applications
ISBN 978-3-030-50612-4 ISBN 978-3-030-50613-1 (eBook)
https://doi.org/10.1007/978-3-030-50613-1



This Springer imprint is published by the registered company Springer Nature Switzerland AG
The registered company address is: Gewerbestrasse 11, 6330 Cham, Switzerland

# Foreword

## Policing in the Era of AI and Smart Societies

By the beginning of 2020 the importance of AI, the Internet of Things and the cyber-spatial context of our lives already was in all our minds. Then events of the Spring of 2020 raised our consciousness to a critical level. Once the Covid-19 lockdown started, and was rolled out in almost every country, perforce we all became knowing inhabitants of the virtual world. Some, working hard from our homes, entered the world of virtual meetings several times daily, across a range of business activities, 'dinner parties', maintaining proximity to family, and entertainment. In much of this we threw caution to the winds, necessarily ignoring security to affect communicative facility. This book is timely, providing focus to our state of knowledge, and to our voluntary (if often unconsidered) sacrifice of confidentiality.

Lawyers constantly are challenged with jurisdictional problems in criminal and civil fraud cases, especially those in which the important evidence is in electronic form. The sharing of such evidence between physical jurisdictions is key to cases being investigated fully or at all, presented ethically, and justice with integrity being done. This will require growing international assent to the reality that the World is becoming a single jurisdiction for these purposes. As the second chapter of the books demonstrates, the policing of space is unable to be controlled by any single jurisdiction or any national interpretation of the Rule of Law. The challenges to finding and assembling evidence in such cases are illustrated by the statistical certainty that by 2025 there will be over 20 billion devices connected to the Internet, each a potential repository for evidence, an invisible needle in a cosmic haystack.

Policing must evolve as quickly as AI. The book argues for the urgent need to develop and adopt proactive and preventive techniques to identify and curb cyber and cyber-enabled crimes. This will need to be done on a fully international basis, if necessary labelling pariah states which choose not to cooperate.

An interesting case is made for the use of blockchain to ensure lawfulness, transparency and governance of organ supply. It is well known that unethical organ supply occurs, sometimes taking cruel advantage of deprived communities. Sophisticated technology would make it much easier to ensure that ethical principles self-evidently applicable to organ transplantation would be followed. This subject is complicated by challenges posed by data protection compliance, but the book rises to meet such challenges in an informed and creative way.

Chapter "Algorithms Can Predict Domestic Abuse, But Should We Let Them?" tackles the issue of the use of algorithms as a predictor of domestic abuse, physical and sexual. Is this a legitimate policing tool? Can we justify the use of the Internet of Things in this context? In many a 'smart home' there are devices which could provide key evidence? How do we reconcile the use of investigatory powers through devices, against the imperative of proportionate privacy for all citizens?

The following chapter addresses control of 'sexting', balancing risk against potentially heavy-handed use of the criminal law against what in some cases might be seen as non-abusive image sharing by young people with equivalent decision-making capacity. The public interest issues encountered in these chapters will test ethicists and computer scientists in the future.

Also much discussed today, and covered fully in the book, are issues of predictive policing through the use of AI. Described as the potential 'ace card' that outstrips and eclipses human minds, AI is capable of digesting vast quantities of data and recognising patterns that escape mere humans. This raises important questions about the structure, powers and accountability of information gatherers, of the technology they use and the consequent changes in society.

All generations have faced quantum challenges of this kind. For example, generations of scepticism delayed the large-scale construction of drains in London until, after the Great Stink of 1858, Parliament realised the urgency of the problem and resolved to create a modern sewerage system. That was a merely local challenge. The legal, political and philosophical matters raised in this excellent book face the whole World, and much is to be learned from the chapters that follow.

April 2020

Lord Alex Carlile
Berriew CBE QC
London, UK

# Contents

# Rethinking Criminal Justice in Cyberspace: The EU E-evidence Framework as a New Model of Cross-Border Cooperation in Criminal Matters

**Oriola Sallavaci**

**Abstract** This chapter analyses the recently proposed EU legal framework on cross-border access to e-evidence for criminal justice purposes. The analysis is placed within the broader context of transformations that the use of technology brings not only on the socio-economic aspects of life but also the increasing challenges posed for the criminal justice in dealing with new forms of crime and globalisation of evidence. This study aims to contribute to the ongoing debate through an analysis of the specific provisions of the E-evidence framework, recommending amendments that would help achieve a balanced approach between efficient criminal investigations and the protection of fundamental rights. At the same time this study addresses what has not received sufficient attention: the challenges posed to traditional principles of cross-border cooperation in the EU and beyond, mutual recognition and mutual trust, the concept of jurisdiction and territoriality, dual criminality, the concept of privacy in the digital age, personal data protection and procedural rights of suspects in criminal proceedings. Through the lens of E-evidence this chapter aims to reflect on these challenges and offer new perspectives.

**Keywords** Electronic evidence · Cross border access · Data protection · Criminal proceedings · European production order · European preservation order · CLOUD Act

## List of Abbreviations

| | |
|---|---|
| AFSJ | Area of Freedom, Security and Justice |
| Art. | Article/Articles |
| CCC | Convention on Cybercrime |
| CFR | Charter of Fundamental Rights of the European Union |
| CJEU | Court of Justice of the European Union |

O. Sallavaci (✉)
University of Essex, Colchester, UK
e-mail: O.Sallavaci@essex.ac.uk



H. Jahankhani et al. (eds.), *Policing in the Era of AI and Smart Societies*, Advanced Sciences and Technologies for Security Applications,
https://doi.org/10.1007/978-3-030-50613-1_1

| | |
|---|---|
| GDPR | General Data Protection Regulation |
| ECHR | European Convention on Human Rights |
| EIO | European Investigation Order |
| EPOC | European Production Order (Certificate) |
| EPOC-PR | European Preservation Order (Certificate) |
| EU | European Union |
| JHA | Justice and Home Affairs |
| LEA/LEAs | Law Enforcement Authority/Authorities |
| MLA | Mutual Legal Assistance |
| MS/MSs | Member State/Member States |
| TEU | Treaty on the European Union |
| TFEU | Treaty on the Functioning of the European Union |
| US | United States of America |

## 1 Introduction: The Changing Nature of Crime and Evidence in Cyberspace

The remarkable developments in computing and information technology in the past decades have transformed every aspect of life. Cyberspace has become an essential element of modern life, crucial to our economies and societies. The growing use of social media, webmail, messaging services and applications to obtain information, communicate, work and socialise result in ever rising data flows across borders. Alongside undeniable benefits, this new reality provides the environment for misuse and abuse, facilitating new forms of criminal activities which did not exist few decades ago. Examples include the spread of viruses and other malicious software, hacking, distributed denial of service (DDoS) attacks and ransomware.[1] At the same time, the use of information and communication technologies (hereafter ICT) has transformed the very nature of some 'traditional' types of crime in terms of the way they are committed, their scale and reach affecting many aspects of life from financial transactions and commercial activities to public security—facilitating disorder, harassment, threatening behaviour and sexual offending among others.[2]

The use of technology has transformed many crimes into crime without borders. The borderless nature of cyberspace, the sophistication of the technologies and offenders' *modi operandi* pose specific and novel challenges for crime investigation and prosecution which in practice may lead to impunity. Cybercrime, in whatever

[1]These are referred to as cyber dependant crimes, also known as computer related crimes. These are offences that can only be committed by using a computer, computer networks, or other forms of information and communications technology (ICT). See Home Office (2013) *Cybercrime: A review of the evidence* Research Report 75, ISBN 978 1 78246 245 3, p. 4 available at https://www.gov.uk/government/publications/cyber-crime-a-review-of-the-evidence.

[2]Cyber-enabled crimes are traditional crimes facilitated by the use of ICT. Unlike cyber-dependent crimes, they can still be committed without the use of ICT. Ibid.

form that it takes, can instantaneously be committed across national borders. Victims of crime can be situated miles away from the offender. Offenders can easily manipulate and hide their location as well as their identity. From a practical perspective, even where authorities manage to identify a suspect, it is challenging to attribute the use of an electronic device to that particular individual i.e. to identify the person behind a screen or keyboard or establish a connection between a computing device and a particular individual.

For all Cybercrime, data remains the key element, both from a crime perspective and from an investigative perspective. Whereas criminals require and target data for most of their crimes, law enforcement agencies (hereafter LEA(s)) need access to relevant data for their investigations. Electronic information (hereafter e-information) can be used for intelligence purposes and crime prevention, to combat ongoing crime by disrupting online criminal activities (e.g. by bringing down websites) and for evidential purposes in criminal proceedings. Electronic evidence (hereafter e-evidence) is paramount for all types of crime that can leave a digital trace, even if that is only some form of electronic communication. These could include serious crimes such as terrorism, child sexual abuse, human trafficking and the like, as well as lower impact, high volume crimes such as spread of malicious software (such as ransomware, spyware etc.).

An increasing number of criminal investigations rely on e-evidence and this goes beyond cyber dependent and cyber enabled crimes. From an evidential point of view, today almost every crime could have an e-evidence element as often offenders use technology, such as personal computers, notepads, camera phones, where they can leave traces of their criminal activity, communications or other information that can be used to determine their whereabouts, plans or connection to a particular criminal activity. E-evidence could include different types of data such as messages exchanged via various social-media applications, information on the holder of email accounts or the content of those emails, information on the timing of online calls via Skype, Viber, WhatsApp etc. These types of data have different levels of relevance in the context of criminal proceedings: subscriber data could be useful in obtaining the identity of a suspect; access logs could be useful in connecting a suspect user to a particular action; metadata and content data can be most relevant as probatory material.[3]

There are several closely linked characteristics of e-evidence that pose particular challenges for crime investigation. First, e-evidence is volatile and can be transmitted, altered or deleted easily. For this reason, effective and timely access by public authorities is vital to enable the investigation and prosecution of crime. External factors such as specific legal requirements contribute to the volatility of e-evidence, increasing challenges for investigations and prosecutions. Examples are (a) the lack of mandatory data retention rules[4] and (b) data minimisation requirements that force service

[3] See below the discussion of different type of data. See European Commission (2018) "Commission Staff Working Impact Assessment" p. 13. Available at https://eur-lex.europa.eu/legal-content/EN/TXT/?qid=1524129550845&uri=SWD:2018:118:FIN.

[4] For instance there are no mandatory data retention rules in the US (which is of importance given that the key SPs operating in the EU are US based) nor in the EU, since The Data Retention Directive

providers (hereafter SPs) to delete data more quickly.[5] Two closely linked problems to volatility of e-evidence, posing challenges for LEAs, concern the availability and location of electronic data. Often data are available only to private infrastructures which may not be located in the same country as the investigating authorities and are therefore subject to different jurisdictions imposing different rights and obligations. Even where the information is publicly available, it might move into systems that require special credentials to access. As a result LEAs require the cooperation of these private infrastructures or other LEAs situated in different countries from where the investigation is taking place.[6]

In addition to the above, determining the location of data may be difficult. Data can be split between different countries and can be copied in multiple countries. It can be moved quickly and effortlessly. Data stored in the cloud are mirrored for security and availability reasons, and can therefore be found in multiple locations within a country or in several separate countries. Data are thus located in different jurisdictions at the same time. Due to this and to cached versions of data, not even the SPs might know where the sought-after data are exactly located. The challenge posed by data moving swiftly across jurisdictions is a consequence of internet governance and the business models of the SPs that have evolved over the past decades across the world.[7]

This state of affairs is referred to as "globalisation of criminal evidence".[8] Crime today often has a cyber component and with it an increasingly prominent cross border dimension. Even crimes that may appear not to have a cross border dimension can actually have one because of e-evidence. In 2018 the European Commission found that in the EU "more than half of all investigations involve a cross-border request to access [electronic] evidence."[9] Yet alarmingly "almost two thirds of crimes involving

2006/24/EC was declared invalid by CJEU in case C-293/12 *Digital Rights Ireland Ltd v Minister of Communications* ECLI:EU:C:2014:238.

[5]Data minimisation is enshrined in the General Data Protection Regulation (GDPR): The processing of personal data must be adequate, relevant and limited to what is necessary—Article 5(1)(c). Data minimisation requirements force service providers to delete data more quickly, increasing the number of cases where data will no longer be available when LEA's request reaches the service provider.

[6]This problem is well recognised. See for instance Eurojust and Europol (2019) *Common challenges in combating Cybercrime* Joint Report, available at https://www.europol.europa.eu/publications-documents/common-challenges-in-combating-cybercrime See also European Commission (2018) "Commission Staff Working Impact Assessment" p. 19.

[7]European Commission (2018) "Commission Staff Working Impact Assessment" p. 13.

[8]Ibid p. 35.

[9]Ibid p. 14 See also data, albeit partial, on crimes that cannot be effectively investigated or prosecuted. The same report also found that "Less than half of all the requests to service providers are fulfilled" p. 15 According to the Commission a request could remain unfulfilled for several reasons, including that the request is sent to a provider who does not hold the data, it is excessively broad or unclear, it fails to specify an (existing) account or sought information, it does not have a valid legal basis or the data sought no longer exists—p. 17.

cross-border access to e-evidence cannot be effectively investigated or prosecuted".[10] The ability of LEAs to access the data needed to conduct criminal investigations is an increasing challenge.[11] This is partly due to technological developments, such as the enhanced use of encryption and other techniques which criminals abuse to obfuscate their tracks, as well as cryptocurrencies to hide their illicit earnings. However, the lack of accessibility to relevant data also comes due to legislative barriers or shortcomings that must be overcome to enhance cross-border access to electronic evidence and the effectiveness of public-private cooperation through facilitated information exchange. These barriers are often related to the principle of territoriality, which sets limits to the scope of jurisdiction and to the investigative powers which law enforcement and judiciary have at their disposal under their national law. As a result, the tools in the hands of LEAs do not provide what is necessary to deal with data flows, for which questions of territoriality are of no relevance as Cybercrime does not recognise borders and e-evidence has become increasingly global.

Improving access to electronic information for law enforcement and intelligence purposes is therefore a pressing issue concerning almost every type of crime. Countries around the world are responding with new legal frameworks and instruments, changes to law enforcement procedures and governance of the internet. The approaches currently taken in an international level span from a government controlled internet characterised by data nationalism and localisation often justified in the name of security, usually resulting in a censored or unfree cyberspace on the one extreme,[12] to a global internet driven by a multi-stakeholder governance model, characterised by free flow of data, which emphases transnational cooperation for the purposes of data access, on the other end of the spectrum.[13] A majority of countries referred to as 'digital deciders' stand somewhere in between and could gravitate toward either end of the spectrum whilst also supporting a third approach that manifests elements of the two extremes.[14] While the global cyber reality is constantly changing and shifting between these two poles, the legislative changes adopted by many countries have consequential effects on the efficiency of criminal investigations and prosecutions as well as on fundamental rights of individuals, including the right to privacy and data protection.

---

[10]Ibid at p. 17 This is partly due to lack of timely access i.e. leads disappear or lack of access i.e. access denied.

[11]See Eurojust and Europol (2019) *Common challenges in combating Cybercrime* Joint Report.

[12]Data nationalism refers to measures taken by some countries to require that data be stored, processed, or handled within their borders in an attempt (or rather justification) to protect privacy and security and to promote economic growth. Russia, China, India and other countries, have enacted laws that require such *data localization*. https://www.itic.org/public-policy/SnapshotofDataLocalizationMeasures7-29-2016.pdf.

[13]Robert Morgus, Jocelyn Woolbright, & Justin Sherman The Digital Deciders: How a group of often overlooked countries could hold the keys to the future of the global internet, October 2018, available at https://www.newamerica.org/cybersecurity-initiative/reports/digital-deciders/.

[14]Ibid. Every jurisdiction has sought to exercise certain degree of control from the early days of the internet, see e.g. Lessig and Resnick [38] 'Zoning speech on the internet: a legal and technical model' *Michigan Law Review*, Vol. 98, No. 2 (Nov., 1999), pp. 395–431.

This study focuses on an important and recent legislative initiative: the EU legal framework on cross-border access to e-evidence for criminal justice purposes. The important legislative package referred to as "E-evidence", aimed at facilitating the access to e-evidence by European LEAs, contains two texts: a draft Regulation[15] providing two new mechanisms for LEA's cross border access to e-evidence (European Production Order (EPOC) and European Preservation Order (EPOC-PR)) and a draft Directive[16] which requires every online service provider (hereafter SP) "established" in or that has "substantial connection" to at least one EU Member State (hereafter MS) to appoint a legal representative in the territory of an EU MS of choice as an addressee for the execution of the above Orders. While both the texts will be discussed, the following analysis shall be based heavily on the draft Regulation.

The proposed legal framework was introduced by the EU Commission in April 2018. On 7 December 2018 the Council adopted its own draft[17] (known as Council's "general approach") which was forwarded to the EU Parliament. The EU Parliament is yet to adopt its position[18] before the 'trilogue' procedures amid the EU Parliament, the Council and the Commission can start in order to agree to a common text.[19] Given that the E-evidence framework is currently being negotiated, the following analysis and findings aim to contribute to achieving the best version of the forthcoming instruments. This study is based on the legal provisions currently contained in the Commission's proposal, the Council's draft and the recently published draft report of the LIBE's rapporteur Birgit Sippel, to be presented to the EU Parliament in 2020,[20] which at the time of writing, is yet to receive academic attention.

---

[15]European Commission "Proposal for a Regulation of the European Parliament and of the Council on European Production and Preservation Orders for electronic evidence in criminal matters" Strasbourg, 17.4.2018 COM (2018) 225 final, 2018/0108(COD) available at https://ec.europa.eu/info/policies/justice-and-fundamental-rights/criminal-justice/e-evidence-cross-border-access-electronic-evidence_en.

[16]European Commission "Proposal for a directive of the European Parliament and of the Council laying down harmonised rules on the appointment of legal representatives for the purpose of gathering evidence in criminal proceedings" Strasbourg, 17.4.2018, COM(2018) 226 final, 2018/0107(COD) available at https://ec.europa.eu/info/policies/justice-and-fundamental-rights/criminal-justice/e-evidence-cross-border-access-electronic-evidence_en.

[17]Council of the EU "Regulation of the European Parliament and of the Council on European production and preservation orders for electronic evidence in criminal matters—general approach" (10206/19) Brussels, 11 June 2019 available at https://data.consilium.europa.eu/doc/document/ST-10206-2019-INIT/en/pdf.

[18]During 2018–2019 EU Parliament has been advancing very slowly. E-evidence has been assigned to the LIBE Committee. Partly due to the European 2019 elections, LIBE is still to adopt its report, which would then be submitted to the Plenary of the Parliament for adoption.

[19]It is expected that the framework will be approved by 2020 and will come into force in 2022.

[20]European Parliament "DRAFT REPORT on the proposal for a Regulation of the European Parliament and of the Council on European Production and Preservation Orders for electronic evidence in criminal matters (COM(2018)0225—C8-0155/2018—2018/0108(COD))" Committee on Civil Liberties, Justice and Home Affairs, November 2019, Rapporteur: Birgit Sippel Available at https://www.europarl.europa.eu/doceo/document/LIBE-PR-642987_EN.pdf.

The following analysis of the E-evidence framework is placed within the broader context of transformations and challenges posed by the use of technology for the criminal justice in dealing with cross border crime and globalisation of evidence. This study aims to contribute to the current debate in what is mainly practice/practitioner oriented literature[21] through an analysis of specific provisions of the framework itself and by proposing improvements to the draft instruments through a set of recommendations. At the same time, this study addresses what has not received sufficient attention in the academic literature: the challenges E-evidence poses for, and the perspectives it opens up in relation to traditional principles of cross-border cooperation in the EU and beyond such as mutual recognition and mutual trust, the concept of jurisdiction and territoriality, personal data protection and the concept of privacy in the digital age as well as dual criminality, equality of arms and procedural rights of the suspects. Building on existing literature[22] it demonstrates how these principles are being challenged and developed in the context of E-evidence.

The EU E-evidence framework is of particular importance in shaping the future of similar instruments and the terms of cooperation between countries all over the world. This study explores the framework's position with regard to specific aspects of the US CLOUD Act 2018[23] which in itself marks a major change in how cross-border access to e-evidence may develop in the rest of the world. At the time of writing, the US has just negotiated the first CLOUD Act executive agreement with

---

[21] See European Data Protection Board (EDPB) (2018) "Opinion 23/2018 on Commission proposals on European Production and Preservation Orders for electronic evidence in criminal matters" available at https://edpb.europa.eu/sites/edpb/files/files/file1/eevidence_opinion_final_en.pdf; European Data Protection Supervisor (EDPS) (2019) "EDPS Opinion on Proposals regarding European Production and Preservation Orders for electronic evidence in criminal matters" Opinion 7/2019, November 2019 available at https://edps.europa.eu/sites/edp/files/publication/opinion_on_e_evidence_proposals_en.pdf; European Criminal Bar Association ECBA (2019) ECBA Opinion on the European Commission's Proposals, available at http://www.ecba.org/extdocserv/20190213-ECBAonEPOsEPROs_Final.pdf; Statement of Article 29 Working Party (2017) "Data protection and privacy aspects of cross-border access to electronic evidence" Brussels 29 November 2017 available at https://www.hldataprotection.com/files/2018/02/20171129-Art.-29-WP-e-Evidence_Statement.pdf; The Council of Bars and Law Societies of Europe (CCBE) (2019) CCBE recommendations on the establishment of international rules for cross-border access to electronic evidence 28/02/2019; The Council of Bars and Law Societies of Europe (CCBE) (2018) CCBE position on the Commission proposal for a Regulation on European Production and Preservation Orders for electronic evidence in criminal matters 19/10/2018; Theodore Christakis (2019) "E-evidence in a Nutshell: Developments in 2018, Relations with the Cloud Act and the Bumpy Road Ahead" Cross-border Data Forum available at https://www.crossborderdataforum.org/e-evidence-in-a-nutshell-developments-in-2018-relations-with-the-cloud-act-and-the-bumpy-road-ahead/.

[22] See inter alia V. Mitsilegas (2016) EU Criminal Law after Lisbon: Rights, Trust and the Transformation of Justice in Europe, Oxford/Portland: Hart Publishing; S. Peers (2016) EU Justice and Home Affairs Law, Vol II. Oxford University Press; Bermann PS (2018) "Legal Jurisdiction and the Deterritorialization of Data" Vanderbilt Law Review, Vol. 71: 11; J. Daskal (2015) "The Un-Territoriality of Data" Yale Law Journal, Vol. 125 (2), 326; C. Janssens (2013) The principle of Mutual Recognition in EU Law, Oxford University Press;.

[23] Clarifying Lawful Overseas Use of Data Act—CLOUD Act provides the legal basis for the United States government to conclude agreements with foreign governments on access to data held by United States service providers and vice-versa.

the United Kingdom[24] which is to be followed by another one with Canada.[25] The EU E-evidence framework shall influence and at the same time needs to conform to a number of new agreements currently being negotiated. In 2019 the EU Commission received negotiating mandate to achieve an agreement between the EU and US[26] as well as to shape the second amending protocol of the Cybercrime Convention (hereafter CCC).[27] Both these instruments need be negotiated from the perspective of the forthcoming provisions of the E-evidence framework therefore it is important that the latter offers provisions that increase the efficiency of investigations and prosecutions by surpassing challenges in cross border cooperation, while maintaining safeguards to fundamental rights of individuals.[28] This study aims to contribute in achieving this objective especially given that, in the global arena, E-evidence framework represents the model to be followed by countries that have embraced or are willing to adopt a free internet governance model as noted above. This is particularly important in the context of recent counter developments taking place in the United Nations General Assembly which seem to favour a state control over the internet and data nationalism model.[29]

---

[24]Available at https://www.gov.uk/government/publications/ukusa-agreement-on-access-to-electronic-data-for-the-purpose-of-countering-serious-crime-cs-usa-no62019?utm_source=b4d391f0-3d36-4077-8793-d5b2b06944c1&utm_medium=email&utm_campaign=govuk-notifications&utm_content=immediate.

[25]The Canadian Association of Chiefs of Police has passed a resolution calling for negotiation of an executive agreement with the U.S. under the CLOUD Act. See https://www.cacp.ca/resolution.html?asst_id=1694.

[26]Council of the EU "Decision authorising the opening of negotiations with a view to concluding an agreement between the European Union and the United States of America on cross-border access to electronic evidence for judicial cooperation in criminal matters" (9114/19) Brussels, 21 May 2019, available at https://data.consilium.europa.eu/doc/document/ST-9114-2019-INIT/en/pdf.

[27]Council of the EU "Decision authorising the European Commission to participate, on behalf of the European Union, in negotiations on a Second Additional Protocol to the Council of Europe Convention on Cybercrime" (CETS No. 185) Brussels, 21 May 2019 available at https://data.consilium.europa.eu/doc/document/ST-9116-2019-INIT/en/pdf In June 2017, the 61 parties to the Budapest Convention on Cybercrime agreed to launch the preparation of an additional Second Protocol to the Convention to help law enforcement secure evidence on servicers in foreign, multiple or unknown jurisdictions. This Second Protocol is expected to be agreed by the end of 2020. See Council of Europe (2019) available at https://rm.coe.int/summary-towards-a-protocol-to-the-budapest-convention/1680972d07.

[28]As noted by the Cybercrime Convention Committee (T-CY) "close coordination in the drafting of the Additional Protocol to the Budapest Convention and the preparation of relevant legal instruments by the European Union should be pursued". Ibid.

[29]On 18 November 2019, the Third Committee of the United Nations General Assembly adopted the resolution "Countering the use of information and communications technologies for criminal purposes" favouring a state control over the internet and data nationalism model. The resolution was backed by Russia and sponsored by a coalition of 45 countries including China, Cuba, North Korea, Nicaragua, Syria, Venezuela, and passed 88–58 with 34 abstentions. It is reported that a committee of experts will meet to draft the treaty in August 2020. Ahead of the adoption, a coalition of countries with the United States in the lead encouraged opposition to the resolution with the argument that it would increase state-backed control over the internet. It was also reported that Russia has presented the resolution as an alternative to the Budapest Convention, ratified

While the future remains uncertain, this study posits that the globalization of criminal e-evidence is driving historic change in the rules as to how LEAs can gain access to communications and other electronic information which has to be consistent with privacy and human rights protection standards. Through the lens of the E-evidence framework, this study throws light on the challenges and transformations that lie ahead of relevant aspects of EU criminal law. These challenges and transformations are often perceived as a weakening of the safeguards and threats to traditional methods of cooperation.[30] This study argues that in order to deal adequately with these challenges, new legal instruments such as E-evidence are required to offer the mechanisms necessary to facilitate the investigation and prosecution of crime while at the same time providing safeguards and guarantees that the rights and interests involved will be adequately protected. While these may manifest as competing objectives, in fact they serve a common purpose, for the public interest is equally invested in efficiently combating crime *and* protection of fundamental rights. Tensions that arise in the balancing process need be addressed by imaginative and forward thinking measures. It is not possible to move forward by resisting challenges and change, by hanging on to outdated mechanisms that ought to evolve, or by aiming to achieve something new whilst not changing anything of essence in the process.

This study is presented in two parts. By analysing the status quo, the first part explores the position that the proposed legal framework takes within the existing instruments for cross border access to e-evidence within the EU and beyond. It explores its impact in the development of the concept of territorial jurisdiction, sovereignty and the principle of mutual recognition. The second part takes a closer look at the provisions of the framework and the proposed instruments from a safeguards perspective. The detailed analysis of the Commission's proposal, Council's draft and the LIBE's rapporteur draft report for the EU Parliament informs this study's recommendations for a balanced and principled approach to cross-border e-evidence access and efficient prosecutions, whilst maintaining respect for fundamental rights and affected states' interests.

---

in 2001 by 64 member states but which has never been adopted by Russia. For a critique see the US position available at https://usun.usmission.gov/statement-on-agenda-item-107-countering-the-use-of-information-and-communications-technologies-for-criminal-purposes/.

[30] See for instance The Council of Bars and Law Societies of Europe (CCBE) (2019) CCBE recommendations on the establishment of international rules for cross-border access to electronic evidence 28/02/2019; The Council of Bars and Law Societies of Europe (CCBE) (2018) CCBE position on the Commission proposal for a Regulation on European Production and Preservation Orders for electronic evidence in criminal matters 19/10/2018.

## 2 Part 1: The E-evidence Framework: A New Paradigm of Transnational Cooperation in Criminal Matters

### *2.1 From Mutual Legal Assistance Requests to Extraterritorial Unilateral Orders: An Organic and Necessary Development?*

Transnational cooperation in criminal matters, including cross border access to evidence located outside the jurisdiction of the investigating or prosecuting authority, has traditionally been regulated via international agreements establishing respective terms and conditions for Mutual Legal Assistance (hereafter MLA). MLA entails the formal cooperation between the competent authorities of different countries on a *request* to collect and transfer the evidence from the country where the evidence is located to the requesting state. MLA agreements are a cornerstone of global cooperation on law enforcement and one of the most widely used mechanisms for requesting foreign assistance in domestic criminal investigations and prosecutions.[31] However, MLA agreements have struggled to keep pace with the changing nature of crime and evidence, especially considering the globalization of data. At the same time the number of MLA requests has increased significantly and the matters involved have grown increasingly more complex. MLA requests take too long to process (from 1 to 18 months), there are no fixed deadlines for responding and the mechanism is complex and diverse from country to country.[32]

Figure 1 illustrates the stages and actors involved in the traditional MLA process. On the one hand, the formal procedures and multiple authorities involved act as safeguards for the protection of individual rights and national interests, yet at the same time they contribute to significant delays and the recognized inefficiency surrounding the MLA system which is problematic especially considering the volatility of E-evidence.[33] The admissibility and execution of MLA requests is subject to the receiving country's national legislation which may result in a refusal of the MLA request on various grounds such as the difficulty to establish a probable cause, lack

[31]The MLA treaties are generally broadly worded to allow for cooperation on a wide range of law enforcement issues including locating and extraditing individuals, freezing assets, requesting searches and seizures etc. They are a necessary tool in combating transnational crime such as money laundering and human trafficking and in prosecuting criminals who attempt to evade domestic law enforcement by operating abroad. See for example the European Convention on Mutual Assistance in Criminal Matters For an account see Steve Peers (2016) EU Justice and Home Affairs Law, Vol II. Oxford University Press.

[32]See Council of EU Non Paper (15072/16) available at http://data.consilium.europa.eu/doc/document/ST-15072-2016-INIT/en/pdf.

[33]Ibid para 2.2.1 See also Council of Europe T-CY report (2013) available at https://rm.coe.int/16802e726c.

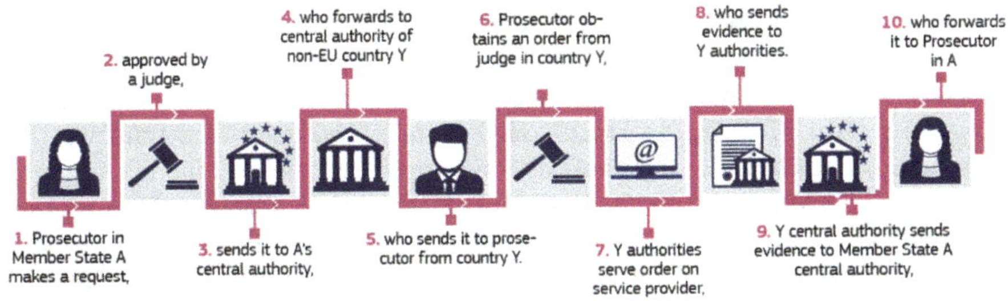


**Fig. 1** MLA process
*Source* European Commission "Security Union: Facilitating Access to Electronic Evidence" Factsheet, April 2018 available at https://ec.europa.eu/info/sites/info/files/placeholder_2.pdf

of dual criminality, data not available due to deletion, incomplete or inadequate requests.[34]

The general framework established by MLA treaties[35] has been further developed by the Council of Europe Convention on Cybercrime (CCC)[36] that entails specific rules for access to e-evidence. These include inter alia: the expedited preservation of stored computer data (Art. 16 CCC); the expedited preservation and partial disclosure of traffic data (Art. 17 CCC); production orders (Art. 18 CCC).[37] In order to address the deficiencies and the ambiguities of the treaty framework, the Cybercrime Committee is working on a second additional protocol to the CCC which shall provide for more effective MLA proceedings, rules allowing for direct cooperation with service providers in other jurisdictions, a clearer framework and stronger safeguards, including data protection requirements for existing mechanisms of cross-border access to computer data. It is expected that the draft protocol shall be finalised by the end of 2020.[38]

[34]Council of EU Non Paper (15072/16) available at http://data.consilium.europa.eu/doc/document/ST-15072-2016-INIT/en/pdf.

[35]Such as European Convention on Mutual Assistance in Criminal Matters of 20 April 1959.

[36]Council of Europe Convention on Cybercrime of 23 November 2001. To date the Cybercrime Convention has been ratified by most EU MSs (except for Ireland and Sweden) and several non-European countries including the US. See the chart of signatures and ratifications https://www.coe.int/en/web/conventions/full-list/-/conventions/treaty/185/signatures?p_auth=w8r6xLCC.

[37]The list of measures covers not only investigative powers (Art. 18 ff. CCC), but also provisional measures aimed at the preservation of electronic evidence (Art. 16, 17 CCC). The powers are subject to conditions and safeguards that seek to balance the requirements of law enforcement with the protection of human rights (Art. 15(1) CCC) and include both procedural (judicial or other independent supervision) and substantial (proportionality, limitation of certain measures to serious offences) requirements in accordance with the principles of the respective national criminal justice system (Art. 15(2) CCC).

[38]Cybercrime Convention Committee (T-CY), Terms of Reference for the Preparation of a Draft 2nd Additional Protocol to the Budapest Convention on Cybercrime, approved by the 17th Plenary of the T-CY on 8 June 2017, T-CY (2017)3, p. 3 available at https://rm.coe.int/summary-towards-a-protocol-to-the-budapest-convention/1680972d07.

Within the EU, the traditional MLA framework for cross border access to evidence has been replaced by the European Investigation Order (EIO)[39] which provides for the gathering and transfer of evidence between MSs, based on the principle of *mutual recognition* (Art. 67(3), 82(1) TFEU). EIO replaces the traditional framework of MLA proceedings based on a *request* by a system of transnational judicial cooperation between the MS that issues the EI *order* (the issuing MS, formerly the requesting state) and the MS that recognises and executes the EIO (the executing MS, formerly the requested state). Similarly to MLA, the EIO mechanism entails a formal cooperation between investigative and judicial authorities of different MSs. A key difference is that the mechanism is triggered by an *order* issued by the requesting MS rather than a *request* as is the case with MLA agreements. The EIO mechanism still requires a decision of another MS to recognise and execute the production order, which is done under the same conditions as if the investigative measure had been ordered by an authority of the executing MS (Art. 9(1) EIO Directive). In this regard, several traditional obstacles to MLA haven been abolished (such as the exceptions for political and fiscal offences). Nevertheless, the obligation to recognise and execute the EIO is still subject to a number of grounds for refusal (Art. 11(1) EIO Directive).

The scope of the EIO covers any investigative measure aimed at gathering evidence, including electronic evidence (Art. 3 EIO Directive). An EIO may only be issued if it is in conformity with the proportionality principle and the investigative measure could have been ordered in a similar domestic case (Art. 6(1) EIO Directive). Furthermore, the EIO must be issued or validated by a judicial authority (judge, court, investigating judge, public prosecutor, Art. 2(c) EIO Directive). EIO has significantly facilitated cross-border cooperation by streamlining the procedure and reducing cooperation obstacles. The EIO Directive provides for deadlines of 120 days (30 days for the executing authority to make a decision on the recognition or execution of the EIO and 90 days to carry out the investigative measure),[40] which is faster than the MLA procedure. This improvement in deadlines is still considered insufficient for accessing e-evidence in criminal investigations, for which the EIO process would still be too long and therefore ineffective.[41]

Due to the limitations and inefficiencies of the judicial cooperation channels, MSs regularly obtain *non-content data* through *direct cooperation with service providers*

[39]Directive 2014/41/EU of the European Parliament and of the Council of 3 April 2014 regarding the European Investigation Order in criminal matters, O.J. L 130/1.

[40]See article 12 of EIO Directive for time limits.

[41]See EU Commission (2018) "Impact Assessment" p. 24. Even though the EIO Directive allows for shorter time-limits where necessary "due to procedural deadlines, the seriousness of the offence or other particularly urgent circumstances" (Art. 12(2)) and article 32(2) provides for a 24 h deadline to decide on provisional measures, arguably these shorter deadlines cannot address the specific needs of e-Evidence: the first is an exception rather than the general rule, requiring reasons for urgency in every case, and the second is specifically aimed at preservation of the data only which in itself is insufficient as timely access need be provided not only preservation of data.

(SPs) on a *voluntary*[42] basis. In direct cooperation situations, the public authorities of country A directly contact the SP established in country B via production orders/requests pursuant to their national rules of criminal procedure, to request information to which the SP has access. According to CCC, a state party may unilaterally and directly access computer data stored abroad if this data is publicly available (Art. 32(a)) or if the data is accessed or received through a computer system in its territory, but located in another state party and if the accessing State Party obtains the lawful and voluntary consent of the person who has the lawful authority to disclose the data through that computer system (Art. 32(b)). The latter provision is considered to provide a legal basis for non-mandatory production requests to foreign SPs established in another State Party.

According to the European Commission, direct cooperation with SPs has become the main channel for authorities to obtain non-content data, as reflected by the significant number of this type of requests.[43] However its efficiency is impeded by a number of factors especially related to existing legal frameworks. Within the EU, the Telecommunications Framework[44] prohibits national telecommunications providers from responding directly to requests from foreign authorities. In addition, there is no legal framework allowing direct cooperation in other communication sectors. Therefore, it is rare to non-existent and mainly used in emergency situations.[45] LEA's requests for direct cooperation to US SPs operating in the EU, are typically redirected to the US, where the SP holds the data or where the management of these requests within the company takes place. Under section 2701(2) of the Electronic Communications and Privacy Act 1986 (ECPA), US based SPs are allowed to cooperate directly with European public authorities with regard to *non-content data*.[46] The cooperation is voluntary from the perspective of ECPA, even though LEAs in some MSs may be using nationally binding orders in making the request. SPs have created their own policies or decide on a case-by-case basis as to whether and how to cooperate. Reported problems in public-private cooperation between LEAs and SPs which have hampered effective investigations and prosecutions concern the lack of standardised procedures across SPs, unreliability of cooperation, unequal treatment of MSs, lack of transparency and of accountability.[47]

A third channel used by LEAs to access e-evidence, relies on mandatory instead of voluntary cooperation. Some states have established an obligation of foreign

---

[42] Ibid p. 26 "Voluntary" means that there is a domestic legal title which cannot be enforced directly in the recipient country. This legal instrument may be an 'order' or 'request' hence, in the absence of a clear legal framework, the distinction between voluntary and mandatory cooperation is not always easy to establish and causes disagreements between LEAs and SPs.

[43] E.g. more than 120 000 in 2016, based on the 2016 transparency reports by Google, Facebook, Microsoft, Twitter and Apple. Ibid. p. 26.

[44] On EU Communication Framework see https://ec.europa.eu/digital-single-market/en/policies/telecom-laws.

[45] See EU Commission (2018) Impact assessment.

[46] ECPA prohibits SPs to give access to content data on a voluntary basis, except in cases of emergency.

[47] EU Commission (2018) Impact assessment pp. 25–28.

SPs to disclose relevant data irrespective of the location where the data is stored or processed, and thereby extended their enforcement jurisdiction to any provider offering electronic communication services within their territory.[48] This may even extend to *direct access* to data in cases where authorities access data without the help of an intermediary, for instance following the seizure of a device or following the lawful acquisition of login information. The national law in a number of MSs empowers authorities, subject to judicial authorisation, to seize and search a device and remotely stored data accessible from it, or to use credentials for an account to access and search data stored under that account.[49] This direct access mechanism has become more relevant as data is regularly stored not on the local device but on servers in different locations, possibly outside of the MS concerned or even outside of the EU. The location of data or of the perpetrator may not be known to LEAs or even SPs and it may be practically impossible to determine (referred to as "loss of knowledge of location").[50] As a result, it can lead to difficulties in establishing whether such searches have a cross-border component and of the enforcing jurisdiction in cyberspace, which requires determining the competence of relevant authorities to undertake an investigative measure across the border.

The proposed E-evidence framework seeks to address the problems and obstacles to criminal investigations associated with the existing mechanisms for cross-border access to e-evidence. During the recent years there have been repeated calls for action by the EU MSs, EU Parliament and Council which have recognised the need to improve the efficiency of mutual legal assistance and judicial cooperation instruments as well as the cooperation between MSs' authorities and SPs based in non-EU countries.[51] The proposed E-evidence framework tackles three key problems identified under the current channels of cooperation that hinder effective investigations and prosecutions: 1. The impact of the current slow procedures under existing judicial cooperation channels to access e-evidence across borders, especially given its volatile nature; 2. Multiple inefficiencies in the public-private cooperation between service

---

[48]Eg. Art. 46 of the Belgian Code of Criminal Procedure; for the application to foreign providers see the judgment of the Hof van Cassatie [Belgian Court of Cassation], Judgment of 1 December 2015, P. 13.2082.N, Yahoo. See European Parliament Policy Department for Citizens' Rights and Constitutional Affairs (2018) Report.

[49]Member States have different approaches to direct access and the data storage location—see section 2.2.3 EU Commission (2018) Impact Statement.

[50]Ibid p. 32.

[51]See Communication from the Commission to the European Parliament, the Council, the European Economic and Social Committee and the Committee of the Regions: The European Agenda on Security, COM (2015) 185 final; Communication on delivering on the European Agenda on Security to fight against terrorism and pave the way towards an effective and genuine Security Union, COM/2016/0230 final; Conclusions of the Council of the European Union on improving criminal justice in cyberspace, ST9579/16; Council of the EU, Final report of the seventh round of mutual evaluations on "The practical implementation and operation of the European policies on prevention and combating Cybercrime", ST 12711 2017 INIT, 2 October 2017. In October 2017 the European Parliament adopted the Resolution of 3 October 2017 on the fight against Cybercrime (2017/2068(INI) calling on the Commission to put forward a European legal framework for electronic evidence.

providers and public authorities; 3. Shortcomings in defining jurisdiction, limitations in how authorities can use investigative measures in cross-border situations and lack of clear frameworks for cooperation with SPs.[52]

The proposed framework creates two new cooperation instruments, namely the European Production Order Certificate (EPOC) and the European Preservation Order Certificate (EPOC-PR) and provides for an obligation of SPs to designate a legal representative in the Union for the receipt of, compliance with and enforcement of the new cooperation instruments. EPOC provides a faster tool for obtaining electronic evidence with deadlines of no longer than 10 days and 6 h for emergency situations. EPOC-PR shall be used to avoid deletion of electronic evidence. Since the electronic data will no longer travel back through multiple steps and authorities but go directly from the legal representative to the authority requesting the data, the procedure will technically be faster and more efficient.[53] In addition, the use of pre-translated and standardized forms is expected to facilitate the cooperation between judicial authorities and SPs, by providing an efficient and fact transmission of e-evidence, standardized exchange of information and cost reduction.

While EIO and the MLA channels will continue to exist, the European E-evidence framework provides a fast track alternative for the specific case of e-evidence. Its material scope is limited to criminal proceedings during the pretrial and the trial phase.[54] Unlike the EIO, the E-evidence framework of cooperation is not to be engaged in proceedings on the imposition of an administrative fine.[55] Ultimately the MSs' authorities decide on whether to cooperate under MLA, EIO or under the E-evidence framework.[56]

Despite expected improvements in the efficiency of investigations and prosecutions by simplifying and speeding up the procedures, the necessity of having *a new instrument* to organize cross border access to electronic evidence has been questioned.[57] The proposed E-evidence framework is considered as adding another layer to the already complex tableau of existing, multiple channels for data access and transnational cooperation.[58] While alternative approaches have been considered and could have been taken by the Commission,[59] in this author's opinion, a specific framework dedicated to improving access to e-evidence is more suitable to help achieve that goal than amendments to existing procedures and instruments that are general in scope and do not provide for the specific e-data related challenges. Procedural

---

[52] EU Commission (2018) Impact study; EU Commission "Security Union: Facilitating Access to Electronic Evidence" Factsheet, April 2018 available at https://ec.europa.eu/info/sites/info/files/placeholder_2.pdf.

[53] As it will be discussed below the authorities of the host country will only be involved in cases where there are specific legal concerns or where the Order needs to be enforced.

[54] Article 3(3) draft Regulation.

[55] Article 4(b) EIO Directive.

[56] Article 23 draft Regulation.

[57] See for example EDPB Opinion 23/2018.

[58] Ibid.

[59] In response to this criticism it is worth noting that several alternatives were considered by the Commission in its Impact assessment (2018).

improvements to existing instruments are necessary, but not by themselves sufficient to overcome the difficulties present in the current channels of cooperation.

According to EDPB, an alternative option to e-evidence framework "could have been … the use of preservation orders to freeze the data for as long as a formal request based on a MLAT is issued" which would have allowed "maintaining the safeguards provided in these instruments while ensuring that the personal data sought is not deleted".[60] As discussed further below, while it is important that the E-evidence framework has adequate safeguards, the proposed alternative measure alone would not be a sufficient improvement to the current status quo. Preserving the data alone is not sufficient as LEAs also need speedy access to those data to be able to progress with the investigation. This is particularly important in the context of Cybercrime where e-evidence is in many cases the only significant lead for investigators. Timely access is important, not only in terms of data volatility which *can* in fact be addressed by the execution of preservation orders, but also for the progress of the investigations itself.

Criminal investigations have to procced step by step, identifying first leads and then following further indications provided by those leads. These steps will often necessitate repeated, iterative requests for access to electronic information across different SPs and different jurisdictions. If the first requests are fulfilled slowly, the chances to find any data in response to further requests decrease significantly.[61] Any delays enable ongoing crimes to progress with detrimental effects on the victims of crime and society as well as enabling the perpetrators to hide or change their *modi operandi*. It is therefore important that the final e-evidence framework provides not only for the preservation of data—which in itself should allow sufficient time taking into consideration that criminal investigations are generally time consuming—but also for the fast access of those data by investigative or judicial authorities. This is an aspect that the proposed framework addresses and provides for through faster mechanisms and procedures albeit not ideal ones.[62]

It has been argued that modifications and improvements to the EIO Directive should have been explored instead of introducing some aspects of the E-evidence framework.[63] The key concern for the critics' is that the existing instruments such as EIO are perceived to have more safeguards in place than the proposed E-evidence framework, such as longer deadlines for the executing authorities to assess whether the request for execution is well founded and respects all the conditions for issuing

---

[60] EDPB opinion 23/2018 pp. 5–6.

[61] EU Commission (2018) Impact assessment p. 20.

[62] The standard time limit for the provision of data is 10 days—which could still be long in terms of data volatility and/or the progress of investigation. Furthermore, the proposed framework does not provide for ongoing investigations and live data collection through surveillance—see the discussion further below.

[63] See Art. 37 of the EIO Directive; EDPB 23/2018 Opinion; EU Parliament, Policy Department for Citizens' Rights and Constitutional Affairs (2018) Report.

and transmitting an EIO.[64] It is important to note here that EIO is a general instrument that is used for various forms of evidence including searches, interception of telecommunications, the gathering of witnesses and experts testimony. It is difficult to reconcile in a single instrument all the specific requirements for different types of evidence and certainly, e-evidence presents specific characteristics that require to be dealt with by specific rules and time lines. Given the general nature of the EIO instrument, even if shorter deadlines were to be introduced, these may not be adequate for other types of evidence while still being too long to adequately deal with the requests for e-evidence considering the volatility of data, data minimization requirements and investigative needs. The instruments proposed by the E-evidence framework are fundamentally different from EIO, a difference that is also reflected in procedural details. It is not possible to adequately respond to novel challenges with old mechanisms embedded in lengthy procedures and bureaucratic complexities. As it will be argued further below, the answer is to provide adequate safeguards that protect the rights and interests of all stakeholders, suited to the new type of instruments created by the E-evidence framework, albeit not identical to the ones found in existing mechanisms of transnational collaboration.

## 2.2 A Paradigm Shift: The Extraterritoriality of the E-evidence Framework

The E-evidence model builds upon the existing models of cooperation, yet is fundamentally different. The Commission did not pursue the idea of direct cross-border access to provider data but proposed a new framework for *mandatory cross-border direct cooperation with SPs.* Unlike current MLA/EIO procedures where the judicial authorities in both issuing and executing countries are involved, the proposed e-evidence framework allows the judicial authority of the issuing MS to address directly the legal representative of the SP established in another EU country via mandatory orders to preserve and/or produce e-evidence. The enforcing MS authorities will only get involved where necessary to ensure compliance with an order by the addressee represented in its territory. The element of 'voluntary cooperation' currently present in the *direct cooperation channel* is thus replaced by a 'mandatory cooperation order' with sanctions to be imposed on the SP in case of non-compliance.[65]

There are two major characteristics of the e-evidence framework that require further attention. First, the instruments proposed by the E–evidence framework have an extraterritorial reach. This extraterritorial dimension is in itself twofold and affects the traditional concept of territorial sovereignty and jurisdiction. On the one hand, the proposed cooperation instruments will create a transnationally binding obligation

[64]According to EIO Directive, the executing authority has 30 days to take its decision on the recognition of the request and then should execute the order within 90 days see Art. 12(3) and (4) EIO Directive. See also Art. 6 EIO Directive.

[65]See recital 59 of the draft Regulation.

of its addressee within the EU that fundamentally differs from the existing mechanisms under the current legal framework of international cooperation in the Area of Freedom Security and Justice (AFSJ). On the other hand, the proposed instruments may interfere with the territorial sovereignty of a third country by extending the enforcement jurisdiction of the issuing MS to SPs established in and data located in the third country. Both aspects will be explored further below.

The second major characteristic of the proposed framework is that it applies *regardless of the location of data* including where e-evidence is stored outside the EU. The jurisdiction that must be complied with is that of the issuing country. The distinction between domestic and cross-border access is no longer based upon the place where the data is stored, but upon the MS where the SP is established or represented.[66] Consequently the proposed framework departs from the traditional rule of international cooperation that cross-border access to computer data requires consent of the state where the data is stored.[67] Jurisdiction is no longer linked to the location of data, but to the place where the addressee of the measure provides its services.[68] According to the new approach, the jurisdiction of the EU and its MSs can be established over SPs *offering their services in the Union* and this requirement is met if the SP enables other persons in (at least) one MS to use its services and has a substantial connection to this MS.[69] In this way the proposal avoids the difficulties in establishing the place where the data is actually stored and the "loss of location" problem highlighted above.

This approach is in line with recent developments in the international arena which demonstrate a departure from data location as the determining factor for establishing enforcement jurisdiction. This tendency is clearly reflected in the Cybercrime Convention Committee's guidance note on production orders and the existing laws of a number of MSs providing for cross-border access to computer data.[70] Article 18(1)(a) of the Cybercrime Convention requires each party to the Convention to

---

[66] Article 1(1) draft Regulation.

[67] Article 25 ff. CCC.

[68] Article 2(4) draft Regulation.

[69] Article 3(4) draft Regulation.

[70] See Cybercrime Convention Committee (T-CY), Ad-hoc Sub-group on Jurisdiction and Transborder Access to Data, Transborder access and jurisdiction: What are the options?, Report of the Transborder Group, adopted by the T-CY on 6 December 2012, T-CY (2012), p. 32. According to Belgian law, any provider of electronic communication services active in Belgium must, upon request of the public prosecutor, disclose identification data irrespective of whether or not the data is stored within Belgian territory. The Belgian Court of Cassation held that criminal sanctions for a failure to comply with such a request does not violate international law because the sanction and the request refer to a conduct within Belgian territory and, therefore, do not affect the territorial sovereignty of another state. (Art. 46 bis of the Belgian Code of Criminal Procedure; for the application to foreign providers see the judgment of the Hof van Cassatie [Belgian Court of Cassation], Judgment of 1 December 2015, P. 13.2082.N, Yahoo.). Similarly, the Irish Supreme Court found that an Irish court, if certain conditions were met, had the power to order the production of documents from an Irish company even if the required objects were located on foreign territory. (Supreme Court of Ireland, 25 January 2013, Walsh v. National Irish Bank, Appeal No. 267/2007, [2013] 1 ESC 2, para. 9.3.). Similarly the German legislator has adopted the Network Enforcement Act ("Netzwerkdurchsetzungsgesetz") that establishes a mandatory cooperation regime for service

adopt national laws under which relevant authorities can compel providers in their territory to disclose electronic data in their possession or control. This requirement contains no exception for data that a company controls but chooses to store abroad. A similar approach has been taken by the US in the CLOUD Act.[71] From a data protection perspective, EU data protection law applies regardless of where the data of persons concerned are stored. The applicability of the GDPR depends either on the fact that the data controller or processor is established within the EU, or on whether EU data subjects' data are processed, even when the controller or processor are not established on the territory of the EU (in which case they have to designate a legal representative in the EU).[72] The extended territorial scope of GDPR and the disappearance of location criteria aim at providing a more complete protection to EU data subjects regardless of where the company processing their data is established.

Considering that data is moved between servers in varying locations or—as in cloud computing systems—even scattered over several jurisdictions, reference to the place where the data is actually stored i.e. location of evidence, has become an outdated concept and irrelevant factor in determining enforcement jurisdiction. As some commentators put it, electronic data itself has become an "unterritorial" medium for which the concept of territoriality no longer fits.[73] This is a new development in criminal law. Jonson and Post 'predicted' over two and a half decades ago that "separated from doctrine tied to territorial jurisdictions, new rules will emerge to govern a wide range of new phenomena that have no clear parallel in the non-virtual world".[74] Yet it can be argued that, in the context of criminal justice and LEA's access to e-evidence, the concept of territorial jurisdiction itself has not become irrelevant; it simply is not—and need not—be linked to the location of the requested data. The 'de-territorialisation' or 'globalisation' of electronic-data and criminal evidence does not abolish the concept of territorial jurisdiction as such; it does not allow unlimited and uncontrolled cross-border access to electronic data in cyberspace. Instead, it encourages the development of the concept through replacing (or supplementing) the

---

providers whose services can be accessed from German territory. Network Enforcement Act of 1 September 2017, Bundesgesetzblatt 2017, part I, p. 3352.

[71] The first part of the CLOUD Act mooted the Supreme Court case of United States v. Microsoft Corp., 584 U.S. ___ (2018). Microsoft argued that the U.S. warrant had no legal force because the emails being sought were stored outside the United States, in Ireland. The United States argued that Microsoft could access the data from within the United States and thus the place where the data happened to be stored did not matter. The CLOUD Act resolved the legal issue, providing that the kind of compelled disclosure orders at issue in the Microsoft Ireland case apply "regardless of whether such communication, record, or other information is located within or outside of the United States".

[72] See Art. 3, in particular (2) and Art. 27 GDPR.

[73] See J. Daskal (2015) "The Un-Territoriality of Data", in Yale Law Journal, Vol. 125, p. 326; Bermann (2018) "Legal Jurisdiction and the Deterritorialization of Data", Vanderbilt Law Review, Vol. 71, p. 11.

[74] D. Johnson and D. Post (1996) "Law And Borders—The Rise of Law in Cyberspace" Stanford Law Review Vol. 48, p. 1367.

location of data by other grounds—connecting factors—that can be used to establish enforcement jurisdiction.[75]

E-evidence framework is a clear example of the development of the territorial jurisdiction concept and the evolvement of connecting factors. The E-evidence framework defines jurisdiction as follows: A SP offers services in the Union if it enables natural or legal persons to use its service in one or more MS(s) and has a substantial link to this MS respectively these MS(s).[76] This definition corresponds to the interpretation of Art. 18(1)(b) CCC.[77] Accordingly, a substantial link shall be considered to exist where the SP is established in the Union,[78] has a significant number or users in one or more MSs or targets its activities toward one or more MSs (by local advertising or advertising in a local language, by making an application ("app") available in the relevant national app store, providing customer service in a local language).[79] On the other hand, the provision of services in view of mere compliance with the prohibition to discriminate based on customers' nationality cannot be considered as targeting activities towards one or more MS(s).[80] The scope of the Commission's proposal is limited to data pertaining to services offered in the EU and does not allow for access to provider data related to services offered exclusively outside the EU.[81] In addition, the fact that EPOC and EPOC-PR can only be addressed in the context of criminal investigations implies a territorial link with the EU—either because the crime was committed in the territory of a MS or because the victim or the criminal is a citizen of a MS.

Currently, MSs follow divergent approaches on establishing enforcement jurisdiction for obtaining access to provider data. Connecting factors to establish jurisdiction are based on the location of data, the establishment of service providers, the place where the provider was offering services, the nationality of the person the electronic data pertain to etc. This fragmentation creates legal uncertainty for both the providers and the individuals concerned. According to the Charter of Fundamental Rights (Art. 8 CFR), legal certainty and transparency are essential to ensure that individuals are able to exercise their rights to data protection, to decide on whether to make use of a particular information or communication service and to take the risk of their personal data being accessed by law enforcement authorities. Overall the

[75] EU Parliament, Policy Department for Citizens' Rights and Constitutional Affairs (2018) Report p. 33. As in the proposed E-evidence framework, a territorial link can be based on other connecting factors such as the place where the service provider is established or where its services are offered.

[76] Article 2(4) draft Regulation, Art. 2(3) draft Directive.

[77] According to the Cybercrime Committee's guidance note.

[78] Article 2(4) draft Directive.

[79] Recital (13) draft directive.

[80] Recital (13) draft directive, referring to Regulation (EU) 2018/302 of the European Parliament and of the Council of 28 February 2018 on addressing unjustified geo-blocking and other forms of discrimination based on customers' nationality, place of residence or place of establishment within the internal market, O.J. L 60 I/1.

[81] Article 3(3) draft Regulation.

proposed E-evidence framework establishes criteria that allow for a determination of enforcement jurisdiction in line with basic requirements of legal certainty.[82]

## 2.3 *E-evidence Framework and the Principle of Mutual Recognition*

E-evidence proposes a new model of direct cooperation with SPs which differs from the traditional forms of judicial cooperation under MLA or EIO. The extraterritorial and unilateral dimensions of EPOC and EPOC-PR affect in principle the territorial sovereignty of the states where SPs are established or represented as well as that of any third countries where data may be located. Within the EU, state sovereignty is not an issue in the relations between MSs as far as MSs have conferred their sovereign powers on the EU. Therefore a new cooperation regime established by EU law, does not violate the sovereignty of the MS as long as there is a valid treaty basis for this legislation.[83] Herein lays a controversial matter: the novelty of the E-evidence approach to transnational cooperation challenges the traditional principle of 'mutual recognition'—challenge which is reflected in the debate regarding the very legal basis of the proposed framework.

The draft Regulation refers to Article 82(1) [and (2)] TFEU as the appropriate legal basis for the adoption of the new legislation on cross-border access to e-evidence.[84] Article 82(1) specifies that "*judicial cooperation in criminal matters shall be based on the principle of mutual recognition*". It has been questioned whether this is an adequate legal basis. Traditionally Article 82 TFEU and the principle of mutual recognition relate to cooperation between judicial or equivalent authorities of different MSs, which is considered a specific and crucial feature concerning its scope *ratione personae*.[85] Whereas the proposed measures under the E-evidence framework establish a direct and mandatory cooperation between the issuing MS and the SP established/represented in another MS. According to the CJEU Opinion 1/15 on the EU-Canada PNR agreement, SPs are not to be considered equal to the judicial authorities of a MS. In that case the involvement of non-judicial authorities threw doubt on the legality of Art. 82(1) as the appropriate legal basis for concluding that agreement,

---

[82] EU Parliament, Policy Department for Citizens' Rights and Constitutional Affairs (2018) Report.

[83] See EU Parliament, Policy Department for Citizens' Rights and Constitutional Affairs (2018); European Data Protection Board (EDPB) Opinion 23/2018; Statement of Article 29 Working Party (2017) "Data protection and privacy aspects of cross-border access to electronic evidence" Brussels 29 November 2017 available at https://www.hldataprotection.com/files/2018/02/20171129-Art.-29-WP-e-Evidence_Statement.pdf.

[84] See the Preamble of the draft Regulation.

[85] C. Janssens (2013) The principle of Mutual Recognition in EU Law, Oxford University Press, p. 152.

especially as the envisaged text did not seem to contribute to facilitating cooperation between judicial authorities.[86]

It should, however, be noted that according to the E-evidence framework the process of enforcing production or preservation orders will require the involvement of a judicial authority in the enforcing MS in a more traditional sense, in cases where a receiving SP does not comply with its obligations, thus triggering the need to call for an ex-post enforcement of the order.[87] However this is intended as an ancillary procedure as the main objective of the proposed procedures is not to involve a receiving authority. The core of the Commission's proposal, a framework of direct cooperation between judicial authorities of the issuing MS and private companies in another MS, goes beyond the traditional legislative practice and understanding of mutual recognition of judicial decisions (Art. 82(1)2(a) TFEU) as cooperation between judicial or equivalent authorities of the MS (Art. 82(1)2(d) TFEU).[88] As it will be discussed further below, this is also reflected in that the issuing MS's law governs the enforcement of an order, not that of the enforcing MS—unlike the traditional basic principle of mutual recognition[89] whereby the executing MS's law governs the execution.

However, the choice of Art. 82(1) TFEU as legal basis is not accidental. The Commission's proposal suggests that the enforcing state generally recognizes any EPOC or EPOC-PR issued against an addressee located/represented within its territory.[90] This concept is already applied in the framework of judicial cooperation in civil matters whereby judicial decisions are enforced directly by private parties without the intervention of public authorities of the MS where the enforcement takes place.[91] Similarly, Art. 82(1) is considered by the Commission a suitable legal basis for the proposed direct cooperation with service providers, in which *the authority*

---

[86]Case 1/15, 27 July 2017, §103: "As the Advocate General has observed in point 108 of his Opinion, none of the provisions of the envisaged agreement refer to facilitating such cooperation. As for the Canadian Competent Authority, that authority does not constitute a judicial authority, nor does it constitute an equivalent authority". Although the issues at stake differ to some extent and the reasoning of the Court in one cannot be fully transposed to the other, some have drawn a parallel with the compatibility issues that arose in Case 1/15 on the EU-Canada PNR agreement. (WP29 p. 1); see also E. Sellier and A. Weyenbergh, "Criminal procedural laws across the European Union—A comparative analysis of selected main differences and the impact they have over the development of EU legislation", study Commissioned by the European Parliament's Policy Department for Citizens' Rights and Constitutional Affairs at the request of the LIBE Committee, PE 604.977, August 2018, p. 31. https://www.europarl.europa.eu/RegData/etudes/STUD/2018/604977/IPOL_STU(2018)604977_EN.pdf.

[87]Article 14(2) draft Regulation.

[88]See EU Parliament, Policy Department for Citizens' Rights and Constitutional Affairs (2018) p. 34; European Data Protection Board (EDPB) Opinion 23/2018.

[89]See C. Janssens (2013) The principle of Mutual Recognition in EU Law, Oxford University Press, p. 171.

[90]EU Commission (2018) "Impact assessment" part 3.1, p. 37.

[91]Article 36(1) Regulation (EU) No. 1215/2012 of the European Parliament and of the Council of 12 December 2012 on Jurisdiction and the Recognition and Enforcement of Judgments in Civil and Commercial Matters, O.J. L 351/1.

*in the issuing Member State would directly address an entity (the service provider) in the executing State and even impose obligations on it.* It is questionable however whether this approach sufficiently takes account of the particularities of cooperation in criminal matters, reflected in the different wording of Art. 81(2)(a) and Art. 82(1)(a) TFEU. Arguably: "laying down 'rules and procedures for ensuring recognition' would be superfluous if an involvement of the recognizing MS would not be required at all".[92]

The extraterritorial reach of judicial and state authorities' decisions in the E-evidence framework introduces a new dimension in mutual recognition, beyond the traditional judicial cooperation in the EU in criminal matters, so far based on procedures involving two judicial authorities: one in the issuing State and another in the executing State.[93] This important aspect of the e-evidence framework entails a fundamentally different approach that demonstrates the (need for) development of the EU law traditional concepts so as to respond to the new challenges with adequate mechanisms. From the perspective of the proposed e-evidence framework, the scope of Article 82(1) requires further clarification from CJEU or an amendment (albeit difficult).

In the meantime, the consensual introduction by the Council of a mandatory notification mechanism for cases involving content data (to be discussed below) means that the enforcing MS shall be involved more often in the e-evidence access process than originally proposed by the Commission. Yet such involvement differs from traditional forms of judicial cooperation as it is without rights to reject an order issued by another MS. The inclusion of the notification mechanism in the Council approach and the mandatory notification mechanism recently proposed by the LIBE's rapporteur[94] clearly reflect that some MSs are not ready to move beyond the traditional concepts and mechanisms of cooperation. In this author's opinion, instead of justifying new measures with unsuitable (perhaps outdated) legal provisions, or introducing changes to proposed instruments that could affect their very *raison d'etre*, efforts should be directed in exploring and developing further the emerging concepts in the criminal justice context and in providing new legal bases accordingly.

---

[92]EU Parliament, Policy Department for Citizens' Rights and Constitutional Affairs (2018) p. 36.

[93]This is the case for final judicial decisions imposing, for instance, a custodial sentence (Framework Decision 2008/909/JHA) or a fine (Framework Decision 2005/214/JHA), but also for decisions relating to the investigation such as a European arrest warrant (Framework Decision 2002/584/JHA) or a European investigation order (Directive 2014/41/EU—'EIO Directive').

[94]European Parliament "DRAFT REPORT on the proposal for a Regulation of the European Parliament and of the Council on European Production and Preservation Orders for electronic evidence in criminal matters (COM(2018)0225—C8-0155/2018—2018/0108(COD))" Committee on Civil Liberties, Justice and Home Affairs, November 2019, Rapporteur: Birgit Sippel Available at https://www.europarl.europa.eu/doceo/document/LIBE-PR-642987_EN.pdf.

## 2.4 Resolving Conflicts of Laws with Third States

The E-evidence Framework was proposed shortly after the passing of the CLOUD Act by the US Congress in 2018. Despite differences in scope and procedures, both instruments display similarities that make them examples of a novel approach that other countries around the world are invited to follow with regard to cross border access to e-evidence. (For a comparison of the key provisions see Table 1). The foundation of both these legal instruments is the extraterritorial reach of the unilateral orders for the production/preservation of e-evidence. They are subject to prior agreements with the states involved in the transnational cooperation, albeit not all the states affected by the cross border access of data. Both the instruments provide for the state authorities ordering SPs to provide data irrespective of data location. Another similarity concerns the procedure to be followed in resolving the potential conflicts of laws with third parties to which the attention now turns.

Often e-evidence is held by SPs with global operations. The SPs may be established outside of the EU, in other third countries[95] in which case they will have an obligation to comply with the laws and blocking statutes of those third States[96] as well as the EU framework. Since SPs and the data they control may be subject to more than one country's laws, conflicting legal obligations may arise when a SP receives an order from authorities of one country requiring the disclosure of data, but another country restricts disclosure of that same data. These potential legal conflicts present significant challenges to LEA's ability to acquire electronic evidence that may be vital to conduct criminal investigations in an efficient manner. With regard to E-evidence framework, two different approaches can be observed corresponding respectively to the original Commission's proposal and the Council's draft Regulation.

According to Art. 15 of the Commission's proposal, a SP may refuse the data disclosure to the issuing MS if compliance with an EPOC would conflict with laws' of a third country prohibiting the disclosure of data so as to protect fundamental rights and interests of such third States, including national security and defence interests, trade secrets or human rights considerations. The SP shall inform the issuing authority of its reasons for not executing the EPOC. If the issuing authority intends to uphold the EPOC, it shall request a review by the competent Court within that MS. If the competent Court finds that there is no conflict (either because the third country's law does not apply, or because it does not prohibit disclosure of the data requested, or because it manifestly seeks to protect other interests than the ones mentioned above), then the Order will be upheld. If, on the other hand, the Court finds that there is a conflict, it has an obligation to "transmit all relevant factual and legal information as regards the case, including its assessment, to the central authorities in the third country concerned". The third country is then entitled to object to the Order within a

[95]Note that under the E-evidence Directive all SPs offering their services in the EU will be obliged to nominate and establish a legal representative in the EU irrespective of where they are established.

[96]In the United States, for example, the Stored Communications Act (SCA), in Title II of the Electronic Communications Privacy Act (ECPA), is a blocking statute that prohibits US-based providers from turning over the content of communications to foreign governments.

**Table 1** US CLOUD Act and EU E-evidence Regulation: a comparison of the key provisions

| Provisions compared | US CLOUD Act | EU E—Evidence Regulation |
|---|---|---|
| Applicable agencies | Domestic agencies of any 'qualifying foreign government'* (18 USC §2703 (h) 1A) | Issuing authority of a Member State |
| Applicable entities/addressees | "A provider of 'electronic communication service' and 'remote computing service' including foreign providers subject to a requirement under this section; (S.103 CA; 18 USC §2713 'The Stored Communications Act) | – Provider of 'electronic communication services' and 'information society services' that store and 'internet domain name and IP numbering services';<br>– Offering services in the Union;<br>– Established or represented in another Member State<br>(see Art. 2) |
| Applicable crimes | Serious crime (for direct access only), including terrorism (18 USC § 2523(b)(4)(D)(i)) | Production order (Art. 5): Subscriber or access data—All criminal offences; Content or transactional data: 3 years prison or listed offences;<br>Preservation order (Art. 6): All criminal offences; |
| Data | – Contents of a wire or electronic communication and any record or other information pertaining to customer or subscriber;<br>– In provider's possession, custody or control, including prospective (e.g. ongoing surveillance and live collection);<br>– Regardless of data location; (18 USC § 2713) | – Content data; subscriber data; access data and transactional data<br>– Stored "at the time of receipt of an order" i.e. no live collection<br>– 'Regardless of the location of data' (Art. 1(1)) |
| Obligation | Preserve, backup or disclose; binding (18 USC § 2713) | Preserve or produce—'a binding decision'(Art. 1(1)) |
| Issuance standard | Purposive approach (i); specific identifier (ii); "a reasonable justification based on articulable and credible facts, particularity, legality and severity regarding the conduct under investigation" (18 USC § 2523(b)(4)(D)(iv)) necessary and proportionate[a] (vi) | "necessary and proportionate" (Art. 5(2) & 6(2)) |

(continued)

**Table 1** (continued)

| Provisions compared | US CLOUD Act | EU E—Evidence Regulation |
|---|---|---|
| Challenge process | – US and foreign providers<br>– Provider has right to file a motion to modify or quash disclosure content (§ 2703 (h)(2)) | – Any addressee i.e. service provider 'offering services in the Union'<br>– 'Reasoned objection' to production of any data to issuing authority (Art. 15(2), 16(2))<br>– Issuing authority requests review by a competent court 'in its Member State' (Art. 15(3) |
| Basis for challenge | – Provider 'reasonably believes': (i) not a US person [or resides in US] and (ii) 'material risk' that provider would violate laws of qualifying foreign government | – Provider 'considers' conflict with laws of 3rd country on fundamental rights and interests (Art. 15(1))[b];<br>– Provider 'considers' conflict with laws of 3rd country on other grounds (Art. 16(1)) |
| Court decisions | The court may modify or quash the legal process where:<br>– The required disclosure would cause the provider to violate the laws of a qualifying foreign government;<br>– Comity analysis (based on the totality of circumstances the interests of justice dictate that the legal process should be modified or quashed);<br>– The customer or subscriber is not a US person and resident<br>§2703 (h)2 B | The court may uphold or lift the order where:<br>– Conflict exists<br>– Does 3rd country law 'manifestly seek' to protect other interests or shield<br>– Action: notification to competent authority of 3rd country<br>– Comity analysis (Art. 16(5)) |
| Comity analysis factors | 1. US government interests;<br>2. Qualifying foreign government interests;<br>3. Provider interests (eg. penalties) and ties to the US<br>4. Suspect related (location, nationality and connection to requesting state)<br>5. Investigation related (Importance; proportionality; efficiency) (§2703 (h) 3 A-H) | 1. Government interests (both)<br>2. Person related: suspect and victim (location; nationality and residence of person; place offence committed)<br>3. Provider related (connection to 3rd country and penalties) |

(continued)

**Table 1** (continued)

| Provisions compared | US CLOUD Act | EU E—Evidence Regulation |
|---|---|---|
| Provider immunity | §2520 (d) (3) including 'good faith determination' that §2511(3); 2511 (2) (i), or 2511 (2) (j) permitted the conduct complained of | None |
| Defences against enforcement action | None | "The possibility to oppose the enforcement", but only to the 'enforcing authority' on the following grounds (Art. 14(4)):<br>1. Procedural non-compliance<br>2. Impossible/force majeure<br>3. Data not stored<br>4. No provision of applicable service<br>5. Manifest violation of Charter or abusive Administrative law remedy |
| Costs reimbursement to provider | §2706: "such costs as are reasonably necessary and which have been directly incurred in searching for, assembling, reproducing, or otherwise providing such information" | Art. 12 but only: "if this is provided by the national law of the issuing State for domestic orders in similar situations" |
| Proximity principle | None, but see US DoJ, Seeking Enterprise Customer Data Held by Cloud Service Providers (December 2017) | Art. 5(6): "may only be addressed to the service Provider where investigatory measures addressed to the company or the entity, are not appropriate" |
| Notification to subject | By provider, unless governmental entity obtains warrant (§ 2703(b) (1)(A) or delayed notice (§ 2705) | By provider, unless requested not to by issuing authority (Art. 11(1))<br>Issuing authority must notify, but not if necessary and proportionate for criminal proceedings (Art. 11(2)) |

[a]This term is not used but the factors included in the provision could amount to an assessment of proportionality
[b]Note that this box and the one below are affected by changes in the Council approach version of the Regulation where art 15 is struck out

timeframe of a maximum of 50 days, *in which case the Court shall lift the Order*. In addition, article 16 establishes a "Review procedure in case of conflicting obligations" based on "*other grounds*" than the ones mentioned in article 15, according to which, the competent Court has *no obligation* to notify the authorities of the third State of a potential conflict of laws and has *no obligation to dismiss* the Order if it concludes that there is such a conflict of laws. Article 16 gives *discretion* to the Court in this respect, while setting out the factors to be considered in determining whether to uphold or withdraw the Order.

Article 15 of the Commission's proposal, provides for a review mechanism which allows affected third States to exercise their protective functions in relation to their fundamental rights and interests by objecting and preventing the execution of an EPOC, where the specified conditions are met. The possibility for third States to object to the execution of an EPOC in case of conflict of laws is a significant departure from the "comity analysis" mechanism introduced by the CLOUD Act in the US to deal with disputes where an executive agreement is in effect.[97] The CLOUD Act does not impose an obligation to a US Court to inform the affected third country, nor does it impose an obligation to lift the order if the US Court finds that such a conflict of laws exists. Instead, the CLOUD Act gives discretion to the US Court to modify or quash such an order, taking into account a series of considerations appearing in §2713(h3).

Taking into consideration its capacity to prevent conflict of laws, the introduction of article 15 was welcomed and it was even suggested that it should be more widely applied by providing for a "wider obligation to consult the competent authorities of the concerned third countries in order to ensure that the procedure will more systematically ensure that the arguments of both sides will be taken into consideration and to show even more respect for the laws of third countries".[98] However, the Council's draft follows a different approach by deleting article 15 in its entirety and introducing a single article 16 entitled: *"Review procedure in case of conflicting obligations"* which provides both for *fundamental rights and interests* and *any other grounds* of conflict. The essential element of the Council's approach consists in substantially reducing the influence that the authorities of a third country can have in the process. There is no obligation to inform third countries in case of a conflict anymore—unlike under article 15(5) of the Commission's proposal. Article 16 instead provides for a possibility for the reviewing Court to "seek information from the competent authority of the third country [...] to the extent that such a transmission does not obstruct the

[97] The CLOUD act created a new "comity" provision for addressing possible conflicts between U.S. law and the laws of other countries, albeit applicable in limited situations. The second major part of the CLOUD Act creates a new mechanism for other countries to access the content of communications held by U.S. service providers. The CLOUD Act enables the bypassing of access restrictions in specified circumstances, based on the adoption of "executive agreements" between the U.S. and other countries, and subject to a number of baseline substantive and procedural requirements. The CLOUD Act authorizes these executive agreements only for countries meeting human rights and rule of law requirements, and only with a long list of requirements for each request.

[98] See European Data Protection Board (EDPB) Opinion 23/2018 pp. 17–18.

relevant criminal proceedings". In addition, according to Council's draft the competent Court of the issuing country no longer has an obligation to dismiss the Order if it finds that there is a conflict of laws, but only a *discretion* to dismiss the Order after weighing a series of relevant factors appearing in article 16(5).

The Council's approach is almost identical with the comity provisions in the CLOUD Act. Despite the criticism addressed to the extraterritorial reach of the CLOUD Act, the Council's approach demonstrates that this has become a preferred model in dealing with conflicts that may arise where e-evidence is involved. It is undeniable that the original article 15 has merits and is the better approach in order to avoid future conflicts of law and disputes with and within the EU. This is because it is based on dialogue and cooperation and provides for the protection of the interests of SPs and of the fundamental rights of the EU and foreign citizens.[99] Yet the decision of the MSs to depart from it was consensual. It remains to be seen how the e-evidence framework will affect the future negotiations of the forthcoming agreement between the US and the EU which will complement the EU-U.S. Data Protection and Privacy Agreement,[100] and the U.S. Judicial Redress Act (JRA), extending the benefits of the U.S. Privacy Act to EU.[101] It is likely that the aim of deleting article 15 was to place the US and the EU on a level playing field concerning these issues during the negotiations. Indeed, any US concerns about the extraterritorial reach of E-evidence and eventual future conflicts with the SCA blocking statutes have as a mirror European concerns about the extraterritorial reach of CLOUD Act and eventual conflicts with the GDPR as well as blocking statutes in the EU Member States. Mitigating the risks of such conflict of laws on a reciprocal basis via enhanced mechanisms for the prevention and resolution of conflicts of laws is considered as an issue for negotiation, not a "right" to be granted to third states by E-evidence Framework.[102] The recent report of LIBE's rapporteur, Birgit Sippel,[103] follows the footsteps of the Council's draft by proposing a similar procedure with clear, shorter deadlines albeit with the difference

[99] See the interventions during the Council's meeting are available under the E-evidence tab (below the video) here: https://video.consilium.europa.eu/en/webcast/2e938e2f-a272-420f-81b9-a058d9da74a8.

[100] Otherwise known as the "Umbrella Agreement" which entered into force on 1 February 2017.

[101] The Commission believes that an EU-US Agreement with the E-evidence proposals as the baseline could help settle any conflicting obligations for service providers and would allow them to deliver content data directly to law enforcement and judicial authorities in the EU or the United States, as the case may be. See https://ec.europa.eu/commission/presscorner/detail/en/MEMO_19_863 See also https://ec.europa.eu/info/policies/justice-and-fundamental-rights/criminal-justice/e-evidence-cross-border-access-electronic-evidence_en.

[102] See Theodore Christakis (2019) "E-evidence in a Nutshell: Developments in 2018, Relations with the Cloud Act and the Bumpy Road Ahead" Cross-border Data Forum available at https://www.crossborderdataforum.org/e-evidence-in-a-nutshell-developments-in-2018-relations-with-the-cloud-act-and-the-bumpy-road-ahead/.

[103] European Parliament "DRAFT REPORT on the proposal for a Regulation of the European Parliament and of the Council on European Production and Preservation Orders for electronic evidence in criminal matters (COM(2018)0225—C8-0155/2018—2018/0108(COD))" Committee on Civil Liberties, Justice and Home Affairs, November 2019, Rapporteur: Birgit Sippel Available at https://www.europarl.europa.eu/doceo/document/LIBE-PR-642987_EN.pdf.

of the involvement of the executing MS unlike the previous drafts that included only the issuing MS.[104] It is highly likely therefore that the final instrument will adopt an amended version of the Council's approach.

## 3 Part 2: The E-evidence Framework and Fundamental Rights

One of the key aims of the proposed E-evidence framework is to facilitate state authorities' cross border access to e-evidence through procedures that respect fundamental rights and the principles enshrined in the Charter of Fundamental Rights (CFR) of the EU and other key international instruments. These include the right to liberty and security, the respect for private and family life, the protection of personal data, the freedom to conduct a business, the right to property, the right to an effective remedy and to a fair trial, the presumption of innocence and right of the defence, procedural rights set out in EU directives, principles of legality and proportionality and the right not to be punished twice in criminal proceedings for the same criminal offence.[105]

In order to achieve a balanced approach in respecting these principles and the criminal justice aim to protect the public and achieve swift punishment of offenders through effective criminal investigations and prosecutions facilitated by speedy access to e-evidence, the proposed framework introduces a number of safeguards as follows[106]:

- EPOC must be approved by a judicial authority in the issuing MS
- for transactional and content data, the EPOC is limited to serious crimes
- individuals will be notified that their data were requested
- individuals will be notified of their rights
- criminal law procedural rights shall apply.

A number of important matters arise that require attention as the most sensitive and controversial aspects of the proposed framework.

---

The draft report is to be presented to the European Parliament after being amended and voted in the LIBE committee during February-March 2020.

[104]Ibid. See amendment 173 proposing a new article 14. Note the role to be played by the executing authority.

[105]See recitals 12 and 14 of the draft Regulation.

[106]See the draft Regulation.

### 3.1 *The Relationship Between the Issuing MS, the Enforcing MS and SPs—a Safeguards Perspective*

According to the E-evidence framework, a prosecutor or investigating authority in a MS issues an order for the preservation and/or production of electronic data (EPOC-PR and EPOC respectively). EPOC and EPOC-PR shall be reviewed by a judicial authority of the issuing country where they involve content and transactional data.[107] According to the draft Regulation, the key role of ensuring the adequacy and legitimacy of the E-evidence Orders rests with the judicial or investigative authorities of the issuing MS. The original procedure proposed by the Commission contains a limited *a posteriori* power of review of the enforcing MS which is triggered under two mechanisms:

(a) Under Article 5(7) the issuing MS *must consult* the enforcing MS at the time of issuing the order if it has reasons to believe that transactional or content data requested is protected by immunities and privileges granted under the law of the enforcing MS, or its disclosure may impact fundamental interests of that MS such as national security and defence. If either is found to be the case, the issuing authority shall not issue an order under the Regulation.[108] While this provision is well intended, it is left solely to the discretion of the issuing authority. Allowing the SPs or other MSs to raise these concerns with the issuing authority would provide for an improvement on the current draft.
(b) According to Article 14(2) the enforcing MS can refuse to enforce an EPOC if it considers "that the data concerned is protected by an immunity or privilege under its national law or its disclosure may impact its fundamental interests such as national security and defence". This mechanism is triggered only at the stage of *enforcement* of an EPOC where a SP does not comply with an Order. A likely problem with this approach is that, in cases where SP complies with an Order which may happen to affect the fundamental interests of another MS or the fundamental rights of its citizens, the affected MS (be it the enforcing MS or another) might not be made aware of that fact and therefore unable to object.

The limited involvement and reviewing powers of the enforcing MS are among the most controversial aspects surrounding the e-evidence proposal. A number of MSs have expressed concerns and dissatisfaction with the proposed procedure due to fears that the authorities of the issuing State will prioritize their own interests over any foreign ones which could lead to them issuing illegitimate requests that could affect the interests of other Member States and their citizens.[109] As it will be

[107]According to the original Commission's proposal.

[108]This provision was further modified by the Council into limiting the enforcing MS's intervention for transactional data, specifying that it applies where issuing MS has 'reasonable grounds to believe' that the person whose data is sought does not reside on the territory of the issuing MS and that data is subject in that MS to rules on determination and limitation of criminal liability relating to freedom of press and freedom of expression in other media'.

[109]The debates are available, listed by country, under the E-evidence tab (below the video) here: https://video.consilium.europa.eu/en/webcast/ffa13ca3-8e18-4bc1-9c80-8fdaa18265ac.

discussed further below, e-evidence is perceived by some as "a unilateral regime of mandatory cooperation with foreign service providers which may bear risks for the interests of the EU and its MSs and the rights of its citizens".[110]

The Commission's approach, however, should not come as a surprise: mutual recognition and mutual trust are fundamental principles well embedded in the EU acquis. As the proposal specifies, the E-evidence framework "can only work on the basis of a high level of mutual trust between the Member States".[111] This is the reason behind the limited powers of review, given that MSs are expected to trust the legal and judicial systems and decisions of each other. As held by CJEU in its Opinion 2/13, mutual trust is a principle "of fundamental importance in EU law … that allows an area without internal borders to be created and maintained."[112] This has resulted in the establishment of "a comprehensive system whereby national judicial decisions in criminal matters are recognised and executed across the EU quasi-automatically, with a minimum of formality and with the aim of speedy execution."[113] At the same time, mutual recognition was designed "not only to strengthen cooperation between MS but also to enhance the protection of individual rights."[114] Its implementation hinges on the mutual trust of MS in each other's criminal justice systems and that trust "is grounded, in particular, on their shared commitment to the principles of freedom, democracy and respect for human rights, fundamental freedoms and the rule of law."[115]

However the mutual trust principle should not be perceived as equal to "blind faith".[116] In today's reality in the EU, *mutual trust* is an objective to be achieved; it has to be earned and not assumed. The debate regarding E-evidence framework has exposed the tensions between theoretical ambitions and the existing reality. Such tensions are fueled by recent concerning examples of the rule of law backsliding in some EU MSs.[117] For as long as disparities in the standards and protections

---

[110]See for example EU Parliament, Policy Department for Citizens' Rights and Constitutional Affairs (2018) part 4.1.3, p. 34.

[111]See Recital 11 of the draft Regulation.

[112]CJEU, Opinion 2/13 of the Court on Accession of the European Union to the European Convention for the Protection of Human Rights and Fundamental Freedoms, 18 December 2014, para 191.

[113]V. Mitsilegas (2016) *EU Criminal Law after Lisbon: Rights, Trust and the Transformation of Justice in Europe*, Oxford/Portland: Hart Publishing, p. 124.

[114]Programme of measures to implement the principle of mutual recognition of decisions in criminal matters, OJ C 12, 15 Jan. 2001, p. 1 available at http://www.ecba.org/extdocserv//CriminalJustice/OtherEUdocs/Programmeofmeasuresimplementprinciplemutualrecogofdecisions.pdf.

[115]Ibid.

[116]S. Peers, EU Justice and Home Affairs Law, Oxford: Oxford University Press, 2016 p. 160.

[117]In July 2018, the European Commission launched legal action against the Polish government over allegations that the changes regarding the way judges are appointed in the country undermine the independence of its Courts. In October 2018 the European Court of Justice ordered the Polish government to suspend "immediately" changes to the country's Supreme Court. In September 2018, the EU Parliament asked EU Member States to determine, in accordance with Treaty Article 7, whether

provided by MSs still exist, the way forward should include innovative mechanisms that allow for the control, improvement and maintenance of those standards within each MS as opposed to fostering a lack of trust, prejudicial treatment and unjustifiable differentiation between MSs within the EU.

In response to debates,[118] as a compromise, the Council introduced article 7a which provides for a limited notification mechanism to be given to enforcing MS by the issuing MS in cases where the EPOC concerns *content data* and the issuing authority has reasonable grounds to believe that the person whose data are sought is not residing on its own territory. This mechanism allows for the enforcing MS to inform the issuing authority within 10 days of any circumstances described s 5 (7) (b) in which case the later may withdraw the Order. This notification mechanism has been criticized as *limited* by MS advocating a more effective provision that includes transnational data and a fundamental rights clause and by other MSs that deem it unnecessary by expressing preference for the Commission proposal.[119]

It has been pointed out that, while the notification is to be made to the enforcing MS, this may not necessarily be the MS whose interests or whose citizens' rights are affected by the disclosure of data. The latter could be the state of nationality or residence of the suspect. A number of MSs have argued that notices need be issued to the affected MSs as well as to the executing MS.[120] It needs, however, to be pointed out that MSs potentially affected may be unknown and even if known, involving multiple parties in the process will undoubtedly result in further delays and inefficiencies akin to those in the existing judicial cooperation channels which would undermine anything close to a solution to the problems faced in practice.

Under the Council's approach, the notified enforcing MS cannot refuse the execution of an EPOC. While traditional MLA agreements provide "grounds for refusal" and the power of the receiving State to determine whether evidence should be produced, no such grounds are prescribed by article 7(a). This approach is logical as the mechanism created by the e-evidence framework is not one which requires judicial cooperation between two MSs. It is a direct relationship between the issuing MS and a SP established or represented in another MS. However it can be further

Hungary is at risk of breaching the EU´s founding values. See https://ec.europa.eu/commission/presscorner/detail/en/IP_17_5367 See also https://ec.europa.eu/info/policies/justice-and-fundamental-rights/upholding-rule-law/rule-law/initiative-strengthen-rule-law-eu_en on the Commission's 2019 initiative to strengthen the Rule of Law in the EU.

[118]The debates are available, listed by country, under the E-evidence tab (below the video) here: https://video.consilium.europa.eu/en/webcast/ffa13ca3-8e18-4bc1-9c80-8fdaa18265ac.

[119]Ibid.

[120]See T. Christakis (2019) "E-evidence in a Nutshell: Developments in 2018, Relations with the Cloud Act and the Bumpy Road Ahead" Cross-border Data Forum available at https://www.crossborderdataforum.org/e-evidence-in-a-nutshell-developments-in-2018-relations-with-the-cloud-act-and-the-bumpy-road-ahead/ See also European Parliament "DRAFT REPORT on the proposal for a Regulation of the European Parliament and of the Council on European Production and Preservation Orders for electronic evidence in criminal matters (COM(2018)0225—C8-0155/2018—2018/0108(COD))" Committee on Civil Liberties, Justice and Home Affairs, November 2019, Rapporteur: Birgit Sippel Available at https://www.europarl.europa.eu/doceo/document/LIBE-PR-642987_EN.pdf.

improved. Under the Council's draft, the executing MS can only react if its *own* laws and interests are violated.[121] Under article 51 of the Charter of the Fundamental Rights of the EU all MS have an obligation to respect the Charter in all cases when they are implementing EU law. This obligation exists irrespective of the place where the targeted person resides or the explicit provisions of E-evidence framework. In this context, a better version of article 7(a) would substitute the wording 'enforcing member state' to 'any Member State'. This would allow the enforcing MS to object, even where it is not directly affected, on behalf of other MSs that may be.

The notification mechanism introduced by the Council has been considered as 'limited' and 'toothless'. The LIBE Rapporteur, in her draft report introduced the automatic and mandatory notification of the 'executing State' for all orders issued irrespectively of the type of data involved. The change in terminology from 'enforcing MS' to 'executing State' corresponds to newly proposed review and refusal powers of the latter. According to the rapporteur, "notwithstanding the principle of mutual trust, the executing authority should be able to refuse the recognition and execution of an order, where such refusal is based on specific and limited grounds listed…in the draft report, in line with grounds adopted in the Directive 2014/41/EU on the European Investigation Order…".[122] In many respects, the approach proposed by the rapporteur marks a significant departure from the original Commission's proposal and the Council's draft. It replicates the existing mutual judicial cooperation mechanisms and despite the artificial improvement to existing instruments by maintaining the 10 day deadlines for the execution of orders, it throws serious doubt as to whether the E-evidence framework is necessary at all.[123]

In this author's opinion, the reasonable way forward is not the unilateral rejection of access to data, nor the mandatory involvement of the enforcing MS for every order. The proposed scheme may fail to achieve its very *raison d'etre* by opening the doors to bureaucratic procedures and delays in executing orders similar to existing judicial cooperation channels. Given the fundamental differences between these channels and the originally proposed framework, it is justifiable that the country where the SPs is represented should have only exceptional involvement in the enforcement of orders following decisions made by authorities of the issuing MS. This is the

---

[121] According to Art. 7a the notified authority "may as soon as possible (and no later than 10 days) inform the issuing authority" of any eventual problems that concern situations where content data requested is protected by (i) immunities and privileges granted under the law of the enforcing State, or (ii) impacting fundamental interests of this enforcing State such as national security and defence, or (iii) affecting special legal protections in the enforcing State related to freedom of press and freedom of expression (but not other human rights).

[122] European Parliament "DRAFT REPORT on the proposal for a Regulation of the European Parliament and of the Council on European Production and Preservation Orders for electronic evidence in criminal matters (COM(2018)0225—C8-0155/2018—2018/0108(COD))" Committee on Civil Liberties, Justice and Home Affairs, November 2019, Rapporteur: Birgit Sippel p. 146 Available at https://www.europarl.europa.eu/doceo/document/LIBE-PR-642987_EN.pdf.

[123] Ibid. Amendments 5, 6, 8 (and overall) seems to take away the very justification and basis for this instrument provided in the original Commission's proposal. Taken together with the other changes proposed by the rapporteur, it is likely that the framework is to be considered superfluous. See amendment 13, 42, 43, 46 and 48, regarding the receiving MS's power to execute and refuse orders.

case not only because the enforcing MS may not be a party directly involved in the proceedings concerning specific criminal cases, in terms of crime location, suspect's nationality or residence, but also because it would be unfair and inefficient to put a heavy burden on particular MSs hosting more SPs representatives than others and would thus receive the highest number of Orders. The question therefore becomes whether what is provided in the draft provisions ensures that an adequate mechanism exists in contested cases.

Overall the Commission's proposal is the better balanced alternative. Once the Council gave way to the pressure of introducing a limited notification mechanism, it opened up the door to it being introduced on every case, including those involving non content data. This state of affairs clearly demonstrates the lack of mutual trust between MSs as a core value which risks undermining the effectiveness of a mechanism that could otherwise adequately be used to combat crime and serve the public interest. The way forward is to raise and harmonize standards across Europe as a means of achieving mutual trust. The proposed e-evidence mechanism builds on forms of cooperation and access channels that already exist. Undermining it will mean returning to the inefficient status quo or producing a superfluous mechanism similar to what already are in place.

### 3.1.1 The Role of Service Providers

The proposed Regulation applies to three groups of service providers:

- Providers of electronic communications services that include inter-personal communications such as voice-over-IP, instant messaging and e-mail services—as defined in Article 2(4) of the Directive (EU) 2015/1535 establishing the European Electronic Communications Code (Recital (16).
- Providers of information society services including storage data, social networks, online marketplaces and other hosting services including cloud computing. Service provider for which storage of data is only of an ancillary nature is excluded from the scope of the proposals even if they fall within the definition on information society services as per Directive (EU) 2015/1535 defining the information society services (Recital (16).
- Providers of Internet infrastructure services related to assignment of names and numbers (domain registers, privacy and proxy service providers, etc.)—as defined in Article 2(3) of the proposed Regulation on E-evidence (Recital 18).

According to the draft Regulation, SPs are natural or legal persons that offer services in the EU i.e. enable legal or natural person in one or more MSs to use the above services and have a substantial connection with that/those MS(s). SPs are obliged to designate a legal representative in the EU for the receipt of, compliance with and enforcement of decisions and orders, regardless of where their headquarters are established. This is to ensure that all SPs that offer services in the EU are subject of the same obligations. The application of the same rules and procedures for access to all SPs aims to improve legal certainty and clarity both for businesses and SPs and the LEAs which is currently lacking under the existing mechanisms of cooperation.

Under the Commission's proposal, the limited powers of review of the enforcing MS are balanced through a variety of options to challenge the legality of, and/or refuse to execute an Order given to SPs. These powers were significantly reduced by the Council in its draft. Articles 9 and 10 establish SP's obligation to inform the issuing authority whenever it cannot comply with its obligations due to an incomplete Order, manifest errors, lack of sufficient information to execute it, or due to a de facto impossibility (for example because the person whose data is sought is not a customer or the data has been deleted before receiving the Order). In addition and controversially, the original Commission proposal provided SPs with a number of reviewing functions that were subsequently deleted or amended in the Council draft. Art. 9(5b) and 14(4f) of the Commission proposal provide that a SP can oppose the execution if it considers that the EPO "manifestly violates the Charter of Fundamental Rights of the European Union or that it is manifestly abusive". In addition, a SP may oppose the enforcement of an EPOC if it "has not been issued or validated by an issuing authority" (Art. 14(4a) or if it "has not been issued for an offence provided for" by the Regulation (Art. 14(4b). These grounds of non-compliance were deleted from the Council's draft.

The Commission and Council have adopted two different approaches with regard to the role of SPs. The Commission's proposal conferred several review powers to the SPs which led to criticism regarding a 'reallocation of protective functions' from public authorities of enforcing MSs to SPs[124] in the context of the limited involvement of the former. The capacity of SPs and the legitimacy to adequately exercise these protective functions have been questioned which led to a downgrade of SPs' review powers on the Council's draft. According to the Council's approach, the role of SPs is to be confined within the framework of cooperation with issuing authorities and compliance with the Orders. The common view is that SPs are not able and should not be put in a position to challenge a court's or public authority's decision. This is in line with the foundation of the E-evidence model according to which the scrutiny and compliance with rights and interests lies with the judicial authorities of the issuing MS. According to Council's approach, a SP should not refuse information or the preservation of data, save in specific and straightforward circumstances contained in Articles 9 and 10.

A controversial provision in the Council's draft has been the introduction of pecuniary sanctions of up to 2% of the total worldwide annual turnover of the SP's preceding financial year which can be imposed in case of their non-compliance.[125] On the one hand, this provision ensures that the obligations imposed on SPs by the Regulation shall be fulfilled, thus 'guaranteeing' the effectiveness of the proposed mechanism. On the other hand, it can be argued that the imposition of such significant sanctions could stop SPs from challenging the legality of an EPOC. This adds

---

[124]See EU Parliament, Policy Department for Citizens' Rights and Constitutional Affairs (2018) p. 41.

[125]Article 13 of the Council's draft.

to the difficulty discussed above, concerning potential conflicts of SP's obligations under a third country's legislation where they may be established or operating. Art. 15–16 of the Commission's proposal provided that a SP may refuse the execution of an EPOC if it considers that compliance with the EPOC would be in conflict with the applicable laws of a third country. Part IV of the Council's draft maintains this option, but downgrades the review mechanisms by deleting article 15. This means that, contrary to the Commission's proposal, the SP might find itself compelled to execute an EPOC despite the fact of a conflict of laws with a third country or risk considerable sanctions.

The way forward remains unclear. From a SP's perspective, a greater involvement of the enforcing MS in reviewing the orders' compliance with rights and interests could relieve substantial judicial and financial burdens which are significant especially for the smaller providers. The notification mechanism introduced by the Council could contribute to that effect despite its limits in the proposed form. Article 7a emphasizes that the notification shall not have suspensive effect on the obligations of the SP to respond to an EPOC which means that, even if the enforcing MS has objections to the production of data, the SP will have to provide them to the issuing MS within the same timeframe. The notification mechanism would be more effective and protective if it were to have a suspensive effect for the SPs that have been informed that the enforcing MS objects to the Order, in suspending the production of data until the matter has been reviewed and decided by the issuing authority according to the proposed Regulation.

Regardless of the notification and reviewing mechanisms to be adopted (or not) in the future, one thing remains certain: SPs should still be able to play a role in protecting the interests of their clients and public at large. While the ability and appetite of private operators to challenge orders on grounds of breach of fundamental rights is deeply questionable, as is their legitimacy to do so, SPs are in a unique position to understand the data being or that should be requested, to identify reasons why an order is deficient and/or to flag issues that may have not been identified by the issuing or enforcing authorities. Maintaining such reviewing powers and facilitating the collaboration between SPs and issuing authorities would enhance the safeguards and protections provided by the E-evidence framework and should be the focus of the forthcoming instrument.

## 3.2 *Beyond Definitions: E-evidence and Data Protection*

The right to data protection stems from a number of legal instruments binding on the EU MSs including: Art. 12 of the Universal Declaration of Human Rights (UDHR); Article 8 European Convention on Human Rights (ECHR); OECD Guidelines on the Protection of Privacy and Trans-border Flows of Personal Data; Convention of the Council of Europe Nr. 108 for the protection of individuals with regard to automatic processing of personal data; Articles 7 & 8 Charter of Fundamental Rights of the European Union (EU Charter). Two fundamental instruments of the EU legislation on the area of data protection are the General Data Protection Regulation (GDPR)[126] and the Law Enforcement Directive 2016/680 (LED).[127] In the context of the procedures laid down in the E-evidence framework, the processing of personal data by SPs will fall under the GDPR, while the processing of personal data by LEAs for the purposes of prevention, investigation, detection or prosecution of criminal offences will fall under LED. The E-evidence framework must therefore ensure compliance with all the above instruments.

### 3.2.1 Defining E-evidence

According to Art. 2.6 of the proposal, electronic evidence "means evidence stored in electronic form by or on behalf of a service provider at the time of receipt of a production or preservation order certificate, consisting in stored subscriber data, access data, transactional data and content data". The term evidence is not defined as such but is described as consisting of 4 types of data—see Table 2. In its technical documents, the Commission acknowledges the lack of precise definition and interpretation of what is understood by "electronic evidence" and the need to define specific categories of electronic evidence. A clear definition of E-evidence is essential when assessing the impact of the proposed measures on the rights of the data subject and on the obligations incumbent to LEAs and SPs. Since Art. 1(1) does not specify the meaning of electronic evidence, this author proposes the following definition in order to avoid differences in interpretation:

> Electronic evidence is information (or data) stored in electronic form which can be used to prove facts in criminal proceedings.

The concept of data and evidence are used interchangeably throughout the instrument. This reflects misconceptions that become source of the tensions reflected in the debates surrounding the proposed instruments. There is a clear difference between data and evidence: while electronic evidence consists of data and information, not all data/information are/is evidence. Data become evidence when collected, processed, analysed and/or used for purposes of proving facts in specific criminal proceedings.[128] This difference is not clear in the e-evidence framework which reflects a confusion between the concepts of personal data more broadly and data to be used as

---

[126]Regulation 2016/679 on the protection of natural persons with regard to the processing of personal data and on the free movement of such data, and repealing Directive 95/46/EC.

[127]Directive 2016/680 on the protection of natural persons with regard to the processing of personal data by competent authorities for the purposes of prevention, investigation, detection or prosecution of criminal offences or the execution of criminal penalties, and the free movement of such data, and repealing Council Framework Decision 2008/977/JHA.

[128]These differences have been dealt with in depth elsewhere, see O.Sallavaci (2014) *The impact of scientific evidence on the criminal trial*, Routledge. More generally on the meaning of evidence see for example P. Roberts and R. Zuckerman (2010) *Criminal Evidence*, Oxford University Press Chap. 1; see also D. Nicolson (2019) *Evidence and Proof in Scotland: Context and Critique*, Edinburgh University Press Chap. 1.

**Table 2** Categories of Data under the E-evidence draft Regulation

| | |
|---|---|
| Art. 2. (7): 'subscriber data' | Any data pertaining to:<br>(a) the identity of a subscriber or customer such as the provided name, date of birth, postal or geographic address, billing and payment data, telephone, or email;<br>(b) the type of service and its duration including technical data and data identifying related technical measures or interfaces used by or provided to the subscriber or customer, and data related to the validation of the use of service, excluding passwords or other authentication means used in lieu of a password that are provided by a user, or created at the request of a user;<br>It should be noted here the exclusion of passwords and authentication means from subscriber data category |
| Art. 2(8) 'access data' | Data related to the commencement and termination of a user access session to a service, which is strictly necessary for the sole purpose of identifying the user of the service, such as the date and time of use, or the log-in to and log-off from the service, together with the IP address allocated by the internet access service provider to the user of a service, data identifying the interface used and the user ID. This includes electronic communications metadata as defined in point (g) of Article 4(3) of the Regulation concerning the Respect for private life and the protection of personal data in electronic communications<br>It need be noted here that this is incorrect as it should be referring to point (c) not (g) of the Regulation[a] |
| Art. 2(9) 'transactional data' | Data related to the provision of a service offered by a service provider that serves to provide context or additional information about such service and is generated or processed by an information system of the service provider, such as the source and destination of a message or another type of interaction, data on the location of the device, date, time, duration, size, route, format, the protocol used and the type of compression, unless such data constitutes access data. This includes electronic communications metadata as defined in point (g) of Article 4(3) of [Regulation concerning the respect for private life and the protection of personal data in electronic communications];<br>Again, this provision refers to the wrong provision of the above Regulation. There is need for greater clarity of the different type of data |
| Art. 2(10) 'content data' | Any stored data in a digital format such as text, voice, videos, images, and sound other than subscriber, access or transactional data;<br>This is a negative definition of content data. Greater clarity is needed as to what is included. Since passwords and similar information are excluded from the above categories, it means that they will be considered content data |

[a]According to Art. 4(3)(c):'"electronic communications metadata' means data processed in an electronic communications network for the purposes of transmitting, distributing or exchanging electronic communications content; including data used to trace and identify the source and destination of a communication, data on the location of the device generated in the context of providing electronic communications services, and the date, time, duration and the type of communication". While this is still in the draft version there have been major changes in the definition by the Council and Parliament. Draft e-Privacy Regulation is available at https://eur-lex.europa.eu/legal-content/EN/TXT/?uri=CELEX%3A52017PC0010

electronic evidence. The lack of a definition, or rather the equalisation of e-evidence with data as in the current draft Regulation could lead to a misunderstanding of the scope of the Regulation and of the way it protects the rights involved.

An analogy can be made here: a firearm is subject to general rules concerning their control and Regulation. When used in the context of the criminal proceedings to prove a contested fact it becomes ballistic/real evidence and is subject to technical and procedural rules in terms of its collection, analysis, presentation and use. Similarly personal data are subject to general data protection laws. The question is how far e-evidence should abide to the principles enshrined in the general data protection instruments, considering the specific purposes for which they will be collected and used, that is the investigation and prosecution of crime. Can e-evidence rules depart from the application of general data protection principles given the specific purpose for their preservation, production and use?

Insufficient thought is given in the framework as to how data become evidence and proof. In some cases data will only be used for intelligence or investigative purposes as circumstantial evidence, in other cases (especially involving content data) electronic information will become vital substantive evidence. In this context procedures agreed for the preservation and production of e-evidence, safeguards to protect the fairness of the proceedings and individual rights are directly linked to the admissibility of such evidence on trial. It is therefore important to consider an issue which has not received sufficient attention so far: the provisions of the e-evidence framework have the potential to ultimately affect the admissibility of the e-evidence itself and the fairness of the subsequent criminal proceedings.

The proposed framework does not approximate the rules on the admissibility of e-evidence, leaving it to the MSs to decide what the potential consequences of violation of the procedural rules regarding EPOC and EPOC-PR are. In case of any procedural breaches, if the SP does not oppose the execution, it is for the issuing MS to decide on the admissibility of the illegally obtained e-evidence to secure a conviction. This aspect differs significantly from that created by the EIO Directive, according to which the executing MS will check if the legal requirements set by the EIO are met (e.g. Art. 9(3) EIO Directive) and which provides for a clear—cut inadmissibility rule in certain cases (Art. 31(3) EIO Directive). It is therefore proposed that a specific provision providing for the inadmissibility of evidence obtained in breach of the E-evidence framework in the specific criminal proceedings be included in the final draft.

### 3.2.2 Categories of Data and Safeguards

The proposed E-evidence framework applies only to ongoing criminal investigations. It does not involve mass surveillance or crime prevention instruments.[129] The material

[129] As highlighted by the European Economic and Social Committee Brussels, 2 August 2018, 11533/18 (points 1.3 and 3.3) available at http://data.consilium.europa.eu/doc/document/ST-11533-2018-INIT/en/pdf.

scope of the instruments created by the Regulation (EPOC and EPOC-PR) is limited only to stored data at the time an order is issued. If LEAs need access to data stored after the order, they need to issue subsequent orders. Unlike the CLOUD Act, the E-evidence framework does not provide for the real time collection of data which not only limits the scope but arguably the usefulness of the instrument.[130] Given the pressures and legal challenges that the police are facing as reflected in a number of recent cases brought to the CJEU[131] and considering the difficulties and the time involved in negotiating the currently proposed instruments, let alone any future amendments, the choice to exclude data which are not stored at the time of issuing the order is a missed opportunity at best. While the national sensitivities with regard to real time interceptions, due to constitutional and/or historical factors, create obstacles for direct cooperation with SPs, it is questionable whether the distinction between real time collection of data and the gathering of stored data is still as relevant in the digital age.[132]

The proposed framework creates four new subcategories of personal data as specified in Table 2. This categorisation differs from other legal frameworks such as CCC. The four categories of data proposed are not clearly delineated: the definition of "access data" in particular is vague compared to the other categories. Similarly IP addresses could both be classed as transactional data and subscriber data. The lack of clear definitions will create difficulties for issuing authorities in their evaluation as to which category the requested data will belong. This evaluation is fundamentally important as the proposed categories of data are associated with different levels of safeguards regarding the substantive and procedural conditions for access. Since the rationale behind the proposed categories is to differentiate between the levels of intrusion to fundamental rights that access to those data bears, it is so much more important that they are clearly delineated and defined.

In the E-evidence framework the Commission seems to follow a different direction from its proposal for e-Privacy Regulation,[133] where it considers that "electronic communications data should be defined in a sufficiently broad and technology neutral way so as to encompass any information concerning the content transmitted or

[130]The conditions for an investigative measure relating to data gathered in real time, continuously and over a certain period of time are outlined in Article 28 EIO. As regards the content data for interception of telecommunications, Articles 30 and 31 EIO apply. These articles define an additional non-recognition ground for these type of data in addition to the the general non-recognition grounds, namely "if the execution of the investigative measure concerned would not be authorised in a similar domestic case".

[131]E.g. *Tele2 Sverige AB and Watson* see also Frank Verbruggen, Sofie Royer, and Helena Severijns (2018) "Reconsidering the blanket-data-retention-taboo, for human rights' sake?" available at https://europeanlawblog.eu/2018/10/01/reconsidering-the-blanket-data-retention-taboo-for-human-rights-sake/.

[132]For instance it is not always clear whether data produced via emails or chat services are in transmission or already stored. See Vanessa Franssen https://europeanlawblog.eu/2018/10/12/the-european-commissions-e-evidence-proposal-toward-an-eu-wide-obligation-for-service-providers-to-cooperate-with-law-enforcement/.

[133]Regulation concerning the respect for private life and the protection of personal data in electronic communications (e-Privacy Regulation).

exchanged (electronic communications content) and the information concerning an end-user of electronic communications services processed for the purposes of transmitting, distributing or enabling the exchange of electronic communications content; including data to trace and identify the source and destination of a communication, geographical location and the date, time, duration and the type of communication".[134] The forthcoming E-evidence framework should therefore either clearly define the four categories of data above or provide an alternative categorisation compatible with the e-Privacy framework. Given that the latter as well as the related limitations to the right to privacy will also apply to LEAs access to e-evidence, consistent definitions of electronic data between related legal frameworks should be ensured as well as consistent safeguards and conditions for access to both 'non-content' and 'content data'.[135]

The Regulation recognises that "all data categories contain personal data, and are thus covered by the safeguards under the Union data protection acquis".[136] However, both the Commission and Council drafts draw a distinction between different categories, in particular between subscriber data and access data, on the one hand, and transactional data and content data, on the other hand, in terms of "the intensity of the impact on fundamental rights".[137] According to the Commission, "orders to produce subscriber data and access data can be issued for any criminal offence. Transactional and content data should be subject to stricter requirements to reflect the more sensitive nature of such data and the correspondingly higher degree of invasiveness of Orders for such data, as compared to subscriber and access data."[138] According to the Council, "as opposed to non-content data, content data is of particularly sensitive nature because persons may reveal their thoughts as well as sensitive details of their private life. This justifies a different treatment and an involvement of the authorities of the enforcing State early on in the procedure."[139] The Council approach makes no distinction between transactional data vs other non-content data as in the Commission proposal. However, this is inconsistent as it will be discussed below.

In the current draft, the definition for both transactional data and access data could involve 'electronic communications (EC) metadata' as defined by Art. 4(3) (c) of the Commission Proposal for an e-Privacy Regulation. The question arises whether EC metadata in itself should be treated differently from content data. Examples of metadata are subscriber data, data on traffic, location etc. The CJEU and ECtHR case law shows that non content data can be just as important and sensitive as content data from a fundamental rights perspective. In *C-203/15—Tele2 Sverige*[140] at para 99, CJEU held that metadata "is liable to allow very precise conclusions to be drawn concerning

[134] Recital 14 e-Privacy Regulation.

[135] See LIBE's rapporteur Draft Report (2019) amendments 25–27 and 91–97 for an alternative classification of data, to be discussed further below.

[136] Recital 23 E-evidence Regulation.

[137] Ibid.

[138] See the Explanatory Memorandum to the draft Regulation as proposed by the Commission.

[139] Recital 35c of the Council's General Approach.

[140] Available at http://curia.europa.eu/juris/liste.jsf?num=C-203/15.

the private lives of the persons whose data has been retained, such as everyday habits, permanent or temporary places of residence, daily or other movements, the activities carried out, the social relationships of those persons and the social environments frequented by them … In particular, that data provides the means … of establishing a profile of the individuals concerned, information that is no less sensitive, having regard to the right to privacy, than the actual content of communications."

Both the CJEU and the ECtHR require that metadata be treated the same as content data from a data protection perspective. The ECtHR in *Big Brother Watch v UK*[141] stated at para 356: "the Court is not persuaded that the acquisition of related communications data is necessarily less intrusive than the acquisition of content. For example, the content of an electronic communication might be encrypted and, even if it were decrypted, might not reveal anything of note about the sender or recipient. The related communications data, on the other hand, could reveal the identities and geographic location of the sender and recipient and the equipment through which the communication was transmitted. In bulk, the degree of intrusion is magnified, since the patterns that will emerge could be capable of painting an intimate picture of a person through the mapping of social networks, location tracking, Internet browsing tracking, mapping of communication patterns, and insight into who a person interacted with". Similarly in *Benedik v Slovenia*,[142] ECtHR stated that: "The view that metadata does not deserve the same level of protection as content data is shattered as it is confronted with present-day realities: there are currently so many forms of metadata—from phone calls, e-mails, web engines showing your surfing history, to Google Maps showing your location, etc.; and if this data are aggregated, an outstandingly intrusive portrait is obtained of the person concerned, revealing his or her personal and professional relationships, ethnic origin, political affiliation, religious beliefs, membership of different groups, financial status, shopping or disease history, and so on."

According to the Commission's proposal "The European Production Order and the European Preservation Order are investigative measures that can be issued only in criminal investigations or criminal proceedings for concrete criminal offences. *The link to a concrete investigation distinguishes it from preventive measures or data retention obligations set out by law* and ensures the application of the procedural rights applicable to criminal proceedings"[143] (emphasis added). The reason why the Commission departs from the Courts' interpretation of metadata in the context of data protection, by differentiating between categories of metadata and content data, is the link to a concrete criminal investigation and the contribution that particular types of data make to it. Subscriber data and access data are considered useful for investigatory purposes to obtain first leads about the identity of a suspect, while

[141]CASE OF BIG BROTHER WATCH AND OTHERS v. THE UNITED KINGDOM (Applications nos. 58170/13, 62322/14 and 24960/15) available at https://hudoc.echr.coe.int/eng#{"itemid":["001-186048"]}.

[142]CASE OF BENEDIK v. SLOVENIA (Application no. 62357/14) available at https://hudoc.echr.coe.int/eng#{"fulltext":["benedik"],"documentcollectionid2":["GRANDCHAMBER","CHAMBER"],"itemid":["001-182455"]}.

[143]Recital 23 E-evidence Regulation.

transactional and content data are deemed as the most relevant as probative material. Due to the differences in their use and the type of information these data can reveal, they are considered to manifest different degrees of interference with fundamental rights which has led to different access conditions for obtaining subscriber and access data on the one hand, and transactional and content data on the other.

The difference between subscriber data and content data is recognised in several existing criminal justice instruments. Both EIO and the CCC provide a different treatment regarding subscriber data—the data category required the most in trans-border cases, and needing swift action in order to start a criminal investigation, to identify a suspect or link a suspect with a certain communication. Subscriber data are considered the category with the lowest intrusion into fundamental rights hence the EIO removes some non-recognition grounds for requests for this type of data (for example, no dual criminality and applicability to all offences).[144] Furthermore, requests for such data have to be always possible under the system of the other Member state. The same applies to the CCC whereby subscriber data can also be requested from a provider operating on its territory (but not necessarily stored there).[145]

However, the differences between the data categories proposed in the draft Regulation need be clearly delineated. For instance, it is not clear whether IP addresses are access, subscriber or transactional data.[146] ECtHR held in *Benedik v Slovenia* at para. 109: "The sole purpose of obtaining the subscriber information [including a dynamic IP address] was to identify a particular person behind the independently collected content revealing data he had been sharing… Information on such activities engages the privacy aspect the moment it is linked to or attributed to an identified or identifiable individual … Therefore what would appear to be peripheral information sought by the police, namely the name and address of a subscriber, must in situations such as the present one be treated as inextricably connected to the relevant pre-existing content revealing data … To hold otherwise would be to deny the necessary protection to information which might reveal a good deal about the online activity of an individual, including sensitive details of his or her interests, beliefs and intimate lifestyle."

The case law demonstrates that the differences between content and non-content data (metadata) from a rights perspective may not be as significant as presented in the proposed Regulation, suggesting that a similar degree of protection should be

---

[144]See Art. 10(2) and 11(2) EIO.

[145]Due to the fact that not all Member States are part of these two instruments, that some service providers are not covered and that the deadlines might be quite long with regard to the volatile nature of e-evidence, both the EIO and the Budapest Convention have limitations that the e-evidence framework seeks to address.

[146]According to recital 21 of the Commission's proposal "Access data is pursued for the same objective as subscriber data… to identify the underlying user and the level of interference with fundamental rights is similar to that of subscriber data. Access data is typically recorded as part of a record of events… to indicate the commencement and termination of a user access session to a service. It is often an individual IP address (static or dynamic) or other identifier that singles out the network interface used during the access session. If the user is unknown, it often needs to be obtained before subscriber data related to that identifier can be ordered from the service provider".

afforded to content and not content data. Given the specificities of the collection and use of data for the purposes of criminal justice, any difference in access procedures for different categories of data requires clear justification. The gathering and use of data should conform to the necessity, proportionality and speciality principles.[147] In order to address the criticism and bring the draft Regulation in line with the jurisprudence of ECtHR and CJEU, LIBE's rapporteur has proposed a different categorisation of data divided into three categories: content, traffic and subscriber data.[148] Traffic data include 'access' and 'transactional' data (i.e. the metadata referred to by the courts as shown above) and are subject to the same conditions for access as the content data. The draft report distinguishes the subscriber data category by acknowledging the lesser degree of intrusion in fundamental rights, reflected in different accessibility conditions. The approach of LIBE's rapporteur seems to provide a better alternative to the categorisation of data than that adopted by the Commission and Council and could reconcile concerns related to the protection of fundamental rights with the needs of LEAs, while ensuring clarity and compatibility in definitions with other legal instruments.[149]

### 3.2.3 Judicial Validation of Orders

According to Article 4 of the draft Regulation there are distinctions with regard to the issuing authorities respectively for EPOC and EPOC-PR depending on the type of data (see Table 3).

According to the Commission's proposal transactional and content data deserve greater 'protection' as only a judge or investigating judge can issue or validate an order, not a prosecutor.[150] It is interesting to note that in article 4 the Council's draft has retained the different treatment of transactional and content data as compared to access and subscriber data. This approach is not consistent throughout the document as for instance the notification mechanism introduced in article 7a discussed above is triggered only for content data. Furthermore, in recital 35 (c) the Council clearly distinguishes between content and non-content data. It is not clear whether the Commission's proposal was deliberately or accidentally followed but this is certainly

[147]See recitals 24 and 56 on necessity and proportionality; regarding the Specialty principle see Art. 12 b of the Council's draft.

[148]European Parliament "DRAFT REPORT on the proposal for a Regulation of the European Parliament and of the Council on European Production and Preservation Orders for electronic evidence in criminal matters (COM(2018)0225—C8-0155/2018—2018/0108(COD))" Committee on Civil Liberties, Justice and Home Affairs, November 2019, Rapporteur: Birgit Sippel Available at https://www.europarl.europa.eu/doceo/document/LIBE-PR-642987_EN.pdf.

See Amendment 25, 91–97 which change the classification of data into subscriber data, traffic data and content data; amendment 26 distinguishes subscribed data only as a less sensitive category of data then others—note the difference with Commission's categorisation of access vs subscriber data; amendment 27 equalises transactional data with traffic data.

[149]Ibid explanatory notes.

[150]Note that as per recital 30, judicial authority comprises either a judge or a prosecutor.

**Table 3** Issuing/validating authorities

| Type of data | European production order issuing/validating authorities | European preservation order Issuing/validating authorities |
|---|---|---|
| Subscriber and access data | A judge, a court, an investigating judge or prosecutor, other competent authority | A judge, a court, an investigating judge or prosecutor, other competent authority |
| Transactional and content data | A judge, a court or an investigating judge competent in the case concerned (NOT a prosecutor), other competent authority | (same as above) |

not in line with Council's justification in the recitals. There is need for a consistent position throughout the instrument.

The draft Regulation does not define what could be qualified as a 'competent investigating authority'. This is left to the issuing MSs which is likely to lead to diversity between MSs and arguably legal uncertainty that could impact rights' protection. Some MSs give investigatory powers to a wide range of bodies.[151] Should they be subject to the Regulation, it will lead to a very high number of orders being issued. A classification of investigating authorities by means of a schedule in the proposed framework would help to better define the permitted activities within the scope of the Regulation. In any case, judicial validation of orders issued by non-judicial authorities should be imperative for all types of data as a form of control and safeguard against abuse or overuse.

According to CJEU in *Digital Rights Ireland*[152] there should be objective criteria "by which the number of persons authorised to access and subsequently use the data retained is limited to what is strictly necessary in the light of the objective pursued".[153] Moreover, the access by the competent national authorities to the data retained should be made dependent on a "prior review carried out by *a court or by an independent administrative body* whose decision seeks to limit access to the data and their use to what is strictly necessary for the purpose of attaining the objective pursued and which intervenes following *a reasoned request of those authorities* submitted within the framework of procedures of prevention, detection or criminal prosecutions" (emphasis added).[154] Similarly the CJEU held in *Tele2*[155] that: "it is essential that access of the competent national authorities to retained data should, as

[151] In the UK see Investigatory Powers Act 2016 Schedule 4.

[152] Digital Rights Ireland Ltd (C-293/12) available at http://curia.europa.eu/juris/document/document.jsf?text=%2522charter%2Bof%2Bfundamental%2Brights%2522&docid=150642&pageIndex=0&doclang=EN&mode=req&dir=&occ=first&part=1&cid=16565#ctx1.

[153] At para 62.

[154] Ibid.

[155] *Tele2 Sverige AB* (Case C-203/15) available at http://curia.europa.eu/juris/document/document.jsf?text=charter%2Bof%2Bfundamental%2Brights&docid=186492&pageIndex=0&doclang=en&mode=lst&dir=&occ=first&part=1&cid=230304#ctx1.

a general rule, except in cases of validly established urgency, be subject to a prior review carried out *either by a court or by an independent administrative body,* and that the decision of that court or body should be made following a reasoned request by those authorities submitted, inter alia, within the framework of procedures for the prevention, detection or prosecution of crime" (emphasis added).[156] In a similar vein, the ECtHR has held that "the failure to disclose the relevant information … to *the courts* deprives them of the power to assess whether there is a sufficient factual basis to suspect the person in respect of whom operational-search measures are requested of a criminal offence or of activities endangering national, military, economic or ecological security"[157] and "control by an *independent body, normally a judge* with special expertise, should be the rule and substitute solutions the exception, warranting close scrutiny"(emphasis added).[158]

According to the above jurisprudence of both CJEU and ECtHR, it can be argued that EPOCs should be issued or validated by a court or by an independent administrative body following reasoned requests by investigative authorities. Since the division of data in 4 categories is likely to prove problematic in practice and considering the jurisprudence of both CJEU and ECtHR, it would be preferable that the same conditions in terms of judicial validation are provided for both content and non-content data. This is particularly important given that the duty to check the Order's compliance with fundamental rights and to avoid breaches or conflicts with privileges and/or national interests of other MS lies primarily with the authorities of the issuing MS. This procedural difference in access for different data categories could be easily aligned by requiring judicial authorisation or validation for all types of data.

### 3.2.4 The [Lack of] Harmonisation of Substantive Criminal Law and the Dual Criminality Principle

Matters become more complex with regard to the substantive conditions for access to data. The draft Regulation provides that orders to produce subscriber and access data can be issued for *any criminal offence* whereas access to transactional and content data is limited to *serious crimes* which comprise offences that carry at least a three year maximum sentence and a number of specific offences listed in article 5(4).[159] For critics, the choice of this threshold condition i.e. a maximum custodial sentence depending on the nature of the data sought contradicts the Commission's argument in that the framework is dedicated to fight terrorism and child abuse offences

---

[156] Ibid at para 120.

[157] *Roman Zakharov v Russia* (Application no. 47143/06) at para 261 available at http://statewatch.org/news/2015/dec/echr-russian-secret-surveillance-judgment.pdf.

[158] *Szabó and Vissy v. Hungary* (Application no. 37138/14) at para 77 available at http://www.statewatch.org/news/2016/jan/echr-case-SZAB-%20AND-VISSY-v-%20HUNGARY.pdf.

[159] See recitals 31 and 32 of the draft Regulation.

i.e. the most serious crimes carrying higher sentences.[160] It is important to note however that there are a number of specific offences, both cyber-dependant and cyber related ones, which, even though they may not be considered serious in and of themselves, may have a great impact and cause considerable damage. Similarly, for instance, a number of terrorism related offences attract less than a maximum of 3 years penalty. It is therefore justifiable that the Regulation should not confine the instruments use solely to what it considers 'serious offences'. To do otherwise would be a missed opportunity which would lead to impunity especially for those offences where evidence is typically available only in electronic form. For this reason this author disagrees with the amendment proposed by LIBE's rapporteur to change the classification of offences by increasing the sentence they attract to 5 years. This would seriously undermine the scope of the E-evidence framework and its usefulness for LEAs.

The E-evidence framework exposes two underlying issues that require consideration. First, there is no harmonisation between MSs with regard to substantive law both in terms of what constitutes a criminal offence and in terms of the maximum custodial sentence. The lack of harmonisation in substantive criminal law causes difficulties in the execution of cooperation measures. Critics point out that in conditions where there is no harmonization of maximum custodial sentences in the EU there will be uncertainty and lack of uniformity of the application of the Regulation by MSs. They propose as an alternative the introduction of a consensual list of serious crimes punished in all MSs and to reserve EPOC requests only for the investigations concerning such crimes.[161] In this author's opinion, taking into consideration the importance of the framework in enhancing the fight against crime and public protection as well as the length of time it takes to be negotiated and/or amended, a closed list of offences would significantly reduce its scope which would be particularly problematic and limiting. For this reason the approach adopted by both the Commission and Council is the preferred one. The EU institutions could explore the value of greater approximation of the substantive criminal law of MSs alongside the harmonisation in criminal procedure which has taken priority.[162]

Secondly, the draft Regulation departs from the principle of dual criminality as a condition for the execution of orders.[163] The production and preservation orders may be issued in proceedings for a criminal offence recognised in the issuing MS only, without any condition of liability in the enforcing MS. Concerns have been expressed that the proposed framework results not only in the deletion of the usual formalities of mutual recognition but also in the deletion of safeguards linked to the

[160] See ECBA Opinion on European Commission Proposals (2019) available at http://www.ecba.org/extdocserv/20190213-ECBAonEPOsEPROs_Final.pdf.

[161] See European Data Protection Board (EDPB) (2018) "Opinion 23/2018 on Commission proposals on European Production and Preservation Orders for electronic evidence in criminal matters" available at https://edpb.europa.eu/sites/edpb/files/files/file1/eevidence_opinion_final_en.pdf.

[162] For the actual harmonisation achieved in both the substantive and procedural criminal law see Steve Peers (2016) EU Justice and Home Affairs Law, Vol II. Oxford University Press.

[163] See Art. 3(2) and 5(2).

dual criminality principle itself.[164] Critics argue that in absence of the dual criminality requirement, the proposed framework would risk the issuing of EPOC for trivial or political offences.[165]

The dual criminality principle has been an essential ingredient of the traditional MLA instruments and has been considered as a way for a MS to maintain its sovereignty.[166] It ensures that a State cannot rely on the assistance of another to apply a criminal sanction which does not exist in the law of the other State. However, dual criminality has been increasingly considered as an obstacle to efficient judicial cooperation and MSs have been more willing to cooperate even if the investigative measures relate to acts that are not considered as an offence in their national law.[167] This has also been reflected in the EIO directive.[168] The E-evidence Regulation's departure from dual criminality is closely linked to the new model of cooperation that it establishes, which differs fundamentally from the traditional ones. Given that under the proposed framework the relationship is primarily between the issuing MS and SP, the traditional link with the substantive criminal law of the enforcing MS, especially in the view of the limited involvement of the latter, is debilitated. According to the E-evidence framework, the enforcing MS cannot refuse or prohibit the production of e-evidence. Even where there may be concerns that the case in question does not involve an offence recognised in the enforcing MS jurisdiction, an acceptable and fair response would not involve an outright rejection of electronic data. This is especially so considering that it is the SP, not the enforcing MS, the one that processes and controls the data.

## *3.3 Confidentiality, Notification of Data Subject and Procedural Rights of Individuals*

The proposed Regulation requires SPs and their legal representatives to ensure confidentiality regarding the orders. At the same time Recital 43 and article11 of the draft Regulation provide that individuals/data subjects will be notified that their data were requested. Overall the proposed provisions give priority to the confidentiality of the orders versus the individual's right to be notified according to the GDPR and LED. The confidentiality requirement aims to avoid jeopardising criminal investigations. In the draft Regulation EPOC-PR is considered less intrusive that EPOC. This leads to a different approach between the two types of orders regarding the right of the data subject to be informed. The issuing authorities of the EPOC-PR have no obligation to inform the data subject.

[164] See EDPB Opinion 23/2018 above.

[165] Ibid. ECBA (2019) Opinion on European Commission's Proposals above.

[166] See Steve Peers (2016) EU Justice and Home Affairs Law, Vol II. Oxford University Press.

[167] See C. Janssens (2013) The principle of Mutual Recognition in EU Law, Oxford University Press, p. 170, 176–179.

[168] See Art. 10(2) and 11(2) EIO.

The right of data subjects to be informed is an essential element in enabling review and judicial redress and is thus closely linked to the enforcement of their rights, which is vital for the defence. As CJEU held in *Tele2/Watson* "the competent national authorities to whom access to the retained data has been granted must notify the persons affected, under the applicable national procedures, as soon as that notification is no longer liable to jeopardise the investigations being undertaken by those authorities. That notification is, in fact, necessary to enable the persons affected to exercise, inter alia, their right to a legal remedy [...]".[169] Similarly, the ECtHR held in *Roman Zakharov v Russia* that "after the surveillance has been terminated, the question of subsequent notification of surveillance measures is inextricably linked to the effectiveness of remedies before the courts and hence to the existence of effective safeguards against the abuse of monitoring powers".[170]

Both the GDPR[171] (Art. 23) and LED[172] (Art. 13) provide for delays, restrictions or omissions in the provision of the information to the data subject, where such measure is *necessary and proportionate* in order to: avoid obstructing official or legal inquiries, investigations or procedures; avoid prejudicing the prevention, detection, investigation or prosecution of criminal offences or the execution of criminal penalties; protect public and national security as well as the rights and freedoms of others. The Council and the Commission however, take two different approaches in their respective drafts.

The Commission's proposal (Art. 11(1)) provides that the SP shall provide notice to the client/person whose data is being sought by an EPO *unless* it is requested not to do so by the issuing authority. The Council's draft entirely reverses the situation by imposing non-notification by default and making the informing of data subject an exception. According to the Council's opinion, SPs shall only inform the person whose data are being sought if explicitly requested by the issuing authority. In this case, the issuing authority shall also provide information about the applicable remedies to SP to be transmitted to the individual concerned. Where the issuing authority did not request SPs to inform the data subject, the former shall do so, subject to delays that constitute *necessary and proportionate* measures.

It is questionable whether the draft Regulation, especially the Council opinion, strikes the right balance between the right of individuals to be informed and their ability to exercise the available legal remedies versus the needs to safeguard the investigation of criminal offences. Both the GDPR and LED intend that *safeguarding investigations* should be an exception to the rights of data subject to be informed and not the rule. The risk is that over-prudence towards safeguarding criminal investigations could translate into unnecessary and disproportionate intrusion on individual rights, especially if there are no adequate protections and there is potential for further breaches in terms of disclosure, if the case progresses from the investigative stage, to prosecution and trial. The disclosure of EPOC/EPOC-PR to data subjects would then

[169] At para 121.

[170] At para 234.

[171] Regulation (EU) 2016/679.

[172] Directive (EU) 2016/680.

depend entirely on the domestic disclosure arrangements of the issuing MS. Failure to disclose could lead to inadmissibility of evidence on trial and even the collapse of proceedings. It also need be noted that there is no real harmonization in practice regarding notification and disclosure in different MSs which would only add further to the uncertainty.

On a related point it can be noted that the volatility of e-evidence works both ways. If innocent individuals who have come to police attention are not informed in time, they cannot defend themselves adequately, not only in terms of their ability to exercise legal remedies but also in terms of collecting any e-evidence that supports the defence case. For example, another person might have access to the suspect's electronic devices. By the time the suspect is informed, the real offender might disappear or it might be difficult to collect evidence that exculpates the suspect. The proposed E-evidence framework is solely concerned with prosecution, thus arguably ignoring the principle of equality of arms in criminal proceedings recognized by Art. 6 ECHR. No provisions in the draft Regulation enable defendants or other parties in the criminal proceedings to access or request e-evidence. Nor do any provisions ensure that defendants' legal advisors have access to electronic data which are useful to assert effectively their rights.[173] This important aspect need be provided for in the final draft of the framework.

Overall the Commission's approach towards confidentiality and individual notification is better balanced as it requires authorities to make an informed decision regarding confidentiality, which can later be justified rather than taking the situation for granted (i.e. that confidentiality is required) and risking delayed disclosure of even non-disclosure.[174] On the other hand, the Council's draft fills a gap in the initial Commission's proposal by introducing an obligation for the issuing authority to inform the person whose content or transactional data are sought in all cases (even though delays are permitted). This means that the targeted person shall always receive a notification, either by the SP (if explicitly requested to do so by the issuing authority) or by the issuing authority itself. The final provision therefore could be a combination of both these elements from the two draft proposals.

Both the Commission's proposal and the Council's draft provide in article 17 for *effective remedies* available to the person whose data is sought. Both texts emphasize that "such right to an effective remedy *shall be exercised before a court in the issuing State* in accordance with its national law and shall include the possibility to challenge the legality of the measure, including its necessity and proportionality" (Art. 17(3), emphasis added). This could be highly problematic if the affected person does not reside in this country for many reasons. It would require travel to another jurisdiction and knowledge of the legal system of another MS. Inability to understand and communicate in the issuing MS's official language would add to these practical difficulties. It would be an improvement to the current provisions if the affected person would be given options to challenge an illegal order and request reparation

[173] See CCBE Recommendations of 28/2/19 and CCBE Position of 19/10/18.

[174] It has been also suggested that the confidentiality restrictions should be subject to independent judicial approval see CCBE recommendations of 28/2/19 and position of 19/10/18.

in his country of residence or in the enforcing MS where these would be better alternatives than having to engage in costly and highly uncertain judicial procedures in the issuing MS. The principle of mutual recognition could allow for the decision of a court in the country of residence or enforcing MS to be followed by the issuing MS.

The Council's draft also constitutes an improvement by introducing a recital 12a according to which an EPOC should not be issued if the issuing MS has indications that this would be contrary to the *ne bis in idem* principle, i.e. if parallel criminal proceedings may be ongoing in another MS. The principle is transformed by the Charter of Fundamental Rights from a traditional principle of criminal procedure to a fundamental right of undisputed importance in EU law.[175] However, nothing appears in this respect in the articles themselves. It is not clear how the issuing MS will come to know about parallel criminal proceedings. The cross-border nature of the proceedings and e-evidence makes the breach of the principle more likely, therefore its protection needs to be more clearly expressed in the E-evidence Regulation. A provision that clearly prohibits the production or use of e-evidence in cases contrary to the *ne bis in idem* principle would be welcome. Further attention to the above issues would improve the proposed framework and achieve a balance between the needs for effective access to data by LEAs and the protection of fundamental rights.

## 4 Conclusion

The changing nature of crime and evidence in cyberspace has brought new challenges for the effective investigation and prosecution of crime. The E-evidence framework is the response of the EU institutions to the increasing calls for action to address the inefficiencies in cross-border access to information by LEAs. It addresses problems present in the traditional channels of cooperation such as delays and bureaucratic procedures, inefficiencies in public—private cooperation between LEAs and SPs and shortcomings in defining jurisdiction. The legal and policy environment surrounding this initiative is complex. E-evidence framework affects many areas: while cross-border access to evidence by public authorities is governed by the acquis in the area of judicial cooperation in criminal matters, the initiative involves the exchange of personal data, which is subject to data protection and e-Privacy frameworks. There are several co-existing levels of Regulation: EU legislation, MSs' domestic legislation governing criminal investigations, international Conventions, bilateral agreements and the legislation of third countries under whose jurisdiction SPs operate.

At the same time, the legal environment is currently subject to change. Several EU instruments are under revision including the e-Privacy Directive. Work is undergoing for an additional protocol to the Council of Europe Convention on Cybercrime, which is the main international framework governing access to e-evidence by public authorities. A new agreement is currently being negotiated between USA and the EU.

---

[175]See A. Kargopulos (2014) 'Ne bis in idem in criminal proceedings' in European Police and Criminal Law Co-operation, M. Bergstrom and A. Jonsson Cornell eds. Hart Publishing pp. 86–126.

Countries all over the world are addressing challenges posed by the cross-border access to e-evidence through legislative measures. While there is a great degree of uncertainty and the process of adopting the E-evidence framework is ridden in complexity, tensions and disagreements between EU MSs, this study posits that the globalization of criminal e-evidence is driving historic change in the rules as to how LEAs can gain access to communications and other electronic information. Therefore, it is paramount that the e-evidence framework sets standards that can and should be followed.

Through the lens of the E-evidence Framework, this study threw light on the challenges that affect relevant aspects of EU criminal law. In order to deal adequately with these challenges, new legal instruments such as E-evidence are required to offer the mechanisms necessary to facilitate the investigation and prosecution of crime while at the same time provide safeguards and guarantees that the rights and interests involved will be adequately protected. The E-evidence model builds upon the existing models of cooperation, yet is fundamentally different. The extraterritorial dimension of the framework affects the traditional concept of territorial sovereignty and jurisdiction. It departs from the traditional rule of international cooperation that cross-border access to computer data requires consent of the state where the data is stored.[176] Most importantly, jurisdiction is no longer linked to the location of data. According to the new approach, the jurisdiction of the EU and its MSs can be established over SPs *offering their services in the Union* and this requirement is met if the SP enables other persons in (at least) one MS to use its services and has a substantial connection to this MS.[177] In this way the proposal avoids the difficulties in establishing the place where the data is actually stored and the "loss of location" problem. E-evidence framework is a clear example of the development of the territorial jurisdiction concept and the evolvement of connecting factors that establish it, in line with the requirements of legal certainty.

The extraterritorial reach of judicial and state authorities' decisions in the E-evidence framework introduces a new dimension in mutual recognition, beyond the traditional judicial cooperation in the EU in criminal matters, so far based on procedures involving two judicial authorities in the issuing and executing State respectively. This important aspect of the e-evidence framework entails a fundamentally different approach that demonstrates the (need for) development of the EU law traditional concepts so as to respond to the new challenges with adequate mechanisms. From the perspective of the proposed e-evidence framework, the scope of article 82(1) TFEU requires further clarification from CJEU or an amendment (albeit difficult). Reliant on the principle of mutual trust, the debates surrounding the e-evidence framework reveal that in today's European reality this principle is still an objective to be achieved. For as long as disparities in the standards and protections provided by MSs still exist, the way forward should include innovative mechanisms that allow for the control, improvement and maintenance of those standards within

---

[176] Article 25 ff. CCC.

[177] Article 3(4) draft Regulation.

each MS as opposed to fostering a lack of trust, prejudicial treatment and unjustifiable differentiation between MSs within the EU.

The E-evidence framework generally achieves what it sets out to do: i.e. to increase the effectiveness of cross-border access to e-evidence. The application of the same rules and procedures for access to all SPs will improve legal certainty and clarity both for SPs and LEAs which is currently lacking under the existing mechanisms of cooperation. In several aspects the framework serves as a model to be followed in the international arena. However further improvements can be recommended:

- There should be only an exceptional involvement of the enforcing MS as proposed by the Council, so that the framework does not repeat the existing mutual judicial cooperation models.
- The wording of Article 7a could be changed to allow for the enforcing MS to raise objections on behalf of any affected state.
- SPs should maintain their reviewing powers given the unique position they are in to understand the data.
- The framework should specify the meaning of e-evidence and should provide for its inadmissibility in cases of breaches of the requirements specified therein.
- The data categories need to be better defined and brought in line with other EU and international legal instruments, as well as the jurisprudence of CJEU and ECtHR.
- Judicial validation of orders issued by non-judicial authorities should be imperative for all types of data as a form of control and safeguard against abuse or overuse.
- A classification of investigating authorities by means of a schedule in the proposed framework would help to better define the permitted activities within the scope of the Regulation.
- A provision that clearly prohibits the production or use of e-evidence in cases contrary to the *ne bis in idem* principle should be included in the final draft.
- The final instrument should adopt the approach proposed by the Commission regarding confidentiality and subject notification with an obligation for the issuing authority to inform the person whose content or transactional data are sought in all cases (even though delays shall be permitted).
- The right to exercise legal remedies should be extended to the enforcing MS and/or the MS of residence of the suspect.
- There should be provisions that enable defendants or other parties in the criminal proceedings to access or request e-evidence. The accessibility of electronic data to the suspects/defendant's lawyer should be ensured in order to assert effectively their rights.

If implemented, these recommendations would improve the E-evidence framework by ensuring a balance between effective criminal investigations/prosecutions and respect for fundamental rights. A balanced and principled approach should be at the core of any existing or forthcoming instruments concerning cross-border access to electronic information.

**Acknowledgements** The author wishes to thank Sabine Michalowski and Donald Nicolson for their comments on an earlier draft.

## References


1. Bermann PS (2018) Legal Jurisdiction and the deterritorialization of data. Vanderbilt Law Rev 71:11
2. Canadian Association of Chief Police Officers (2018) Resolution #02–2018 reasonable law to facilitate cross-border access to data related to Canadian criminal offences or held by Canadian Providers available at https://www.cacp.ca/resolution.html?asst_id=1694
3. Christakis T (2019) E-evidence in a Nutshell: developments in 2018, relations with the cloud act and the bumpy road ahead. Cross-border Data Forum available at https://www.crossborderdataforum.org/e-evidence-in-a-nutshell-developments-in-2018-relations-with-the-cloud-act-and-the-bumpy-road-ahead/
4. CJEU (2014) Opinion 2/13 of the court on accession of the European Union to the European Convention for the protection of human rights and fundamental freedoms, 18 December 2014 available at https://www.europeansources.info/record/opinion-2-13-accession-european-union-european-convention-protection-human-rights-fundamental-freedoms/
5. Council of Europe "Enhanced international cooperation on Cybercrime and electronic evidence: Towards a Protocol to the Budapest Convention" 5 September 2019 available at https://rm.coe.int/summary-towards-a-protocol-to-the-budapest-convention/1680972d07
6. Council of Europe "Preparation of the 2nd additional protocol to the Budapest Convention on Cybercrime: state of play" available at https://rm.coe.int/t-cy-2019-19-protocol-tor-extension-chair-note-v3/16809577ff
7. Council of Europe "T-CY assessment report: The mutual legal assistance provisions of the Budapest Convention on Cybercrime" December 2014 available at https://rm.coe.int/16802e726c
8. Council of the EU "Decision authorising the opening of negotiations with a view to concluding an agreement between the European Union and the United States of America on cross-border access to electronic evidence for judicial cooperation in criminal matters" (9114/19) Brussels, 21 May 2019, available at https://data.consilium.europa.eu/doc/document/ST-9114-2019-INIT/en/pdf
9. Council of the EU "Decision authorising the European Commission to participate, on behalf of the European Union, in negotiations on a second additional protocol to the Council of europe Convention on Cybercrime" (CETS No. 185) Brussels, 21 May 2019 available at https://data.consilium.europa.eu/doc/document/ST-9116-2019-INIT/en/pdf
10. Council of the EU "Regulation of the European Parliament and of the Council on European production and preservation orders for electronic evidence in criminal matters—general approach" (10206/19) Brussels, 11 June 2019 available at https://data.consilium.europa.eu/doc/document/ST-10206-2019-INIT/en/pdf
11. Council of the EU (2018) Opinion of the European Economic and social committee, Brussels, 2 August 2018 (11533/18) available at http://data.consilium.europa.eu/doc/document/ST-11533-2018-INIT/en/pdf
12. Council of the EU, Final report of the seventh round of mutual evaluations on "The practical implementation and operation of the European policies on prevention and combating Cybercrime", ST 12711 2017 INIT, 2 October 2017 available at http://data.consilium.europa.eu/doc/document/ST-8178-2017-REV-1-DCL-1/en/pdf
13. Council of the EU "Non-paper: Progress Report following the Conclusions of the Council of the European Union on Improving Criminal Justice in Cyberspace" Brussels, 2 December 2016 (15072/16) available at http://data.consilium.europa.eu/doc/document/ST-15072-2016-INIT/en/pdf
14. Council of the EU "Conclusions of the Council of the European Union on improving criminal justice in cyberspace" ST9579/16 available at https://ec.europa.eu/home-affairs/sites/homeaffairs/files/what-we-do/policies/organized-crime-and-human-trafficking/council_conclusions_on_improving_criminal_justice_in_cyberspace_en.pdf

15. Cybercrime Convention Committee (T-CY), Ad-hoc Sub-group on Jurisdiction and Transborder Access to Data, Transborder access and jurisdiction: What are the options?, Report of the Transborder Group, adopted by the T-CY on 6 December 2012, T-CY (2012)
16. Daskal J (2015) The un-territoriality of data. Yale Law Journal 125(2):326
17. European Commission (2018) "Commission Staff Working Document: IMPACT ASSESSMENT Accompanying the document 'Proposal for a Regulation of the European Parliament and of the Council on European Production and Preservation Orders for electronic evidence in criminal matters' and 'Proposal for a Directive of the European Parliament and of the Council laying down harmonised rules on the appointment of legal representatives for the purpose of gathering evidence in criminal proceedings' Brussels, 17. 4. 2018, SWD (2018) 118 final available at https://eur-lex.europa.eu/legal-content/EN/TXT/?qid=1524129550845&uri=SWD:2018:118:FIN
18. European Commission "Proposal for a Regulation of the european parliament and of the Council on European production and preservation orders for electronic evidence in criminal matters" Strasbourg, 17.4.2018 COM(2018) 225 final, 2018/0108(COD) available at https://ec.europa.eu/info/policies/justice-and-fundamental-rights/criminal-justice/e-evidence-cross-border-access-electronic-evidence_en
19. European Commission "Proposal for a directive of the european parliament and of the Council laying down harmonised rules on the appointment of legal representatives for the purpose of gathering evidence in criminal proceedings" Strasbourg, 17. 4. 2018, COM (2018) 226 final, 2018/0107(COD) available at https://ec.europa.eu/info/policies/justice-and-fundamental-rights/criminal-justice/e-evidence-cross-border-access-electronic-evidence_en
20. European Commission "Recommendation for a COUNCIL DECISION authorising the opening of negotiations in view of an agreement between the European Union and the United States of America on cross-border access to electronic evidence for judicial cooperation in criminal matters" 05 February 2019 available at https://ec.europa.eu/info/policies/justice-and-fundamental-rights/criminal-justice/e-evidence-cross-border-access-electronic-evidence_en
21. European Commission "Recommendation for a COUNCIL DECISION authorising the participation in negotiations on a second Additional Protocol to the Council of Europe Convention on Cybercrime (CETS No. 185) 05 February 2019, available at https://ec.europa.eu/info/policies/justice-and-fundamental-rights/criminal-justice/e-evidence-cross-border-access-electronic-evidence_en
22. European Commission "Security Union: Facilitating Access to Electronic Evidence" Factsheet, April 2018 available at https://ec.europa.eu/info/sites/info/files/placeholder_2.pdf
23. European Commission (2016) "Communication on delivering on the European Agenda on Security to fight against terrorism and pave the way towards an effective and genuine Security Union", COM/2016/0230 final available at https://ec.europa.eu/commission/presscorner/detail/en/IP_16_1445
24. European Commission (2015) "Communication from the Commission to the European Parliament, the Council, the European Economic and Social Committee and the Committee of the Regions: The European Agenda on Security" COM(2015) 185 final available at https://ec.europa.eu/home-affairs/sites/homeaffairs/files/e-library/documents/basic-documents/docs/eu_agenda_on_security_en.pdf
25. European Data Protection Board (EDPB) (2018) "Opinion 23/2018 on Commission proposals on European Production and Preservation Orders for electronic evidence in criminal matters" available at https://edpb.europa.eu/sites/edpb/files/files/file1/eevidence_opinion_final_en.pdf
26. European Data Protection Supervisor (EDPS) (2019) "EDPS Opinion on Proposals regarding European Production and Preservation Orders for electronic evidence in criminal matters" Opinion 7/2019, November 2019 available at https://edps.europa.eu/sites/edp/files/publication/opinion_on_e_evidence_proposals_en.pdf
27. European Parliament "DRAFT REPORT on the proposal for a Regulation of the European Parliament and of the Council on European Production and Preservation Orders for electronic evidence in criminal matters (COM(2018)0225 - C8-0155/2018—2018/0108(COD))" Committee on Civil Liberties, Justice and Home Affairs, November 2019, Rapporteur: Birgit

Sippel Available at https://www.europarl.europa.eu/doceo/document/LIBE-PR-642987_EN.pdf
28. European Parliament, Policy Department for Citizens' Rights and Constitutional Affairs (2018) "An assessment of the Commission's proposals on electronic evidence" (external author Martin Bosse) available at https://www.europarl.europa.eu/thinktank/en/document.html?reference=IPOL_STU(2018)604989
29. European Parliament, Policy Department for Citizens' Rights and Constitutional Affairs (2018b) Criminal procedural laws across the European Union: A comparative analysis of selected main differences and the impact they have over the development of EU legislation available at http://www.europarl.europa.eu/thinktank/en/document.html?reference=IPOL_STU(2018)604977
30. European Parliament Resolution of 3 October 2017 on the fight against Cybercrime (2017/2068(INI) available at http://www.europarl.europa.eu/doceo/document/TA-8-2017-0366_EN.html?redirect
31. Eurojust and Europol (2019) Common challenges in combating Cybercrime Joint Report, available at https://www.europol.europa.eu/publications-documents/common-challenges-in-combating-cybercrime
32. European Criminal Bar Association ECBA (2019) ECBA Opinion on the European Commission's Proposals, available at http://www.ecba.org/extdocserv/20190213-ECBAonEPOsEPROs_Final.pdf
33. Frank Verbruggen, Sofie Royer, and Helena Severijns (2018) "Reconsidering the blanket-data-retention-taboo, for human rights' sake?" available at https://europeanlawblog.eu/2018/10/01/reconsidering-the-blanket-data-retention-taboo-for-human-rights-sake/
34. Home Office (2013) Cybercrime: A review of the evidence Research Report 75, ISBN 978 1 78246 2453 available at https://www.gov.uk/government/publications/cyber-crime-a-review-of-the-evidence
35. Janssens C (2013) The principle of Mutual Recognition in EU Law, Oxford University Press
36. Johnson D, Post D (1996) "Law and Borders—the rise of law in cyberspace. Stanford law review Vol 48, 1367
37. Kargopulos A (2014) Ne bis in idem in criminal proceedings. In: Bergstrom M, Jonsson A (eds) Cornell European police and criminal law co-operation, Hart Publishing, pp 86–126
38. Lessig L, Resnick P (1999) Zoning speech on the internet: a legal and technical model. Michigan Law Rev 98(2):395-431
39. Mitsilegas V (2016) Eu criminal law after lisbon: rights, trust and the transformation of Justice in Europe. Hart Publishing, Oxford/Portland
40. Morgus R, Woolbright J, Sherman J (2018) The digital deciders: how a group of often overlooked countries could hold the keys to the future of the global internet, October 2018, available at https://www.newamerica.org/cybersecurity-initiative/reports/digital-deciders/
41. Nicolson D (2019) Evidence and proof in Scotland: context and critique. Edinburgh University Press
42. Peers S (2016) EU justice and home affairs law. Vol II. Oxford University Press
43. Programme of measures to implement the principle of mutual recognition of decisions in criminal matters, OJ C 12, (15 January 2001) available at http://www.ecba.org/extdocserv//CriminalJustice/OtherEUdocs/Programmeofmeasuresimplementprinciplemutualrecogofdecisions.pdf
44. Roberts P, Zuckerman R (2010) Criminal evidence. Oxford University Press
45. Sallavaci O (2014) The impact of scientific evidence on the criminal trial. Routledge
46. Statement of Article 29 Working Party (2017) Data protection and privacy aspects of cross-border access to electronic evidence. Brussels 29 November 2017 available at https://www.hldataprotection.com/files/2018/02/20171129-Art.-29-WP-e-Evidence_Statement.pdf
47. The Council of Bars and Law Societies of Europe (CCBE) (2019) CCBE recommendations on the establishment of international rules for cross-border access to electronic evidence 28/02/2019

48. The Council of Bars and Law Societies of Europe (CCBE) (2018) CCBE position on the Commission proposal for a Regulation on European Production and Preservation Orders for electronic evidence in criminal matters 19/10/2018
49. Vanessa Franssen (2018) The European Commission's e-evidence proposal available at https://europeanlawblog.eu/2018/10/12/the-european-commissions-e-evidence-proposal-toward-an-eu-wide-obligation-for-service-providers-to-cooperate-with-law-enforcement/

## *Legislation*

50. Directive 2014/41/EU of the European Parliament and of the Council of 3 April 2014 regarding the European Investigation Order in criminal matters, O.J. L 130/1
51. Directive 2016/680 on the protection of natural persons with regard to the processing of personal data by competent authorities for the purposes of prevention, investigation, detection or prosecution of criminal offences or the execution of criminal penalties, and the free movement of such data, and repealing Council Framework Decision 2008/977/JHA (LED)
52. Electronic Communications Privacy Act (ECPA) US
53. European Convention on Mutual Assistance in Criminal Matters
54. European Convention on Cybercrime (Budapest Convention) available at https://rm.coe.int/CoERMPublicCommonSearchServices/DisplayDCTMContent?documentId=0900001680081561
55. Proposal for a Regulation of the European Parliament and of the Council concerning the respect for private life and the protection of personal data in electronic communications and repealing Directive 2002/58/EC (Regulation on Privacy and Electronic Communications) COM/2017/010 final—2017/03 (COD)—Draft e-Privacy Regulation available at https://eur-lex.europa.eu/legal-content/EN/TXT/?uri=CELEX%3A52017PC0010
56. Regulation (EU) No. 1215/2012 of the European Parliament and of the Council of 12 December 2012 on Jurisdiction and the Recognition and Enforcement of Judgments in Civil and Commercial Matters, O.J. L 351/1
57. Regulation (EU) 2016/679 of the European Parliament and of the Council of 27 April 2016 on the protection of natural persons with regard to the processing of personal data and on the free movement of such data, and repealing Directive 95/46/EC (General Data Protection Regulation) (GDPR)
58. UK/USA: Agreement on Access to Electronic Data for the Purpose of Countering Serious Crime [CS USA No.6/2019] available at https://www.gov.uk/government/publications/ukusa-agreement-on-access-to-electronic-data-for-the-purpose-of-countering-serious-crime-cs-usa-no62019

# Policing in the Era of AI and Smart Societies: Austerity; Legitimacy and Blurring the Line of Consent

**Mark Manning and Stuart Agnew**

**Abstract** The policing of space, in the traditional sense, can no longer be defined by physical boundaries and is unable to be controlled by any single legal jurisdiction or one rule of law. In a time of artificial intelligence (AI) and smart technologies, arguably policing has reached the limits of policing by public consent in the sense that the new police were introduced in 1829 to counter the problems of rising crime which were becoming a threat the existing social and political order [9]. Policing threats such as cybercrime—whilst experiencing several years of simultaneous budgets cuts, the evolution of new technologies, and the changing nature of crime has created challenges for the governance of policing [54]. This is the context in which this chapter will explore the capacity and limits of policing in an age of austerity, to combat the ever-increased risk of becoming a victim of some form of cybercrime whilst practicing within the global context of AI and smart technologies.

**Keywords** Policing · Threats · Criminology · AI · Smart societies · Austerity · Police budgets

## 1 Introduction

In the opening of his book 'Policing Space', Herbert [34] highlighted the importance to policing of controlling territory to the extent that it is central to the exercise of police power. Arguably, this exercise of power over space through enforcement of the rule of law also defines the limits of police crime control responsibilities [34]. Dixon [22] also highlights the importance of subordination to the rule of law as key to police claims to legitimacy. Of course, the context in which these claims were made, preceded a time when policing space could no longer be defined by physical

M. Manning (✉) · S. Agnew
University of Suffolk, Ipswich, UK
e-mail: mark.manning.1@uos.ac.uk

S. Agnew
e-mail: s.agnew@uos.ac.uk



H. Jahankhani et al. (eds.), *Policing in the Era of AI and Smart Societies*, Advanced Sciences and Technologies for Security Applications,
https://doi.org/10.1007/978-3-030-50613-1_2

boundaries; to a time when police space is, like the universe, endless and unable to be controlled by any single legal jurisdiction or one rule of law. It is in this time of artificial intelligence (AI) and smart technologies where policing has also, arguably, reached the limits of policing by public consent in the sense that the new police were introduced in 1829 to counter the problems of rising crime which were becoming a threat the existing social and political order [9]. To a time when Morrell and Bradford [54] argue that policing threats such as cybercrime—whilst experiencing several years of simultaneous budgets cuts, the evolution of new technologies, and the changing nature of crime has created challenges for the governance of policing. Millie [53] has also recently argued that the police task has continually widened by the periodic adding of responsibilities in which policing risk has become a recent feature of social policy and police practices. This is the context in which this chapter will explore the capacity and limits of policing in an age of austerity, to combat the ever-increased risk of becoming a victim of some form of cybercrime whilst practicing within the global context of AI and smart technologies. In a context where AI and smart technologies will also be necessary tools to aid the police in their quest whilst simultaneously presenting them with significant legislative constraints and stretching the limits of public consent and legitimacy. The fiscal landscape facing 21st century policing also requires police leaders of today and tomorrow to consider not just the economic impact of austerity but politics (local, national and international), technology and social change [69]. Critical discussions surrounding the framing of 'austerity' naturally follow a radical austerity program by central government.

## 2 Austerity and Contemporary Policing in a Cyber-Enabled World

It is not the intention here to regurgitate the plethora of arguments and debates relating to the causes and impacts of the global financial crisis and the most suitable reaction to it. However, it is important to consider the political dimensions relating to the response of the global financial meltdown and the implications this had on individual nation states as this directly affects the level of investment made to public services, in this case policing. Mews [52] and Konzelmann [45] provide illuminating analysis of both the causes and some of the impacts of the financial crisis, placing emphasis on the consequences that governmental policy responses had on its own citizens, highlighting that numerous responses were available, all with their own implications. The initial response of the international monetary community provided a highly coordinated fiscal stimulus program to steady the international financial markets, eventually leading to the "governmental rescues of banks and financial institutions deemed 'too big to fail'" [45]. The resulting increase in public sector debt together with strategies to tackle a growing global recession enabled the revival of neoclassical economic orthodoxy that national budget deficits and public debts reduced opportunities for private economic investment and risked the wrath of credit rating agencies [45, 75]. The misleading political debate that followed the crisis (at least in the UK), which if it was not so serious would be laughable, was clearly framed around party political ideology enabling the construction of an argument that repositioned what was explicitly a financial crisis to that of a UK national debt crisis [13, 78].

This reframing permitted politicians to construct a narrative surrounding fiscal responsibility, ensuring that lines were blurred with regards to the causes of the crisis with an emphasis on fiscal consolidation and taking decisive interventionist actions [79]. Arguments presented by the Coalition government included claims that the budget deficit and national debt restricted private sector investment and growth; placed financial burdens on future generations due to the failures of the day and most prominently, the government would lose the faith of the financial markets resulting in a reduction in the nation's credit rating and increased costs of government and private borrowing, all of which has subsequently been critically discredit [75]. As such, it is important to understand that the austerity related policies implemented, initially under the Conservative-Liberal Democrats coalition government in 2010 were ideological in nature and not imposed upon the UK government by external bodies. The term 'austerity' tends to relate to forms of spending cuts by government with an aim to "reduce a country's current fiscal deficit—the difference between government spending and revenues—and to contain its mounting public debt" [45]. Such policies often include programmes that contain measures to reduce public expenditure, increase tax revenues and other government income streams such as releasing capital by selling off non-financial assets [45]. It is clear how such policies would appeal not only to traditional conservative party with a focus on small state and fiscal responsibility but also to 'right wing Orange Book liberals' such as Nick Clegg, David Laws and Vince Cable who published a collection of essays in 2005 that were critical of their party's lack of focus on traditional Liberalism with an aim to resurrect a change of political direction to the right. It is interesting to note that they all held substantial posts within the Coalition government. That said, the concept of fiscal consolidation is nothing new within political discourse and the implementation of such policies have been seen within the EU periphery states such as Greece and Portugal [79] and "the International Monetary Fund's 'structural adjustment' policies" on Global South countries in terms of access to international bail outs [13, 78].

'The Coalition: our plan for government' document published by the Coalition government in 2010 highlighted in the foreword that "the most urgent task facing this coalition is to tackle our record debts, because without sound finances, none of our ambitions will be deliverable" (HM Government [36]; 7). Here what is being depicted is what Clarke and Newman [13] argue is the presentation of a "paradoxical position of 'virtuous necessity'", in other words austerity policies that reduce government spending are necessary and by making these hard decisions the Coalition government is displaying political virtue. The framing of this strategy was to ensure that the public knew that the government did not want to inflict short term pain (in terms of accessing services and welfare cuts) on its citizens however by aiming to balance the budget by 2015 [79], this would enable future spending on what really mattered, public services rather than servicing national debt. This was emphasised by George Osborne in February 2010 during his Mais Lecture—A New Economic Model when he drew against the now discredited research of "Professor Ken Rogoff, former Chief Economist at the IMF, and his co-author Carmen Reinhart who demonstrate convincingly, all financial crises ultimately have their origins in one thing—rapid and unsustainable increases in debt" ([65], online) as a major justification of seeking to introduce austerity measures should a conservative government be elected.

However, history has demonstrated time and again across the continents, austerity measures aimed at reducing national debt and stimulating growth is a myth that lacks evidence of success yet it appears to be the 'go to' approach for central governments and international financial bodies such as the IMF and World Bank [13, 45, 75]. This was highlighted again when the UK government had to acknowledge that it would not achieve the intended goal of a balanced budget in 2015 as such, the finishing line was moved with even the latest report from the Office of Budget Responsibility (OBR) ([62]; 2) highlighting that the UK is yet to achieve a 'balanced budget' and in fact public sector net borrowing is increasing and that "in the first half of 2019–20, the deficit is up £7.2 billion (21.6%) on the first half of 2018–19".

## 3 Focus of Austerity Policies

Care must be taken when discussing public spending as this can be measured in several ways, for example it can be based upon what money is spent on:

- Departmental Expenditure Limits (DEL)—This covers the elements of public spending that central government has a large element of control over as it is centrally funded
- Annually Managed Expenditure (AME)—This relates to areas where central government has less control such as the demands placed on welfare benefits or the receipts local authorities receive through local taxation.

Alternatively, the focus could be based around the investment focus of central government both in terms of capital and resources:

- Resource Spending—this relates to the day to day operations of a department and covers aspects relating to staffing, administration and program costs
- Capital Spending—this relates to fixed assets such as buildings and equipment together with infrastructure spending on roads/rail for example [6, 43].

A result of the Comprehensive Spending Review (CSR) in 2010, the coalition government introduced a strategy to reduce public spending by approximately 19% across government departments including the Home Office (responsible for policing) and the Ministry of Justice (responsible for courts, prisons and probation services) with an aim to ensure that there was a balanced budget in 2015. However as has been previously identified, the CSR in 2015 required the Conservative government to continue with austerity cuts as the balanced budget objectives were never achieved.

The figure below provides an overview of the cuts that affected government departments. Although the Home Office and Ministry of Justice did not receive the heaviest cuts there has been approximately a 25% reduction in spending in these departments that directly affect public safety and the broader criminal justice system [43]. Cuts to the Department of Work and Pensions (DWP) and the Ministry for Housing, Communities and Local Government (MHCLG) were far more drastic.

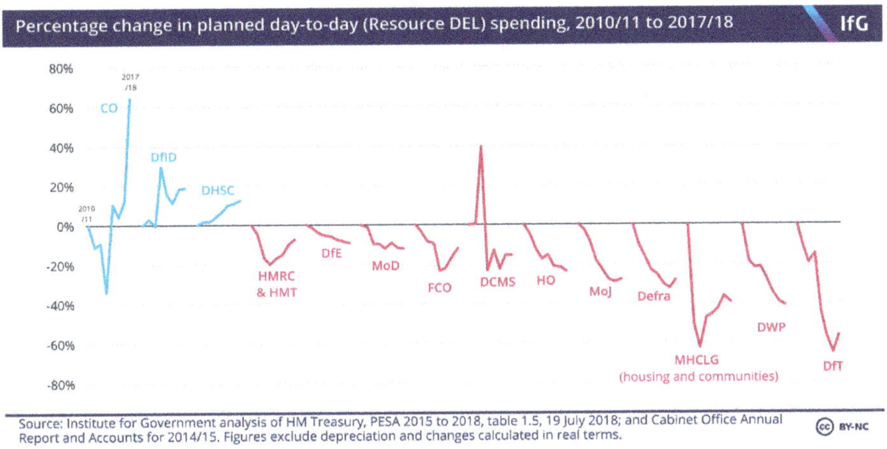


When it is considered that these departments provide support to citizens regarding quality of life issues, such as welfare payments, support services, housing and community outreach programs, it becomes evident that although there may have been a political rhetoric that "we are all in it together" [64], it is clear those that rely on key public services have been impacted the most irrespective of the claim from David Cameron [12] whilst leader of the opposition at the Conservative Party Conference in 2009 that "in a phrase, you get more for less." Arguably recent history would suggest that with regards to the provision of public services and matters relating to policing and criminal justice, 'you get less for less'.

## 4 Austerity, Police Budgets and Demands on Resources

The figure below demonstrates specifically the level of fiscal cuts that the police service has faced since 2009 which has had a direct result in the level of service that they are able to provide [44].

**Spending has declined by 16% since 2009/10, and forces are becoming more reliant on revenue raised locally**

Figure 9.1 **Change in day-to-day spending on police services in England and Wales since 2010 (real terms)**

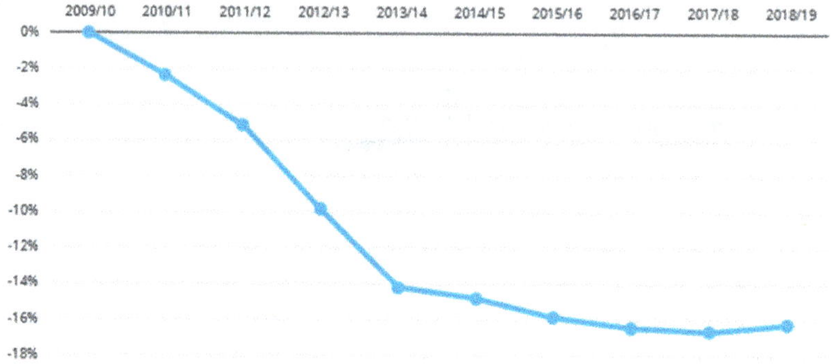


Note: This chart represents the percentage change in gross expenditure over time, in 2018/19 prices.

Source: Ministry of Housing, Communities and Local Government, 'Local Authority Revenue Expenditure and Financing in England, individual local authority data - outturn: Revenue outturn central, protective and other services (RO6)'; StatsWales, 'Revenue outturn expenditure summary'.

Although overall there has been a reduction of 16% in real terms since 2009 to the police budget this should be seen within the context of a 30% reduction in central grants that has resulted in local constabularies seeking to mitigate these large scale financial cuts through a number of strategies, including drawing against monetary reserves, selling assets, careful consideration of how policing is operationalised and a reduction in police strength [44, 4, 24]. It is this reduction in both available budget and police strength that has a direct consequence on the ability of the police service to meet the growing demands placed upon them. The table below demonstrates that police officer strength in England and Wales has reduced by 14% between 31 March 2010 and 31 March 2019, equivalent to 20,560 officers [4], yet there is no evidence of a reduction on the expectations of the police service to not only meet responses to current traditional crime and disorder incidents but also to investigate a growing number of historical sexual abuse cases, crime prevention activities, complex frauds [24] and also continue to service non-criminal emergencies such as traffic accidents and missing persons highlighting what Bowling, Reiner and Sheptycki ([9]; 102) identify as an "omnibus role".

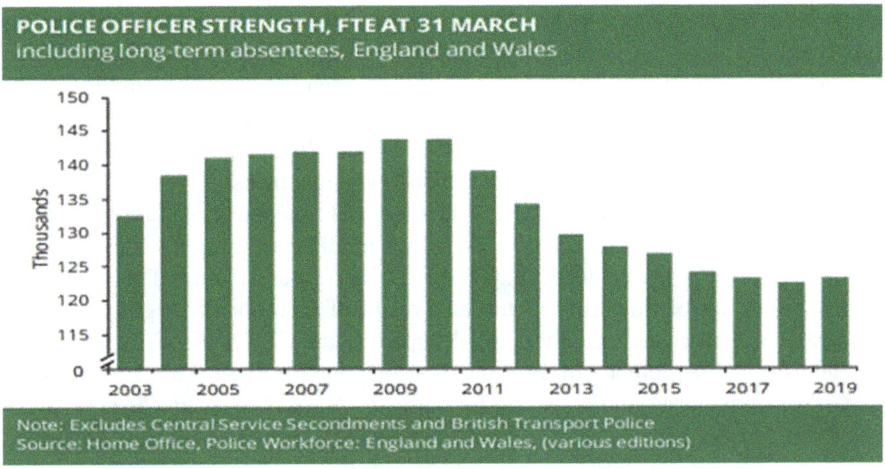


Fleming and Graborsky ([27]; 282) highlight how the police service have become a victim of their own marketing, arguing that as they have over the years been "presenting themselves as omniscient, omnipotent and omnipresent" the public (and arguably even politicians) have come to expect far more than what is actually achievable creating an 'expectation gap'. Although it is quite probable that public demand for police assistance has exceeded capacity for many years, the impact of budget and staffing reductions has brought more clearly to the public and the media, elements of rationalising of police responses to requests for assistance. It is interesting to note the how Chief Officers responses to reduced available budgets were similar to that of politicians with regards budget deficits and a growing national debt, 'cut-backs'. In an attempt to quantify demands placed upon the police, the College of Policing (2015) published its estimation of the scale, scope and costs associated with policing. Even accepting the limitations and criticisms of this report (Elliott-Davies 2016), it does demonstrate some of the more challenging and resource intensive investigations that are becoming more prevalent. For example, it is is argued that there is an increasing trend for more cases to be tried in the Crown Court and increases in fraud cases suggesting more complex and serious cases; there has been a considerable increase in investigations into child sexual exploitation and historical sexual abuse that require substantial resources, increased dissemination from Child Exploitation and Online Protection Centre (CEOP) to regional forces of potential abusers for investigation; an increase in complex investigations into human trafficking and modern slavery (which can also be linked to contemporary crimes associated with County Lines which is receiving considerable national interest) and a number of forces highlighting challenges in specialist units such as High Tech Crime Units (HTCU) due to the number of digital devices that require to be examined as part of investigations (College of Policing 2015).

The growth of mobile digital devices amongst the public must be acknowledged as having consequences for the police. The Fraud Advisory Panel ([28]; 6) claims "by far the greatest setback to the state's efforts to protect its citizens from fraud has been the explosion of inexpensive, powerful and portable communications and computing devices connected by cheap, fast networks." Moreover, the latest Ofcom [61] 'Adults: media use and attitudes' report states that 96% of adults in the UK use a mobile phone and that their findings suggest that the participants regularly access "social media, messaging, shopping, and watching and listening to streaming services and YouTube". Here it becomes apparent that should any investigation be undertaken where the victim and accused have had any form of contact, it may be appropriate to sift through text messages, call logs, social media posts, photos and videos to determine if there is any evidence that could substantiate any claims. The importance of this should not be downplayed and as a result of a number of high profile rape and sexual assault cases recently being dropped by the CPS due to failures relating to disclosure to the defence of evidence that may support their case by the Police and CPS, a review was conducted. By February 2018 3,637 cases had been reviewed with 47 cases being stopped, 18 of the 47 cases having disclosure issues had already been charged using the Threshold Test prior to fully examining all communication evidence [15]. "Common themes identified included communications evidence such as texts, emails and social media being examined too late in the process" [16] all of which undermine public confidence in the Police, CPS and the broader criminal justice system in addition to potentially ruining the lives of law-abiding citizens and increases the likelihood of possible miscarriages of justice.

In addition to the above, fairly recent reports published by the National Crime Agency [55, 56] highlight the growing challenge of cybercrime. The Cyber Crime Assessment 2016 highlighted the lack of reporting of cybercrimes, the lack of understanding of the scale and scope whilst acknowledging that "Cyber-crime activity is growing fast and evolving at pace, becoming both more aggressive and technically proficient" (NCA [55]; 6). Furthermore whilst exploring pathways into cybercrime, key findings suggested that the average age of suspects in NCCU cases was 17 years whereas for other offences dealt with by the NCA it was in the late 30 s (drug and economic crimes); the apparent ease of which to purchase low level, easy to use hacking tools in addition to a perception that there is limited likelihood of being caught helps facilitate these types of crimes and financial gain is rarely a key motivator for young people engaging in cybercrime as status recognition carries far more currency (NCA [56]). It is clear that cybercrime is a complex arena with a diverse range of perpetrators seeking to engage in deviant and illegal activities all with equally diverse motivations and demographics. Whether it be large scale state sanctioned or supported cyber attacks, international serious organised crime groups or individual hackers, the targeting and investigation of such activities require considerable investment and resources. However when considering broader public perceptions on crime and victimisation, the trend still focuses on 'traditional' street-crimes such as violence and property related offences with a disconnect between the reality of actual crime statistics and the public's understanding (ONS [63]). As such, in times when police resources are stretched, this again exacerbates the 'expectation gap' calling into question elements of legitimacy in the eyes of the public relating to what is seen as 'policing', which is often framed through a very narrow lens.

Although it could be that what is needed is for the Police and Home Office to educate the public to what could arguably be seen as a greater risk in terms of potential victimisation. When the Office for National Statistics included fraud and cybercrime for the first time in the Crime Survey for England and Wales in 2016, it highlighted 5.8 million crimes, not previously recorded, suggesting that the public were far more likely to be a victim of these tyes of offences than any other and dramatically transformed conventional wisdom regarding the typology of victimisation [47]. This is not to say that no efforts have been made with respect to highlighting the dangers of fraud and cybercrime, however irrespective of what has occurred to date, public understanding and police capacity to tackle fraud and cybercrime, is still limited. Ten years after the initial fraud review conducted by the then Lord Chancellor, Lord Peter Goldsmith QC PC, evidence presented by the Fraud Advisory Panel ([28]; 6) suggests that there are still too few investigations; still a lack of understanding and lack of strategic co-ordination to tackle fraud, the government's response to austerity reduced budgets that tackled fraud and "Police resources are focused on those [frauds] involving organised crime gangs or linked to the national security threats from terrorism or cybercrime. Since many of these are committed from abroad, very few perpetrators are brought to justice." In addition, the National Fraud Profile for April 2018–March 2019 as reported by Action Fraud [2] identified 741,123 frauds reported with total victim losses of £2.2 billion. Furthermore, of the reported frauds, 86% were cyber-enabled and resulted in 42,127 disseminations to regional forces for enforcement. When considering the National Cyber Profile (based upon cyber dependent offences) over the same period, 23,525 offences were reported totalling a loss by victims of £40 million, with the vast majority of reporting coming from individuals and not businesses (84% and 16% respectively) highlighting the majority of losses resulting from the hacking of social media and emails (Action Fraud [3]).

As has been highlighted, the challenging impacts of austerity politics on the Police's ability to reduce the 'expectation gap' in terms of tackling traditional crimes has only become more difficult with the changing nature of crime, notably as a result of increase use of technology. The availability of affordable computers and Information and Communication Technology (ICT) together with access to easy to use illicit software has enabled opportunities for potential offenders to reap rewards [48]. More needs to be done by the Police Service should it wish to tackle cyber related crimes and this will be explored below.

## 5 Challenges for Policing—Identifying the Scope of the Problem

Identifying the size and scope of the police role in cyberspace is therefore complicated, firstly by variance in defining the meaning of cyber crimes and differences in the way such crimes are recorded by the police or identifed as self reports to surveys such as the Crime Survey of England and Wales. Yar and Steinmetz [89] observe that part of the difficulty is that the term cybercrime cannot be applied to a single crime type, rather, it is a collective term used to identify a range of activities committed in cyberspace. Many of which will necessarily involve in the police use use of AI and smart technologies to combat them. These crimes may be variously recorded as computer misuse or fraud, but may extend to pornography and child sexual exploitation. Many of these activities may also be recorded without specific mention of digital or internet involvemement.

For these reasons, Yar and Steinmetz [89] recognise the considerable problems presented to the criminal justice system by policing the realm of cyberspace, not least of which is because 'policing has historically followed the organisation of political, social and economic life within national terroritories'. As an example, in a study by Her Majesty's Inspector of Constabularies (HMIC FRS) exploring digital crime and policing in England and Wales, a number of factors pertinent to policing were explored. These included: the views of victims; the extent of knowledge and training provided to the police service including frontline and specialist teams, and issues of governance at force and national level [33]. Whilst the report was broadly supportive of existing policies and practices and it identified the need for chief officers to continue developing appropriate training and capabilites for responding to digital crime, the report also clearly identified a need 'to establish the scale and impact of digital crime, at both the national and local level, and how to respond to it' [33]. It is significant that many of the victims interviewed for this study were unaware of the risks posed by digital crime, were unaware that they had become a victim and often, too embarrassed to admit they were a victim and subsequently failed to report the matter. This is a common problem especially for those who fall victim to identity crimes [86].

All of these factors contribute to the 'dark figure of crime' and present difficulties in identifying the scope of the problem [58, 85]. In consequence, this presents the 43 chief officers responsible for policing in England and Wales with significant difficulties concerning how they should develop effective strategies of governance over crime control and assessing risk, whilst also facing increased calls for demand in response to more high-profile, high-harm, crime areas. These include knife crimes and homicides, the investigation of which would arguably, make a larger contribution to the public good [54]. However, in April 2019, Chief Constable Peter Goodman—the National Police Chiefs Council lead for cybercrime—announced that, as part of the developing NPCC National Cybercrime Programme, forces had been able to access £7 m of funding from the Home Office and the National Cyber Security Programme to develop a network of local, regional and national cybercrime units. This funding is supported by a further five year investment pledge of £1.9b under the auspices of the National Cyber Security Strategy [57]. On face value, providing the police service with the requisite funding to respond to the perceived challenges of cybercrime seems a good step forward, but it also raises a number of questions concerning how the police service situate themselves in networks of security within cyberspace; whether they posses the requisite tools and knowledge to do so; whether it is their role to do so; whether legislation is robust enough for policing to operate in this space; whether there are sufficient protections in place to protect human rights and unecessary risks to privacy and finally, whether the general public regard this activity as legitimate?

## 6 Challenges for Policing—Identifying the Field

The policing of cyberspace and operating in networks of security within cyberspace has been a field of developing interest [46, 85–87]. Yar and Steinmetz [89] argue that part of the problem for policing is in recognising the fact that the law and criminal justice systems are not easily adaptable to crimes not committed in the physical, territorial sense that Herbert [34] referred to. Where the legal situation becomes tenuous, the legitimacy of the public police to operate in this sphere becomes equally tenuous as they lose their subordination to the rule of law in a conventional sense [22] and requires them to redefine previously 'taken for granted understanding of police territory, powers and jurisdiction' [54]. Further, Wall [85] identified that for the police to be successful in this quest requires more than the acquisition of knowledge; it requires them to engage and develop new relationships within broader networks of internet security. Arguably, whilst these networks are essential, the police may not maintain the sovereignty usually provided to them by the rule of law. For this reason, it is also necessary for them to develop and maintain 'parity of legal definitions across boundaries, broadly accepted frameworks of accountability to the public, shared values, multi-agency and cross-sectoral dialogues, and more' [85], p. 199).

Here, Morrell and Bradford [54] offer a useful contribution to understanding police modes of governance in which they link governance to ethics, and how the governance of policing contributes to the public good. This is an important consideration when reflecting upon the demand management dilemmas facing policing and how policing in the 21st century requires them to increasingly explore the use of AI and smart technology. In doing so, similar questions arise when considering how these technologies contribute to the public good and whether the public recognise the legitimacy of the police service to use them and grant their consent for its use. Kremer [46] provides a useful example which is more likely to gain public consent when the use of technology supports an identified physical security threat at an airport, for example, where physical procedures and smart technologies are used to detect potential threats. It is generally accepted that their use may breach or interfere with citizens fundamental rights, but are accepted by the public as legitimate in the context of the security mindset [46]. However, other technologies may be viewed less favourably as exemplified in a recent study into the use by the police of live facial recognition (LFR) technology in London [29].

## 7 Challenges for Policing—Human Rights, Privacy and Surveillance Technologies

There are a number of police practices which are unlikely to gain immediate public support, whatever the claims made by the police service to justify their use, and this is especially true for their use of surveillance technologies for intelligence gathering and/or criminal investigations. On these occasions, questions may reasonably be asked about interference with individual human rights by public authorities, where citizens may have an expectation of privacy. The following example is a useful, but not exhaustive illustration of the pitfalls for policing. Between 2016 and 2019, the London Metropolitan Police conducted trials of live facial recognition (LFR) technology in and around 10 sites in central London. Six of which were observed by independent researchers from the University of Essex operating under the auspices of the Human Rights, Big Data and Technology Project—funded by the Economic and Social Research Council. The subsequent report, without reaching any firm conclusions concerning the future use of this technology by law enforcement agencies, highlighted a number of concerns arising from the use of the technology and the legal justifications for its use; consideration of interference with human rights and testing the boundaries of public consent. Of these, consent is of particular interest as it defines what maybe regarded as the legitmate boundaries of police power and practices and whether normative compliance may follow [83]. One issue raised by the report was the fact that the Metropolitan Police regarded its use of LFR technology as overt public space surveillance in the same sense that CCTV is deployed in public spaces. Whilst the use of CCTV is so ubiquitious that its use may now be regarded by the public as banal [31] the same may not be said of all public space surveillance technologies when its use is directed towards identified individuals. As in the case of LFR and other technologies, arguments may be raised that such usage by the police service falls, as previously stated, into the legal realm of the Human Rights Act (HRA) [40]; the Regulation of Investigatory Powers Act (RIPA) [71]; the Investigatory Powers Act [41]; General Data Protection Regulation (GDPR) and the [21] (DPA [21]). For this reason, brief consideration will now be given to 3 areas of law, policy and practice which impact directly upon the police use of AI and smart technologies for surveillance of the population—overtly and covertly; or are used in the course of criminal investigations. This includes consideration of the obligations placed upon the police service by the Criminal Procedures and Investigations Act (CPIA) (1996) to record, retain and disclose their use of these technologies in any subsequent criminal proceedings.

Dealing first with the main points concerning human rights. The HRA 1998 details the statutory rights afforded to citizens of the UK and how they are protected from some actions of public authorities. For the purpose of this chapter, consideration will be given to article 6 for reasons associated with disclosure of material in accordance with CPIA (1996) and article 8 for reasons of privacy.

Article 6-Right to a Fair Trial:

In the determination of his civil rights and obligations or of any criminal charge against him, everyone is entitled to a fair and public hearing within a reasonable time by an independent and impartial tribunal established by law. Judgment shall be pronounced publicly but the press and public may be excluded from all or part of the trial in the interest of morals, public order or national security in a democratic society, where the interests of juveniles or the protection of the private life of the parties so require, or to the extent strictly necessary in the opinion of the court in special circumstances where publicity would prejudice the interests of justice' [40].

Article 8-Right to respect for private and family life:

1. Everyone has the right to respect for his private and family life, his home and his correspondence.
2. There shall be no interference by a public authority with the exercise of this right except such as is in accordance with the law and is necessary in a democratic society in the interests of national security, public safety or the economic well-being of the country, for the prevention of disorder or crime, for the protection of health or morals, or for the protection of the rights and freedoms of others [40].

It can be seen that article 8 is not absolute as within 8.2 there is a provision to interfere with this right if it is in accordance with the law and is necessary in democratic society for the reasons stated. The law enacted to allow this to happen and to provide the legal requirements to do so is RIPA [71]. The relevant section states that:

surveillance is directed for the purposes of this Part if it is covert but not intrusive and is undertaken—

(a) for the purposes of a specific investigation or a specific operation;

(b) in such a manner as is likely to result in the obtaining of private information about a person (whether or not one specifically identified for the purposes of the investigation or operation); and

(c) otherwise than by way of an immediate response to events or circumstances the nature of which is such that it would not be reasonably practicable for an authorisation under this Part to be sought for the carrying out of the surveillance.

It is helpful for this illustration that consideration was given to human rights legislation and of RIPA [71] by Fussey and Murray [29] in their evaluation of the use of LFR technology. They explored compatibility with article 8 HRA [40]—whether such technology was justified as necessary in a democratic society and in respect of RIPA, whether LFR fell within the realm of covert directed surveillance. The Metropolitan Police service claimed that their trial of LFR technology in London was lawful—non intrusive overt surveillance and did not breach Human Rights legislation. This was premised upon several factors: the trials took place in public spaces; consent was implied by the use of uniformed police officers alerting the public that the LFR technology was being used in the vicinity (affording them the opportunity to choose a different route) and this was supported by advertising, leafleting and signage used to alert members of the public, and finally, the police had carefully considered the legal implications for this practice even though they did not claim any specific lawful authority for their deployment [29].

Having entered the area, the LFR technology scanned the faces of those who entered and compared these scans electronically against an already prepared watchlist of individuals whose presence was sought by the police. Where a match was detected, a police officer confirmed the identification by a physical observation of the individual concerned. Whilst the subsequent report by Fussey and Murray [29] raised a number of concerns relating to the use of LFR technology, a similar deployment by South Wales Police was subject to a judicial review and its use was upheld by the authority of R (Bridges) v The Chief Constable of South Wales [2019] EWHC 2341 (Admin). The use of LFR was also subject to a report by the Information Commmissioners Office (ICO) (2019). Whilst, the legal judgment required some future consideration of the legal standards required to operate LFR technology and for a periodic review of its use (See: ICO, 2019), there is some evidence in the ICO report that the use of LFR has broad support from the public. The ICO conduced a survey in January 2019 which received responses from 2002 adults over 18 years, the findings suggested that '82% of those surveyed indicated that it was acceptable for the police to use LFR; 72% of those surveyed agreed or strongly agreed that LFR should be used on a permanent basis in areas of high crime; 65% of those surveyed agreed or strongly agreed that LFR is a necessary security measure to prevent low-level crime; and 60% of those surveyed agreed or strongly agreed that it is acceptable to process the faces of everyone in a crowd even if the purpose is to find a single person of interest' (ICO [42], p. 9). The survey findings seem to add some weight in a general sense to the issue of public consent and their perception of the legitimacy of the practice as something that morally, the police service should or ought to do.

For now, it seems the police service has overcome the first hurdle with their use of LFR, but with an implication that the legal landscape may change in the near future. However, whilst the legal requirements for the use of other technologies in public and private spaces for directed and covert surveillance are more clear (see: RIPA [71]), the increased monitoring of public spaces; surveillance of social media networks and interest groups and, big data surveillance by the police service will remain under scrutiny and are the subject of a developing body of academic literature [10, 26, 66, 74, 86, 88]. Further, the investigation of mobile phone technology for investigation is an area which has placed significant additional burdens on the police service and led them towards some criticism from victims of crime and by civil liberty groups. In an independent review of the investigation of rape in London, mobile telephone technology examined as part of a criminal investigation came under scrutiny (Rt Hon Dame Elish Angiolini DBE QC, [72]. The report highlighted the additional demands placed upon investigators to recover evidence within multi-media devices and across telecommunications networks (Rt Hon Dame Elish Angiolini DBE QC [72], p. 44). Further, how investigation of these devices whilst time consuming, also presents significant disclosure issues (Ibid, p. 93). As an example, the report revealed that in the year 2013/14 the Metropolitan Police Sapphire Units responsible for rape investigation submitted 3,433 mobile telephones for examination by the Communications Intelligence unit and a further 1,105 devices submitted for analysis (comprised of phone handsets, computers and video/audio devices). This represented 27% of the total requests for forensic services on behalf of the Metropolitan Police service leading to a recommendation that they should review the level of forensic support required for rape investigation. A similar recommendation was made in respect of reviewing CPS prosecutors workloads in the light of the additional burdens placed upon them to review unused material as part of the duty to disclose, required by CPIA 1996 (Rt Hon Dame Elish Angiolini DBE QC [72]. This final recommendation was endorsed in a subsequent report by HM Crown Prosecution Service [35]. However, whilst this report highlighted the importance of the proper and thorough investigation of digital technology, another report from Big Brother Watch [7] is more sceptical.

The report by Big Brother Watch [7] raises a number of concerns for breaches of civil liberties by increased intrusive investigation of mobile telephone technologies and by the use of artificial intelligence to gain data from them [7]. Whilst the report recognises the importance of gathering some data for the purpose of thoroughly investigating complaints made by victims of crime, they claim that victims are essentially signing a blank cheque to hand over personal information which far exceeds the purposes for which the data is collected. The report claims that often, if a victim does not cooperate, they are threatened with discontinuance of any investigation being carried out on their behalf. As such, it seems that policing in an age of AI and Smart technologies presents them with the number of legal and ethical dilemmas which are extremely difficult to navigate. The examples that follow in the next section will provide further examples of why this is so.

## 8 Contemporary Policing and Digital Surveillance

This section serves as an introduction to two main areas of concern relating to the use of digital technologies to assist the police in fulfilling their duties. The areas being focused upon initially explore the use of digital imagery captured by CCTV and Automatic Number Plate Recognition (ANPR) cameras as this is the most likely areas that the majority of citizens will be monitored by the police, this is then supplemented by a discussion surrounding the policing of aspects of the internet and social media. There is no doubt that an image of a perpetrator committing an offence clearly assists in ensuring that the correct offender is apprehended, prosecuted, found guilty and receives the appropriate punishment in a timely fashion. However irrespective of how popular TV, films and books portray policing and the use of captured images as a fundamental way to catch offenders, this rarely is the case [70]. The use of images to assist the police or those in authority to identify, categories and track individuals is not a new phenomenon nor is the development and implementation of surveillance techniques to monitor society [59]. Although at times very useful in police investigations, the use of images is only one of many avenues that will be followed, inevitably, assistance from the public, in way of witness statements or tip-offs still provide valuable insight.

## 9 CCTV

There is no need for us to discuss the development, introduction, political debates (or lack thereof) or theoretical underpinnings regarding CCTV use in the UK as one thing for certain is that on this issue, pandora's box is certainly open (see [14, 59, 67, 49, 60]) for an excellent introduction to key discussions that are largely still relevant today). The introduction of CCTV in the UK has passed its 25th anniversary and dominant arguments presented justifying their deployment tends to form around community safety, crime control and assisting with investigations. Although no accurate figures exist it is believed that there could be as many as 6 million CCTV cameras operating in the UK (estimated at 20% of all cameras in the world) and there appears to be little to suggest that this will not continue to grow both under the auspices of the state (Home Office, Local Authorities, Ministry of Defence for example); private industry (not just security but all areas of industrial life) and certainly a growing arena of personal and home security (technological advances enabling low cost home surveillance via cameras attached to homes or embedded into doorbells for instance) [9, 59, 70]. Although serious questions should be asked regarding the effectiveness of CCTV as a crime prevention and crime detection tool especially when current rates of prosecution of offences in England and Wales is an appalling 8% [38]. One would certainly hope that in a society where not being captured on a CCTV camera is a herculean challenge [23, 59, 70], one would also expect a better rate of return for the investment.

Although regularly highlighted as a crime prevention and community safety initiative, the deployment of CCTV cameras initially offered a limited amount of 'protection' as they relied upon poorly paid and often un-motivated staff to monitor screens to identify if any incidents required follow-up action by the police [59, 70]. Arguably though, developments regarding how integrated CCTV has become in modern policing: assisting in the deployment of resources to potential problem areas, crowd and traffic monitoring, town centres, all provide examples of how valuable a resource it is. In addition, it is not unusual for the press to report that the police are reviewing all available CCTV footage when a serious incident occurs, and they even ask for the public to submit their own camera footage if any exists. However contemporary developments now permit for video footage to be automatically reviewed using computer algorithms against set parameters that highlight specific 'timeframes' of footage that may need human evaluation [23, 70].

In January 2020 the Metropolitan Police announced that it intended to formally launch Live Facial Recognition (LFR) technology to aid them in identifying and locating individuals who are of interest, moving on from just pilot testing the technology [51]. It must also be acknowledged that there is widespread use of LFR across the globe, the US, Canada, Russia and China all have various forms of LFR being used although not without controversy [18]. As had been previously mentioned, the use of LFR is a contentious matter as serious questions persist around the legitimacy of this form of surveillance both in terms of its effectiveness in a policing context but also in relation to potential infringements on citizen's human rights [5, 29]. Dwyer [23] highlights that as surveillance networks become more inter-connected and complex, relying less on human intervention and more on AI, a major concern relates to the component elements that make up the system, should one area have an issue this then affects outputs. Put another way, if the database that the AI is relying upon is flawed in any way this will produce flawed results, even if the AI software functions perfectly. An example of this has been identified by AI Now in their annual report when discussing the use of AI recognition software in relation to emotion-detecting or more formally identified as affect recognition. The report states that this software claims to be able to assist in understanding people's emotional state through the interpretation of micro expressions, walking gait or even voice analysis to discover whether or not an individual secretly feels anger, stress, or anxiety for example, some of which have been marketed to law enforcement agencies. Converus, software that examines eye movement and pupil dilation to detect deception has now been sold to police services in both the US and UK. Yet according to AI Now "there remains little to no evidence that these new affect-recognition products have any scientific validity" [18].

However arguably an area of success relates to the implementation of Automatic Number Plate Recognition (ANPR) cameras. Currently there are approximately 11,000 ANPR cameras nationally and they submit 50 million 'reads' daily to a central database [68], to identify vehicles of 'interest' to the police [70]. Originally installed to help protect the City of London as part of the 'ring of steel' to prevent terrorist attacks from the IRA in the early 1990s, once a vehicle passes an ANPR camera, a digital image is taken of the licence plate using optical character recognition software that also records the date, time and location of the vehicle. This is then mapped to the Police National Computer (PNC) the Driver and Vehicle Licensing Agency (DVLA) and the Motor Insurance Bureau (MIB) to "identify stolen, uninsured, unregistered, unlicensed vehicles or those in violation of some other law" [32]. Presented to the public as a crime prevention tool that will enable the capture, arrest and prosecution of 'real criminals', ANPR implementation has received a more favourable introduction than traditional speed cameras that also only capture images of 'real criminals' although those captured for speeding may disagree with the terminology [32, 70]. Burry and Kozitsky [11] identified that evaluations of the use of ANPR (also known as Automatic License Plate Recognition ALPR) by some police forces in the U.S. claimed to have "increased the recovery of stolen vehicles by 65% and increased arrests by 55%". This should not be a surprise as when a vehicle is located on a 'hotlist', police officers are notified and if appropriate a vehicle will be stopped for further investigation [32]. This live monitoring, the sifting of huge databases and active relay of information to local police officers is possible due to the technological advances in computer algorithms [11]. However, it could be that the use of ANPR appears to hold more success due to its superficial simplicity, whereas LFR software is required to 'interpret' human emotions and complex facial features, a rather more challenging scenario.

## 10 The Police and the Internet

The internet environment provides new dilemmas for the police. Challenges surrounding anonymity (actual or perceived), the limited impact of geographical boundaries, limited or the delay in developing appropriate expertise in the area, not forgetting a lack of consensus regarding how to regulate and police the internet are just some of the issues to be navigated (Curran, Fenton and Freedman [20, 89]. Everett [25] identifies that a major aspect of attempting to police the internet and associated deviant and illegal behaviours is due to nation states, should they have any legislation relating to cybercrime, being framed around their perceptions of how to define the issue. Furthermore, she suggests that should international harmonisation occur, no matter how unlikely, agreeing and ratifying legislative changes takes too long and as a result of the recent financial crisis, most law enforcement agencies are still struggling to recover from budget cuts. Therefore, as "the incidence of e-crime inexorably continues to rise in direct correlation with the growing amount of online activity taking place, the funding, staffing and training of suitable agencies and personnel has so far simply not kept pace" [25]. Yar and Steinmetz [89] provide an excellent account of the "lack of organizational stability and continuity in the field of cybercrime policing [that] may itself disrupt efforts to effectively tackle the problem of online crime." They highlight many of the 'so-called' international agencies that appear to respond to cybercrime but emphasise their primary role tends to be supporting local law enforcement agencies rather than conducting investigations and that as greater understanding and political focus changes relating to cybercrime, so does structures and policing responsibilities.

This is particularly problematic when considering the broad spectrum of offences that may be perpetrated online: hacking, the development and introduction of malware, digital piracy and intellectual property theft, economic crimes and online fraud, the distribution of pornography (depending on local legislation), prostitution and sexual offences, child abuse and sexual exploitation, online harassment and stalking not forgetting extremism, cyberterrorism and cyberwarfare [37, 89]. Therefore, it is understandable that any police service may struggle to appropriately manage the risks associated with cybercrime when, from inception, their priority has primarily been around social control, crime investigation and detection, crime prevention and more recently public reassurance. Indeed, it must be recognized that the police are only one of a myriad of actors within the plural policing of the internet, albeit they are a state sanctioned agency [37, 50, 70, 89].

The technological advances in the late 20th and early 21st centuries have enabled a 'computer revolution' that has provided opportunities to legitimately enhance peoples' lives but also facilitated the commission of crime and deviance. Current computer-related crimes may require complex and time consuming investigations as a result of many devices having: encryption facilities that protect the content from unauthorised access; huge data storing capacities that need analysing; networked capacity that requires the interrogation of communication data; the identification of specific IP addresses to provide location data for suspects [89]. Like 'traditional policing', the police have available to them an element of discretion regarding which cyber-related offences they will investigate [9, 70] often under the guise of the seriousness of the offence. This can be seen as a pragmatic response to a growing demand on police resources for crimes that are often perceived to be "low-impact in nature, entailing minimal harm to many discrete victims" [89], therefore not justifying a formal police response. However, as identified earlier, due to a lack of investment in training, many police officers lack the required expertise to competently understand the impact of cybercrimes on victims therefore limiting their ability to accurately estimate the level of harm and distress caused. Bond and Tyrell ([8]; 13) highlighted that "inconsistent and incomplete knowledge is likely to lead to ineffective management of cases as well as increased victim dissatisfaction" as a result of their research into revenge pornography in England and Wales.

## 11 Analysing Devices

As has been identified earlier, electronic devices may need to be analysed to identify evidence is present that may assist an investigation. Depending on the nature of the investigation being undertaken, the digital forensic teams (HTCU) can utilize several computer programs "to facilitate digital evidence acquisition and analysis" [89]. For example when searching for images of child abuse, a forensic investigator could employ programs such as EnCase or RedLight that use AI computer vision technology that scans devices against a range of metrics such as a high concentration of skin tone and edges that may be attributed to people, and then highlights to investigators any specific image for further consideration [37, 89]. A major challenge facing the police service is that it is no longer just desktop computers and laptops that require attention but numerous devices such as: mobile telephones, wireless routers, smart watches, games consoles, building security access logs, CCTV and GPS equipment [37]. This growth of potential sources of evidence has been reported to potentially cause delays of up to 12 months for some devices to be fully analysed [39]. Furthermore, police officers investigating an incident may be able to 'Triage' elements of digital forensic evidence by deploying a 'Triage Kiosk' that downloads digital files and provides an initial scan for potentially problematic files/images. It is envisaged that the use of Triage Kiosks will improve drastically the time taken to verify if digital devices have anything that relates to the investigation [39], Scottish Police Federation [76]. Although every investigation is different, the Digital Forensics Process detailed below provides an overview of the procedures followed:

- Recovery—the data is extracted, which often involves making a copy of a hard disk, downloading data from a mobile, or recovering data from a remote system. The data is then processed to allow an examiner to work on it. This can include decrypting data and recovering files.
- Interpretation—the data is analysed and interpreted, which often involves synthesising information from different sources. This may require significant expertise.

- Presentation—the findings from the analysis are communicated to the investigation team, as a written report or verbally and on occasions they may be used as part of court proceedings.

(adapted from [39])

It should be noted that it is the role of the forensic investigator to also highlight the limitations of the evidence provided. For example, even though indecent images of children may be present on a computer this does not necessitate that the owner can be charged with possession of indecent images as there is a requirement to establish that the owner/user knew of their presence [1].

## 12 Analysing Social Media

The requirements for online material to be considered during investigations also provides the police with a headache. In 2019 there were 45 million active social media users and of that 39 million were active mobile social media users in the UK [80]. The challenge therefore is about identifying an effective way to interrogate social media accounts (public and private) to capture any relevant data, if account holders either have not password protected their account or that the password has been provided to investigators. The ability to make amendments to online forums and cloud based websites provide additional issues for investigators to overcome as ‘messages’ or ‘threads’ may no longer resemble the ‘threat or image’ that a victim claimed existed or has been deleted and overwritten (Taylor, Haggerty, Gresty, Almond and Berry [39, 81]. It is possible that some data may be recoverable from the existing device used using tradition digital forensic techniques, however the police may seek information from internet service provider (ISP) hosting the website or the website owner [37, 81].

Urbanik and Haggerty [84] argue that social media has transformed the dynamics of some existing crimes and provides opportunities for new varieties to flourish such as ‘revenge porn’. The ability of such platforms to enable individuals to share their views and life experiences with little to no moderation operationalises the concept of free speech. Yet, the freedoms that permit unfettered access to cyberspace provides an opportunity for content deemed illegal or problematic to also be uploaded. The range of online content that can be deemed problematic ranges from discriminatory content, illegal and offensive images, instructions on how to commit illegal activities, terrorist related documentation and even individuals filming or posting claims of their own criminal or deviant activities or future plans to engage in criminal activity [82, 84, 89]. As identified earlier, there are multiple agencies that monitor and police the internet, primarily the host website, for example Facebook, Twitter and YouTube, however, in an attempt to tackle gang related crime, the Home Office has allocated £1.38 million to create a dedicated specialist unit that will monitor gang related social media activity based within the Metropolitan Police. It is anticipated that this unit will be able to seek “out both covert and overt threats, messages, or incitements to violence related to gangs. Such content will then be flagged to social media companies to be taken down" [82]. Although it is too early to comment on the likelihood that this initiative will provide positive results, there is clear academic evidence that in the main, the police and other authorities tend to inflate the impact of social media postings on gang-related crime [84].

## 13 Conclusion

The challenges facing contemporary policing with regards to technological developments and the impact and opportunities these provide (legitimate and illegitimate), should not be under-estimated. It would certainly appear that governments, international bodies, legislation and law enforcement agencies will always be playing catch-up to those that seek to do harm or exploit technology to their own end. The challenge of tackling offences that have no geographical boundaries and even at times, victims that either lack the power to voice their concerns or do not even know they are victims and even the broad range of potential offences that can have catastrophic impacts on an individual's life, needs further investigation and understanding. This chapter should be read as an introduction to issues that affect the public police in relation to an era of AI and smart societies, taking into consideration wider political and legal concerns. As the integration of AI expands into all aspects of life, more emphasis must be placed upon ensuring that the component aspects of AI networks actually produce the outcomes that is claimed by the developers and never taking for granted the protection provided to the public by the [40].

## References

1. ACPO (2012) ACPO good practice guide for digital evidence, March 2012, http://library.college.police.uk/docs/acpo/digital-evidence-2012.pdf
2. Action Fraud (2019a) National fraud profile https://data.actionfraud.police.uk/cms/wp-content/uploads/2019/06/National_Fraud.pdf
3. Action Fraud (2019b) National cyber profile https://data.actionfraud.police.uk/cms/wp-content/uploads/2019/06/National-Cyber-2019.pdf
4. Allen G, Zayed Y (2019) Police service strength, briefing paper, Number 00634, 31 October 2019. House of Commons Library
5. Amnesty International UK (2020) UK: Met Police's use of facial recognition technology 'a huge threat to human rights', https://www.amnesty.org.uk/press-releases/uk-met-polices-use-facial-recognition-technology-huge-threat-human-rights, 24th January 2020
6. Bailey S (2002) Public sector economics: theory, policy and practice. Palgrave, Hampshire
7. Big Brother Watch (2019) Digital Strip Searches The police's data investigations of victims. Online@ https://bigbrotherwatch.org.uk/wp-content/uploads/2019/07/Digital-Strip-Searches-Final.pdf: Big Brother Watch
8. Bond E, Tyrrell K (2018) Understanding revenge pornography: a national survey of police officers and staff in England and Wales. J Interpers Viol, 1–16

9. Bowling B, Reiner R, Sheptycki J (2019) The politics of the police, 5th edn. Oxford University Press, Oxford
10. Brayne S (2017) Big data surveillance: the case of policing. Am Sociol Rev 82(5):977–1008
11. Burry A, Kozitsky V (2017) Automatic License Plate Recognition. In: Loce R, Bala R, Trivedi M (eds) Computer vision and imaging in intelligent transportation systems. Wiley, New York
12. Cameron D (2009) Spring conference Speech. https://www.politics.co.uk/comment-analysis/2009/04/27/tory-spring-conference-speeches-in-full
13. Clarke J, Newman J (2012) The alchemy of austerity. Crit Soc Policy 32(3):299–319
14. Cohen S (1985) Visions of social control. Polity Press, Cambridge
15. CPS (2018a) Rape and serious sexual offence prosecutions: Assessment of disclosure of unused material before trial. https://www.cps.gov.uk/sites/default/files/documents/publications/RASSO-prosecutions-Assessment-disclosure-unused-material-ahead-trial_0.pdf
16. CPS (2018b) CPS publishes outcome of sexual offences review. https://www.cps.gov.uk/cps/news/cps-publishes-outcome-sexual-offences-review
17. Criminal Procedures & Investigation Act 1996
18. Crawford K, Dobbe R, Dryer T, Fried G, Green B, Kaziunas E, Kak A, Mathur V, McElroy E, Sánchez A, Raji D, Rankin J, Richardson R, Schultz J, West S, Whittaker M (2019) AI Now 2019 Report. New York: AI Now Institute, https://ainowinstitute.org/AI_Now_2019_Report.html
19. Criminal Procedures and Investigations Act 1996
20. Curran J, Fenton N, Freedman D (2012) Misunderstanding the Internet. Routledge, London
21. Data Protection Act 2018
22. Dixon D (1997) Law in policing: legal regulation and police practices. Clarendon Press, Oxford
23. Dwyer T (2015) Convergent media and privacy. Palgrave, Basingstoke
24. Elliott-Davies M, Donnelly J, Boag-Munroe F, Van Mechelen D (2016) Getting a battering: the perceived impact of demand and capacity imbalance within the Police Service of England and Wales: A qualitative review. Police J: Theory Pract Princ 89(2):93–116
25. Everett C (2009) Who is responsible for policing the internet? Comput Fraud Secur 2009(5):5–6
26. Ferguson A (2018) The legal risks of big data policing. Criminal Justice 33(2):4–7
27. Fleming J, Grabosky P (2009) Managing the Demand for police services, or how to control an insatiable appetite. Policing: J Policy Pract 3(3):281–291
28. Fraud Advisory Panel (2016) The Fraud Review: Ten Years On. https://www.fraudadvisorypanel.org/wp-content/uploads/2016/06/The-Fraud-Review-Ten-Years-On-WEB.pdf
29. Fussey P, Murray D (2019) Independent report on the London metropolitan police service's trial of live facial recognition technology. Colchester: Human Rights Centre, University of Essex
30. General Data Protection Regulation
31. Goold B, Loader I, Thumala A (2013) The banality of security: the curious case of surveillance cameras. Br J Criminol 53(6):977–996
32. Haines A, Wells H (2011) Persecution or protection? Understanding the differential public response to two road-based surveillance systems. Criminol Criminal Justice 12(3):257–273
33. Her Majesty's Inspectorate of Constabularies (2015) Real lives, real crimes: a study of digital crime and policing. Available online: https://www.justiceinspectorates.gov.uk/hmic
34. Herbert S (1997) Policing space: territoriality and the los Angeles police department. University of Minnesota Press, Minneapolis
35. HM Crown Prosecution Service Inspectorate (2019) 2019 rape inspection: a thematic review of rape cases by HM Crown Prosecution Service Inspectorate. London: HMCPSI Publication No. CP001:1267
36. HM Government (2010) The Coalition: our plan for government, https://www.gov.uk/government/publications/the-coalition-documentation
37. Holt T, Bossler A, Seigried-Spellar K (2018) Cybercrime and digital forensics: an introduction, 2nd edn. Routledge, London
38. Home Office (2019) Crime Outcomes in England and Wales: year ending March 2019, Statistical Bulletin HOSB 12/19, July 2019. https://assets.publishing.service.gov.uk/government/uploads/system/uploads/attachment_data/file/817769/crime-outcomes-hosb1219.pdf

39. Houses of Parliament (2016) Digital Forensics and Crime. Research Note, Number 520, March 2016. Parliamentary Office of Science and Technology. https://researchbriefings.parliament.uk/ResearchBriefing/Summary/POST-PN-0520 https://nationalcrimeagency.gov.uk/who-we-are/publications/357-cyber-crime-assessment-2016/file
40. Human Rights Act (1998)
41. Investigatory Powers Act (2016)
42. Information Commissioners Office (ICO) (2019) ICO investigation into how the police use facial recognition technology in public places. Available online https://ico.org.uk/media/about-the-ico/documents/2616185/live-frt-law-enforcement-report-20191031.pdf: Information Commissioners Office
43. Institute for Government (2019a) Whitehall Monitor 2019. https://www.instituteforgovernment.org.uk/publication/whitehall-monitor-2019/finances
44. Institute for Government (2019b) Performance Tracker 2019 A data-driven analysis of the performance of public services. https://www.instituteforgovernment.org.uk/publications/performance-tracker-2019
45. Konzelmann S (2014) The political economics of austerity. Camb J Econ 2014(38):701–741
46. Kremer J (2014) Policing Cybercrime or militarizing cybersecurity? Security mindsets and the regulation of threats from cyberspace. Inf Commun Technol Law 23(3):220–237
47. Loveday B (2017a) Still plodding along? The police response to the changing profile of crime in England and Wales. Int J Police Sci Manag 19(2):101–109
48. Loveday B (2017) The shape of things to come. Reflections on the potential implications of the 2016 Office of National Statistics Crime Survey for the police service of England and Wales. Policing 12(4):398–409
49. Lyon D (1994) The electronic eye: the rise of surveillance society. Polity Press, Cambridge
50. Mawby R (2008) Models of policing. In Newburn T (ed) Handbook of policing (2nd ed). Cullompton: Willan
51. Metropolitan Police (2020) Live facial recognition, https://www.met.police.uk/live-facial-recognition-trial/
52. Mew S (2013) Contentious politics: financial crisis, political-economic conflict, and collective struggles-a commentary. Soc Justice 39(1):99–114
53. Millie A (2014) What are the police for? Re-thinking policing post austerity. In: Brown J (ed) The Future of policing. Routledge, London
54. Morrell K, Bradford B (2019) Policing and public management: governance, vices and virtues. Routledge, London
55. National Crime Agency (2016) Cyber Crime Assessment 2016. https://www.nationalcrimeagency.gov.uk/who-we-are/publications/357-cyber-crime-assessment-2016/file
56. National Crime Agency (2017) Pathways into Cyber Crime. https://nationalcrimeagency.gov.uk/who-we-are/publications/6-pathways-into-cyber-crime-1/file
57. National Police Chiefs Council (2019) Dedicated Cyber Crime Units Get Million Pound Cash Injection. news.npcc.police.uk: NPCC
58. Newburn T (2017) Criminology, 3rd edn. Routledge, London
59. Norris C, Armstrong G (1999) The Maximum surveillance society: the rise of CCTV. Berg, Oxford
60. Norris C, Moran J, Armstrong G (eds) (1998) Surveillance, closed circuit television and social control. Ashgate, Aldershot
61. Ofcom (2019) Adults: Media use and attitudes report 2019. https://www.ofcom.org.uk/research-and-data/media-literacy-research/adults/media-lives
62. Office of Budget Responsibility (2019) Commentary on the Public Sector Finances. September 2019, https://obr.uk/docs/dlm_uploads/October-2019-Commentary-on-the-Public-Finances.pdf
63. Office of National Statistics (2017) Public perceptions of crime in England and Wales: year ending March 2016. https://www.ons.gov.uk/peoplepopulationandcommunity/crimeandjustice/articles/publicperceptionsofcrimeinenglandandwales/yearendingmarch2016

64. Osborne G (2009) We will lead the economy out of crisis. https://conservative-speeches.sayit.mysociety.org/speech/601293
65. Osborne G (2010) A New Economic Model, the Mais Lecture, 24 February. https://conservative-speeches.sayit.mysociety.org/speech/601526
66. Owen S (2017) Monitoring social media and protest movements: ensuring political discourse order through surveillance and surveillance discourse. Soc Ident 23(6):688–700
67. Painter K, Tilley N (eds) (1999) Surveillance of public space: CCTV, street lighting and crime prevention, crime prevention studies, vol 10. Criminal Justice Press, New York
68. PoliceUK (2020) Automatic Number Plate Recognition. https://www.police.uk/information-and-advice/automatic-number-plate-recognition/
69. Rogers C (2014) Police accountability in the age of austerity. Police J: Theory Pract Princ 87(1):1–2
70. Rowe M (2018) Introduction to policing, 3rd edn. Sage, London
71. Regulation of Investigatory Powers Act (2000)
72. Rt Hon Dame Elish Angiolini DBE QC (2015) Report of the Independent Review into The Investigation and Prosecution of Rape in London. London: Commissioner of the Metropolitan
73. Police and Director of Public Prosecutions Jointly
74. Sanders C, Sheptycki J (2017) Policing, crime and 'big data'; towards a critique of the moral economy of stochastic governance. Crime Law Soc Change 68:1–15
75. Sawyer M (2012) The tragedy of UK fiscal policy in the aftermath of the financial crisis. Camb J Econ 2012(36):205–221
76. Scottish Police Federation (2019) 'Cyber kiosks' to be rolled out by summer after use is found to be "lawful", https://spf.org.uk/cyber-kiosks-to-be-rolled-out-by-summer-after-use-is-found-to-be-lawful/
77. Smith R (2016) Policing in austerity: time to go lean? Int J Emerg Serv 5(2):174–183
78. Stanley L (2016) Legitimacy gaps, taxpayer conflict, and the politics of austerity in the UK. Br J Politics Int Relat 18(2):389–406
79. Stanley L (2016) Governing austerity in the United Kingdom: anticipatory fiscal consolidation as a variety of austerity governance. Econ Soc 45(3–4):303–324
80. Statista (2019) Total number and the share of population of active social media and mobile social media users in the United Kingdom (UK) in January 2019. https://www.statista.com/statistics/507405/uk-active-social-media-and-mobile-social-media-users/
81. Taylor MJ, Haggerty J, Gresty D, Almond P, Berry T (2014) Forensic investigation of social networking applications. Network Secur 11:9–16
82. Trendall S (2018) Government and police to set up £1.4m anti-gang social-media unit, Public Technology. https://www.publictechnology.net/articles/news/government-and-police-set-%C2%A314m-anti-gang-social-media-unit
83. Tyler T (2006) Why people obey the law. Princeton University Press, Princeton
84. Urbanik M, Haggerty KD (2018) 'It's Dangerous': the online world of drug dealers, rappers and the street code. Br J Criminol 58(6):1343–1360
85. Wall D (2007) Policing cybercrimes: situating the public police in networks of security within cyberspace. Police Pract Res 8(2):183–205
86. Wall D (2013) Policing identity crimes. Policing and Society: An International Journal of Research and Policy 23(4):437–460
87. Wall D, Williams M (2013) Policing cybercrime: networked and social media technologies and the challenges for policing. Policing Soc: Int J Res Policy 23(4):409–412
88. Williams M, Edwards A, Housley W, Burnap P, Rana O, Avis N, Morgan J, Sloan L (2013) Policing cyber-neighbourhoods: tension monitoring social media networks. Policing Soc 23(4):461–481
89. Yar M, Steinmetz KF (2019) Cybercrime and society, 3rd edn. Sage, London

# Behavioural Analytics: A Preventative Means for the Future of Policing

**Alireza Daneshkhah, Hamid Jahankhani, Homan Forouzan, Reza Montasari, and Amin Hosseinian-Far**

**Abstract** Without sufficient intelligence, police response to crimes occurs in the form a reactive retort. This is even more so in the case of cyberspace policing, as digital platforms increase the complexities involved in the overall police incident response development. In this paper, we briefly introduce cybercrime and the necessities that police forces have to deal with. We argue that there is an urgent need for development and adoption of proactive and preventive techniques to identify and curb cyber and cyber-enabled crimes. We then present topic modelling as one of effective preventive techniques for predicting behaviours that can potentially be linked to cybercrime activities on social media.

**Keywords** Future of policing · Topic model · Information security · Machine learning · Predictive inference · Behavioural analytics

## 1 Introduction

More and more people and organisations are relying on electronic devices and the Internet to store personal information, and this consequently increases also increase the opportunity for crime. Cyber criminals have no jurisdiction as they can operate from anywhere in the world. The complicity of investigation of such crimes is extremely challenging, if staff are not adequately trained or educated on the subject matter in being able to identify the offenders and bring them to justices [22]. As

---

A. Daneshkhah
Coventry University, Coventry, UK

H. Jahankhani (✉)
Northumbria University, London, UK
e-mail: Hamid.jahankhani@northumbria.ac.uk

H. Forouzan · A. Hosseinian-Far
University of Northampton, Northampton, UK

R. Montasari
Huddersfield University, Huddersfield, UK



H. Jahankhani et al. (eds.), *Policing in the Era of AI and Smart Societies*,
Advanced Sciences and Technologies for Security Applications,
https://doi.org/10.1007/978-3-030-50613-1_3

technology has become a pivotal point in our society, the dependency is intensified and critical for all, ranging from people to business and instead a larger scale to the government organisations becoming more cyber resilient. In addition, it is vital to have in place measures and processes in place that are adequate and sufficient in securing information security across all technological platforms. Such processes will provide safeguarding of data, information, network and devices from any form of hacking, breach or attack. Moreover. it is important that the police forces and cyber security specialists valuing, protecting and processing available information and intelligence with confidentiality, integrity and availability (CIA), as this would have a direct impact on the public's trust and confidence on those parties [10]. If the security of this information protection is breached, this could have a detrimental effect on the service that police forces deliver, public confidence and the organisations reputational values. Therefore, it is extremely imperative that the right level of training and education be provided to police officers to be able to protect and safeguard the information on their Information Communications and Technology (ICT) systems.

## 2 Technology and Crime

The term cybercrime describes acts, which incorporates the unlawful usage of computer technology and the Internet [14]. The question that is raised here is how aware, educated and knowledgeable the police services are in safeguarding their information and preventing a cyber-attack on their infrastructures.

As cyber criminals can operate from anywhere around the world with no jurisdiction this makes it extremely difficult for the law enforcement agencies to track and bring to justice those responsible. Such investigations are very complex and resource intensive for the police. What is key here is that the police services need to be aware, educated and trained to be able to identify their weaknesses and vulnerabilities to prevent their devices being subject to a breach or an attack. Previously cybercrime was not on the government and law enforcement agencies agenda, however more recently due to the rapid rise of cyber-enabled crime within the UK in 2010 the UK Government have classified cybercrime as a 'Tier 1' threat by The Government's 2010 National Security Strategy [5]. The Government's 2010 National Security Strategy has grouped threats into three tiers, where 'Tier 1' threat is classified as the highest threat. Within the report, it has been highlighted that companies, industries and government organisations need to protect their devise and prevent potential attacks within the UK [10]. Tackling the risks and the impacts associated with cyber and cyber enabled crimes can be more challenging for Small to Medium Enterprises (SME) compared to larger organisations, due to the lack of relevant resources (both human and financial).

As the society is seeing a surge in the use of technology and the dependency is becoming greater day by day, it is vital that there is an adequate and secure information security to safeguard the information, data, network and devices from any form of attack [35]. The term cybercrime is used to describe acts, which incorporates the unlawful usage of computer technology and the Internet. The question that could be asked here is how equipped, trained and educated are the police forces in tackling such a vast growing crime. Cyber criminals have no jurisdiction as they can operate from anywhere in the world the complicity of investigation of such crimes will make it difficult if the police are not adequately trained or educated on the subject matter in being able to identify the offenders and bring them to justices.

The Office for National Statistics (ONS) Survey of Crime in England and Wales report In March 2016 [8], noteworthy saw an important change in cybercrime. Due to the surge in cyber enabled crimes the ONS devoted a cybercrime and fraud section on the report for a very first time. This illustrated the importance of cybercrime and the need for government and law enforcement agencies needing to take cybercrime more seriously than ever before. The report highlighted the fact that an estimate of 5.8 million cyber enabled crime and fraud had been committed in England and Wales. The data estimated out of the 12 million crimes committed across England, Wales nearly over half of those crimes were cyber enabled, and fraud related [9]. Such statistics were an eye opener to the government and the law enforcement agencies as traditional crimes was making a significant shift towards cyber enabled crime. The question that might be considered is the fact that are police forces across England and Wales adequately trained, educated and equipped to tackle cyber enabled crime to bring those responsible to justice and to serve justice for the victims of those crimes. Due to the advancement of technology, criminals are using the cyber space more and more in carrying out their criminal conducts, the governments national statistics has highlighted that cyber enabled crime victims are on an increase year by year [44].

## 3 Traditional Crime Versus Cyber Crime

Typically, criminals who intended to gain personal information from others would have committed identify theft by intercepting the intended targets post, looking at their trash and trying to piece their office shredded documents together. With the advancement of technology and the social dependency for people to interact with the Internet, more and more personal information has become readily accessible for criminals. As people are using their smart phones, tablets, TV's and computers more to purchasing goods of the internet, paying their bills via applications, using social media applications to engage with others and to share personal information.

Traditional Personal identity theft tactics have not changed but what has changed is their method in which they are acquired. As previously criminals used to physically trawl through the trash of others now through hacking, breaches and attacks they search the systems recycle bin for deleted items, cache memory, temporary files and cookies for recent accessed data and so on. There are many more methods that criminals use to obtain personal or financial information from others for example the use of phishing emails to get the intended victim to provide their personal or financial information to the criminal. Benefits of obtaining personal information could be financial, revenge, personal or to misrepresent that person and to commit a criminal conduct [6, 10].

Both traditional crime and cybercrime have one thing in common and that is the word 'crime' which includes an unlawful act or conduct. One uses the Internet and or a computer device to carry out the criminal conduct, where the perpetrator has no jurisdiction and can operate from anywhere across the world in committing that crime. On the other hand, traditional crimes require the perpetrator to be present at the crime scene where the crime has been committed [6, 10].

For both traditional and cybercrime, the perpetrator will leave evidential footprints behind. For instance, for traditional crimes, the offender will leave DNA, fingerprints and physical traces of evidence behind at the crime scene. The same applies for cybercrime, cyber criminals will leave digital footprints and evidential traces behind through the use of the internet or digital devices [10, 40].

As the police services in the UK have been investigating traditional crimes since the 1890s, they have become experts and masters in identifying and bringing offenders to justice through their evolving methods and tactics. However, the police service has recently began investigating cybercrime and are still by far nowhere near in being able to master such methods and tactics. With traditional crimes the police would have looked at the physical footprints left by the perpetrator (DNA, finger prints, shoe prints etc.), review CCTV footages of the incidents, speak with witnesses and interview suspects to obtain further information. This is not always possible with cyber criminals who could be in another country, using proxy servers from another country or other genuinely devices to carry out their attack on the intended target in a third country. Due to such complexities and lack of knowledge and training by police services across the world the police are finding it very difficult to investigate such offences and bring those responsible to justice. Due to such complications and difficulties faced by the legal authorities the investigations of cyber-attacks are more resource intensive, financial very expensive and require a lot of time in order to identify and prosecute those responsible [19].

Traditionally perpetrators would have taken a high risk in order to commit a theft, robbery or a burglary offence in compression to the benefit that they would have obtained from committing such offences. There was a high risk that law enforcement agencies would have caught and brought them to justice. However, in the world of cybercrime similar or even higher profits are achievable with much lesser risk of being caught and prosecuted. Criminals are becoming wiser and cyber knowledgeable by balancing out the risk of being caught against the benefits [12].

## 4 Digital Platforms and Social Media

The rise of digital platforms for business and personal use has necessitated further engagement with preventive measures in security management. The landscape of cyber crime and cyber enabled crime classification and categorisation is now very dissimilar to the earlier cataloguing as illustrated in Jahankhani et al. [21]. Social media have become an integral part of the day to day lives; furthermore, several business models nowadays leverage the potentials of data generated within social media. Twitter, Facebook, Instagram, Snapchat, and LinkedIn are some of the examples of platforms that have seen a significant increase in the number of its users from both personal and business realms. Figure 1 illustrates the total number of Twitter users in the 9 years from 2010 until the first quarter of 2019, presenting a significant growth in the number of users in 9 years.

Some perpetrators will use the internet and the social media to cause the cyber bullying, stalking and harassment either for their own pleasure or to gain financial means from them [37].

Big Data (BD) that is being produced in such online platforms can potentially offer valuable insights [18, 19], yet inferring and identifying perilous crimes from the data have become very challenging. The complexities arising in BD and the challenges in BD analysis are not only caused by the high volume of data, and can be due to the high velocity, variety, velocity or veracity of data generated in social media platforms [18]. The cyber criminology of social media can occur in a reactive manner where the law enforcement teams and/or security specialists attempt to infer from the available data after the cyber crime has occurred. In the contrary, a predictive approach is a preferred method for envisaging a crime that is to occur prior to it happens [7]. In the section below, we examine behavioural analytics as an emerging method for businesses to gain competitive advantage, and how behavioural analytics could be used for facilitating cyber criminology in social media platforms. As an instance of these crimes, we can discuss some of these in more details.

As the Internet is becoming a key part of our life's and the majority of us are becoming more and more dependent on the usage of social media in order to keep in

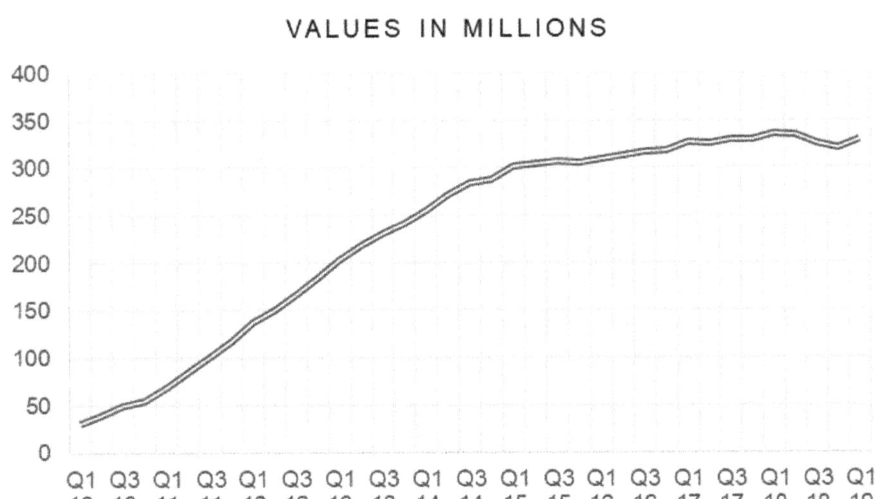


**Fig. 1** Number of Twitter users from Q1 2010 to Q1 2019. Data from Statista [38]

contact with our relatives, friends, colleagues, associates or even find new friends. However, this presence on the cyberspace comes with worries:

- The majority of social media users are blind to cyber bullying and its effects on victims as they might not consider or beware that sending an inappropriate messages/pictures/comments could cause the receiver or the intended victim anxiety, humiliation, depression and ultimately lead to a suicide [16]. Cyber Bullying has a number of different types, as there are numerous ways of bullying someone online.
- Online Harassment—This involves the act of sending insulting, rude, offensive messages to the intended victim. Such messages/comments/photos are abusive or humiliating in nature [16].
- Trickery and Outing—This involves an act when one shares another's personal information in order to trick that person or has the purpose to divulge secrets with the intention of on warding that to others. Such acts may involve private photos, images and videos too [4].
- Cyber Stalking—This involves an act of constant messages being repeatedly send to another or a group with threatening, intimidating and abusive behaviour in nature. Such acts may also be illegal and could be treated as a criminal offence depending on the contexts that is be circulated. This would also include sending out false rumours and gossip to others on social media applications. This may also include altering images of others with the intention of posting in online for the purpose of bullying.
- Exclusion from a Group—This is an act where others deliberately leave the intended victim out of a group such as online apps, gaming sites, group messages and other online meetings. Unfortunately, this form of cyber bullying is very common among the younger generation [16].
- Impersonation—This act involves one hacking into another's email or social networking account with the intention of using the account to send malicious and humiliating posts, images to/about others. This act also involves the setting up of fake profiles on applications, social network sites, and online boards, such activities are very hard to get rid of.

## 5 Preventive Versus Reactive Policing

Ratcliffe [33] views intelligence-led policing as a strategic effort to reduce crime and to adopt a preventive approach to tackle crimes. He defines it as "the application of criminal intelligence analysis as an objective decision-making tool in order to facilitate crime reduction and prevention through effective policing strategies and external partnership projects drawn from an evidential base". He goes on to argue that the police authorities act as the decision maker in the context and the impact made by the police within the criminal environment is influences by the intelligence provided (see Fig. 2).

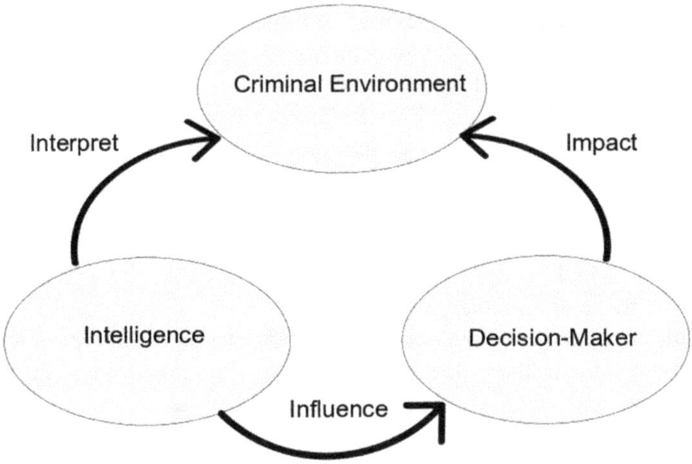


**Fig. 2** Intelligence-led policing. Redrawn with contents adapted from Ratcliffe [33]

Lum et al. [29] introduced a crime prevention matrix that sees reactive approaches to policing on the other side of the spectrum where the police acts after the crime has occurred or in the best scenario when the crime is taking place. The preventive approaches on the other hand, attempt to prevent a crime from occurring [36]. One of the dilemmas that the police will need to consider is the accuracy of ex-ante approaches to crime prevention, and to minimise bias through reasonable approaches such as risk management [25].

Technology can play an important role in pricing the intelligence required for implementation of preventive policing. Artificial intelligence (AI) and machine learning techniques can play a vital role in proving reliable intelligence to police forces [7]. In a social media context. the data for such techniques could be provided by the social media platforms themselves. The interactions between individuals or groups may provide some valuable input to these AI approaches. In the following sections, we discuss behavioural analytics in social media.

## 6 Behavioural Analytics

Behaviour Analytics emerged with the advances in Web 2.0 and the introduction of numerous online business models [39]. Many technologies have been developed to assess the behaviour of the online users on different social media platforms and predict their behaviours and interests according to the current posting, liking, commenting, etc. The behaviour data can be categorised into individual and collective behaviours [46]. Zafarani and Liu [46] further define the individual behaviour as the behaviour shown by a user when interacting with another user, a community or an entity (an example of a user-entity individual behaviour is a user liking a post).

The collective behaviour is the behaviour exhibited by individuals as part of group behaviour. The inherent complexity of behaviour analysis and the multifaceted interactions seem to be very challenging, however such analysis can potentially bring numerous benefits to businesses. The collected behaviour data are then fed into complex computational algorithms to market the products or services to the right audience based on the users' already shown predictive behaviour and interests. Such business intelligence and insights clearly contribute to businesses gaining competitive advantage over their competitors. Ghostery is a browser extension developed in 2009 [13] by which website visitors can gain a detailed site analysis by recognising the site trackers and analytics extensions. Some of these trackers are aimed at improving targeted advertisements by analysing the users' interests, interactions and social behaviour in the online platforms. For instance, Lotame provides such a holistic overview on the consumers behaviours collected through various online sources [28]. Full Circle Studies is another firm with a tracker used facilitating Internet market research by providing targeted advertisements to consumers, irrespective of the industry [11]. Matomo is another web analytics platform by which businesses can gain a richer perspective of their visitors through the log analytic facility provided by the technology [30].

The online behaviour is representative of the behaviour that individuals embody in real life [27]. This would indicate that online consumer transactions and behaviour could also benefit other disciplines such as cyber threat analysis, crime data mining and prediction [7]. The UK Cyber Security Strategy first introduced in July 2009, highlights three strands by which UK businesses could get more vigilant when combatting cybercrime. The first two elements i.e. Reduce Risk and Exploit Opportunities are directly reliant on the third strand to improve knowledge, capabilities and decision making [43].

To make informed decisions within a context, computational and predictive techniques could be applied on behavioural data to facilitate combatting potential cyber and cyber enabled crimes. The datasets on consumer behaviour is typically generated in the form of XML and JSON [1]. Gephi (open source) or the Excel plug-in NodeXL are some instances of the analytics tools which then crunch the collected data and produce meaningful insights. Such an approach could be applied in the cyber defence context with a view to identify patterns of behaviour and predict potential cyber and/or cyber-enabled crimes, [26]. Below are the proposed computational techniques that can be applied on behaviour data on social media, together with some examples where the techniques are applied in different contexts.

The behaviours that are widely observed on the social media, online networks, and other intelligent systems, are very complex. It has become increasingly challenging to search and extract useful information from the collective knowledge stored digitally in the various forms including blogs, web pages, images, sounds, videos, and social networks [20]. It would be then very important to develop appropriate tools to efficiently identify behavioural patterns between individuals, groups and population directly or indirectly producing digitised information. Retrieving information from the web search, using keywords is very tedious task and normally does not produce accurate and detailed findings. An alternative approach to the keyword search is Topic modelling. This specific machine learning approach is presented in Sect. 7.

## 7 Topic Models

Topic Modelling is an unsupervised machine learning algorithm in Natural Language Processing that identifies relationships and associations within textual data. The application of Topic Modelling has been widely used on raw text data, where meaningful clusters (topics) are generated by the model. Several predictive solutions have been presented for selected research problems by means of topic models. These have been applied in a variety of subject areas namely bioinformatics, multilingual data and machine translation, sentiment analysis in social sciences, and inference for document analysis.

Topic Models were nitially introduced by Blei et al. [3], Latent Dirichlet Allocation (LDA) has gained its popularity over the years in its success at modelling topics in discrete data. Blei described a way to uncover hidden topics from documents by determining the hidden per-document topic distribution. LDA is an unsupervised generative probabilistic model, often used for the purpose of topic modelling documents. The model assumes that topics within documents can be represented as probabilistic distributions over the words in a document and the word distributions across topics share a common Dirichlet prior [23]. The concept behind LDA is the assumption that words from a particular topic will occur over a probabilistic distribution.

LDA assumes that documents can be represented as a mixture of latent topics, and within these documents are words that follow certain probabilities. In order to understand how topics are determined by the model, we first have to understand how a document is generated. The number of words within a document is determined possibly following a Poisson distribution. Since a document will contain a mixture of topics, the topic mixture of the document can be characterized as following a Dirichlet distribution over a fixed number of topics. Each word in the document are then selected based on the topic distribution within the document. With this process in mind, LDA uses this knowledge to break down the structure of a document to identify topics within them.

Based on Fig. 3, it can be observed that words (Wd, n) within documents (N) and the collection of documents (D). The number of topics is denoted by K, is set by the model user. The collection of documents contains several hidden topics and dependencies. The hidden topics are uncovered by the process of computing the posterior distribution of topics within a document, where the numerator is the joint distribution of all random variables:

$$p(\beta_{1:\mathrm{K}}, \theta_{1:D}, \mathrm{Z}_{1:D} | W_{1:D}) = p(\beta_{1:\mathrm{K}}, \theta_{1:D}, \mathrm{Z}_{1:D}, W_{1:D}) / p(W_{1:\mathrm{D}})$$

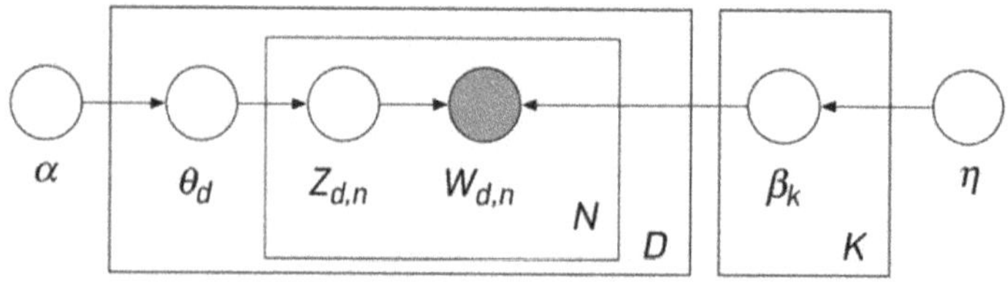


**Fig. 3** Plate notation of LDA [2]

Topic models have been widely applied for various purposes, and slightly altered to fit the task at hand. While the models differ from one another slightly, LDA has been commonly used as the foundation of a topic model.

Topic modelling [2] methods learn a latent space in observed data (as a collection of documents, images, videos and other digital formats) allowing to represent them in a low-dimensional space of so-called topics. Typical activities or behaviours can be viewed as sets of features that often come together. Topic modelling can be then viewed as a method to identify these types of statistical regularities. As a result, a topic model has become a promising tool for probabilistic behaviour modelling and detecting anomaly. Although, the technique was initially developed for text mining [3, 17], it has been applied in a wide range of other fields including computer vision and social network analysis [41]. For instance, topic models can be viewed as a suite of algorithms that discovers the hidden thematic structure in the collected documents retrieved from a web search. These algorithms are very helpful in modelling the users' behaviours based on more efficient methods of searching, browsing and summarising very large amounts of texts (or images and video clips). In other words, topic modelling ca be used as an efficient algorithm for Behaviour modelling in social networks; this is in line with the core framework of "data-to-knowledge-to-service" pipeline (see Fig. 4) where behavioural data are considered as the input to support services and systems of the online social networks including precise recommendation and anomaly detection.

Probabilistic topic modelling algorithms categorise the retrieved topics based on the themes identified by the algorithms. The models which are widely used in topic modelling, are Latent Semantic analysis (LSA), Probabilistic Latent Semantic Analysis (pLSA) and Latent Dirichlet analysis (LDA) [17]. By applying these models on the search history or online data of users, valuable searched topics including any suspicious activities or anomaly behaviours can be detected. LDA can be used to automatically group documents into topics according to dependencies between words and documents [3]. This method can be extended for the personalised preference analysis [32] with an application in discovering the topic-level social dynamics in social media text-based data (e.g., Twitter). Nevertheless, LDA suffers from the limitation that is uninterpretable and the representations are too general. As a result, mining the entities and events, the attributes and aspects related to the entities and events, and the users' sentiments will facilitate the modelling of behavioural contents and users' intentions underlying the User-generated content.

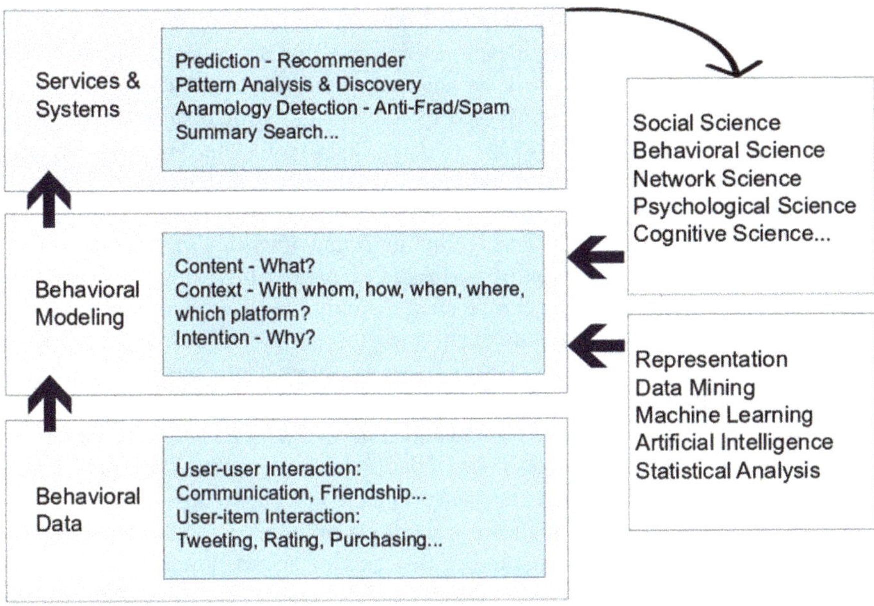


**Fig. 4** Behaviour modelling is a core framework of the "data-to-knowledge-to-service" pipeline. Redrawn with contents adapted from Jiang [24]

## 8 Proposed Refinements

An alternative approach to the above method is the Hierarchical Dirichlet Process (HDP) [42], which is widely used in probabilistic topic modelling, where the data under consideration could be documents, clips or videos and the components would be the distributions of terms that reflect recurring patterns (or "topics") within the collection. One limitation of HDP analysis is that the proposed Bayesian inference algorithms require multiple passes through all data [45]. This would make them intractable for very large-scale applications in the social media context. A method to overcome this challenge will be to investigate various inference algorithms for the HDP, including online variational inference algorithms or Expectation Propagation algorithm [31] so that the resulting method can be easily applicable to massive and streaming data. The variational and Expectation Propagation algorithms have been significantly promising in analysing massive data and are considerably faster than traditional inference algorithms in the HDP. Nonetheless, their applications on behavioural modelling are very limited. Therefore, it would be essential to develop new online inference methods to efficiently analyse very large data sets, such as streaming texts, image or videos, which are very common in social media. Using probabilistic models, accurate prediction and detection of user behaviour can be evaluated online. Such methods could be used to detect the complex behavioural interactions between users/groups and predict how they are likely to act in the future, in the real time. Such a behaviour model can also effectively used for anomaly detection or any abnormal activities in social media. Our proposed topic model provides a probabilistic framework for anomaly detection. Under this framework a normality measure can be represented as the likelihood of data or the posterior probability of the specific aspect or topic of the online stream data. Anomaly detection in other data types such as images and video, is conducted differently compared to text data. For the intelligent vision systems for instance, anomaly detection can be investigated in two contexts: observing any abnormal activities as violating typical activities allowed in social media or as a rapid change in behaviour. However, the proposed behavioural modelling can be used to analyse former abnormal activities, a proper probabilistic change point detection methodology is required for the latter. We propose to develop an efficient online framework by which change points can be detected; This can be used for behaviour analysis, and anomaly detection. A change is defined as a breakpoint between normal and abnormal behaviours, and changes can be then viewed as functional breaks in input data. Existing methods [20] for Gaussian Process (GP) regression over non-stationary data include clustering and change point detection algorithms. Even though these methods require significant computation, they do not provide provable guarantees in terms of accuracy and computational speed, since most algorithms only work in batch settings [15]. This computational complexity can be overcome by combining Bayesian online change point detection algorithm [34] with Gaussian processes.

## 9 Conclusion and Discussion

The rise of cyberspace has created a growing variety of crimes that are occurring or are enabled on digital platforms. These crimes are either occurring within the cyberspace, or the digital means are considered as an enabler of traditional crimes. With the ever-growing adoption of Internet technologies and digital cyberspace, the landscape of crimes is shifting. Social media adoption has seen a continuous growth in the past decade, and so the crimes occurring or enabled by such digital platforms. This necessitates a change in policing strategies to put more emphasis on preventive and intelligence-led policing. In this paper, we presented topic modelling as an AI based technique for analysing patterns of behaviour in social media data. Such intelligence, can potentially provide reliable intelligence to police forces to curb cyber and cyber enabled crimes.

## References

1. Batrinca B, Treleaven PC (2015) Social media analytics: a survey of techniques, tools and platforms. AI & Soc 30(1):89–116
2. Blei DM (2012) Probabilistic topic models. Communications 55(4):77–84

3. Blei DM, Ng AY, Jordan MI (2003) Latent Dirichlet allocation. J Mach Learn Res 3:993–1022
4. Button M, Cross C (2017) Technology and fraud: the 'Fraudogenic' consequences of the Internet revolution. The Routledge handbook of technology, crime and justice. Routledge, London
5. Cabinet Office (2010) A strong Britain in an age of uncertainty: the national security strategy, vol 7953. The Stationery Office
6. Clough J (2015) Principles of cybercrime. Cambridge University Press
7. Farsi M, Daneshkhah A, Hosseinian-Far A, Chatrabgoun O, Montasari R (2018) Crime data mining, threat analysis and prediction. In: Jahankhani H (ed) Cyber criminology. Springer, pp 183–202
8. Flatley J (2016) Crime in England and wales: year ending Mar 2016. Stat Bull 29
9. Ford R (2016) Fraud doubles the number of crimes. The Times, p 22
10. Forouzan H, Jahankhani H, McCarthy J (2018) An examination into the level of training, education and awareness among frontline police officers in tackling cybercrime within the Metropolitan Police Service. In: Cyber criminology. Springer, Cham, pp 307–323
11. Full Circle Studies (2018). About full circle studies. http://www.fullcirclestudies.com/about.aspx
12. Gaidosch T, Adelmann F, Morozova A, Wilson C (2019) Cybersecurity risk supervision. J Iss 2019:15
13. Ghostery (2018) About ghostery. https://www.ghostery.com/about-ghostery/
14. Gillespie AA (2019) Cybercrime: key issues and debates. Routledge
15. Grande RC (2014) Computationally efficient gaussian process change point detection and regression. PhD thesis, Massachusetts Institute of Technology, Boston
16. Hinduja S, Patchin JW (2014) Bullying beyond the schoolyard: preventing and responding to cyberbullying. Corwin Press
17. Hofmann T (1999) Probabilistic latent semantic indexing. ACM, Berkley, pp 50–57
18. Hosseinian-Far A, Ramachandran M, Sarwar D (eds) (2017) Strategic engineering for cloud computing and big data analytics. Springer
19. Hosseinian-Far A, Ramachandran M, Slack CL (2018) Emerging trends in cloud computing, big data, fog computing, IoT and smart living. In: Technology for smart futures. Springer, Cham, pp 29–40
20. Isupova O (2018) Machine learning methods for behaviour analysis and anomaly detection in video, 1st edn. Springer Theses
21. Jahankhani H, Al-Nemrat A, Hosseinian-Far A (2014) Cybercrime classification and characteristics. In: Cyber crime and cyber terrorism investigator's handbook. Syngress, pp 149–164
22. Jahankhani H, Hosseinian-Far A (2014) Digital forensics education, training and awareness. In: Cyber crime and cyber terrorism investigator's handbook. Syngress, pp 91–100
23. Jelodar H, Wang Y, Yuan C, Feng X, Jiang X, Li Y, Zhao L (2019) Latent Dirichlet allocation (LDA) and topic modelling: models, applications, a survey. Multimedia Tools and Applications 78(11):15169–15211
24. Jiang M (2017) Behavior modeling in social networks. In: Encyclopaedia of social network analysis and mining, pp 1–11
25. Kamin KA, Rachlinski JJ (1995) Ex post $\neq$ ex ante. Law Hum Behav 19(1):89–104
26. Kowalski RM, Giumetti GW (2017) Bullying in the digital age. In: Cybercrime and its victims. Routledge, pp 167–186
27. Kularathne SD et al (2017) Consumer behavior analysis for social media. Int J Adv Eng Manag Sci (IJAEMS) 3(1):11–21
28. Lotame (2018) About Lotame. https://www.lotame.com/about-lotame/
29. Lum C, Koper CS, Telep CW (2011) The evidence-based policing matrix. J Exper Criminol 7(1):3–26
30. Matomo (2018) What is Matomo? https://matomo.org/what-is-matomo/
31. Minka TP (2001) Expectation propagation for approximate Bayesian inference. In: Proceedings of the seventeenth conference on uncertainty in artificial intelligence. Morgan Kaufmann Publishers Inc., pp 362–369

32. Narang K et al (2013) Discovery and analysis of evolving topical social discussions on unstructured microblogs. Springer, Moscow, pp 24–27
33. Ratcliffe J (2003) Intelligence-led policing, vol 248. Australian Institute of Criminology, Canberra
34. Saatci Y, Turner RD, Rasmussen CE (2010) Gaussian process change point models. Haifa, IBM
35. Schjolberg S (2014) The history of cybercrime: 1976–2014. BoD–Books on Demand
36. Sherman LW, Eck JE (2003) Policing for crime prevention. In: Evidence-based crime prevention. Routledge, pp 309–343
37. Shinder DL, Cross M (2008) Scene of the cybercrime. Elsevier
38. Statista (2019) Number of monthly active Twitter users worldwide from 1st quarter 2010 to 1st quarter 2019. https://www.statista.com/statistics/282087/number-of-monthly-active-twitter-users/
39. Squicciarini A, Rajtmajer S, Griffin C (2017) Positive and negative behavioral analysis in social networks. ACM Trans Web (TWEB) 7:1–12
40. Swire P (2009) No cop on the beat: underenforcement in e-commerce and cybercrime. J Telecomm High Tech L 7, 107
41. Tang J, Sun J, Wang C, Yang Z (2009) Social influence analysis in large-scale networks. ACM, Paris, pp 807–816
42. Teh YW, Jordan MI, Beal MJ, Blei DM (2005) Sharing clusters among related groups: Hierarchical Dirichlet processes. In: Advances in neural information processing systems, pp 1385–1392
43. UK Home Office (2011) Social and behavioural science: countering the terrorist threat. https://www.gov.uk/government/publications/social-and-behavioural-science-countering-the-terrorist-threat
44. Wall DS (2013) Policing identity crimes. Policing and Society 23(4):437–460
45. Wang C, Paisley J, Blei, D (2011) Online variational inference for the hierarchical Dirichlet process. In: Proceedings of the fourteenth international conference on artificial intelligence and statistics, June 2011, pp 752–760
46. Zafarani R, Liu H (2014) Behavior analysis in social media. IEEE Intell Syst 29(4):1–4

# Securing Transparency and Governance of Organ Supply Chain Through Blockchain

**Nicanor Chavez, Stefan Kendzierskyj, Hamid Jahankhani, and Amin Hosseinian**

**Abstract** The governance and supply chain of organs is a complicated process throughout the life cycle; from the outset of pre-assessment of organ placement, it's supply chain journey and important post donor analysis. Healthcare organisations face a huge challenge in the diverse collation of data that are held in systems which are mostly in silo operation and little scope for interoperability or accessibility of medical data. Lack of data access or trust in its accuracy makes the task more challenging and problematic for healthcare institutions whose preference undoubtably would be to focus their energies on the decision making side of a patient's health in assessing organ donor suitability and urgency to organ match due to the receiving patient criticalities, rather than time and resources spent on validating data authenticity, etc. There are further complications that can occur in potential mix-ups of organs, contamination of DNA during organ transplant, non-ethical organ supply and audit trail transparency related to these activities. There is a serious question on how to create a single source of the truth and blockchain may provide the best possibilities. Blockchain is becoming a more sought after technology being used in the healthcare space due to its attributes of immutability, traceability and security whilst providing that assurance of transparency and audit trail. Blockchain looks to be a good fit to manage the supply chain of organ procurement/placement and an audit control method to analyse data in any pre or post operation event. Combined with the right processes, in the form of a cyber security framework/maturity model for the healthcare industry, would ensure that all those who signed up to the blockchain deployed for the supply chain logistics would respect the ethics and requirements and expect transparency for those authorised to access. However, some challenges exist in GDPR compliancy of data that would exist on a certain proposed blockchain models and needs further exploring with regards to benefits in data held off-chain.

N. Chavez · S. Kendzierskyj · H. Jahankhani (✉)
Northumbria University, London, UK
e-mail: Hamid.jahankhani@northumbria.ac.uk

A. Hosseinian
Northampton University, Northampton, UK



H. Jahankhani et al. (eds.), *Policing in the Era of AI and Smart Societies*, Advanced Sciences and Technologies for Security Applications, https://doi.org/10.1007/978-3-030-50613-1_4

**Keywords** Blockchain · Supply chain · GDPR · Organ transplant · Organ trafficking · Transplant tourism · Maturity model · Governance · Risk

## 1 Organ Supply Chain Through Blockchain

Organ transplant is a critical area of healthcare as those patients in need will have an urgency and priority that puts additional pressure across those involved in the touch points of organ supply chain. The following data underlines this pressurised situation. According to the UK National Health Service (NHS) Blood and Transplant most current online information (circa April 2019), there have been 1735 people who have received an organ transplant and 6282 people who are still waiting to get a transplant in the UK. This equates to the unfortunate result of people dying daily while they wait for the correct match. In its 2018 reports, The Global Observatory on Donation and Transplantation (part of the World Health Organization, WHO) reported a total of 44,219 organs transplanted within the European Union; while the European Commission (in its European Organs Directive) reported that during 2017, there was a total of 34,000 organ transplants while 60,000 patients were on waiting lists in 800 different organ transplant programmes. The organ transplantation cycle is composed of several types by activities that involve the donation and extraction of human organs, most commonly being the kidneys, liver, lungs and heart that get transplanted (NHS Blood and Transplant, April 2019). During all phases of this cycle, a big amount of data related to donors, organs and patients gets recorded in different computer systems and printed in multiple ways to provide health organizations and physicians the information needed to take proper decisions on organ allocation and medical procedures, which then is read, analysed and moved around in hardcopy format that could potentially be lost, copied or printed with typographical errors, thus potentially leading to erroneous decisions or violating medical and data regulations.

The difficulty is further heightened with the challenge of system accessibility and interoperability of medical records and other data sets, due to the disparate and diverse type of systems and infrastructure. Typically, it is not just the disparate infrastructure but types of structured/unstructured data and its applications and how to access all in a single source of the truth. There is an enormous volume of data held amongst hospitals, clinics, pharmacies and labs that also makes difficult to authenticate, track its journey and audit. Since data is a key element but there is also supply chain physical components (the organs) then there needs to be a mechanism that can ensure all data is captured, interoperable, cannot be tampered, etc.

To improve efficiency and transparency it is suggested in this chapter to propose the use of blockchain and smart contracts as a way of governing the organ donor matching and transplantation. Also, to help organise the pre/post-surgery medical activities by trying to identify whether there could be a mix-up of organs or contamination of DNA during the organ transplant cycle that could affect the proposed system, as well as activities related to DNA sampling and recording in a public blockchain. Finally, data protection and ethics that are inherent to supply chain governance where activities and practices related to public health are involved. To support ethics and governance it is beneficial to operate a cyber security maturity model (CSMM) alongside blockchain requirements. That means all organisations that require to be part of organ supply chain run on blockchain architecture must comply with the supply chain prerequisites and a maturity model can effectively monitor all through control methods, training and other that help keep a high discipline and compliance. It is then easier to warn those that consistently fail to comply, are below standard and deploy methods to change the behaviour. Through blockchain all information related to a patient's health as well as to the entire organ donation and transplant related activities (analysing potential organ donors, donor-recipient matching, laboratory tests, transplantation, pre/post operation and DNA sampling) can be tracked. The data will come from multiple systems and record specific non-patient identifiable information in the blockchain.

Blockchain technology offers great potential in the healthcare industry; it is estimated that 55% of healthcare applications will have adopted blockchain for commercial deployment by 2025 (Mikulic, 2017), while at the same time the healthcare sector suffers the highest toll of system data breaches with 2.5 times the global average when comparing to other industries, being about $380 per single patient record compromised in 2017 (Arnold, 2018).

One key concern in healthcare is the management of sensitive information, its data sharing and security due to the application of the General Data Protection Regulation (GDPR) in the UK and the European Union. Blockchain can help to avoid sensitive data retention by enabling the 'disclosing without exposing' of data, with the use of its cryptographic techniques and methods.

## 2 Organ Trafficking and Transplant Tourism

Compounding the structural issues of data interoperability, transparency and so on is the darker side of organ supply where the urgency to source organs creates and stimulates a demand where criminals often interact and thrive in. The WHO reports this international trade on the rise where those vulnerable may sell their kidney for $1000 [37]. This crosses ethics where criminals contaminate supply chain with 'non-ethical' sourced organs (those that sell organs and illegally traffic) and transfers across a number of third parties where organisations who require to be bona fide and ethical can end up procuring trafficked organs. The US Department of State [35] quotes how a lot of criminal activity is mapped in and around human trafficking and as mentioned often affecting the most vulnerable in society.

Organ trafficking, and transplant tourism takes place when a person who needs the transplant travels to a different country to purchase the required organ, often from a donor who is in financial need. Organ commercialism is on the rise and several business models and job roles have been created as of result of this [30]. Jafar [30] refers to such business models and job roles as 'profitable enterprises' and goes on to argue that such activities exploit poor donors in an illegal and unregulated form. In 2008 at the Istanbul Summit, a declaration was signed by participating members, with a view to promote regulation of organ procurement, and assert that physicians and regulatory bodies of the donor's and recipient's counties should prohibit transplant tourism [2]. This summit symbolised one of the key collective international efforts to curb the unethical practices involved in organ trafficking and exploitation of the vulnerable and the poor. Soon after the declaration of Istanbul Summit, and in response to that, the Canadian Society of Transplantation and the Canadian Society of Nephrology introduced a similar policy document to inform Canadian healthcare stakeholders when conducting transplant healthcare [26]. In a more recent study, Ambagtsheer [4] conducted a qualitative study on kidney procurement and organ trafficking in Netherlands and affirms that identifying such unethical trades is a challenging task, due to poor reporting, and the complexities involved. Bagheri and Delmonico [6] anticipated that the key solution to the problem would be an international agreement that is formal, biding that imposes legal liability. There are already some existing regional and international rules and policy guidelines related to organ, tissue and cell trafficking [8, 13], however, Pietrobon [33] argues that implementing such conventions is not a straightforward task, due to the transnational nature of the convention implementation, and low willingness shown by some of the participating countries and authorities. One of the solutions to overcome this would be to enhance cross-border collaboration, information sharing, joint prosecution efforts, and transnational law enforcement structures [27]. Ambagtsheer [4] assessed two case studies of Trafficking in Human Beings for the purpose of Organ Removal (THBOR) where both cases were investigated by police and they went through prosecution. He concluded that in both cases, the complexities, the number of stakeholders and other relevant obstacles have made the process extremely challenging. Furthermore, the lack of awareness by different stakeholders contributes to the poor implementation of such transnational efforts [27]. Ambagtsheer [4] argues that investigation and prosecution should not be deemed as the only key approach in tackling THBOR, and therefore, efficient legal organ supply and procurement, and processes for victims' protection should be enhanced, irrespective of the processes involved for investigation and prosecution. Another perspective to this is the role that physicians and healthcare providers play. Caulfield et al. [9] believe that health care professionals and physicians can enact a significant role in curtailing organ trafficking. Patients (the donor, the recipient, or both) discuss the available options in the first instance with the medical professionals. The second phase of communication occurs when they provide their medical solution choice related to the transplantation, and the final interaction phase, referred to as 'post-transplantation' phase, is when the operation has been completed. Therefore, physicians and medical professional can potentially curtail the illegal organ trade throughout all the above three phases [9]. Considering the existing information, it is apparent that there is little or no comprehensive research work on the adoption of suitable technologies to monitor and regulate organ procurement and operation, and more importantly to restrain illegal activities within the context.

Crucially, it is why a blockchain mechanism could potentially solve many issues of authenticity, tracking and for those institutions in the supply chain that need that security there but a transparency to be able to view data where permissioned.

## 3 Blockchain and Healthcare Operability

Blockchain is a decentralised network of different peers interconnected as an open distributed ledger (or database) which can efficiently record transactions in a permanent and verifiable manner. Bitcoin is today perhaps the most widely used P2P (peer to peer) digital currency which was first released in a white paper at the end of 2008 by the pseudonym of Nakamoto [32]. Bitcoin's enormous success triggered a massive surge of 'crypto currencies' where hundreds of alternative currencies were created and traded, making a total market cap of $215.00B traded in October 2019 (Coincap 2019). Although having its roots in cryptocurrency, blockchain technology, besides from offering decentralization, offers industry real tangible benefits in the form of a high level of transparency, immutability and security via algorithmic consensus mechanisms. One of the key features of blockchain and particularly important for this study is that it provides a mechanism of unfalsifiable time-stamping transactions (smart contracts) which stores and tracks them in a secure and verifiable way, enabling the share of the information in real time. This is extremely useful for patients and healthcare organizations as this helps them to control their records and provides a higher level of transparency and security to all participants within the blockchain and instilling a sense of authenticity when analysing multiple data sets. A key benefit to blockchain technology is that "every user can maintain their own copy of the ledger" [40]. This is an important statement regarding one of the basic features of a blockchain, because when there is a central repository of data, a user needs to trust that the administrator keeps regular and proper backup of the system, as centrally managed databases might be lost, destroyed or corrupted. Moreover, whenever a new user (or node) joins a blockchain network, it 'scans' or looks for other nodes and gets a full copy of the blockchain ledger, making it very difficult for the ledger to be destroyed or lost, and being in a P2P configuration, the blockchain is resilient to the loss of individual or multiple nodes.

Blockchain is already implemented for healthcare organizations, and Agbo et al. [3] make the case for the increased privacy and security in the access of data through the use of cryptographic algorithms that encrypt data stored in blockchain, ensuring that only the users who get access permissions are able to decrypt it; moreover since the patient identity gets pseudonymized by the use of cryptographic keys, their data can be shared by all stakeholders without revealing the identity of the patient in question and therefore cam respect certain privacy aspects.

There are various types of blockchains depending on the data that will be managed, its availability and the type of actions that participants will be able to perform in the system. The following Table 1 details the comparison between these types of architectures:

**Table 1** Comparison among blockchain architectures

| | Permissionless public | Permissionless private | Permissioned public | Permissioned private |
|---|---|---|---|---|
| Participation | Anyone can join and act as a node | Anyone in the private network act as a node | Only nodes in a predetermined criterion can act as a node | Only chosen nodes in a private network can act as a node |
| Security | Very high | Low | Medium | Low |
| Speed | Very low | Fast | Slow | Very fast |
| Trust level | Trustless | Trusted | Trustless | Trusted |

As mentioned, one of the benefits of blockchain is that it removes the need of a central authority that enables the system to administer transactions; this allows participants in the blockchain to perform transactions in a distributed environment and eliminates the problem of a single point of failure improving their speed without being affected by the delay that a central authority adds. Instead blockchain uses a consensus mechanism which determines the conditions that need to be met for the nodes within a system whether to accept to add a block in the blockchain, this way reconciling discrepancies and agreeing the transaction is valid or not. There are numerous types of consensus algorithms. Some of the most relevant/popular below are discussed by Fernández-Caramés, and Fraga-Lamas while reviewing the use of blockchain for the Internet of Things [25]:

- **Proof of Work (PoW)** used in Bitcoin, it requires the miners to solve complex problems to get the right to verify new transaction.
- **Proof of Stake (PoS)** requires less computational power than PoW, consuming less energy.
- **Practical Byzantine Fault Tolerant (PBFT)** solves the Byzantine Generals Problem for asynchronous environments. PBFT assumes that less than a third of the nodes are malicious. For every block to be added to the chain, a leader is selected to be in charge of ordering the transaction. Such a selection has to be supported by at least 2/3 of the all nodes, which have to be known by the network.
- **Delegated Proof-of-Stake (DPoS)** is similar to PoS, but stakeholders instead of being the ones generating and validating blocks, they select certain delegates to do it. Since less nodes are involved in block validation, transactions are performed faster than with other schemes.
- **Delegated BFT (DBFT)** is a variant of BFT where, in a similar way to DPoS, some specific nodes are voted to be the ones generating and validating blocks.
- **Ripple consensus algorithm** was proposed to reduce the high latencies found in many blockchains, which are in part due to the use of synchronous communications among the nodes. Thus, each node relies on a trusted subset of nodes when determining consensus, what clearly reduces latency.
- **Stellar Consensus Protocol (SCP)** is an implementation of a consensus method called Federated Byzantine Agreement (FBA). It is similar to PBFT but, whilst in

PBFT every node queries all the other nodes and waits for the majority to agree, in SCP the nodes only wait for a subset of the participants that they consider important.
- **Sieve** is a consensus algorithm proposed by IBM Research that has already been implemented for Hyperledger–Fabric. Its objective is to run non-deterministic smart contracts on a permissioned blockchain that makes use of BFT replication.

The healthcare organisation would need review its objectives, network and way of working in order to select the blockchain model and consensus algorithm. The following Table 2 shows a summary comparison between the different types of blockchain and consensus algorithms [1].

## *3.1 Blockchain Governance*

A common misconception regarding blockchain networks is that they run wild without ownership or control. This is not particularly true as permissionless blockchain networks are governed often by software developers who have a large degree of influence on where blockchain should deploy. The users can reject any change from the developers by declining to install any updates, or publishing nodes which have some degree of control as they create and publish any new block; they all play an important role in the blockchain governance, even when there is not a central authority. Permissioned blockchain networks rely on a governance structure that controls access and enforces rules, responding to incident including cyber threats—because of the degree of trusts among the participants, this type of network commonly uses less computationally intensive consensus mechanisms [20].

There are two areas that must be considered when creating a blockchain system:

- Blockchain Governance—which refers to the processes and structure that determine how the blockchain will be maintained and will evolve over time.
- Solution Governance—this refers to the set of rules that will regulate how different groups or organizations will interact with each other.

Complementing the points mentioned above, The IBM Corporation in their paper "The Founder's Handbook" (IBM 2018) includes six governance elements to consider when working in the governance strategy for a blockchain:

1. **Data**: Questions like who will own the data, what will be the data-related security need of the network? A defined security strategy along a distinct ownership of data must be in place before the blockchain is deployed into production.
2. **Marketplace**: This element is aimed for blockchains which are created to generate revenue, so the main question will be what will be the model in place, how this revenue will be shared and if the participants of the network will get incentives to join if they will be allowed to generate income-related applications over the blockchain.

Table 2 Comparison among consensus mechanisms

| Consensus algorithms | Blockchain platform | Launched since | Programming languages | Smart contracts | Pros | Cons |
|---|---|---|---|---|---|---|
| PoW | Bitcoin | 2009 | C++ | No | Less opportunity for 51% attack | Greater energy consumption |
| | | | | | Better mecurity | Centralization of miners |
| PoS | NXT | 2013 | Java | Yes | Energy efficient | Nothing-at-stake problem |
| | | | | | More decentralized | |
| DPoS | Lisk | 2016 | JavaScript | No | Energy efficient | Partially centralized |
| | | | | | Scalable | Double spend attack |
| | | | | | Increased security | |
| LPoS | Waves | 2016 | Scala | Yes | Fair usage | Decentralization issue |
| | | | | | Lease coins | |
| PoET | Hyperledger sawtooth | 2018 | Python, JavaScript, Go, C++, Java, and Rust | Yes | Cheap participation | Need for specialized hardware |
| | | | | | | Not good for public blockchain |
| PBFT | Hyperledger Fabric | 2015 | JavaScript, Python, Java REST and Go | Yes | No need for confirmation | Communication gap |
| | | | | | Reduction in energy | Sybil attack |
| SBFT | Chain | 2014 | Java, Node, and Ruby | No | Good security | Not for public blockchain |
| | | | | | Signature validation | |
| DBFT | NEO | 2016 | Python, NET, Java, C++, C, Go, Kotlin, JavaScript | Yes | Scalable | Conflictions in the chain |
| | | | | | Fast | |
| DAG | IOTA | 2015 | Javascript, Rust, Java Go, and C++ | In process | Low cost network | Implementation gaps |
| | | | | | Scalability | Not suited for smart contracts |
| POA | Decred | 2016 | Go | Yes | Reduces the probability of the 51% attack | Greater energy consumption |

(continued)

**Table 2** (continued)

| Consensus algorithms | Blockchain platform | Launched since | Programming languages | Smart contracts | Pros | Cons |
|---|---|---|---|---|---|---|
| | | | | | Equal contribution | Double signing |
| PoI | NEM | 2015 | Java, C++, XEM | Yes | Vesting | Decentralization issue |
| | | | | | Transaction partnership | |
| PoC | Burstcoin | 2014 | Java | Yes | Cheap | Favoring bigger fishes |
| | | | | | Efficient | Decentralization issue |
| | | | | | Distributed | |
| PoB | Slimcoin | 2014 | Python, C++, Shell, JavaScript | No | Preservation of the network | Not for short term investors |
| | | | | | | Wasting coins |
| PoWeight | Filecoin | 2017 | SNARK/STARK | Yes | Scalable | Issue with incentivization |
| | | | | | Customizable | |

3. **Participation**: This covers all actions related to network access and enrolment (on boarding/off boarding) of participants, and what will happen to data when a participant leaves the blockchain.
4. **Technology**: This must be covered during the early stages of the blockchain creation, as questions on infrastructure costs, coding related, level of privacy required, and other tech strategies must be thought with the aim to support the solution as it continues to grow.
5. **Transactions**: As different types of solutions that will run on the blockchain are evaluated, questions related to the number of participants and the types of transactions must be discussed and answered.
6. **Smart Contracts**: A very key and important aspect, as a blockchain depends on smart contracts, which help to establish trust within the network via the rules that help to govern them.

It will be important for any organization to follow tested cybersecurity standards and their guidelines in order to assure the security of all systems that interact with/or that the blockchain network will use. These standards will provide a strong base to protect a blockchain network from attacks, for example: any organization who aims to build a blockchain network, must ensure that all networks, systems and computer equipment used is patched and accesses are properly administered following best practices in order to avoid compromising it due to security breaches. This is where the concept of adhering to a cyber security maturity model can be of effective potential to the whole supply chain and provide a methodology to benchmark for a high level of compliance and security.

# 4 The Organ Transplantation Life Cycle

The lifecycle of organ transplantation is not a straightforward process. On the one side is the complex and ethical approach to define the matching and delicate management of this and all its associated data. On the other side is the physical element to supply chain of the organ and the convoluted process of packaging, storage and transportation often against a time driven requirement [38]. Supply chain needs to ensure time is keep to a minimum as 'time the organ is without vascularization'.

To help define a human organ, tissue and cell donation can come from three sources: Living, Non-living and Cadaveric. Within the living donor type, there are the 'living related donors' (a blood related of the potential recipient of the organ), the 'living un-related donors' (not a blood related but with emotional ties to the recipient), and there can be also a third type which is the 'altruistic donor' who volunteer to donate an organ (most commonly a kidney) without previous knowledge of the recipient. Sometimes there is an 'offer' from a brain-dead patient, and the hospital needs an agreement from the relatives in order to approve the donation of the organ.

In a formal hospital environment, only these types of living donors are allowed to become part of the organ donation cycle in Europe and in the United States of America, otherwise they are blocked as this could potentially be a case of organ trafficking.

Health organizations and hospitals must have a well-established organ allocation system with at least one list of patients waiting for a transplant. Regarding the 'waiting list', the recipient patient gets evaluated along with the donor that potentially will provide the organ with a series of medical tests performed to both on them, and all the information recorded allows the system to perform some complex calculations to reveal whether the donor and the recipient are a match and the organ can be offered.

## *4.1 Donor Matching and Pre-surgery Related Activities*

The detection of potential donors is probably the most difficult activity to be subject of very rigorous standards and protocols. There are three tests that are performed to evaluate donors:

- **Histocompatibility** (or blood matching): Determines if the donor's blood is compatible with the recipient.
- **Crossmatch**: The cross-matching test is very important part of the living donor medical examination analysis and is repeated again just before the transplant surgery: the blood from the donor and the recipient are mixed, and if the recipient's cells attack and kill the donor cells, then the crossmatch is considered positive meaning that the recipient's has antibodies against the donor cells (and therefore they are incompatible); if the crossmatch is negative, then both donor and recipient are 'compatible'.

| Patient | HLA type recipient | | | | HLA type donor | |
|---|---|---|---|---|---|---|
| | A | A | B | B | Acceptable HLA-A antigens | Acceptable HLA-B antigens |
| 1 | A2 | A29 | B7 | B44 | A 69, 68, 74, 31, 32, 33 | B 55, 56, 70, 72, 42, 45, 50, 54, 61, 71, 75, 13, 41, 48, 49, 59, 62, 76, 77, 18, 35, 38, 47, 60, 67,* 39,* 64,* 8,* 65* |
| 2 | A29 | A68 | B14 | | A 69, 33, 34 | B 39, 65, 67, 55, 71 |
| 3 | A2 | A11 | B7 | B51 | A 69, 68, 3, 32,* 74,* 25,* 34,* 66* | B 55, 78, 35, 53, 56, 71, 52, 54, 70, 72, 75, 76, 77, 18, 42, 58, 81, 59,* 64,* 65,* 67,* 38,* 39* |
| 4 | A*0101 | A*0201 | B*0702 | | A 36, 69, 68, 74* | B 55, 42, 81, 67* |
| 5 | A24 | | B7 | B62 | A 23 | B 76, 55, 70, 72, 75, 77, 56, 71, 42, 46, 54, 63, 59,* 64,* 67* |
| 6 | A*0301 | | B*1402 | B*4701 | | B 39, 61, 65, 27, 55, 37, 54, 56, 67, 73, 70,* 71,* 72,* 18,* 50,* 75,* 62* |
| 7 | A*3101 | A*6901 | B*0702 | B*5501 | A 68, 29, 33, 74, 30 | B 54, 56, 42, 81, 67,* 39,* 64* |

**Fig. 1** An example of HLA matching between recipient and donor

- **HLA testing**: The HLA test or 'leukocyte antigen' is a quite complex blood test that involves antigens which are proteins (or markers) inside the cells of the body that distinguish each individual as unique. For organ transplantation, there are six antigens markers that have shown to be most important; both donor and recipient receive an HLA testing in order to determine their level of compatibility of these markers according to a score.

When a donor and a recipient's HLA markers are the same (or at least very close to each other's percentages), then it is determined that they are compatible and the organ then can be used for people (recipients) that are part of the 'waiting list': the very first person with negative crossmatch and closes percentage HLA marker matching from this list takes the organ (Fig. 1).

There are more tests which are used to review and record the health of the donor (Hepatitis, HIV, Blood tests, X-rays, among many others). If during the tests it is found that the donor has a particular disease, then the organ could be used in patients with the same type of disease and blood type if the doctors agree. In the case of children, they can only accept organs from another children, or small or thin people.

## *4.2 Post-surgery Related Information*

After the transplant occurs, the recipient patient undergoes an immunological suppressor treatment to avoid a rejection of the organ for the rest of his/her life or until the organ stops working (an average time of 10 years for cadaveric donors, and 20–25 years from living donors), forcing the patient to return to the 'waiting list', which only accepts people until 65 yrs. old, but there are some programs within the European Union who manage older patients. The patient stays in the hospital for a month and then returns depending on their condition (ex. Every 3 months), to check for antibodies or crossmatch and the sample cells from a donor are kept in liquid nitrogen within deep freezers in order to preserve them. It could also be that the patient experiences a rejection of the organ, as most of them occur during six months after transplantation, but it can also occur several years later, and early treatment can help to reverse the rejection in most cases (University of California San Francisco 2019). This relates to an interesting point as the information related to both the organ donor and recipient must be kept recorded and intact for a long period of time; potentially could have a conflict with GDPR requirements.

## *4.3 Electronic Record Systems Handling as Part of the Transplant Life Cycle*

Expiration of an organ is mostly of a few hours and therefore the organ transplantation needs to be executed within a window of time. A form of audit trail of all organs available and their respective journey through supply chain seems critical. As part of healthcare computing and record management standards, the European Federation for Immunogenetics addresses that a hospital laboratory must "Document each step in the processing and testing of patient specimens to assure that accurate test results are recorded", and that laboratory records must maintain depending on local regulations the following records:

- Logbooks
- Worksheets, that must clearly identify:
  - Sample tested
  - Reagents used
  - Methods used
  - Test performed
  - Date of the test
  - Person performing the test
  - Summary of results obtained
- All donor and patient related recorded information

It also specifies that that "Records may be only saved in computer files, provided that back-up files are maintained to ensure against loss of data" (European Federation for Immunogenetics 2018). Likewise, the European Health Committee of the Council of Europe, as part of their guidelines on standards required for quality assurance that must be achieved on services of transplantation of human organs, requires for hospitals to implement a "computerised record-keeping system that ensures the authenticity, integrity and confidentiality of all records but retains the ability to generate true paper copies" with their hardware and software regularly checked to ensure they are reliable [14]. Similarly the Foundation for the Accreditation of Cellular Therapy (FACT), as part of an extensive explanation of its standards on electronic record management and their validation, stipulates that "For all critical electronic record systems, there shall be policies, Standard Operating Procedures, and system elements to maintain the accuracy, integrity, identity, and confidentiality of all records". It includes several detailed standards than point out the necessity of identifying any individual who interacts with record entries: from simple sign-in sheets to more complex systems that enable the tracking of record entries based on a user's login-credentials. It also points out that the usage of any system whether it is built in-house or commercially acquired must be validated as the calculations must be correct under any circumstances, as they will affect the outcome of a decision related to the patient's health (FACT 2019). These guidelines also indicate that there should be a system that allows traceability from all steps and data performed and obtained during the transplantation cycle, and that it should be able to show the path each organ donation takes tracking them from the donor to the recipient or disposal and vice versa. The system also must respect the confidentiality of donors and recipients.

## 4.4 DNA Sampling as Part of the Organ Transplant Life Cycle

DNA samples are taken as part of the organ transplantation testing for both recipient and donor. In order to prevent that DNA samples are contaminated or maliciously replaced with a different one (for example someone within the hospital trying to bring an illegal organ to be used), a series of checkpoints are put in place. The first checkpoint is implemented is with the use of a method that detects variations in the DNA sampled called 'HLA typing'.

The HLA typing method, as mentioned previously, is used to establish identity, parentage, and family relationship which helps to find out the appropriate matches for organ and tissue transplantation. According to guidelines and standards every blood sample that enters the laboratory takes a code number that is unique and characterizes this particular sample. Samples that are directed for DNA analysis (using molecular methodologies) take a unique code that is kept until the final results. The sample code is included in the final report for HLA typing (this is the second checkpoint) and the donor keeps at the laboratory the same code for further analysis and for different procedures (as crossmatch with the patient). Following these rules, a mix up of the donor's DNA should never occur in the laboratory. The third and final checkpoint is the repetition of the HLA typing for donors and recipients, with new blood sample in order to confirm the results from the first sample.

## 4.5 Recording a DNA Sequence in a Public Blockchain System

The DNA or deoxyribonucleic acid is the hereditary material in humans and almost all other organisms—or a biological blueprint. The human genome is comprised about 3 billion base pairs (letters) which is the equivalent to 3.2 GB of data (Elliot and Gregory, 2015).

Questions on cost storage of the data in a public blockchain, can be found with some calculations based on the paper "Ethereum: A secure decentralized generalized transaction ledger" [39] which most up-to-date blockchain blogs make reference to when making their case for storage costs in the Blockchain shows that in the Ethereum blockchain, one KB of storage will cost 0.032 ETH while a GB will cost 32,000 ETH (the price of ETH while writing this paragraph is at £116 GBP), so to store 1 GB of data will cost around £3.7 million pounds, which for any project type will be a prohibitive cost—even if the price per megabyte could round in the hundreds, to store 3.2 GB of DNA data per patient it wouldn't make any sense. Hence why data storage off-chain is the option, more cost effective and cam comply GDPR privacy questions (if data were stored on-chain).

Most of the work related to DNA storage in a blockchain is in its infancy, and although there have been some proof of concept tests like the one performed by DNAtix in December 2017, where there was a transfer of the complete genome sequence of a virus over the Ethereum blockchain, this test only recorded about 5400 base pairs which equates to 1348 bytes [15]—this hardly grasps the range of the human genome, even with compression algorithms which can reduce the size to 700 MB (some figures even mention the complete raw genome being in the +100 GB range), making inefficient to store this amount of data with the current blockchain technology.

It needs to be understood that the blockchain technology was not conceived as a database for storing large files because it is computationally very expensive. For this purpose, data needs to be compressed and converted into a hexadecimal format, and only the hash of the file in question should get recorded in the blockchain. Not all data needs to be recorded in the blockchain as in some cases it could potentially make the data unusable (e.g. storing Medical image data) as blockchain transactions are slow to confirm, and is extremely slow when dealing with rich applications data flow as they might require many thousands of transactions per second.

Another issue will be the immutability of the blockchain which in some case will be a drawback for data storage of private-related information, as once data gets recorded it cannot be removed (e.g. a patient photo-ID gets stored: even if it gets replaced by a different one, the previous data will reside within the blockchain forever can be seen by anyone). This point is key to the audit system as immutability provides the robustness to keep track of activity stored in the blockchain, so it is very important to understand the type of information that the system will be recording before putting it into production.

One additional drawback will be the storage capacity. If all medical and administrative related applications will keep their data in the blockchain, the size of the blockchain will grow very fast potentially exceeding hard drive capacity on each computer acting as a node becoming computationally very expensive.

## 5 GDPR Data Protection and Ethics

The General Data Protection Regulation is a European Union law implemented in May 2018 and requires organizations to safeguard personal data and uphold the privacy rights of anyone in EU territory [29]. It includes seven principles of data protection and eighth privacy rights, these principles and rights must be implemented and ensured by all members of the EU and its enforcement carries heavy financial penalties for those organizations who incur on violations of the law—even if they are outside the European Union but handle data related to EU citizens.

The Information Commissioner's Office [29], which is the UK's independent body set up to uphold information rights, provides a guide for data protection officers and other roles who have the responsibility for data protection on a daily basis, and covers (Data Protection Act (DPA) 2018), and the General Data Protection Regulation (GDPR) as it applies in the UK. The GDPR requires that all organizations have in place appropriate organizational and technical measures to secure personal data. One of these is encryption, as it is the most suitable electronic method at this moment for securing personal data. In this context, blockchain technology provides a secure and efficient method to create a tamper-proof log of transactions by the means of cryptographic hash functions on each block of the chain and by the use of digital signatures which are used for authentication, integrity of data and non-repudiation ensuring that the data recorded in the blockchain is valid.

## 5.1 *The GDPR—Blockchain Paradox*

The GDPR regulation brought the paradox on whether or not blockchain with its immutability attribute can function within the European Union legislation, and the topic is vastly discussed on the internet. Some groups (mostly from the United States) point that GDPR is fundamentally incompatible with how blockchain works in reality, implying that the European Union could close itself from how the future internet will be. It must be remembered that when the GDPR legislation was implemented, blockchain was mainly used for cryptocurrencies and wasn't taking into consideration this technology for industry use. In the current conditions, blockchain solutions potentially would need to be mutable by consensus or by a central administrator with the advantage that personal data could be deleted from the blockchain when someone requests the 'right to be forgotten' (one of the eight privacy rights of GDPR). The problem with this approach is that immutability is one of the core points in the existence of blockchain, and without it, it then will just be a common database.

GDPR legislation could benefit from the use of blockchain as it is a tool that actually can give better control to individuals of their own personal data; a good example will be through the use of 'Self Sovereign Identity' (SSI), a novel concept from the 'Sorvin Network', part of an open source project aimed to provide individuals with a digital identity "lifetime portable digital identity that does not depend on any central authority and can never be taken away" (The Sorvin Foundation 2018). But in the meantime, organizations are at risk of being non-compliant with the GDPR legislation, as personal identifiable information (PII) cannot be removed from the blockchain, so a different approach must be taken. That approach could be a hybrid solution with data help off-chain in data lakes or other traditional cloud cased models.

### 5.2 Ethics Involved Organ Transplantation

Due to the fact that a living kidney transplantation can be performed with success using a kidney from a non-genetically related donor, adding to the long list of patients waiting for a transplant and the shortage of organs—including the uneven distribution of wealth in the world—this has created a scenario of organ harvesting that goes against the ethical framework followed by the medical transplant community and international organizations. The trafficking of organs and persons for the only purpose of commercialism and organ removal is forbidden by law in most countries, but unfortunately occurs in certain parts of the world [23] and is increasing this criminal activity. Any institution that has a living donor program working within the ethical framework of organ transplantation guided by approved international standards must have all necessary regulatory infrastructure aligned with the European and UK legislations, and should also consider other safeguards that demonstrate the integrity of the program by any independent assessment prior to a transplant, that no reward has been offered (or given) that results in the donation of an organ, and that consent has been provided freely (no coercion to the donor has been made).

Having a model where everything can be recorded on blockchain and monitor audit control in all stages of organ donation makes complete sense for not just the audit, tracking, traceability but also to help deter criminal behaviours. The smart contracts will approve all milestones and consent and help safeguard ethics.

### 5.3 Evaluation of Blockchain and GDPR Compatibility

The objective needs be addressed as part of the paradox between GDPR and blockchain: while GDPR was being created, its main target was conventional databases but not emergent technology such as blockchain. GDPR has among its privacy rights the concepts of 'right to access information related to you', 'the right to be forgotten', 'the right to data portability' and 'the right to make companies edit-correct-change information about you', while blockchain brings with it a some of its strongest points which are immutability and transparency.

There are some similarities between them, and both aim to provide a greater transparency on data and at the same time there are some important differences, the critical one being related to the immutability of blockchain and the rights that GDPR gives to users in order to erase, delete or add their personal identifiable information. GDPR requires user's identity but blockchain prefers anonymity, and as mentioned before, GDPR is focused more in centralized systems or common databases rather than decentralized like blockchains. Most of the GDPR regulations deal with personal data that has already being recorded—as there has been public outcry by knowing that certain social media companies have been collecting and monetizing people's data without their consent; and GDPR requests the users to agree to share their personal information, while blockchain for example of cryptocurrencies never deals with personal data. But blockchain uses public keys which are used to identify who creates a transaction and it potentially be that they could be treated as personal data by GDPR because they are connected to specific users—at this moment this has not been discussed in a court of law, so there is not a clear answer.

Many blockchain companies and consortiums are working to deal with this regulation taking diverse paths, as the pressure to comply with GDPR (and not get fined up to 4% of their annual worldwide revenue) increases. One way could be to issue a legal agreement between all the participants from a permissioned blockchain on which it will be agreed not to export the personal data in question, use it or copy it to an end user application or system (although the information could never be removed); this will need to be reviewed from a regulator point of view. Another method could be to improve the anonymization of information within blockchain in order to be compliant, this however requires more investment and testing.

Most recently in July 2019, the European Commission published a report regarding the impact of the EU data protection rules and how its implementation can be improved. The report shows that member states and businesses are developing a compliance culture and that its citizens are becoming more aware of their rights regarding their personal data. There is also a study performed by the European Parliamentary Research Service aimed to identify whether distributed ledgers be squared with European data protection law; it points out that one of the main divergencies between GDPR and blockchain systems have is that GDPR assumes that data can be modified or erased to comply with its regulations, but blockchain makes these changes extremely difficult (or economically inviable) and this ensures the integrity of the data thus increasing the trust in the network, with the additional uncertain definition of the 'erasure' clause in its Article 17. The study concludes that it will be easier for permissioned or private blockchains to comply with the legal requirements of GDPR and also explains that it is not possible to assess the compatibility between GDPR and blockchain technology. It highlights however that the use of blockchain provides benefits from the data protection perspective, also offers several suggestions on how blockchains could get more legal certainty based on the interpretation of certain elements of the GDPR, and recommends that interdisciplinary research to explore how technical design of blockchains and their governance models could be adapted to GDPR requirements.

## 6 Organ Supply Chain Framework

The scope to create a blockchain framework to manage the lifecycle of organ transplantation is both necessary for efficiency, ethics, transparency and critical to ensure supply chain can manage effectively the many moving components. This will further protect against any contamination and criminal behaviour and safeguard the provision that are both excluded any entry. The framework is recommended to deploy an applied methodology that provides the basis of mandatory requirements/compliance that usually encompasses a cyber security maturity model (CSMM). This will ensure that organisations that require to be part of the blockchain organ transplant supply chain fully understand and comply with compliance regulations and are frequently audited to ensure they are up to date and are following the objectives and requirements set out for when agreements to join take place.

Adopting a CSMM is a matter of selecting what is best suited to this type of supply chain. The same can be said regarding type of blockchain which must be able to operate in a distributed way where the application services involved run on multiple hosts and are not dependent on a centralised authority. Selecting the consensus mechanism is a similar exercise and for the purposes of this healthcare scenario the PBFT consensus mechanism protocol is recommended. The PBFT pilot, as long it runs with less than 100 nodes, can offer 1000 transactions per second with a small payload size. This is considering that health records within blockchain will manage only data text, while it can also manage a good percentage of rogue nodes. For the blockchain model to be able to reach a fast throughput, the number of nodes in blockchain needs to be limited in order that it must be able to provide an efficient auditability and transparency of immutable information. Also, to be able to comply with data privacy regulations, the system must offer control of data access and anonymization of personal health related information.

The audit log process of the system should have also high throughput in order to manage the large number of log transactions and be able to integrate with existing systems with minimal changes or updates in the overall design and should be able to manage transactions of diverse sizes, as these might vary from between systems. The audit process will also provide a time stamped transaction sequence along with an audit trail to verify all transactions coming from each node and for stakeholders, while its architecture should be designed to be modular as well as service oriented so different types of applications can interact and benefit from it. Regarding security, the system will be able to prevent and neutralize any data tampering at its source. As it potentially will interact with other systems such as electronic health record systems, it will integrate its blockchain data transmission activities smoothly for a secure exchange of data, and have the feature of search and retrieval capability to retrieve any set of desired transactions with the length and time of search can be setup; this feature must be quick and responsive to ensure audits can be performed in real time. With regards to GDPR compliancy, some of the reviewed solutions do not get involved in the topic, others make the assumption that organizations who use the system are already compliant, and one offers a service to be 'GDPR compliant'.

The proposed framework is based on theoretical design of an audit and tracking system based on blockchain technology supported by smart contracts with the aim to assist healthcare institutions to keep track and audit the organ transplant data that is recorded as part organ matching related activities. The proposed audit system should count with several features such as been able to convert audit log data to a blockchain compatible format that will be distributed among peers of the blockchain network. It should also have data integrity logic in order to have record authenticity. From the security point of view, it should prevent rogue nodes from changing their transaction timestamps, and as part of a private-permissioned blockchain it should count with provisioned access control to selected users via an access control mechanism. This

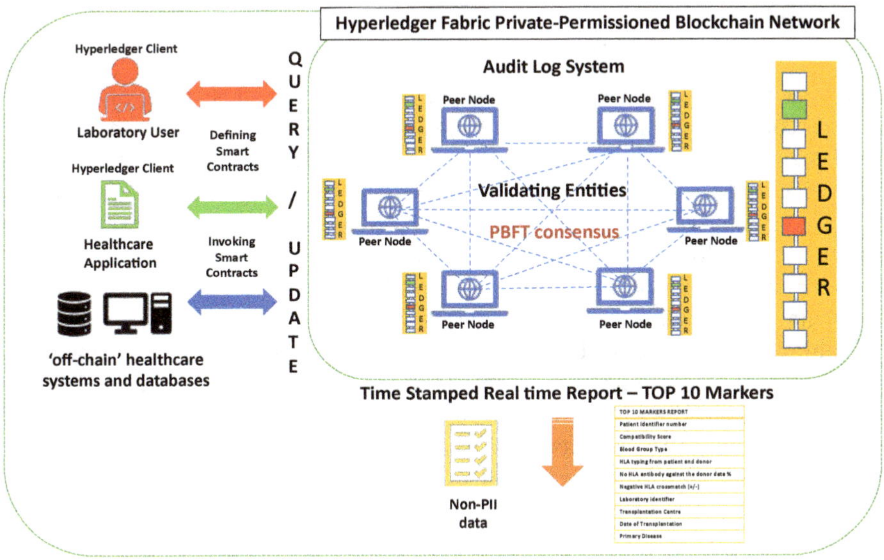


**Fig. 2** Proposed blockchain audit system

should allow auditability and transparency of records along with an end to end tamper-evident audit trail, proof of compliance, integrity and time stamp for authentication of transactions.

The following Fig. 2 shows the idea of the proposed blockchain based audit system and although a high-level design.

It is recommended that further studies be carried out to test and evaluate a Hyperledger installation with PBFT along another consensus mechanism that can compensate the needs of this protocol when having more than a hundred nodes in the blockchain, along with different sizes of data load in order to evaluate the maximum size of data where throughput gets diminished in order to explore different performance bottlenecks and tune-in the system.

Due to the fact that the organ transplantation is extremely complex because of the different types of organs and their transplantation protocols, it can be recommended to gather available detailed information from the NHS transplantation healthcare centres based in the UK, showing per type of organ and evaluate what type of information needs to be recorded within the blockchain. Also, to perform tests with real life data, this with the goal to provide precise information that can be then shown as part of the reports. With the same idea in mind, it will be interesting to see how can this blockchain system can connect to a 'federated' blockchain model, so testing in that way are needed. From the medical side and in order to assure that the proposed system is used in a safe environment, a legal framework surrounding the activities with organ donations against unacceptable practices like organ trafficking, needs to be in place.

## 7 Conclusion

It is clear that organ transplant and supply chain needs some form of audit and tracking control that can help secure and maintain accuracy, ethics and transparency. Blockchain and its unique attributes can help provide this mechanism to further secure data and patient safety. It can also help deter the behaviours that has attracted both the criminal enterprise and desperation from individuals looking to illegally participate in selling their organs and those donors looking to procure.

It can also help post donor analysis of failures that occur and track and trace the origins as to what were exact reasons (in case the organ was not correct match, contaminated etc.). Also, with these questions arising regarding DNA contamination.

Adopting the right type of blockchain for organ supply chain is key and storing the data off-chain is an important consideration for cost effectiveness and privacy. Mixing the right type of cyber security maturity model will further enhance the potential for efficient compliance and ensure those that enter the supply chain are validated and continually audited with consequences for repeated failures to comply.

## References

1. 101 Blockchains (2018a) Consensus algorithms: the root of the Blockchain technology. https://101blockchains.com/consensus-algorithms-blockchain/. Accessed 19 Dec 2019
2. Abboud O, Abbud-Filho M, Abdramanov K, Abdulla S, Abraham G, Abueva AV, Aderibigbe A, Al-Mousawi M, Alberu J, Allen RD, Almazan-Gomez LC (2008) The declaration of Istanbul on organ trafficking and transplant tourism. Clin J Am Soc Nephrol 3(5):1227–1231
3. Agbo C, Mahmoud Q, Eklund J (2019) Blockchain technology in healthcare: a systematic review. Healthcare 7(2):56
4. Ambagtsheer F (2019) Combating human trafficking for the purpose of organ removal: lessons learned from prosecuting criminal cases. In: The Palgrave International handbook of human trafficking, pp 1733–1749
5. Arnold A (2018) Is blockchain the answer to a better healthcare industry? Forbes.com, https://www.forbes.com/sites/andrewarnold/2018/08/26/is-blockchain-the-answer-to-a-better-healthcare-industry/#f839edf75a8b. Accessed 16 Aug 2019
6. Bagheri A, Delmonico FL (2013) Global initiatives to tackle organ trafficking and transplant tourism. Med Health Care Philos 16(4):887–895
7. Budiani-Saberi DA, Delmonico FL (2008) Organ trafficking and transplant tourism: a commentary on the global realities. Am J Transplant 8(5):925–929
8. Caplan A, Dominguez-Gil B, Matesanz R, Prior C (2009) Trafficking in organs, tissues and cells and trafficking in human beings for the purpose of the removal of organs. Joint Council of Europe/United Nations Study
9. Caulfield T, Duijst W, Bos M, Chassis I, Codreanu I, Danovitch G, Gill J, Ivanovski N, Shin, M (2016) Trafficking in human beings for the purpose of organ removal and the ethical and legal obligations of healthcare providers. Transp Direct 2(2)
10. CoinDesk (2019) How to mine ethereum—CoinDesk. https://www.coindesk.com/information/how-to-mine-ethereum. Accessed 7 Sep 2019
11. Coincap (2017) CoinCap.io|Reliable cryptocurrency prices and market capitalizations. https://coincap.io. Accessed 20 Aug 2019

12. ConsenSys (2019)General philosophy—ethereum smart contract best practices. Github.io, https://consensys.github.io/smart-contract-best-practices/general_philosophy/. Accessed 15 Nov 2019
13. Council of Europe (1997) Convention for the protection of human rights and dignity of the human being with regard to the application of biology and medicine: convention on human rights and biomedicine. COE, Oviedo
14. Council of Europe Publishing (2004) Guide to safety and quality assurance for organs, tissues, and cells, 2nd edn. Council of Europe Publishing: The Council of Europe
15. DNATIX (2017) DNA sequences on the blockchain. DNAtix—The secure platform for genetics. https://www.dnatix.com/dna-sequences-on-the-blockchain/. Accessed 8 Dec 2019
16. Data Protection Act (2018) Available at: http://www.legislation.gov.uk/ukpga/2018/12/section/15/enacted [online] Accessed 30 May 2020
17. Dragonchain (2019) Dragonchain|Blockchain as a service. https://dragonchain.com. Accessed 22 Oct 2019
18. Ekblaw A, Azaria A, Halamka J, Lippman A, Vieira T (2016) A case study for Blockchain in healthcare: "MedRec" prototype for electronic health records and medical research data. MIT Media Lab. https://pdfs.semanticscholar.org/56e6/5b469cad2f3ebd560b3a10e7346780f4ab0a.pdf. Accessed 25 Nov 2019
19. Elliott TA, Gregory TR (2015) Do larger genomes contain more diverse transposable elements? BMC Evol Biol 15(1). https://bmcevolbiol.biomedcentral.com/articles/10.1186/s12862–015-0339-8. Accessed 7 Jan 2020
20. English E, Davine A, Nonaka M (2018) Advancing Blockchain cybersecurity: technical and policy considerations for the financial services industry. Chamber of Digital Commerce. https://query.prod.cms.rt.microsoft.com/cms/api/am/binary/RE1TH5G. Accessed 12 Oct 2019
21. European Federation for Immunogenetics (2018) Standards for Histocompatibility & Immunogenetics Testing Version 7.0. Standards and quality assurance committee. https://efi-web.org
22. European Union (2019) FAQ—GDPR.eu. GDPR.eu. https://gdpr.eu/faq/. Accessed 28 Nov 2019
23. European Union 2016 Working Group on Living Donation. Toolbox living kidney donation. [Online]. Available at: https://ec.europa.eu/health/sites/health/files/blood_tissues_organs/docs/eutoolbox_living_kidney_donation_en.pdf. Accessed 30 May 2020
24. FACT Foundation for the Accreditation of Cellular Therapy (2019) Common standards for cellular therapies. http://www.factwebsite.org, http://www.factwebsite.org/WorkArea/DownloadAsset.aspx?id=1970
25. Fernández-Caramés TM, Fraga-Lamas P (2018) A review on the use of Blockchain for the Internet of Things. www.semanticscholar.org, https://www.semanticscholar.org/paper/A-Review-on-the-Use-of-Blockchain-for-the-Internet-Fern%C3%A1ndez-Caram%C3%A9s-Fraga-Lamas/02458904f9bd718bd8c6a1a36e9847ad83b0410b. Accessed 4 Nov 2019
26. Gill JS, Goldberg A, Prasad GV, Fortin MC, Hansen TB, Levin A, Gill J, Tonelli M, Tibbles LA, Knoll G, Cole EH (2010) Policy statement of Canadian Society of Transplantation and Canadian Society of Nephrology on organ trafficking and transplant tourism. Transplantation 90(8):817
27. Holmes P, Rijken C, D'Orsi S, Esser L, Hol F, Gallagher A, Greenberg G, Helberg L, Horvatits L, McCarthy S, Ratel J (2016) Establishing trafficking in human beings for the purpose of organ removal and improving cross-border collaboration in criminal cases: recommendations. Transp Direct 2(2)
28. IBM (2019) The founder's handbook your guide to getting started with blockchain, Edition 2.0. https://www.ibm.com/blockchain/platform. Accessed 30 Nov 2019
29. ICO 2020. The principles. Available at: https://ico.org.uk/for-organisations/guide-to-data-protection/guide-to-the-general-data-protection-regulation-gdpr/principles/ [online]. Accessed 30 May 20
30. Jafar TH (2009) Organ trafficking: global solutions for a global problem. Am J Kidney Dis 54(6):1145–1157

31. Mikulic M (2017) Healthcare blockchain adoption rate worldwide 2017|Statista. Statista. https://www.statista.com/statistics/759208/healthcare-blockchain-adoption-rate-in-health-apps-worldwide/. Accessed 18 Aug 2019
32. Nakamoto S (2008) Bitcoin: a peer-to-peer electronic cash system. Bitcoin.org. https://bitcoin.org/bitcoin.pdf. Accessed 18 Aug 2019
33. Pietrobon A (2016) Challenges in implementing the european convention against trafficking in human organs. Leiden Journal of International Law 29(2):485–502
34. Steering Committee of the Istanbul Summit (2008) Organ trafficking and transplant tourism and commercialism: the declaration of Istanbul. The Lancet 372(9632):5–6
35. The Sovrin Foundation (2018) Sovrin TM: a protocol and token for self-sovereign identity and decentralized trust a white paper from the Sovrin Foundation. The Sovrin Foundation. https://sovrin.org/wp-content/uploads/2018/03/Sovrin-Protocol-and-Token-White-Paper.pdf. Accessed 7 Dec 2019
36. US Department of State (2019) Trafficking in Persons Report June 2019. https://www.state.gov/wp-content/uploads/2019/06/2019-Trafficking-in-Persons-Report.pdf. Accessed 2 Feb 2020
37. University of California San Francisco (2010) Transplant surgery—Kidney transplant. UCSF.edu, https://transplantsurgery.ucsf.edu/conditions–procedures/kidney-transplant.aspx. Accessed 14 Dec 2019
38. Venanzi D, da Silva OR, Palmisano A (2013) Supply chain of human organs: a case study in hospital complex in sorocaba. IFAC Proc 46(24):183–189
39. WHO (2004) Organ trafficking and transplantation pose new challenges. https://www.who.int/bulletin/volumes/82/9/feature0904/en/index1.html. Accessed 2 Feb 2020
40. Wood G (2017) Ethereum: a secure decentralised generalised transaction ledger EIP-150 revision. Dr. Gavin Wood. http://gavwood.com/Paper.pdf. Accessed 22 Dec 2019
41. Yaga D, Mell P, Roby N, Scarfone K (2018) NISTIR 8202—Blockchain technology overview. Nvlpubs.nist.gov, https://nvlpubs.nist.gov/nistpubs/ir/2018/NIST.IR.8202.pdf. Accessed 24 Aug 2019

# IoT and Cloud Forensic Investigation Guidelines

**I. Mitchell, S. Hara, J. Ibarra Jimenez, Hamid Jahankhani, and Reza Montasari**

**Abstract** IoT devices are becoming more prevalent in society, with an expected 21.5 Billion devices connected by 2025 [24], and when an incident occurs in the vicinity of such devices then they should be considered as potential digital evidence. A network of IoT devices is often referred to as a smart environment, or more frequently as a cyber physical system [17]. Is there a need for yet another framework? It could be questioned that: (i) there is no need for such frameworks since the IoT devices are not that important; or, (ii) that there are adequate SOPs and frameworks already in place? This chapter aims to provide answers to these questions.

**Keywords** Cyber physical systems · Digital forensic frameworks · Blockchain · Cloud · IoT

## 1 Introduction

The only thing that is constant is change, has often been attributed to the Greek philosopher, Heraclitus (c.500 BCE). Some 2500 years later never has their been a more apt quote for today's society, with its constant use of technology and hence

I. Mitchell · S. Hara
Middlesex University, London, UK
e-mail: i.mitchell@mdx.ac.uk

S. Hara
e-mail: s.hara@mdx.ac.uk

J. Ibarra Jimenez · H. Jahankhani (✉)
Northumbria University, London, UK
e-mail: Hamid.jahankhani@northumbria.ac.uk

J. Ibarra Jimenez
e-mail: jaime.jimenez@northumbria.ac.uk

R. Montasari
Huddersfield University, Huddersfield, UK
e-mail: r.montasari@hud.ac.uk

 
H. Jahankhani et al. (eds.), *Policing in the Era of AI and Smart Societies*, Advanced Sciences and Technologies for Security Applications,
https://doi.org/10.1007/978-3-030-50613-1_5

change. Currently, it is estimated that $2.5 \times 10^{18}$, or 2.5 quintillion, bytes of data are written every day. This astronomical figure is likely to increase over the next 5 years with the introduction of two major technologies: Blockchain; and, the Internet of Things (IoT). The data generated by the two technologies will be cloud based and hence, the problem for law enforcement and e-Discovery analysts is how is it possible to conceive that every piece of technology has been investigated? Paul Kirk understood in 1953 when he wrote about forensic evidence, "Only human failure to find it, study and understand it can diminish its value" [23]. Combining these pre-technological age quotes, the problem can be defined as, the human failure to find, study and understand digital evidence in an ever changing world of technology will diminish its value.

The starting point is unusual and requires structure. This has been recognised by the call to develop Digital Forensics Frameworks (DFFs) in the inaugural Digital Forensic Research Workshop [29], its response has been phenomenal with over 20,000 papers written on DFFs. This implies that there is no *silver bullet*, and it is no surprise since these frameworks are structured and need refining each time a change in technology occurs. However, guidelines are based on principles *and* procedures and there are some exceptional frameworks that were pioneering in the development of accommodating both. For example, in [5] there is a tiered approach that allows principles and practices to synergize, using Standard Operating Procedures (SOP) to *maintain* principles and opportunities to question and add to the knowledge to *improve* quality. In the UK the over-riding document is ACPOs Good Practice Guide for Digital Evidence, Uribe [36], others have accompanied this document over the years and include, but not limited to, El Ioini and Pahl [14], Palmer [33]. There is a need to research the need for a DFF with principles, SOP, and guidelines for technologies that include IoT and cloud. Joining the two together and treating them as one, rather than deploying different DFFs for each, which the remainder of this chapter investigates.

Section 2 provides some of the background information, including definitions and suggestions to be considered in the IoT network. Section 3 provides a rationale for the approach and the technology used and how this may be involved in illegal activities. Section 4 proposes some guidelines and improvements of SOPs in this area. Finally, Sect. 5 concludes and discusses the findings from the research.

## 2 Background

### 2.1 A Need for Another Framework?

To answer the first question would require some evidence of a security breach in cyber physical systems via an IoT device. There are many systems available but let us consider Body Area Networks (BAN) that include an array of medical devices, e.g., pacemakers. In [4] there is evidence of how to 'hack' a pacemaker provided by the National Health Service (NHS) in the UK. This study [4] shows that pacemakers can be hacked and the severe consequences that a security breach could result in. The study went on to show that Medical Consultants and Coroners, did not consider the security of the device when purchasing, or inspecting the device when it failed, respectively. Whilst these devices transmit on restricted frequencies, this does not deter the criminally minded with malicious intent to break these rules and commit further crimes. This is not an isolated incident, Body Area Network devices, or implantable medical devices, require more sophisticated technology to improve the quality of patients' lives, many of whom their lives depend on this technology. In [6] we can see a range of issues with these devices and there is a need for cyber-security experts to be consulted during the acquisition of implantable medical devices, [38].

The pacemaker attack [4] was not an off-the-shelf attack and required some skill. However, there is evidence of other IoT devices having their security breached with simple attacks using off-the-shelf malware and/or exploiting IoT devices were the users leave the default settings for passwords. In Finland [8] it is reported that a DDoS attack prevented the heating of buildings in sub-zero weather conditions, and was a result of the devices having default passwords. Furthermore, studies in [34] shows that in 2017, 48% of U.S. Companies using IoT devices have suffered a security breach, these included devices from teddy bears to warehouse equipment.

In summary, the consequences of these attacks on cyber physical systems range from life-threatening [4, 6, 8] to denial of service [34]. Regardless of the consequences, an incident has occurred that requires a digital investigation and the collection, preservation, acquisition, analysis, reporting and presentation of material.

This chapter is concerned with providing a framework, under which the digital investigation is guided, and able to produce digital evidence that is acceptable and admissible in a court of law and therefore, to answer the first question, when cyber physical systems are compromised there is a need for the development of investigative techniques, which includes new frameworks (Fig. 1).

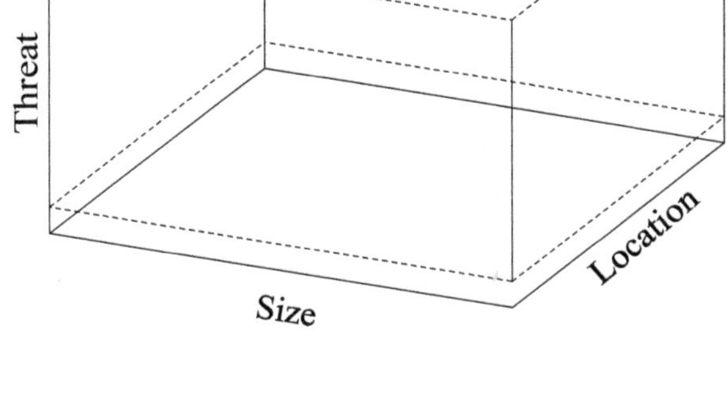


**Fig. 1** IoT classification continuum, derived from a combination of [27, 28, 32]

## 2.2 *IoT Classification Continuum*

To answer the second question a more detailed look at IoT devices is required. There are classifications of IoT devices [27, 28, 32], which relate to three different criterias: Memory size; Physical location; and, threat-level. Combining these three areas into a continuum can help Digital Forensic Investigators, DFIs, to make decisions about how the First Response Team proceed. Based on knowledge about the case type and the smart environment they are about to investigate, a DFI will be guided by the classification of the device and help develop a strategy for seizure (alongside existing recommendations). For example, location can guide the search strategy, whilst memory size may guide the order of volatility and in certain situations give rise to the issue of contamination of the device due to small memory sizes and information being overwritten. This is particularly an issue if first responders do not have information that a digital incident scene is a smart environment. Finally, with many IoT devices threatening critical national infrastructures the search strategy may prioritise the discovery of a particular IoT device. The IoT classification continuum is there to help DFIs and FRTs to search, seize and gather physical IoT artefacts. The need for forensic procedures to collect information from smart environments is in demand and the classification continuum can help.

## 2.3 *Cyber Physical System Forensic Readiness*

In [20] we see a review of current techniques and their approaches, which essentially decomposes the problem into three areas: device; network; and, cloud. IoTDots [1] focuses on the data capture and analysis, and is an important tool in the capture of data from devices and the subsequent reconstruction of events.

In both these papers forensic readiness is touched on, and there is a challenge presented by the range of IoT devices to make the network forensic ready. Some attempts have been proposed [30] and a solution is the use of BlockChain Technology, BCT (for an introduction to blockchain, see [13, 37]).

IOTA [12] is a permissionless BCT that allows the exchange of cryptocurrency via IoT devices on a cyber physical system. During an investigation it would be necessary to look at all devices in the cyber system. There are a combination of three things required in the investigation: device identification; spatio-temporal information of each IoT device, which can be used for exculpatory and inculpatory evidence; and, the state information of the IoT device, which can be used for attribution and who is ultimately responsible and in control.

Like it or not Cyber physical systems are here to stay and increasingly likely to be part of our everyday lives in the future. As already shown is Sect. 2.2, it is not inconceivable that someone could instruct an IoT device to do something illegal. This is where the immutable append-only distributed ledger forged by consensus algorithms, of BCT, would allow DFIs to search the relevant part of the Blockchain representing that cyber physical system. Then it would be possible to reconstruct events by reverse engineering the extracted information from the Blockchain and accounting for every device's state and spatial-temporal information in a cyber physical system.

There would be concerns over confidentiality and privacy of data? There already is concern over this data, e.g. see [3], however, this is no defence. Our brief description of BCT is lacking, we failed to explain that the data is encrypted and IOTA's consensus algorithm, tangle [30] is resistant to quantum computations. The latter part is important and means that our information on our blockchain is resistant to spoliation or direct contamination from adversaries. More importantly, there is no data, the data recorded or generated by the IoT device is still stored on the cloud. The crucial issue is retrieving the data with e-consent. Many IoT devices store data on the cloud that the DFI will not have sufficient privileges to access. This could be for a combination of reasons, but mainly falls on the right of privacy, and incompatible jurisdictions. BCT provides a restricted access to an itinerary of IoT devices' state, ID, and spatio-temporal information related to the investigation. Data relating to these devices would have to be obtained through Special Point of Contacts, SPoCs and subject to normal procedures and processes.

Using something like IOTA [12, 31] would standardise cyber physical systems auditability of IoT devices. Furthermore, there is the use of smart contracts [9, 10] that could prevent IoT devices completing something socially unacceptable or of illegal consequence. Where systems rely on external sources of information to change state, e.g., stock exchange, weather reports, other IoT devices, etc., then there would be an issue of centralisation and trust. To avoid centralisation and dependency on a single source of information an oracle could be introduced and is defined as, "*an interface that delivers data from an external source to smart contracts*" [2]. This would ensure the authenticity and promote trust between objects in the cyber physical system. Therefore, to make cyber physical systems forensic ready, will require a permissionless blockchain using oraclized sources of information in combination with smart contracts.

## 2.4 Proposed Framework/Summary

There exists IoT DFF and our second question is do we require another one? Quality is often misunderstood, and in Digital Forensics we are not proposing a completely new DFF, but more of an improve version of current DFFs. Quality is maintaining principles and improving practices, in this chapter it is proposed that for reasons above a new improved version of DFF for IoT is proposed based on the work thus far. The authors would like to think that in a few years, this model will also be reviewed, distilled and improved.

The proposed framework is Digital Forensic Incident Process Model, DFIPM, and its main purpose is to allow DFIs to recover IoT artefacts from the three categories: device; network; and, cloud. Then based on IoT levels of relevance determine possible root cause of the cyber incident. The basis of our work considers [17, 24], which will be explained in the following Sect. 3.

## 3 Method

Digital forensic frameworks provide theoretical guidance to practitioners of digital forensics but they have become too prescriptive in their approach. Their design was/is to ensure that all evidence that is acquired, handled, processed and presented from crime scene to a courtroom meets the legal jurisdictional requirements. Earlier digital forensic frameworks evolved from dealing with devices that were largely unconnected and stand-alone to more current frameworks that present investigative methodologies for cloud, networks and IoT.

This chapter proposes that SOP should be considered for digital investigations. These SOPs will draw best practice from current guidelines and digital frameworks to produce a single consultative provision with a focus on practical application for evolving technologies for both civil and criminal crimes.

## 4 Digital Forensic Investigation Process Model, DFIPM

The proposed framework, DFIPM, has been developed from high to low-level approach and consists of seven phases, or processes. The seven phases are at a higher abstract level with more detail provided at a low-level in sub-phases. Figure 2 presents the abstract level of the DFIPM. This abstract model work with eight concurrent processes and are known as principles and listed below:

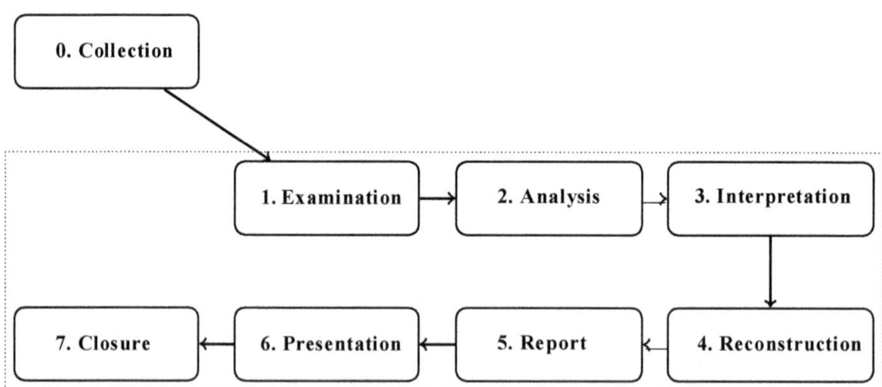


**Fig. 2** Activity diagram for digital forensic investigation process model, DFIPM, for cyber physical systems

1. *Preservation*—Maximising evidential integrity must be maintained, where possible, throughout all stages of the framework. It is paramount that all possible precautions have been taken during the seizure and acquisition of the artefact.
2. *Evidence Continuity*—Using a chain of custody the custodian of the artefact must be recorded each time it is transferred. A record of these events provide an auditable record of evidence movement, see [23] for a more detailed explanation.
3. *Information Flow Management*—Permission for investigators to interact with the variety of laws, regulations and guidelines appropriately due the entire lifecycle of processing the artefact.
4. *Case Management*—Manage, record and keep track of artefacts involved in the case. In [7] it is highlighted the importance of this principle as one of the main components of scaffolding to bind all artefacts, evidence, reports, supporting documentation for the building of a strong case.
5. *Prepared Techniques and Standardised Tools*—DFIs need to use diverse tools and techniques during the investigation and this principle is covered extensively in [21]. Whilst the range of tools that are approved is adequate for traditional computer forensics, it is in much need of updating for IoT devices.
6. *Authorised Consent*—All personal data must have associated permission. This data should not be compromised or disclosed. A further option of a smart contract could be used to ensure that the data permissions are not breached. Mutual Legal Assistants, MLAs, and SPoCs will provide guidance and accessibility to data.
7. *Documentation*—The documentation should record the entire life-cycle of the investigation. All changes, contemporaneous notes and preventative techniques should be included.
8. *Physical Investigation*—Interviews with bystanders or other people in the location is crucial and should be carried out by qualified personnel. However, in a digital incident scene there are more questions relating to digital devices that may require specialisms. Always include an interviewer in your FRT who has both knowledge and expertise in technology and interview techniques. All interviews need recording and added to the report.
9. *Training*—As a principle training and competence of staff is often overlooked. It is now included in the code of conduct in the FSR, which Digital Forensic Laboratories have to comply with for accreditation, [39].
10. *Search*—FRTs always require search strategies at incident scene. Often due to conditions outside the control of the investigation, e.g., weather, budgets, time management, FRTs only get one chance to complete the search and seizure of the area. Some IoT devices are going to be difficult to find, or unintentionally contaminated. Forensic readiness, combined with the classification of IoT devices will at least provide a itinerary of IoT devices to be avoided and seized, if possible, or data to be considered in the reconstruction of events.

## *4.1 Examination*

Pareto's 80/20 rule is not just confined to business, it is also present in digital forensic investigations with 80% of the work dedicated to nearly 20% of the framework's two phases: Examination; and, Analysis. In [7] it is argued that examination and analysis should be one single phase, however, this was before IoTs were available and mass marketed. They indicated that there were slight differences when applying to traditional digital forensic analysis, e.g., HDD and simple network forensics. These slight differences have been exacerbated over the years with the introduction of new technologies and have different goals and aims and therefore they are considered as two different phases.

Examination is primarily concerned with the identification and extraction of potential digital evidence, that could be either inculpatory or exculpatory. Whereas analysis involves detailed and methodical standard operating procedures that factually support the reconstruction of the event. Figure 3 shows an activity diagram followed by a list explaining each of the sub-phases.

1.1 *Survey*—Surveying the Digital Incident Scene is the first sub-phase in the Examination phase and enables DFIs to discover pieces of evidence for a specific case type and depends on the skill level of the suspect, which can be under-estimated. Predicting the suspect's skill level would lead DFIs to decide on procedures, techniques and methods in the analysis phase. The main objective of this sub-phase is to identify potential digital evidence, including in unusual locations of

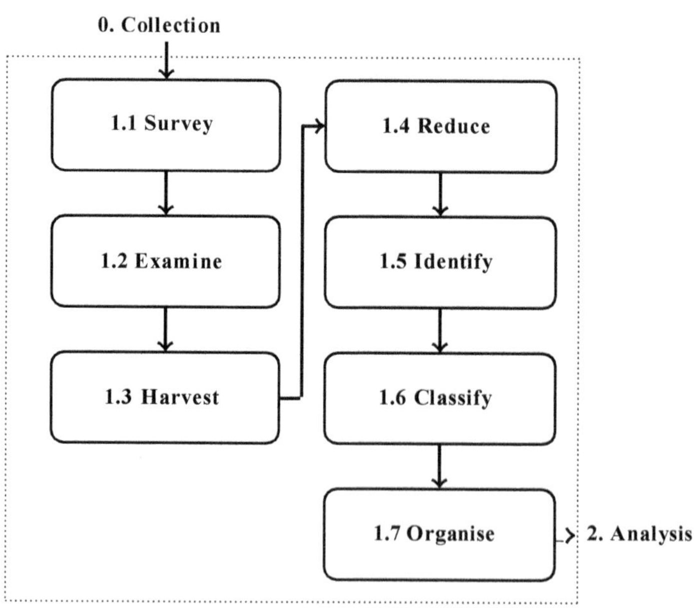


**Fig. 3** Activity diagram for the examination process showing sub-phases

the system architecture [26], again use of BCT and an itinerary of IoT devices can be used here on forensic ready cyber physical systems.

1.2 *Examine*—DFIs must perform a detailed examination of the image acquired. File and folder structure is indexed using NIST approved software, e.g., Access-Data's FTK, Axiom for cloud-based data artefacts.

1.3 *Harvest*—Order the harvest and collected data. File and folder structure is indexed to provide an order of data acquired. The output of this stage is to produce a logical and catalogued data set [25]. This also includes any data gleaned of the forensic ready blockchain and used to identify IoT devices in the survey stage.

1.4 *Reduce*—'Digital litter' is a downside in any investigation, during triage there needs to be ways of identifying relevant and irrelevant files. There are files that are relevant to the system and crucial to it operation, however, may be irrelevant to the investigation. There are many files that are not crucial to the operation of the system and irrelevant to the investigation. Then there are just the many files that have been saved or duplicated and never accessed. Most forensic tools, e.g. AccessData's FTK, will compile a list of all files enabling legal teams to categorise into used or unused data. The DFI has to have an *order of relevancy* to identify files that are important to the investigation and thus reduce and de-duplicate material being searched.

1.5 *Identify*—Once the sub-phases have been completed a clear identification of relevant potential digital artefacts should be recorded.

1.6 *Classify*—Grouping data with similar patterns, which can accelerate the process of analysis focused on the case type.

1.7 *Organise*—After these sub-phases it may be required to re-organise and provide new focus for the investigation.

## *4.2 Analysis*

This is the most intensive phase in the framework due to the amounts of data collected combine with levels of complexity. With the examination phase complete the DFIs have the main patterns and characteristics of the incident encountered identified. This is based on the Evidence searching phase from [7] and is iterative, if the evaluation of results does not yield any attribution or cannot be validated, then a new hypothesis can be form and the analysis life-cycle can continue. The stopping criteria would be when there is definitive attribution (of at least the machine, not the person) and evaluation of the results are valid. Figure 4 shows the activity diagram of the analysis phase, the sub-phases are explained in the list below.

2.1 *Hypothesis*—Using information from previous phases, the DFI can make hypotheses regarding the cyber-crime and map the root cause of the incident by remaking a sequence of events that changes the current state of the system. The hypotheses are built on the following:

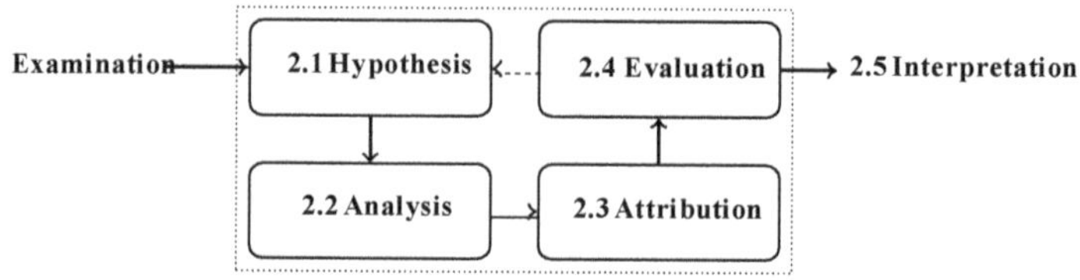


**Fig. 4** Activity diagram for analysis phase

- Assumptions are based on the results of the different stages form the Examination phase;
- Digital evidence organised from the Examination phase; and,
- Documentation of their findings.

2.2 *Analysis*—The DFIs have to perform a deep investigation to the organised information collected form the Examination phase on the hypothesis defined from the previous sub-phase. In addition, it must be completed by competent and train personnel using NIST approved software, [41]. The credibility of the potential evidence should consider the relevance, admissibility and weight. Not all collection of evidence can be analysed using NIST approved software, especially in the domain of IoT, any non-standard software used should be accompanied with detailed contemporaneous notes and reproducibility reports.

2.3 *Attribution*—Attribution is left to courts or tribunals, however, the digital evidence should provide facts that associate a user to the event identified in the analysis stage. For example, in some cases, DFIs can use access logs, traffic, personal device, IoT logs, to associate a user to an event. If no attribution can be found then the next sub-phase, Evaluation, cannot be valid and the DFI revisits the hypothesis.

2.4 *Evaluation*—Once the attribution has been assigned, the validity of the results are tested. On the successful validation of results the hypothesis can be accepted and the output is passed on to the next phase.

## 4.3 Interpretation

The Interpretation phase is for using standardised practices to explain the facts discovered across the investigation with the results obtained from the Analysis phase. After the hypothesis has been accepted and validated the interpretation phase delivers statements with legal context for later reporting and presentation phases. Figure 5 shows the activity diagram for the interpretation phase and the sub-phases are explained below.

3.1 *Interpret Results*—The interpretation of the results will depend on the availability of data and circumstances around the development of the case [18]. In addition DFIs may require information from individuals involved in the operation in order to carry out a more effective interpretation. This sub-phase is

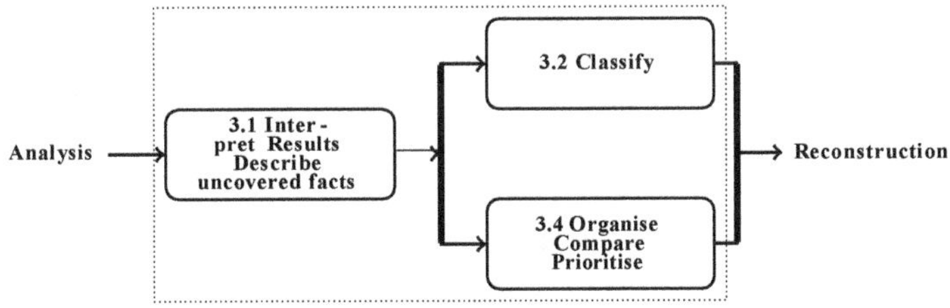


**Fig. 5** Activity diagram for interpretation phase

concerned with mapping the analysis to the goal and scope of the investigation. During this process DFIs must analyse links and use timeline tools in order to reconstruct events.

3.2 *Classify*—The classification of the event under scrutiny may support other facts; it is rare that a single event leads to a single incident, it is normally the amalgamation of a series of events that leads to the incident. These events need to be classified and put in some hierarchical order; this may also benefit timeline analysis, again the forensic readiness can provide a dynamic timeline analysis using the information gleaned from the blockchain.

3.3 *Organise*—Simultaneously, these events can be organised and given priorities.

## *4.4 Reconstruction*

The previous three stages have parallel streams for the device; network; and, cloud data. This phase collates the data from these parallel streams to form an overall picture of the cyber physical system.

The reconstruction of events provides admissible evidence and typically for smart environments will involve a simulator. The simulation of events needs to be reproducible and can be problematic with non-deterministic systems, such as cyber physical systems [16] that rely and respond to user interaction.

There are further problems predicted in the reconstruction of smart environments. Blockchain engineering will undoubtedly be introduce to manage the security, authenticity and integrity of the communication between IoT devices, but this will only help if investigators are given sufficient read access permissions. In the proposed model this information would be governed by a permissionless blockchain, IOTA, and information regarding the identity, spatio-temporal and state would be accessible. The data would be accessed via a different parallel stream, as indicated in Fig. 9.

Blockchain analysis will be required to identify which components were activated and as a result completed transactions which result in the generation of blocks. There are many simulators of smart environments, however, these simulators do not allow for the simulation of blockchain components.

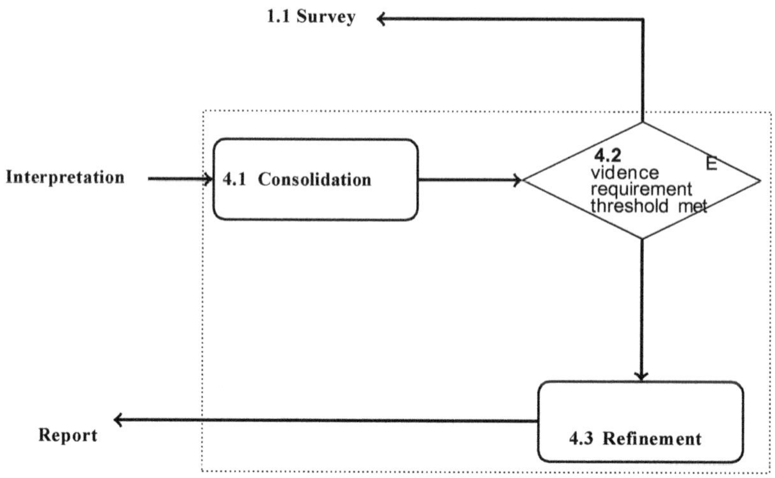


**Fig. 6** Activity diagram for reconstruction phase

The consolidation of events in a smart environment, will require significant work and emphasis on the results from the interpretation phase. Figure 6 shows the activity diagram for the reconstruction phase, followed by the description of the sub-phases.

4.1 *Consolidation*—In the interpretation phase it was mentioned that there may be a number of events that lead to a culminating activity that is considered illegal. The consolidation sub-phase is responsible for putting all the events together and in a simulated environment looking at how these event are accumulated into a single action. For example, in a smart home/environment with many IoT devices, it may be necessary to track a certain device and its changing states over time to exonerate or incriminate some behaviour of the accused. The consolidation phase may indicate multiple actions of an individual using many IoT devices and other digital artefacts.

4.2 *Threshold*—All evidence has to meet a threshold to stand scrutiny in a court of law. Increasingly, it is becoming difficult for the DFIs to explain to legal representatives the details about the information gathered. It is suggested that counsel is arranged between parties and reconstructions to date are demonstrated, showing the output of the consolidation process. If the threshold is reached then the next stage of reporting can begin, however, if the threshold is not met then going back to the survey sub-phase in the Examination phase would be considered or ultimately closing the case.

4.3 *Refinement*—If counsel returns positive feedback and the threshold is met, then refinement of the consolidation process can begin, ensuring reproducibility of the results. To this point the principles are continued throughout all of the sub-phases and therefore the reproducibility is not be a problem.

## 4.5 Report

Documentation is a principle, the report is the phase that collates all the information hitherto, into a comprehensive report with precise details of each phase. All evidence presented should uphold scrutiny [15] and the DFI is to remain impartial and rely on the known facts [5]. Unlike single device or multiple independent device investigations, where the software used can automatically generate the report, IoT investigations are different and some investment is required from the law enforcement agencies to ensure the generation of documentation is integrated, automated and consistent. The report must have conclusions that are reproducible by independent third parties and include the following [35]:

- *Seizure Forms*—Authorisation, Evidence logs, transportation of evidence logs, attendance logs, photo/videos, contemporaneous notes, interview notes, and other documentation used at the incident scene.
- *Evidential Continuity*—The chain of custody forms, showing the transfer of evidence to custodians.
- *Reconstruction & Analysis*—A brief outline of any reconstruction and analysis methods used and the revealed results.
- *Software Licenses*—Provide valid licenses of any software used.
- *Personnel*—Certificates and brief biopics of personnel involved in the case.
- *Other*—And all the information from the other phases.

Due to the multimedia, videos etc., it is advised that the report take on a different structure than traditional linear paper-based reports. The information about the case would be held on a private cloud, the report should take on a multimedia form and be non-linear based, e.g., web-based/html. This would certainly ease the burden on collating evidence and generating a single linear based report. Due to the parallel streams in the DFIPM, multiple teams can work interdependently and when ready make available via a report the information required, this can then be pointed to via an organised hyperlink, [40].

## 4.6 Presentation

The presentation phase is not without peril, but good preparation to a wide range of audience, use of user-friendly and non-technical vocabulary and adhering to the facts should prevail. Figure 7 shows the activity diagram for the presentation phase and the sub-phases are discussed in the following list.

6.1 *Requirements*—Case type will determine the structure of the report. It is recommended that the report is a non-linear collection of documents stored on private cloud. The advancements of technology allows us to record video of the reconstruction of events, which can provide excellent guidelines on reproducibility and show that Standard Operating Procedures (SOP) are being followed. This

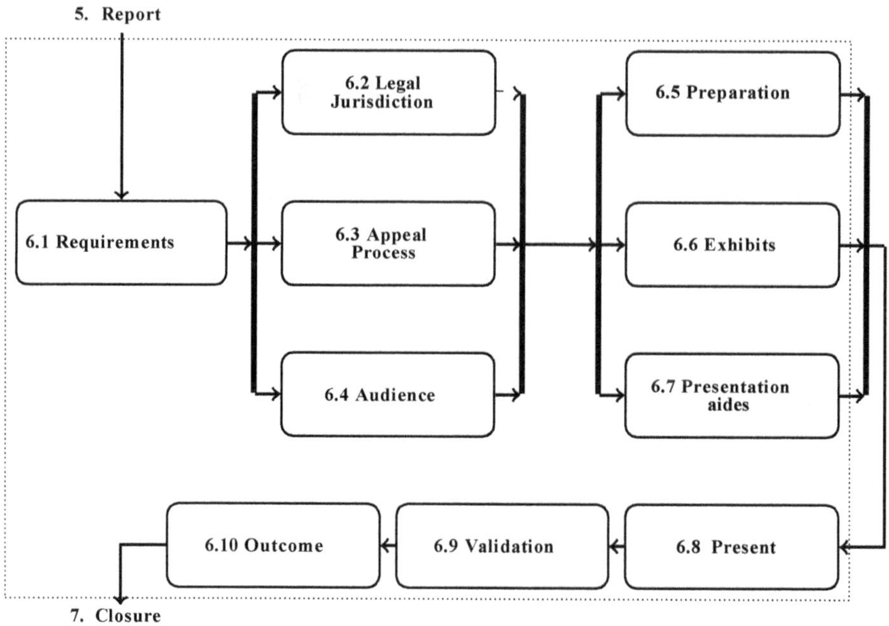


**Fig. 7** Activity diagram for presentation phase

has the consequence of non-linear means that the focus is on the content, there should be a standard set-up for the identified case type and then the DFIs are left to populate and manage the content.

6.2 *Legal Jurisdiction*—Ensure that the seizure of all material was authorised by correct legal authority and appropriate forms are included in the report.

6.3 *Appeal Process*—Whilst the outcome of the case could be successful, the appeal process has to be considered. The documents and related evidence should be archived and stored for no longer than the time required to lodge an appeal.

6.4 *Audience*—Some documents in the report may require some re-writing using a simplified and non-technical vocabulary understood by a wide range of audience.

6.5 *Preparation*—The preparation of appropriate individuals to be called to give evidence. You do not want your expert on Mobile Phones presenting evidence on a WiFi enabled coffee machine that has been used to complete a DDoS attack on an organisation's network. The individual presenting should be involved in the reconstruction, be briefed and defer questions to other experts in the case when unable to provide a direct answer. IoT Forensics may require several experts to give evidence, this opens the opportunity for the defence to build upon any inconsistencies given in their testimonies. There needs to be a coherent and comprehensive narrative based on facts, and therefore it is recommended that during pre-trial briefs everyone is invited.

6.6 *Exhibits*—Ensure evidence bags, labels and accompanying forms have correct and matching information for each artefact presented.
6.7 *Presentation Aids*—Elaborate diagrams and video may be required to explain complexity of the IoT system.
6.8 *Present*—This sub-phase represents the live presentation complete in a legal setting; where possible, it is advised that this be recorded or notes taken of performance of the many individuals that may be involved. This feedback can be useful for the debriefing.
6.9 *Validation*—Did the validation of the hypothesis succeed after the presentation, was there anything omitted?
6.10 *Outcome*—The outcome of the case based on the evidence provided.

## 4.7 Closure

Closure is not only about closing the case. It is also concerned with the destruction or return of evidence and concerned with debriefing and improving quality of the procedures and processes used.

7.1 *Outcome*—The outcome of the case can be used to assess the strengths and weaknesses of the organisation's policies, procedures and regulatory compliance.
7.2 *Hypothesis*—The DFIPM is an iterative process and allows DFIs to visit any of the preceding phases.
7.3 *Critical Review*—Regardless of the outcome, a critical review of the case should be written and should identify good practice and make recommendations.
7.4 *Identify Lessons Learned* —During the critical review and debrief there should be a list of recommendations that should serve to improve the professional practices and overall quality of the digital forensic laboratory.
7.5 *Store, Destroy, Re-cycle or Up-cycle*—Destruction should be a last resort of any material. Many organisations are striving for carbon neutral footprints and the destruction of evidence should be a last resort. Evidence can stay in the evidence store and be used for training personnel. Many of the elements of the artefacts can be re-purposed or sold, if appropriately wiped of any information. The key point here is that only at this point can the artefacts be considered for reuse or destruction, where reuse is chosen ensure that there is a strict guidance policy regarding GDPR [11], e.g. the right to be forgotten, if the suspect is cleared of all charges (Fig. 8).
7.6 *Return Evidence*—Depending on the outcome of the case and the case type, the priority should be to return the evidence. It should be noted that for some case types evidence cannot be returned.
7.7 *Record Case Decision*—A record of the case decision should be included in the critical review.
7.8 *Dissemination And/Or Storage*—Relevant information regarding the case must be disseminated to all authorised stakeholders. It may include notification

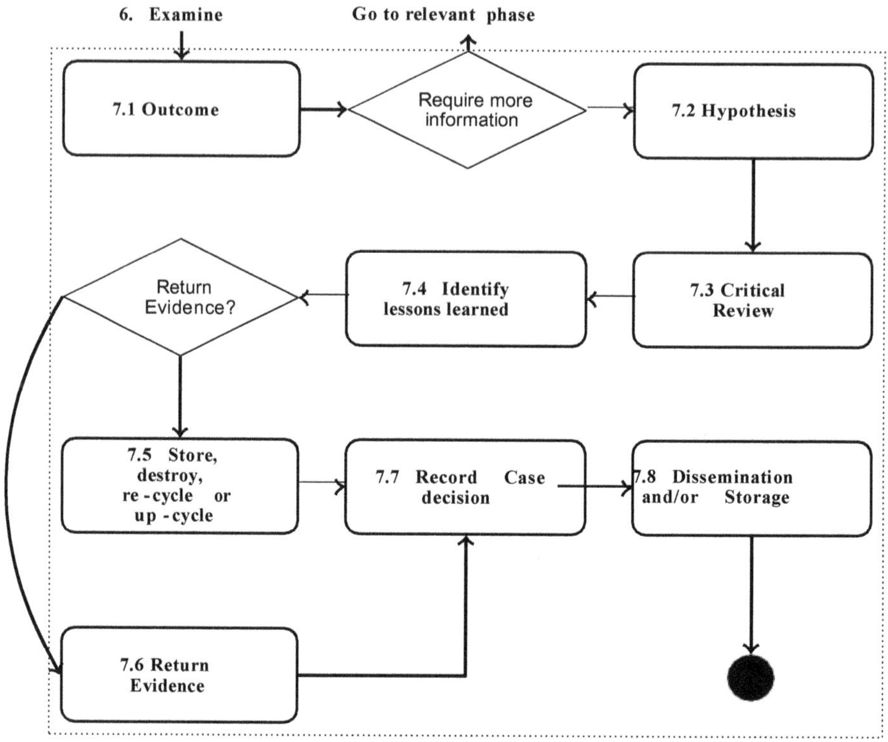


**Fig. 8** Activity diagram for closure phase

regarding the return to previous processes, acceptance or rejection of the hypothesis, a failure to demonstrate in a believable manner the reconstruction of events or other reasons.

## 4.8 Summary

Figure 9 shows the overview of the proposed DFIPM merging multiple architectures that IoT interacts with, the principle that it must have, the "Privacy by Design" principle—remember any digital evidence may uncover private data irrelevant to the case—and the mandatory aspects that would lead to a reliable investigation process assuring data privacy. During the evidence collection or acquisition it is necessary to isolate the type of information gathered, separating them into device, network and cloud forensics. This is because each architecture deals with different tools, methodologies and timelines, leading them to different interpretations. Once each component reaches the interpretation phase, they will all get merged into the event reconstruction phase. Then the remaining phases are completed in a serial manner, with the option of some iteration.

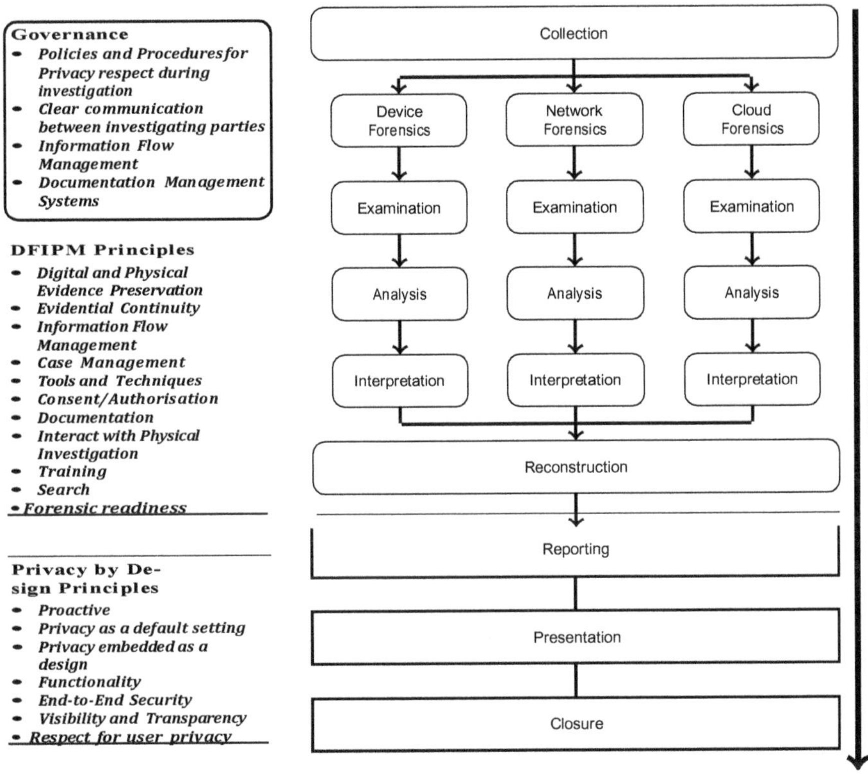


**Fig. 9** Overall view of DFIPM

It is this final overview in Fig. 9 that is important and shows the parallel streams working in the different domains, namely: Device Forensics; Network Forensics; and, Cloud Forensics.

## 5 Conclusions

The main contribution of this paper is the proposed model, DFIPM, which has three parallel streams working in each of the areas identified in cyber physical systems: device; network; and, cloud. The parallel streams produce data for the reconstruction of events phase, from where it continues through more traditional phases until it reaches the closure phase. Each phase's sub-phase is explained in detail in Sect. 4. Whilst the phases are being complete there are some over-riding principles discussed also in Sect. 4 and briefly listed as follows: Preservation; Evidential Continuity; Information Flow Management; Case Management; Tools and Techniques; Interacting with physical investigation; Training; Search strategies; and, Forensic readiness.

The use of blockchain technology, such as IOTA [31], to securely record the information about state is crucial to making cyber physical systems forensic ready. As discussed in Sect. 2.3 blockchain technology would not provide the data that IoT devices may record, however, it can identify the device and then provide provisional access to the data. Essentially, it will allow DFIs to identify which components in the cyber physical system are to be included in the investigation. This may seem odd, but already we are seeing a wide range of devices that could amount to 100's of artefacts being seized for a single smart environment. A crucial contribution of this paper is the benefits of having access to read the records of each IoT device and then consider in subsequent phases what is relevant and whether or not to make a request to the SPoC for the associated data.

In the future this will become important, since it is quite possible that every incident will result in 100's of digital IoT artefacts being seized. By their nature cyber physical systems are constantly changing state and therefore, the challenge for digital forensics is how to capture that dynamic data and reconstruct a timeline of events. This in the past has been accomplished in many textbooks, e.g., see [19], however cyber-physical has a more interactive role with living organisms.[1] The interaction of the investigator has to be kept minimal, especially where the data from that IoT device is unlikely to be provided by the service provider and the memory (data) size of the IoT device is small. In such cases the overwriting of data due to contamination from many physical interactions between the investigators and the IoT device could lead to loss of data. Seizure and preservation have a paradoxical relationship, you cannot seize some IoT devices without contamination. However, DFIs must document every effort that seizure caused minimal changes to the IoT device, whilst maximising the possible amount of data recovered from the IoT device.

Finally we return to Heraclitus and his tenant on flux, and the quote, 'You cannot step into the same river twice'. Whilst this is often seen as a test of resilience, i.e. you will be a different person tomorrow, it also has another interpretation from the river's perspective, which is always changing. By 2025 there will be an estimated 21.5 Bn IoT devices, and hence this flood of technology will make walking into the same smart environment twice an impossibility due to the state change of the IoT devices. Without necessary safeguards it will become difficult for DFIs to investigate incidents due to the number of IoTs involved and the complexity it brings. Creating cyber physical systems with non-registered or unaccountable IoT devices is likely to see a rise in challenging and socially unacceptable behaviour, as witnessed by the introduction of social media [22]. The introduction of standardised blockchain technology will make cyber physical systems not only forensic ready, but could also have the added benefit of minimising challenging or socially unacceptable behaviour, or at least finding some accountability for the incident.

**Conflicting Interests** None identified.

[1]N.B. Many cyber-physical systems with wireless sensors are used with livestock.

## References


1. Babun L, Sikder AK, Acar, A, Selcuk Uluagac A (2018) Iotdots: a digital forensics framework for smart environments. arXiv preprint arXiv:1809.00745
2. Bashir I (2018) Mastering blockchain. Packt, 2 edn.
3. BBC (2020) Ring doorbell' gives Facebook and Google user data. https://www.bbc.co.uk/news/technology-51281476. Accessed Jan 2020
4. Beavers JL, Faulks M, Marchang J (2019) Hacking NHS pacemakers: a feasibility study. In: Global security, safety and sustainability the security challenges of the connected world
5. Beebe NL, Clark JG (2005) A hierarchical, objectives-based framework for the digital investigations process. Digit Invest 2(2),147–167
6. Camara C, Peris-Lopez P, Tapiador JE (2015) Security and privacy issues in implantable medical devices: a comprehensive survey. J Biomed Inform 55, 272–289
7. Carrier B, Spafford EH (2004) An event-based digital forensic investigation framework. In: Digital forensic research workshop, pp 11–13
8. Casey E, Blitz A, Steuart C (2005) Digital evidence and computer crime
9. Chirgwin R (2020) Finns chilling as DDoS knocks out building control system. https://www.theregister.co.uk/2016/11/09/finns_chilling_as_ddos_knocks_out_building_control_system/. Accessed Jan 2020
10. Clack CD, Bakshi, VA Braine L (2016) Smart contract templates: essential requirements and design options. arXiv preprint arXiv:1612.04496
11. Clack CD, Bakshi VA, Braine L (2016) Smart contract templates: foundations, design landscape and research directions. arXiv preprint arXiv:1608.00771
12. Council of European Union. Council Regulation (EU) no 2016/679. http://eur-lex.europa.eu/legal-content/en/LSU/?uri=CELEX%3A32016R0679. Accessed July 2018
13. Divya M, Biradar NB (2018) IOTA-next generation block chain. Int J Eng Comput Sci 7(4), 23823–23826
14. El Ioini N, Pahl C (2018) A review of distributed ledger technologies. In: OTM confederated international conferences "On the Move to Meaningful Internet Systems". Springer, pp 277–288
15. Forensic Science Regulator (FSR). Codes of practice and conduct for forensic science providers and practitioners in the criminal justice system. Technical report, UK Govt, Birmingham, UK
16. Garrie DB (2014) Digital forensic evidence in the courtroom: understanding content and quality. Northwest J Technol Intellect Prop 12, 1–128
17. Griffor ER, Greer C, Wollman DA, Burns MJ (2017) Framework for cyber-physical systems: Volume 1, overview. Technical report, National Institute of Standards and Technology
18. Ibarra J (2019) Digital forensic investigation process model (DFIPM) to IoMT ensuring data privacy. Master's thesis, Northumbria University, Newcastle, UK
19. ISO17025:2017 (2017). General requirements for the competence of testing and calibrating laboratories. Technical report, International Organisation for Standardization (ISO), Geneva, CH
20. Jones KJ, Bejtlich R, Rose CW (2005) Real digital forensics: computer security and incident response. Addison-Wesley Professional
21. Karabiyik U, Akkaya K (2019) Digital forensics for IoT and WSNS. In: Mission-oriented sensor networks and systems: art and science. Springer, pp 171–207
22. Kent K, Chevalier S, Grance T, Dang H (2006). Guide to integrating forensic techniques into incident response. Technical report, National Institute of Standards and Technology
23. Kirk PL (1953) Crime investigation: Physical evidence and the police laboratory, New York
24. Lueth KL (2020) State of the IoT 2018: number of IoT devices now at 7b market accelerating. https://iot-analytics.com/state-of-the-iot-update-q1-q2-2018-number-of-iot-devices-now-7b/. Accessed: Jan 2020
25. Mitchell, I, Cockerton T, Hara S, Evans C. (2018) SMERF: social media, ethics and risk framework. Cyber Criminol
26. Mitchell I, Hara S, Jahankhani H, Neilson D (2019) Blockchain of custody, BoC. Cyber Secur Pract Guide

27. Montasari R (2016) The comprehensive digital forensic investigation process model. PhD thesis, University of Derby
28. Montasari R (2016) A comprehensive digital forensic investigation process model. Int J Electron Secur Digit Forensics 8(4):285–302
29. Montasari R, Peltola P (2015) Computer forensic analysis of private browsing modes. In: International conference on global security, safety, and sustainability. Springer, pp 96–109
30. Mouton F, Venter HS (2011) A prototype for achieving digital forensic readiness on wireless sensor networks. In: IEEE Africon'11. IEEE, pp 1–6
31. Nagasai A (2020) Classification of IoT devices. https://www.ciscoplatform.com/profiles/blogs/classification-of-iot-devices. Accessed Jan 2020
32. Oriwoh E, Sant P, Epiphaniou G (2013) Guidelines for Internet of Things deployment approaches—The thing commandments. Procedia Computer Science 21:122–131
33. Palmer GL (2002) A roadmap for digital forensics research report from the first digital forensics workshop (technical report dtr-t001-01-final). Air Force Research Lab, Rome Research Site, Utica, pp 1–48
34. Serguei Popov. The tangle. http://tanglereport.com/wp-content/uploads/2018/01/IOTA_Whitepaper.pdf. Accessed Jan 2020
35. Popov S, Moog H, Camargo D, Capossele A, Dimitrov V, Gal A, Greve A, Kusmierz B, Mueller S, Penzkofer A (2020) The coordicide, pp 1–30. Accessed Jan 2020
36. Uribe F (2018) The classification of Internet of Things (IoT) devices based on their impact on living things. SSRN: https://ssrn.com/abstract=3350094 or http://dx.doi.org/10.2139/ssrn.3350094. Accessed Jan 2020
37. U.S. Department of Justice (2009) Electronic crime scene investigation: an on-the scene reference for first responders. National Institute of Justice, November 2009
38. Vilandrie A (2020) Survey: Nearly half of U.S. firms using internet of things hit by security breaches. https://www.businesswire.com/news/home/20170601006165/en. Accessed Jan 2020
39. Watson D, Jones AJ (2013) Digital forensics processing and procedures: meeting the requirements of ISO 17020, ISO 17025, ISO 27001 and best practice requirements, 1st edn. Elsevier
40. Williams J (2018) Good practice guide for digital evidence, March 2012. http://library.college.police.uk/docs/acpo/digital-evidence-2012.pdf. Accessed March 2018
41. Yaga D, Mell P, Roby N, Scarfone K (2018) Blockchain technology overview. Technical report, National Institute of Standards and Technology

# Algorithms Can Predict Domestic Abuse, But Should We Let Them?

**Matthew Bland**

**Abstract** As domestic abuse has become a higher priority for law enforcement in England and Wales, so demand and the intensity of resource deployment has increased. With many police struggling to meet demand, some are exploring algorithms as a means to better predict the risk of serious harm and so better target their resources. In this chapter, I set out the case for algorithms playing a role in domestic abuse strategies, within the context of their wider growth in policing. I include examples of how targeting algorithms work now and explore a range of concerns and potential pitfalls. The central argument of this chapter is to promote the cause of regulation in algorithms in policing. This fledgling field has much promise but will not succeed without due regard to the many potential problems that accompany it.

**Keywords** Domestic abuse · Domestic violence · Algorithms · Police · Big data · Analytics · Random forest · Forecasting

## 1 Introduction

Policing domestic abuse has become one of the primary priorities of law enforcement around the world, particularly so in the last two decades. Domestic abuse commonly relates to crimes that occur between current or former intimate partners. In some places (such as England and Wales) it also denotes crimes between siblings or parents and adult children. There is consensus among researchers that much domestic abuse remains hidden [10, 14] and it is thought that the recent rises seen in England and Wales represent greater propensity to report and record accurately rather than an underlying social trend [17, 20]. Regardless of the cause, however, the fact remains that domestic abuse makes up a substantial portion of police demand [40] and requires a resource intensive response [7]. It is also a source of a high proportion of serious criminality, including homicide and sexual crimes [40]. It should be no surprise

M. Bland (✉)
Institute of Criminology, University Cambridge, Cambridge, UK
e-mail: mpb57@cam.ac.uk

 
H. Jahankhani et al. (eds.), *Policing in the Era of AI and Smart Societies*, Advanced Sciences and Technologies for Security Applications,
https://doi.org/10.1007/978-3-030-50613-1_6

therefore, that practitioners have developed an interest in assessing what advantages the burgeoning field of police artificial intelligence may bring.

Early forays into artificial intelligence-led policing tools have shown some promise, including some formative efforts aimed at forecasting future serious domestic crimes. In this chapter, I explore the seeming inevitability that artificial intelligence will be able to predict serious domestic cases before they happen (indeed this is already happening in some places) and test the potentially more important fundamental question—should such tools be allowed to predict these cases in the first place. As the adage goes, just because we can do things, it does not necessarily follow that we should.

This chapter begins by describing the relative growth of algorithms, the building block of artificial intelligence tools, in society in general and policing in particular. This overview repeats themes set out in many previous articles in this field ([2, 4, 42] for example) and my purpose is not to tread old ground but rather to place what follows in the proper context. This brief discussion is framed by consideration of the main ethical issues which run throughout this discourse. The chapter then delves more deeply into the issue of domestic abuse. Firstly, I examine whether there is actually a need for algorithms in this field (spoiler: I think there is a need). I then describe the nature and performance of some of the first models developed in this area and compare these to what is known about current practices. These promising first steps are not without problems, however. The chapter also considers a range of challenges that are currently in front of successful operationalisation.

In the final section of the chapter I try to look forward by discussing a range of key actions for researchers and practitioners alike to consider as they develop these types of technology in future. It seems inevitable that law enforcement agencies will pursue opportunities in this area and it is vitally important that these pursuits take some form of mature structure.

## *1.1 The Development of Algorithms in Society and Policing*

### 1.1.1 Algorithms in Society

The term 'artificial intelligence' conjures images of autonomous robots, often seen replacing or even overthrowing humankind. While these visions (thankfully) remain the object of science fiction stories and movies, artificial intelligence has become a mainstream part of 21st century society. In its broadest sense, the term refers to the undertaking of ordinarily human tasks by machines. Such tasks include decision making or visual recognition and have been enabled by the rapid growth in data availability and computer processing power. Under the hood, artificial intelligence is powered by algorithms. Algorithms are typically mathematical constructs designed to solve problems. In practice they form a series of instructions. Some algorithms are formulated using machine-learning, a branch of artificial intelligence in which a computer refines its own processes based on its findings [24]. In short, machine learning algorithms are behind what many of us identify as artificial intelligence.

This form of technology pervades many aspects of modern life. In many instances the public is well briefed on the influence algorithms have on their lives. Online activity is the most obvious place to start. Millions of people are familiar with the output of algorithms which govern the search results Google provides us, the 'friend suggestions' Facebook makes, the 'recommended for you' viewing offerings of Netflix or the tailored adverts provided on seemingly every website a person visits. Search for an image of the new Nike trainers on a search engine and the next site you visit will probably contain an advertisement for the same or similar trainers. That is an algorithm at work, taking inputs (your browsing history) and using a set of rules (analysis about what the inputs mean you will like) to convert them into outputs (an advert).

Many algorithms are less visible than this and have yet to permeate into wider public discourse. Evening news programmes often contain updates on stock market performance but rarely explain that algorithms conduct most of the daily trading and play a crucial role in that performance. Algorithms also decide whether we are successful in a loan application, how your call to a customer service centre will be prioritised and how much your insurance premium will change by this year. The role of algorithms in these examples is less well discussed than the general debate about the online world, but the influence is no less. These primarily mathematical procedures influence people's everyday lives in tangible and meaningful ways.

One of the primary public debates concerning algorithms in society focuses on the right to privacy. To generalise, individuals are often concerned that their data (which is to say the records of their online activity) is being used for something 'bad'. What constitutes 'bad' is debatable. It could mean something which disrupts the life of the individual to whom the data belongs or it could refer to data being used to alter the individual's behaviour. Agrawal et al. [1] argue that the desire for privacy is inextricably linked to a person's expectation about how the data will be used. Stories such as the Facebook/Cambridge Analytica scandal have done little to quell fears about impropriety of large organisations and it is these kinds of stories which fuel the primary concerns around privacy.

While privacy ranks highly in public discourse of algorithms, it is by no means the only concern. A brief synopsis of the other main issues is a useful primer for a longer discussion about algorithms in policing in general and domestic abuse responses specifically and so these are detailed as follows, in no particular order. Firstly, the fear of over-automation. At one extreme this manifests itself in science fiction-like concerns of machines turning against humankind. In a more pragmatic sense, this fear is a reflection of intelligent machines replacing humans and this fear is at least partly rooted in reality. Algorithms have been replacing humans in the workplace for decades because they can process more information, more quickly and at lower cost due to their ability to capitalise on improvements in computer processing power and data availability. Counter balancing this perspective is the notion that there is more work to be done than before, caused by (1) the same explosion of data that has enhanced the capability of algorithms, (2) technology's propensity to cause new problems that require solutions (see cyber crime as a perfect demonstration) and (3) additional process put in place to manage technology [60].

Another concern, one particularly relevant to the policing context, is the notion that algorithms may enable a 'surveillance state'. This idea is also widely covered in popular culture, embodied by George Orwell's 1984 and more recently by news coverage of the Edward Snowden/National Security Agency affair. The latter incident has been argued as evidence of state surveillance capability beyond the comprehension of previous generations [13] and while algorithms do not play a starring role in Snowden's story per se, they are associated by virtue of the centrality of data and automation. Algorithms are understood to be complex and that complexity brings paranoia. People do not necessarily understand how they work (nor could anyone reasonably hope to) and this leaves a void filled by paranoia and speculation.

Finally, we must note concerns about rights infringements related to algorithms. This debate is principally focussed on human rights and overlaps with discussions of privacy. More broadly however, there are numerous concerns about rights being infringed as a result of unfair, unjust or inaccurate decisions taken by algorithms [28]. These issues are ethically and legally complex with interpretations often needing to balance the rights of the individual with the rights of the community (see [42]). Concerns manifest themselves in ways such as the fear of biased outcomes. If an algorithm is constructed on biased data, say marginalising a certain demographic because this is the way data reflect historic practices, then it is 'baking in' this bias by reinforcing it in future practice. These sorts of problems take on different meanings when translated to a criminal justice environment. It is one thing to be charged a higher insurance premium because of your average postcode demographic and quite another to be sentenced to a longer jail term for the same reason.

### 1.1.2 Algorithms in Policing

Policing has not been exempted from the rise of the algorithm. 14% of UK police agencies have indicated some form of algorithm use [41] covering a range of topics. Four years later I contest that this figure is likely to be much higher. There is also a growing array of examples of algorithms being used in law enforcement from the United States. The rise of the policing algorithm is of course partly to do with availability (this kind of technology is simply more common and lower cost than in the past) but also driven by pressures to cope with increasing demand and shrinking resources [7, 42]. In England and Wales, police forces underwent substantial budget reductions between 2010 and 2018, with accompanying impacts on the numbers of police officer and staff. At the same time, recorded crime increased substantially (see [7]). For stretched organisations seeking to manage these circumstances, algorithms unquestionably offered promising opportunities and forces were openly encouraged to invest in them by the chief inspector of policing [21].

As my intention in this chapter is to consider the issue of algorithms in responding to domestic abuse, a brief exposition of other policing algorithms is an essential ingredient. In one sense, these algorithms establish a form of precedent (whether justifiable or not). In another they suggest a form of baseline with which we might meaningfully compare domestic abuse algorithms. Here is a selection of algorithms used by law enforcement agencies at present.

### 1.1.3 Automatic Number Plate Recognition

Not commonly recognised as an algorithm, but ANPR (as it is known) is in fact powered by an algorithm which 'reads' number plates and cross refers them against a database to trigger alarms (see [23]). ANPR cameras have become a critical policing tool in the last two decades and used in proactive and reactive settings. The technology is also widely used by petrol stations and highway enforcement.

### 1.1.4 Chicago Gun Crime

Faced with high gun crime levels, police in Chicago developed a predictive policing initiative to try to prevent crimes occurring. Part of the initiative involved the creation of a 'Strategic Subjects List' of individuals considered to be most at risk of committing gun violence. The algorithm deployed by Chicago made use of co-arrest network data to estimate relative risk of involvement in a gun-related homicide. Saunders et al. [47] found that there was in fact no difference in risk of victimisation for those identified by the algorithm but there was an increased risk of subsequent arrest. They hypothesised that this may be due to officers using the 'risk list' as an investigative aid for open gun crime cases, rather than a preventative aide as it was intended.

### 1.1.5 Criminal Reduction Using Statistical History (CRUSH)

CRUSH was first used by police in Memphis, Tennessee, USA where police partnered with local academics to model non-crime datasets closely correlated with peaks in crime [59]. Highlighted areas were targeted with concentrated patrols to prevent crimes before they occurred. Crime rates fell in the period Blue CRUSH (as it was known locally) operated but although the initiative was heralded as the cause by media and politicians, longer term statistical analyses cast some doubt on this [18, 55] and to date there has not been a published randomised trial of the initiative.

### 1.1.6 Evidence Based Investigation Tool (EBIT)

Following changes to crime recording practices in 2014 [29] English and Welsh police forces faced large increases in less serious violent cases. In response to this Kent Police developed EBIT, a system for predicting the likelihood of a case being detected. EBIT employed statistical modelling of a small number of solvability factors (such as whether there was an identified suspect or whether there was forensic evidence available) to recommend to officers whether a case should be closed early or sent to an investigator for further work. Kent Police reported substantial increases in investigator capacity but were criticised for focussing on 'easy' cases [22]. The system has since been developed in six further UK police agencies.

### 1.1.7 Facial Recognition

Much controversy has surrounded the trialling of facial recognition in the UK [17]. The tool is potentially very powerful as a surveillance capability for law enforcement agencies seeking to identify dangerous individuals in crowded places. Concerns arise from the potential for the system to be inaccurate, in effect targeting innocent individuals simply because the algorithm is not good enough.

### 1.1.8 Harm Assessment Risk Tool (HART)

In the last decade, the Probation and Parole department in Philadelphia, USA worked with academics to develop a forecasting algorithm to assist in determining what level of response it should give to offenders (see [2]). The algorithm utilised a machine learning procedure known as *random forest* to classify offenders based on calculations of their risk of committing future crimes. Those identified as at risk of committing serious crimes were given more intensive treatments. The procedure was later replicated in Durham Constabulary in the UK with a different purpose in mind. In Durham, HART, which was also constructed using *random forest* was deployed in custody suites where sergeants used it to identify offenders who would be suitable for out of court treatment [42, 58].

### 1.1.9 PredPol

One of the more notorious forms of policing algorithm, *PredPol* is a private entity which deploys an algorithm based on seismology [32] to predict when and where crime will occur within 500 × 500 m ranges. It has been used by police in the USA and the UK with some fanfare but has been criticised for susceptibility to feedback loops [12] and an inability to demonstrate tangible reductions in crime [34]. In some senses the brand *PredPol* has become synonymous with the topic of predictive policing which is in fact much broader [35].

While this short list of algorithms in policing is by no means comprehensive, the descriptions serve to illustrate the general nature of their current use. They also hint at a number of dilemmas that police agencies face, each of which has relevance to any potential deployment of algorithms to deal with domestic abuse. Before I move onto that topic specifically, we should examine these dilemmas in more detail because therein lie the major obstacles for any potential domestic abuse algorithm to overcome.

The popular notion of 'pre-crime' [59], derives from the Philip K. Dick short story, *Minority Report* (later a Steven Spielberg film). The central plot point revolves around a police unit that arrests homicide offenders before the crime is committed. Partly because it is an interesting yet easy to grasp notion and partly because it has been cemented in popular culture, the 'minority report' angle is often cited in discourse of predictive algorithms in policing (see [15, 43, 44, 50, 52]). Fun references aside though, a real dilemma lays at the heart of this parallel: is it ethical to take action against someone for something they have not yet done. Naturally, the answer to this question is at least partly dependent on what the action is and how certain we are that they will do the thing which prompts the action. Indeed, we can never be 100% certain about the future, so is any action justifiable? The counterpoint here is that police already do this. It is the basis of intelligence led policing [44] and proactive evidence based policing strategies [49]. It is not a sustainable position for a police agency to take no proactive actions and any proactivity is predicated on what is judged likely to occur in the future. Accordingly, the dilemma here is not whether it is right to predict the future and take action, but how accurate those predictions are and how proportionate are the subsequent actions to the predicted offence.

If the consensus is that prediction must occur, then it is logical to deduce that some form of data is involved in arriving at the prediction. For algorithms, data are an essential ingredient but not without dilemmas. The devil is of course, in the detail. It matters what data are being used and there are different concerns in play. Is it ethical to use someone's vehicle movements to profile their risk of committing a serious crime? Should the generic socio-classification of someone's address by a marketing company affect the level of crime prevention assistance available to them? These are very real questions faced by agencies operating algorithms today (see [28]) for concerns around Durham Constabulary's use of socio-demographics). Within these issues lies the spectre of perceived bias [9] and the ethical principles of the European Convention for Human Rights, namely necessity, proportionality and foreseeability (see [42]). This is a tricky field to navigate but these dilemmas provide the beginnings of a framework upon which we may construct a useful test for the suitability of algorithms. We will return to this issue later in the chapter with specific reference to the *ALGO-CARE* framework set out by Oswald et al. [42].

## 1.2 Domestic Abuse Context

The primary question for any law enforcement agency considering the use of an algorithm is "why wo we need it?". As obvious as this might seem, algorithms suffer from the same condition as all new technologies in that newness sometimes outshines utility. It is somewhat easy however, to make a case for their potential utility in responding to domestic abuse. As I have already covered, police agencies in England and Wales have been under some pressure to improve their practices since the police inspectorate published a deeply critical report of the services response to domestic abuse [19]. Together with a countrywide initiative to improve crime recording standards, reported levels of domestic abuse have increased substantially—in the year to March 2019 they had risen by 24% [40] following a rise of 23% in 2018 [39]. The 'demand-shock' effect of rises in domestic abuse cases has been exacerbated by high minimum standards of response. Most police agencies in England and Wales operate with something approximating these approaches: (1) a mandatory attendance at all domestic calls, (2) a mandatory risk assessment completed by the officers attending the scene and later by a specialist domestic abuse officer, (3) multi agency risk assessment conferences—meetings of police and partner agencies—for the highest risk cases. In many jurisdictions these occur daily and (4) an advisory policy of arrest where there is the police power to do so (see [7] for a full description of the police response).

Of course, it is logical to argue that domestic abuse cases merit this kind of response. After all, domestic abuse cases make up 20% of all homicides of people over 16 in England and Wales. 40% of rape of females aged over 16 [40] and 35% of all violent related offences. Abuse is widely acknowledged as a largely hidden crime with much concern over the impact of coercive and controlling behaviour and police ability to recognise it [33, 51]. However, these statistics belie a simple fact—most domestic abuse crimes are not 'serious'.[1] Harm has been repeatedly shown to be highly concentrated among a small proportion (less than 5%) of offenders, victims and dyads (see [3, 6, 7, 26]). The current response to domestic abuse is characterised by the representativeness heuristic [25]. Which is to say that the strategy is not founded on base rates. Consider two of proportions I mentioned a moment ago: (1) 20% of homicides of people over 16, and (2) 40% of rapes of females over the age of 16 (I am excluding violence against the person because it is such a broad category). These are striking numbers and paint a picture of high harm. Consider these in pure number terms and they are arguably even worse. In 2019, these proportions constituted 366 homicides and 15,847 rapes. Now however, consider the total number of domestic abuse cases in the same year—1.3 million. Homicide and rape of females make up 1.2% of all domestic abuse [40]. While this is just one definition of serious crime, and we could easily make the case for other forms of crime to be included, this percentage is likely to stay below 5% in most analyses.

Consider then what police officers are being asked to do when they visit the scene of a domestic abuse incident in which they may have no or limited prior knowledge of the parties involved. They sit down with the subject and ask a series of questions from a standard template. These questions probably include things like: "is the abuse getting worse?" and "has the suspect ever attempted to strangle/choke/suffocate/drown you?". The risk assessment templates are normally derived from the Victim Domestic Abuse Stalking and Harassment and Honour Based Abuse (DASH) risk template [45] or an updated version of it focussing on coercive and controlling behaviour [46]. In either version the emphasis is placed

[1] In this chapter I use a loose definition of serious to reflect homicide, serious assault, serious sexual offences and coercive and controlling behaviour. This definition is not a statutory one or formed with any kind of harm index. More detail on severity is included in [7].

on structured professional judgement [27] and the procedure boils down to this: the more questions answered 'yes' the higher the risk. Most police agencies operate with a specific threshold (e.g. 14 yes answers equals high risk). Cases are classified as 'standard', 'moderate' or 'high' risk 'High' risk cases are normally eligible for multi-agency risk assessment conferences (MARACs) whereby partner agencies take a case management approach to reducing the risk by addressing issues such as housing needs.

While this infrastructure may sound thorough and well-established there is a growing body of evidence which suggests it is in fact ineffective. Robinson et al. [46] reviewed the procedures around DASH for the College of Policing and found that it was applied inconsistently and with a greater emphasis on physical violence than was appropriate. Furthermore, several quantitative studies have challenged the predictive validity of the process. The central criticism of these studies is consistent—a high 'false negative' rate (see [11, 16, 54, 56]). Stated plainly—the DASH has a low success rate when it comes to identifying serious or repeat domestic abuse. Given that this appears to be its primary function and given the level of resource intensity maintaining this procedure requires this is an unsustainable position and one ideal for exploring the question of whether an algorithm might improve things.

This exploration has already begun as part of the wider growth of algorithm development in policing. I personally know of ongoing development of risk prediction algorithms for domestic abuse in at least four British police agencies, all of which centre on the use of the machine learning forecasting technique known as *random forest*. Random forest is an algorithm which can be tailored to balance the rates of prediction error as the designer desires. This is highly desirable in this type of forecasting where one might wish to minimise one type of error at the expense of another. For example—imagine you are a police officer using an algorithm to forecast whether the domestic abuse suspect you are dealing with is likely to commit a serious domestic offence in the next year. The algorithm can predict 'yes' or 'no'. If it predicts 'yes' and the officer follows a course of action but the prediction was in fact wrong, then the error has resulted in wasted effort. If the algorithm predicts 'no' and the officer takes no action, but the algorithm was wrong, then the error has resulted in harm taking place. While neither outcome is desirable, most of us would agree that harm is a worse outcome than waste to some degree. The *random forest* algorithm allows the designer to trade errors off against each other. The algorithm can be calibrated to reduce harmful errors at the expense of increasing wasteful errors.

Let us briefly consider two published studies that have covered these developments to date. Berk, Sorenson and Barnes [5, 4] analysed a *random forest* algorithm for domestic abuse arraignment cases. They identified three possible forecasting outcomes (1) no arrests for domestic violence, (2) an arrest but not for an offence involving physical injury and (3) an arrest with physical injury. Their baseline was that 80% of those actually released at arraignment were not subsequently arrested. Their model correctly predicted no arrest 90% of the time, leading to the general conclusion that, if magistrates used the model, they could improve the failure rate of decisions by around half. It predicted the other two outcomes less efficiently, over-compensating its forecasts to avoid harmful errors. Accordingly, while three quarters of all domestic violence with injury was correctly forecast, only 21% of the overall forecasts were correct.

The other study was my own exploration of custody data. I was motivated by a desire to address what I had found in previous studies—that a high proportion of the most serious cases had no prior record for domestic abuse [6, 7]. This meant that no risk assessment procedure based on known abuse could identify such cases. However, a wider screening tool might. I applied a *random forest* algorithm to a set of records of arrest for any offence [7]. As with Berk, Sorenson and Barnes I weighted the algorithm to favour wasteful errors over harmful errors and designed the algorithm to forecast, for each arrestee, regardless of the offence they were arrested for, if they would commit no abuse, less serious abuse or more serious abuse in the future. The algorithm could identify 77% of serious abuse but at a wasteful error rate of 90% (nine in every ten forecasts of serious abuse was incorrect). When predicting no abuse, the algorithm was correct 99.9% of the time.

These two studies show promising signs that the notion of actuarial procedures can out-perform clinical procedures in forecasting the future [30] albeit with costs—some effort would be misplaced in the quest to prevent serious abuse. The practical perspective is that some individuals may receive interventions they do not need. These findings are compounded by the recent works of Turner et al. [56] and Grogger et al. [16] which both ran direct comparisons between DASH and alternative actuarial methods to test effectiveness. Both conclusively found that actuarial methods were superior. The weight of the early evidence it seems, is universally in favour of these procedures showing more promise than the status quo.

However, many immediate challenges must be overcome before algorithm use can become mainstream in domestic abuse responses. While the early studies show promise, there is a danger that widespread implementation would suffer from the same 'doomed to success' mindset as many other policing initiatives. It is therefore worthwhile exploring some of these challenges in brief before I move on to discuss the next steps researchers and practitioners may take.

### 1.2.1 Regulation and Technology

Regulation in the AI/algorithm field is a hot topic, unsurprisingly given the range of concerns we have already discussed. However, establishing regulatory infrastructure in such a specialised area at a time when technology rapidly advancing is a critical challenge [37]. Should police agencies be able to develop these solutions in the absence of such regulation?

### 1.2.2 Trade offs

I have illustrated the potential to calibrate algorithms to minimise certain kinds of error. This is an advantage for certain, but the other side of the coin is deciding where the calibration lies. Is the balance purely a measure of local policy or should there be a national standard? Can more resource-rich agencies afford to be more wasteful, thus penalising communities living in force jurisdictions where resources are less plentiful? Conversely, what is an acceptable level of misapplied interventions?

#### 1.2.3 ICT Infrastructure

Along the same lines, some police agencies have more advanced ICT capabilities than others in terms of data assimilation. At the same time, as data sources grow and agencies become more reliant on these systems, future investments in ICT infrastructure are likely to take on even greater importance.

#### 1.2.4 Justification

The type of algorithm I described from my own work [7] is proactive—it scans a wider population (arrestees) for forecasts about an issue they may not have presented with. While this is necessary to develop a comprehensive domestic abuse strategy, it does not follow necessarily that it is justifiable [31]. Careful planning is required to ensure that such procedures are proportionate. Correlation is not causation (see [48]) and these tools work solely on a correlative basis.

#### 1.2.5 Data Fetishisation

Though an algorithm's results may improve upon the collated results of hundreds of individual officers it does not necessarily follow that the individual's forecast is irrelevant. Algorithms only know what they are told, whereas humans can assimilate wider, unstructured information. It would be easy for agencies seeking efficiency to prioritise the role of a successful algorithm, thus 'fetishising' the role of data but this would be a singular mistake. Algorithms in policing can only be advisory at best if a force is to retain a sense of legitimacy.

### *1.3 Key Issues for Researchers and Practitioners*

So far in this chapter we have considered the rising tide of algorithms in society and policing. We have also seen that domestic abuse policing in England and Wales is one area which may benefit from more accurate predictions and that there is emerging evidence that algorithms could improve on the current situation. Yet at the same time many of the concerns about algorithms in society in general present challenges that are yet to be overcome. What then, should researchers and practitioners do next? This final section outlines four broad principles for the future development of algorithms in policing—all of which touch upon various components of Oswald et al.'s [42] checklist ALGO-CARE. ALGO-CARE (which is a mnemonic for advisory, lawful, granularity, ownership, challengeable, accuracy, responsible, explainable) provides the best published framework for algorithm development to date. My intention in this chapter is not to develop an alternative but a complementary discussion. My hope is that the following principles enable to decision making proposed by ALGO-CARE, rather than contradict it.

### 1.3.1 Expertise

Algorithms are complex by design and complex in implementation. Their deployment 'out-of-the-box' is unlikely. "Every algorithm needs an analyst" as my mentor Professor Lawrence W. Sherman is oft heard to say (personal communication). In fact, I think every algorithm needs a team which includes an analyst alongside a network engineer, an applications developer, a communications specialist and several members of the teams that will use it. All of these roles exist in policing today, but it is unlikely that expertise in handling and developing algorithms is a prevalent skillset. Indeed, as skillsets go, it is ill-defined. Yet the police service is accustomed to dealing with specialisms (see forensic science, surveillance, firearms, advanced driving and hostage negotiation for example) so it is not hard to envision how algorithmic expertise might be developed.

The role of experts should not be underplayed in the development of algorithms. Such are the inherent dangers of misuse that the reputational risks for policing are very high, let alone immediate danger for the public. The European General Data Protection Regulation includes stipulations on the use of algorithms, specifying the role that humans must play [37]. It is vital that the humans involved are sufficiently skilled and knowledgeable in the handling of the subject matter. This knowledge must go beyond the purely technical aspects of maths and computer science and into the areas of accuracy, bias and ethics.

### 1.3.2 Transparency

Many of the concerns we have discussed in this chapter are rooted in the theme of transparency. Transparency does not come naturally to algorithms, particularly those of a *black-box* nature which cannot be easily decoded. The legal standing of algorithms aside, their contribution to or erosion of police legitimacy, a central plank of the policing model in most democratic nations [53, 57] is critical to their success. How to make algorithms transparent however, is a multi-faceted issue. Transparency is restricted by complexity—a *random forest* algorithm can be explained, but it may not be understood—on a practical level they can have hundreds of thousands of lines of code [2, 42]. Communicating each element of the inner workings is far from straightforward particularly compared to an individual explaining what they think their own decision making process was based on.

The ALGO-CARE framework for decision making [42] sets out a useful starting point for transparency. It poses pertinent questions the lawfulness, bias and workings of an algorithm. While each agency may apply a spectrum of detail to answering these questions, if all algorithms had to be accompanied by an ALGO-CARE briefing, the advancement of algorithms in policing would at least be on an equal footing. Commentators and inspectors could compare processes across agencies and even the agencies themselves may be able to learn openly.

### 1.3.3 Accountability

Olhede and Wolfe [36] posed the topical question of who is liable if an algorithm goes wrong. Their answer was complex, dependant on data, decision making, safety testing and fairness factors. They even cite the case of the HART in Durham Police that we discussed earlier in this chapter, underscoring the potential miscarriage of justice that algorithms can do. The simple counterpoint is that such miscarriages almost certainly happen already. Is it enough to simply state that algorithms are satisfactory because they make fewer and more auditable mistakes than humans? At a high level, I would argue that this is correct but the notion does not survive contact with detailed application. Algorithms in policing, and especially in domestic abuse, should be advisory only. Therefore, a human should always be in charge of the final decision. The algorithm is merely 'intelligence' for them to factor into that decision. The weighting of that 'intelligence' is not prescribed though and this is a key point of accountability for agencies to consider—is central guidance necessary or is individual discretion more important? And if the algorithm is owned by a private third party, is that entity accountable for any inaccuracy [8].

Ultimately, while this issue is fundamentally linked to the matter of regulation, it is not impossible to foresee how agencies could introduce their own accountability frameworks in the form of the safety tests that Olhede and Wolfe discuss and to which Oswald et al. [42] allude in their discussion of experimental proportionality. There are many forms that these elements may take, of which the ALGO-CARE framework provides a strong starting point but which would still benefit from more detailed specifications to be prescribed to police agencies.

### 1.3.4 Evaluation

In the absence of a prescribed safety test doctrine, the role of evaluation becomes vital. Although evaluation should not be instigated at the expense of pre-implementation checks, it is of no less importance. In the example of a potential domestic abuse algorithm, pre-implementation testing should include non-training data testing (whereby the designer tests the algorithm on data not used in the construction of the algorithm) and shadowing (in which the algorithm is implemented in parallel with existing practices). However, once implemented, evaluation should move beyond pure assessments of algorithm accuracy.

The bottom line of any algorithm project is the extent to which there is a net benefit to the population. If a domestic abuse algorithm is designed to prevent serious crimes occurring, then an overarching factor is of course whether crimes are prevented at an acceptable level of cost, both economic and individual. There are, however, equally important proxy effects that must be considered, not least those on human behaviour. These might include de-skilling—are police officers becoming over-reliant on the algorithm to the detriment of their own ability to perceive risk. Alternatively, the algorithm may prompt a move toward greater risk aversion through another form of over-reliance. The only way to evaluate these impacts is by thoroughly planned methodologies designed before the onset of implementation. They require mature, multi-disciplinary research skills that stretch beyond the domain of purely data science.

## 2 Conclusions

Algorithms are already operating in law enforcement and show promise in improving the capability of police forces to predict future serious domestic abuse before it occurs. At face value this is an exciting development, particularly given the current context. However, there is the potential to cause waste, de-skill professionals and focus interventions inappropriately. While all of these issues are arguably present in the status quo, there is little to be gained from swapping one set of ills for another. Instead, there is a need to construct a meaningful framework of regulation and control, which enforces the principles set out in Oswald et al. [42] and establishes a set of minimum standards for the development and inclusion of specialist capabilities, transparency, accountability and evaluation. The need for this framework will become more pressing as police agencies further adopt algorithm led solutions on their own terms. The inherent danger in this position is that a small number of 'failures' could cause irreparable harm to this promising area of crime prevention science.

## References


1. Agrawal A, Gans J, Goldfarb A (2018) Prediction machines: the simple economics of artificial intelligence. Harvard Business Press
2. Barnes G, Hyatt JM (2012) Classifying adult probationers by forecasting future offending
3. Barnham L, Barnes GC, Sherman LW (2017) Targeting escalation of intimate partner violence: evidence from 52,000 offenders. Camb J Evid Based Polic, 1–27
4. Berk R (2012) Criminal justice forecasts of risk: a machine learning approach. Springer Science & Business Media
5. Berk RA, Sorenson SB, Barnes G (2016) Forecasting domestic violence: a machine learning approach to help inform arraignment decisions. J Empir Leg Stud 13(1):94–115
6. Bland M, Ariel B (2015) Targeting escalation in reported domestic abuse: Evidence from 36,000 callouts. Int Crim Justice Rev 25(1):30–53. https://doi.org/10.1177/1057567715574382

7. Bland MP (2020). Targeting domestic abuse by mining police records. Doctoral dissertation, University of Cambridge
8. Brauneis R, Goodman EP (2018) Algorithmic transparency for the smart city. Yale JL & Tech, 20, p 103
9. Carlo S (2017) Artificial intelligence, big data and the rule of law, event report. The Bingham centre for the rule of law, 9 October 2017 https://www.biicl.org/event/1280
10. Carrell SE, Hoekstra M (2012) Family business or social problem? The cost of unreported domestic violence. J Policy Anal Manag 31(4):861–875
11. Chalkley R, Strang H (2017) Predicting domestic homicides and serious violence in Dorset: A replication of Thornton's Thames Valley analysis. Camb J Evid Based Polic 1(2–3):81–92
12. Ensign D, Friedler SA, Neville S, Scheidegger C, Venkatasubramanian S (2017) Runaway feedback loops in predictive policing. arXiv:1706.09847
13. Giroux HA (2015) Totalitarian paranoia in the post-Orwellian surveillance state. Cult Stud 29(2):108–140
14. Gracia E (2004) Unreported cases of domestic violence against women: towards an epidemiology of social silence, tolerance, and inhibition. J Epidemiol Commun Health 58(7): 536–537
15. Greengard S (2012) Policing the future. Commun ACM 55(3):19–21
16. Grogger J, Ivandic R, Kirchmaier T (2020) Comparing conventional and machine-learning approaches to risk assessment in domestic abuse cases (CEP Discussion Paper No 1676 February 2020)
17. Hern A (2020) What is facial recognition-and how to police use it? The Guardian. https://www.theguardian.com/technology/2020/jan/24/what-is-facial-recognition-and-how-do-police-use-it. Accessed on 6 March 2020
18. Hickman L (2013) How algorithms rule the world. The Guardian. Accessed on 5 March 2020
19. Her Majesty's Inspectorate of the Constabulary, Fire and Rescue Services (2014a) Everyone's business: Improving the police response to domestic violence. https://www.justiceinspectorates.gov.uk/hmicfrs/wp-content/uploads/2014/04/improving-the-police-response-to-domestic-abuse.pdf. Accessed 15 Oct 2016
20. Her Majesty's Inspectorate of the Constabulary, Fire and Rescue Services (2014b) Crime recording: making the victim count. https://www.justiceinspectorates.gov.uk/hmicfrs/wp-content/uploads/crime-recording-making-the-victim-count.pdf. Accessed 15 Oct 2016
21. Her Majesty's Inspectorate of Constabulary, Fire and Rescue Services (2018) The state of policing: The annual assessment of policing in England and Wales. https://www.justiceinspectorates.gov.uk/hmicfrs/wp-content/uploads/state-of-policing-2017-2.pdf. Accessed 5 March 2020
22. Howgego J (2019) A UK police force is dropping tricky cases on advice of an algorithm. the New Scientist. https://www.newscientist.com/article/2189986-a-uk-police-force-is-dropping-tricky-cases-on-advice-of-an-algorithm/Accessed 6 March 2020
23. Joh EE (2017) Artificial intelligence and policing: First questions. Seattle UL Rev 41:1139
24. Jordan MI, Mitchell TM (2015) Machine learning: Trends, perspectives, and prospects. Science 349(6245):255–260
25. Kahneman D (2011) Thinking, fast and slow. Macmillan
26. Kerr J, Whyte C, Strang H (2017) Targeting escalation and harm in intimate partner violence: evidence from northern territory police, Australia. Camb J Evid Based Polic 1–17
27. Kropp PR (2004) Some questions regarding spousal assault risk assessment. Violence against Women 10(6):676–697
28. Liberty (2019) Liberty report exposes police forces' use of discriminatory data to predict crime. https://www.libertyhumanrights.org.uk/news/press-releases-and-statements/liberty-report-exposes-police-forces'-use-discriminatory-data-0. Accessed 4 March 2019
29. McFadzien K, Phillips JM (2019) Perils of the subjective approach: A critical analysis of the UK national crime recording standards. Polic J Policy Pract
30. Meehl P (1954) Clinical versus statistical prediction: A theoretical analysis and a review of the evidence. University of Minnesota Press, Minneapolis

31. Mittelstadt BD, Allo P, Taddeo M, Wachter S, Floridi L (2016) The ethics of algorithms: Mapping the debate. Big Data Soc 3(2):2053951716679679
32. Mohler GO, Short MB, Brantingham PJ, Schoenberg FP, Tita GE (2011) Self-exciting point process modeling of crime. J Am Stat Assoc 106(493):100–108
33. Myhill A (2015) Measuring coercive control: What can we learn from national population surveys? Violence against Women 21(3):355–375
34. Nillson P (2018) First UK police force to try predictive policing ends contract. Financial Times. https://www.ft.com/content/b34b0b08-ef19-11e8-89c8-d36339d835c0. Accessed 6 March 2020
35. Nix J (2015) Predictive policing. Critical issues in policing: Contemporary readings, p 275
36. Olhede S, Wolfe P (2017) When algorithms go wrong, who is liable? Significance 14(6):8–9
37. Olhede SC, Wolfe PJ (2018) The growing ubiquity of algorithms in society: implications, impacts and innovations. Philos Trans R Soc A Math Phy Eng Sci 376(2128):20170364
38. Office for National Statistics (ONS) (2017) Domestic abuse in England and Wales: year ending March 2017. Statistical Bulletin. London, UK: Office of National Statistics. https://www.ons.gov.uk/peoplepopulationandcommunity/crimeandjustice/bulletins/domesticabuseinenglandandwales/yearendingmarch2017. Accessed 17 March 2018
39. Office for National Statistics (ONS) (2018) Domestic abuse in England and Wales: year ending March 2018. Statistical Bulletin. London, UK: Office of National Statistics. https://www.ons.gov.uk/peoplepopulationandcommunity/crimeandjustice/bulletins/domesticabuseinenglandandwales/yearendingmarch2018. Accessed 2 March 2019
40. Office for National Statistics (ONS) (2019) Domestic abuse in England and Wales: year ending March 2018. Statistical Bulletin. London, UK: Office of National Statistics. https://www.ons.gov.uk/peoplepopulationandcommunity/crimeandjustice/bulletins/domesticabuseinenglandandwales/yearendingmarch2019 Accessed 6 March 2020
41. Oswald M, Grace J (2016) Intelligence, policing and the use of algorithmic analysis: a freedom of information-based study. J Inf Rights Policy Pract 1(1)
42. Oswald M, Grace J, Urwin S, Barnes GC (2018) Algorithmic risk assessment policing models: lessons from the Durham HART model and 'experimental' proportionality. Inf Commun Technol Law 27(2):223–250
43. Phua C, Alahakoon D, Lee V (2004) Minority report in fraud detection: classification of skewed data. ACM SIGKDD Explorations Newsl 6(1):50–59
44. Ratcliffe J (2015) What is the future… of predictive policing. Practice 6(2):151–166
45. Richards L, Letchford S, Stratton S (2008) Policing Domestic Violence. Oxford University Press, Oxford. Blackstone's Practical Policing
46. Robinson AL, Myhill A, Wire J, Roberts J, Tilley N (2016) Risk-led policing of domestic abuse and the DASH risk model. What works: crime Reduction Research. Cardiff & London: Cardiff University, College of Policing and UCL Department of Security and Crime Science
47. Saunders J, Hunt P, Hollywood JS (2016) Predictions put into practice: a quasi-experimental evaluation of Chicago's predictive policing pilot. J Exp Criminol 12(3):347–371
48. Shmueli G, Ray S, Estrada JMV, Chatla SB (2016) The elephant in the room: Predictive performance of PLS models. J Bus Res 69(10):4552–4564
49. Sherman LW (2013) The rise of evidence-based policing: Targeting, testing, and tracking. Crime Justice 42(1):377–451
50. Simmons R (2017) Big Data and Procedural Justice: Legitimizing Algorithms in the Criminal Justice System. Ohio St J Crim L 15:573
51. Stark E (2007) Coercive control: How men entrap women in everyday life. Oxford University Press, New York, NY
52. Stroud M (2014) The minority report: Chicago's new police computer predicts crimes, but is it racist. The Verge, 19
53. Tankebe J (2013) Viewing things differently: The dimensions of public perceptions of police legitimacy. Criminology 51(1):103–135
54. Thornton S (2017) Police Attempts to predict domestic murder and serious assaults: is early warning possible yet? Camb J Evid Based Polic 1–17

55. Tulumello S (2016) The long way to a safer Memphis: Local policies for crime prevention need structural change. Benjamin L. Hooks Institute for Social Change Policy Papers, pp 12–22
56. Turner E, Medina J, Brown G (2019) Dashing hopes? The predictive accuracy of domestic abuse risk assessment by the police, Brit J Criminol, azy074
57. Tyler TR (2004) Enhancing police legitimacy. Annal Am Acad Polit Soc Science 593(1):84–99
58. Urwin S (2016) Algorithmic forecasting of offender dangerousness for police custody officers: an assessment of accuracy for the Durham constabulary model: Master Thesis. University of Cambridge. Wolfson College
59. Vlahos J (2012) The department of pre-crime. Sci Am 306(1): 62–67
60. Willocks L (2019) Are we facing AI Armageddon? What's wrong with the automation and future of work debate. Forbes. https://www.forbes.com/sites/londonschoolofeconomics/2019/08/08/are-we-facing-ai-armageddon-whats-wrong-with-the-automation-and-future-of-work-debate/#461f909a314b. Accessed 6 March 2020

# Tackling Teen Sexting—Policing Challenges When Society and Technology Outpace Legislation

**Emma Bond and Andy Phippen**

**Abstract** Concerns over cyberattacks, identify theft, ransomware and online fraud dominate the language of cybercrime and attract considerable public and political attention. Yet within the discourses of online risk, fears surrounding children and young people online remain at the forefront of media and policy debate. In modern society children have become the object of social concern and increasing anxiety about risk, superimposed on protective discourses, located as vulnerable innocents and sexting has attracted considerable attention as a moral panic. Drawing on data from police forces across the UK, this chapter outlines the ad hoc nature of police responses to the complex challenges of the production and sharing of intimate images by young people and it both raises concerns about the inconsistent application of legislation resulting in the criminalisation of minors who may be victims of abuse, and questions effective use of Outcome 21 as an alternative to arrest for young people in the UK since its introduction in 2016.

**Keywords** Sexting · Children · Young people · Children's rights · Outcome 21 · Legislation

## 1 Introduction

As the outline for this volume suggests it had long been recognised that criminal activity draws together perpetrators of crime. More recently the affordances (see [23]) and interoperability of modern communication technologies, social media, artificial intelligence (AI) and the internet of things (IoT) as facilitating a complex myriad of new ways of communicating, sharing and collaborating for criminals are increasingly acknowledged as transforming the landscapes of crime on a global scale

E. Bond (✉)
University of Suffolk, Ipswich, UK
e-mail: e.bond@uos.ac.uk

A. Phippen
Bournemouth University, Poole, UK
e-mail: aphippen1@bournemouth.ac.uk



H. Jahankhani et al. (eds.), *Policing in the Era of AI and Smart Societies*, Advanced Sciences and Technologies for Security Applications,
https://doi.org/10.1007/978-3-030-50613-1_7

and giving rise to complex new challenges for law enforcement and everyday policing responses.

Many of the challenges for policing in the 21st century are documented and examined in this edition. In an increasingly difficult political and economic environment with fewer resources, completing priorities and changing public perceptions of modern policing, the shift towards evidence-based policing (College of Policing, online) in establishing 'what works' in crime prevention, predictive policing and effectively reducing the prevalence of crime and ameliorating harm. This shift reflects the transformation of risk in late modernity from the traditional risks and hazards to those manufactured as a consequence of modernity itself and that we are living in a risk society [4, 15, 16]. Discourses on risk extend to virtual spaces and online places [8] and these arguments are also highly pertinent to understanding the social construction of risk in relation to policing an increasingly technological engaged society in the knowledge economy.

Concerns over cyberattacks, identify theft, ransomware and online fraud dominate the language of cybercrime and attract considerable public and political attention. Within the discourses of online risk, fears surrounding children and young people online emerged during the last decades of the twentieth century and remain at the forefront of media and policy debate. Central to legal, public and political exchanges in relation to young people's participation in online environments are dominant ideologies of childhood which underpin protectionist discourses. Heins [21] argued that, in relation to the Internet 'the protectionist approach, with its assumption of harm to minors from exposure to explicit sexual information and ideas, is not only intellectually and politically flawed, it is ultimately counterproductive'.

In modern society children have become the object of social concern and increasing anxiety about risk, superimposed on protective discourses, located as vulnerable innocents to be shielded from the dangers of the wider social world [49] which now includes the dangers of the online world [8]. Online harms such as cyberbullying, online grooming, access to violent and sexual content and commercial exploitation have been the focus of academic research and of political and media campaigns to limit children's time online and access to the internet. Recent policy initiatives for example the recent Online Harms white paper [43] arguably reflect such developments. *Sexting* has been the focus of increasing concern amongst parents, teachers, policy makers, law enforcement and organisations working with children and young people [38, 65] suggests that 'no other cybercrime issue has elicited the degree of anxiety as that over the circulation of sexual images of minors on the Internet'.

In 2017 the National Police Chiefs' Council (NPCC) published data on the nature of sexting by children (under 18), as recorded by police forces in England and Wales, under the headline 'Police dealing with rising number [of] 'sexting' cases involving children'. However, a gross disconnection between the law and uses of technology by consenting teenagers has generated problems both for policy, education, legal systems [2] and, as we outline in this chapter, law enforcement and everyday policing in the UK. Furthermore, just as risk is socially and culturally constructed [4, 15, 16] responses to sexting need to also recognise the seriousness of incidents of bullying, harassment, or abuse [2] including coercion and control but also the meaning that sexting has for young people's self-identify and everyday experiences [8, 44].

Young people are using mobile technologies as a virtual space to initiate and maintain romantic, intimate relationships, gossip and exchange pornographic material similar to the physical space of the "bike shed" a few generations ago [5]. Sexual images, both downloaded or assessed online and user-generated are common currency in young people's communication practices as a form of gifting (see [37]) yet whilst many are produced and shared with another consensually often they distributed further without consent or produced under coercion leading to abuse and harm [5, 8, 42, 47]. As such 'incidents of youth sexting can range from consensual interaction between dating partners to coercion, harassment, and abuse' [50] and there is a considerable diversity of sexting behaviours, motivating factors and consequentially myriads of risk, harm and resilience which contribute to young people's self-identify, everyday relationships and experiences [5–8]. However, under UK law sexting practices, the production and distribution of an indecent image of a minor remains illegal as a result of section 1 of the Protection of Children Act introduced in 1978. It is well established that current legal frameworks are insufficient to provide an adequate and appropriate response in many sexting cases due to the diversity of complexity of circumstances relating to sexting behaviours. Fears over the increasing numbers of children being criminalised by the very law designed to protect them, and high profile media cases (see for example [60]) gave rise to the College of Policing issuing new guidance in 2016 allowing a sexting incident involving a young person to be reported and recorded without criminal charges begin brought and the child having a criminal record. According to the [13] 'HOCR requires each crime to be allocated an outcome from a menu of predefined codes. In January 2016, the Home Office launched outcome 21 which states:

> Further investigation, resulting from the crime report, which could provide evidence sufficient to support formal action being taken against the suspect is not in the public interest – police decision.

This outcome code allows the police to record a crime as having happened but for no formal criminal justice action to be taken as it is not considered to be in the public interest to do so.

Drawing on data from a research study undertaken in 2018/2019 from police forces across the UK under the Freedom of Information Act 2000, this chapter outlines the ad hoc nature of police responses to the complex challenges of the production and sharing of intimate by young people which are by definition in law, indecent images of children under the Protection of Children Act 1978 [54] and it both raises concerns about the inconsistent application of legislation resulting in the criminalisation of minors who may be victims of abuse, and questions effective use of Outcome 21 as an alternative to arrest for young people in the UK since its introduction in 2016.

## 2 Understanding Sexting

Sexting has attracted both considerable media and academic attention. Mostly associated with adolescents, sexting, widely speaking, refers to the production of and sharing of a naked or semi-naked image or a sexualized message via digital technology. Whilst there is no definition in law for sexting, the National Society for the Prevention of Cruelty to Children (NSPCC) defines it thus:

> Sexting is when someone shares sexual, naked or semi-naked images or videos of themselves or others, or sends sexually explicit messages.

It has been argued, however, that such broad definitions of sexting mask differences in sexting practices, whether the images were produced and shared consensually or not, and creates misapplications of the term in contexts where it is inappropriate to use it, including media, academic, and court contexts [9]. Jorge 26 offers a more useful definition which considers the concept of age in sexting activities and that current concerns related to sexting focus on children but that many different and multiple platforms of digital communication are used:

> sexting includes sending, receiving, or exchanging images, messages or videos of a sexual nature with other people, be it people children know or not. Sexual communication can, therefore, go from seeing sexy pictures or videos from peers, to having conversations on webcam or chat rooms about sex, being asked on the webcam to take off their clothes, or having their pictures in sexy poses that are shared with others.

The concept of consent is also an important but an all-too-often hidden concept that is often ignored in debates and discourses on sexting. Clear distinctions need to be made apparent in these arenas as to whether the sexting is a consensual practice or whether it is a non-consensual redistribution of images to others or if the images were produced non-consensually through coercive or controlling behaviours [9]. Sexting as a term is also sometimes used to describe an adult sending naked pictures or semi-naked pictures of themselves or another to a young person or a child and/or requesting the child to send images of themselves, which relates to online grooming activity [40]. This activity is clearly of a criminal nature and in a very different context and intent than the sexting activity of two 15 years olds sharing images between themselves in an intimate relationship. It is this 'broad range of behaviours potentially encompassed by the term makes defining, classifying and understanding the motivations for sexting difficult' [32] and for responding effectively. Furthermore, as Hasinoff [20, pp. 449–450] points out, whilst sexting, is often defined as the practice of sending sexually explicit images or text through mobile phones or via internet applications, it is 'teenage girls who create and share images of themselves garner a great deal of anxiety—sexting is typically seen as a technological, sexual and moral crisis' which highlights both the gendered nature of sexting and the moral panic currently associated with it. Moral panics (see [12]) are also related to long standing debates on state intervention, the child and the changing construction of risk [63] in late modern society. Public debates on risk rarely include young people's views and risks to children remain defined and managed by adults and, as such, responsibility and reflexivity accredited to adults is denied to children and young people [19, 48]. Furthermore, there is a growing body of academic work which 'speaks back to a ubiquitous media landscape where children and young people's own experiences of doing, being and becoming sexual are often sensationalized, silenced, caricatured, pathologized and routinely undermined' [46].

## 3 The Prevalence and Emergence of Sexting

Sexting is not new. The term appeared during the middle years of the first decade in the 21st century and was initially associated mainly with webcams and home computers. The attention at the time was focused on child protection concerns through organizations like Child Exploitation and Online Protection Centre (CEOP) in the UK. Concerns over children being groomed online and being coerced or threatened into sending a naked or semi-naked picture by someone seeking sexual gratification have been the focus of policy debate and many public educational campaigns across the globe. Other campaigns have depicted the child or young person as a victim who sends a sexualized image to a peer that is then posted on a social media site or shared widely among a peer group causing the sender humiliation and distress. Whilst undoubtedly well intended in their development, many educational initiatives have been criticized for exploiting 'slut shaming in an effort to responsibilize teenage girls for preventing the purported harms that may flow from sexting' [28]. Campaigns like these and other such examples of extra-legal social control render young people as incomplete, as *becomings* rather than as *beings* [24], as lacking in agency and capacity for choice and self-determination. These dominant perspectives drawn from developmental psychology that categorized children and young people as incomplete, having to pass successfully through one stage before moving onto the next before they are deemed as competent, fail to recognize that young people have both rights and responsibilities in sexual expression and self-representation [9].

Survey data from the UK suggested that 40% of young people aged 14–16 know peers who have engaged in sexting [42]. Unsurprisingly sexting is, however, not specific to the UK. The Pew Research Centre commissioned a study on sexting [33] from a nationally representative survey of young people in the United States aged between 12 and 17 years. They found that 4% of cell phone-owning teens said they had sent sexually suggestive nude or nearly nude images of themselves to someone else via text messaging and 15% of cell-owning teens ages 12–17 said they had received sexually suggestive nude or nearly nude images of someone they know via text messaging. Across Europe the EU Kids Online study [36] found that 15% of 11–16 year olds surveyed had received peer-to- peer sexual messages or images of people naked or having sex, and 3% said they have sent or posted such messages.

Whilst the actual prevalence rates of youth sexting vary due the problematic ethical challenges of researching illegal activities coupled with young people's understandable trepidation to self-report, it is a well acknowledged global phenomena including the countries in the majority south [45]. Understanding sexting behaviours is highly complex and, as outlined above, commonly used definitions do not adequately address the different types of sexting and the different motivations and consequences that sexting and its associated behaviours have. Furthermore, sexting understood as an adult or media-generated concept, does not 'adequately reflect young people's everyday experiences of creating and sharing digital images' [3]. This media-generated word, one that, it is worth noting, young people themselves do not actually use [3, 47], is currently the topic of considerable academic, legal, and public debate. Yet, whilst there is a growing body of research on the topic, 'our knowledge of the practices and perspectives of young people is still relatively limited' [32]. Moreover, policy initiatives and criminal and legal frameworks, remain uninfluenced what academic work is available in this area, preferring instead to drive the prohibitive narrative, whilst young people are simultaneously being victimized and criminalized by inadequate legal frameworks and outdated understandings [9].

Media, legal and public discourses have to date centred on the risks of sexting in relation to children and young people and its legality (albeit laws created far before sexting become common practice and whose intention was not to criminalise minors for these acts), as have policy and policing responses to sexting activity. As such it is argued that the (il)legality of sexting fails to recognize young people's agency and that they may be choosing to produce and share images of themselves by choice. While it is legal to have sex with consent in many countries at age 16, it is still illegal to take a photo of either one's own body or that of another if they are under 18 (even if over 16 and, thus, over the age of consent to have sex in many countries). Thus the legal implications of sexting are according both public and academic attention, yet such debates remain simultaneously both contested and contentious. Young people are being criminalized by the very laws designed to protect them but the majority of young people view sexting (although they do not use such terminology) as a mundane, fairly everyday thing to do, especially in the context of a romantic, intimate relationship and they are often sharing the images with each other within the trusting relationship [41]. However, it is usually when that relationship breaks down that there is a greater likihood that the image will be shared with others or published online with often harmful psychological and emotional consequences for the person depicted in the image.

## 4 Revenge Pornography

It is interesting that many of the existing debates on sexting seem to ignore the fact that adults also engage in sexting behaviours and share images between intimate partners as part of flirting and in developing new or maintaining existing romantic or sexual relationships online just as adolescents do. The normalization of the selfie culture and sexting behaviours in adults as well as young people and recent news headlines are rife with stories of celebrities' sexting activities and politicians appearing in sexting scandals that have attracted considerable media attention. It can be argued that 'given this apparent cross generational adoption of this behaviour, there are clear indicators that this behaviour should be considered within the range of normative human sexual behaviour' [62]. Although often overlooked in academic research on sexting, recent research has found sexting behaviours to be associated with attachment anxiety in adult relationships, as attachment anxiety predicted sending texts that solicit sexual activity for those individuals in relationships and also predicted positive attitudes toward sexting such as accepting it as normal, believing that it will enhance the relationship, and thinking that partners will expect sexting [61]. Commonly referred to as revenge pornography, adults are also victims of digital abuse when the images are shared online or become public, which has been a criminal offence in the UK since 2015. More widely legislation has also been introduced in 26 states in the United States which have laws that relate to revenge pornography and South Australia prohibits the distribution of "invasive images" of another person without that person's consent [17]. Definitions of revenge pornography usually involve an individual, often an adult ex-partner, uploading onto the internet intimate sexual images of the victim, to cause the victim humiliation or embarrassment [14]. This posting of sexual photos of non-consenting others, which often appear alongside identifying personal information, leads to humiliation and embarrassment and may in- crease the potential for online and real-life harassment [51]. Police understanding in the UK of revenge pornography is however poor [11] and many adult victims fail to receive adequate protection from the criminal justice system.

## 5 The Wider Socio-Technical Context

Whilst sexting has been the topic of considerable academic attention, empirical evidence suggests that young people were sexting in the pre-smartphone era using webcams, camera phones, and Bluetooth technology to produce and share images [5, 6, 28, 42]. Young people actively construct, negotiate, reconstruct and renegotiate their online identities, reflexively navigating both their online and offline identities in response to online information and imagery, and communication practices including likes, comments, and feedback on social media profiles. Digital artefacts as both text and image are fundamental to self-identity in late modernity and also to developing, maintaining, and managing everyday relationships [7] and the potential to gain social acceptance as part of a couple or part of a group [5, 6, 47]. Yet just as mobile technologies have become a taken-for-granted, ubiquitous part of everyday life [8, 34], they are important in our understanding of the wider societal and cultural contexts in the trajectory of sexting presented here and to the discussion on police responses to sexting.

It is undoubtedly the interconnectivity of internet-enabled mobile technologies like smartphones, tablets and so on that provide the affordances for both accessibility and privacy and the rapid uptake of these technologies that facilitates the popularity of sexting and the closely associated phenomenon of the selfie. The increase in popularity of the selfie is also important to understanding the occurrence of sexting, as it has become a ubiquitous communication in young people's everyday lives

[30]. This practice of image-based self-representation is afforded by the interoperability and hyperconnectivity of mobile phones, tablets, and Wi-Fi technology and the phenomenon of the selfie has enabled the almost constant documenting of everyday life through image. Many young people take and post several images of themselves on a daily basis [30]. As taking a selfie has become for many young people an everyday, mundane, and taken-for-granted behaviour and hundreds of self-images or self-portraits are posted online, such activities have be- come normalized in everyday life. A generation or so ago it was comparatively difficult to produce and share a naked or semi-naked image of the self, with cumbersome and clumsy technologies, expensive film, and third-party involvement required to develop and produce the image(s). Now with digitization and the technological convergence of mobile technologies, such image production has become mainstream, taken for granted, and a seemingly mundane activity. Furthermore, many social media platforms offer anonymity and some temporality, which are considered to ameliorate some of the risks associated with other social media and the recent plethora of anonymous apps and those that host images that appear to 'disappear' seconds after they are sent have seemingly also changing the landscape of sexting and of harmful digital communication. The anonymity of social media platforms has an impact on risk taking behaviours but also the risk and potential harm encountered [29, 31, 52].

The availability of and ease of access to increasingly hard-core pornography is also having an impact on sexting practices, sexual behaviour, sexuality, and expectations amongst adolescents and is further normalizing sexting behaviours. 'Sexuality in the modern sense' came about when sexual activity 'went behind the scenes' [16, p. 164] and while for many young people their developing sexual identity and indeed sexual activity in the form of sexting remain *behind the scenes* through mobile technologies, but it is when the activity is no longer *behind the scenes* and becomes visible that the discourses on risk emerge. The boundaries between public and private have become blurred. Images shared in the context of a romantic intimate relationship made public when shared with others via text or social media or published online without the consent of the person who is depicted in the image—digital abuse—become agents of humiliation, embarrassment, and shame often with tragic consequences emotionally and psychologically for the person who originally produced the image [1]. It is these tragic cases, which have occasionally resulted in young people taking their own lives and cases when young people have been blackmailed or coerced into sending a furthermore more sexualised image of themselves or communicating online with someone who intends to sexually exploit or abuse them, that have brought the sexting phenomenon to the forefront of public and policy attention.

## 6 Legal Responses to Sexting

In the United Kingdom crimes involving indecent images of a child fall under section 1 of the Protection of Children Act (PCA) 1978, as amended by section 45 of the Sexual Offences Act 2003 to extend the definition of children from under 16

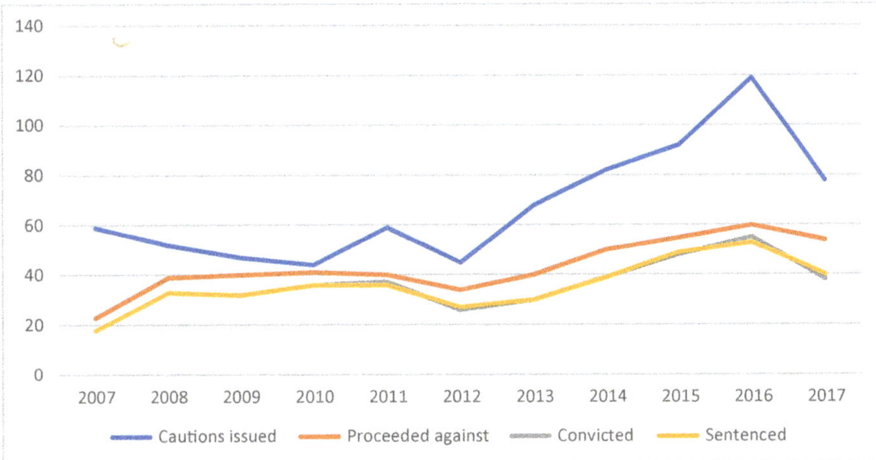


**Fig. 1** Ministry of justice statistics on charges against Home Office crime code 86/2 for juveniles

to under 18. It is a crime to take, make, permit to take, distribute, show, possess with intent to distribute, or to advertise indecent photographs or pseudo photographs of any person below the age of 18. Thus any image of a naked or semi-naked person under 18 in the UK illegal (even though the age of consent for sex is 16).

The following section of this chapter presents the findings of research (see [10]) exploring arrest and crime recording of young people minors for the generation or distribution of indecent images of children, under section 1 of the 1978 Protection of Children Act [54]. The study, funded by the Marie Collins Foundation,[1] was conducted using Freedom of Information requests under the Freedom of Information Act 2000 [56] to police forces in the UK to collect data that would give an indication of the volume of arrests of minors made between December 2016 and March 2019. The start date for the data requested relates to the introduction of Outcome 21 practices (allowing the recording of a crime that is not considered worth pursuing because it is not in the public interest to do so). The new recording method was introduced and guidelines produced by the [13] in the UK specifically to address the increasing number of young people who were being charged under s1 of the PCA as a result of engaging in sexting. Data from the Ministry of Justice (2018) on juveniles entering the criminal justice system as a result of charges under section 1 of the Protection of Children Act (related to Home Office crime code 86/2 see [55] doubled between 2007 and 2016 (see Fig. 1).

It is interesting to note that since the introduction of outcome 21 recording in 2016, charge statistics have reduced.

[1]Marie Collins Foundation is a charitable, UK based organisation who work with children, their families and wider stakeholders to raise awareness of and effectively respond to online child sexual abuse https://www.mariecollinsfoundation.org.uk/mcf/what-we-do.

For youth sexting, the UK legislation that is applied centres on section 1 of the Protection of Children Act (1978):

> it is an offence for a person—
>
> (a) to take, or permit to be taken [or to make], any indecent photograph [or pseudo-photograph] of a child…; or
>
> (b) to distribute or show such indecent photographs [or pseudo-photographs]; or
>
> (c) to have in his possession such indecent photographs [or pseudo-photographs], with a view to their being distributed or shown by himself or others; or
>
> (d) to publish or cause to be published any advertisement likely to be understood as conveying that the advertiser distributes or shows such indecent photographs [F4or pseudo-photographs], or intends to do so

While the legislation was updated in:

> s45 2003 Sexual Offences Act [57]—extending PCA offence from under 16 under 18.
>
> s67 2015 Serious Crime Act [58]—extending legislation to include sexual communication with a child.

the act of production and distribution of an indecent image of a minor remained fundamentally connected with the 1978 legislation.

Given the year that the law reached ascent (1978), it could not have been in the minds of the legislators that the subject of the image, the taker of the image, and the distributor of the image, could all be the same person. Concern has grown around the criminalisation of minors, with a criminal record that would follow them into adulthood, as a result of a practice that was being broadly adopted with the advent of mobile technologies and camera phones [5, 6, 8, 42] and the application of a law being applied for a purpose for which it was not intended.

This legislation makes it illegal for someone to generate and distribute an indecent image of a child and in the event of self-generation and sharing, the victim will also be the perpetrator under this legislation reflecting the victim/treat dualism often associated with post-modern childhoods. The *child* has thus become both the victim and threat [25] in discourses on sexting, which mirror more traditional constructions of childhood especially in public, albeit virtual, space. On the one hand, they are seen as asexual, or blank slates on which the cultural is written; on the other, as highly sexualised 'dangerous', and needing the assistance of a civilized hand [39]. The conceptualization of the child is simultaneously an innocent victim in need of protecting and an evil threat in need of punishment. Children and young people are seen to be both the victims of sexting and the perpetrators, punishable by law, but more recently studies have argued that it is important to understand that many sexting activities are undertaken by young people as consensual acts of intimacy and sharing in a romantic relationship and within the normative landscape of adolescence in what is an increasingly sexualized society. Children and young people are therefore positioned in contradictory ways within discourses of sexuality.

Therefore, in the modern digital world, we have a legislative tension between protecting the victim on the one hand and addressing the illegality of the generation and sharing on the other hand. Those who produce images of themselves and send to others, sometimes voluntarily, sometimes as a result of pressure or coercion [59] risk criminalisation should knowledge of this self-generation be made public and reported to the police. According to UKCCIS [53, p. 8]:

> Where the police are notified of incidents of youth produced sexual imagery they are obliged, under the Home Office Counting Rules and National Crime Recording Standards, to record the incident on their crime systems. The incident will be listed as a 'crime' and the young person involved will be listed as a 'suspect.'

However, the National Police Chiefs Council (NPCC) has made clear that incidents involving youth produced sexual imagery should primarily be treated as safeguarding issues [53] and while many instances of youth self-generation were private and went no further than the intended recipient, there are also many that do. And as a result of further distribution victims were often abused or pressured into other harmful behaviours [44]. Therefore, victims would disclose the abuse to adults with responsibility for their safeguarding (parents, school teachers, etc.), which would often result in police involvement and if police were made aware of the production and distribution of an indecent image of a minor, it would have to be recorded as a crime. The UKCCIS produced guidance for schools and colleges in 2016 to support schools in developing procedures to respond to incidents involving youth produced sexual imagery states:

> All incidents involving youth produced sexual imagery should be responded to in line with the school's safeguarding and child protection policy'….. 'and at any point in the process if there is a concern a young person has been harmed or is at risk of harm a referral should be made to children's social care and/or the police immediately.

Yet it should be noted that even if no further action was taken, the recording of a crime could be recalled in the event of a future criminal records check (for example a Disclosure and Barring Service check) which could severely impact on the young person's future.

## 7 Outcome 21

As a result of high-profile cases (see for example, [60]) and resultant media pressure that the criminalisation of a minor for the self-generation of an indecent image seemed disproportionate, the [13] issued its own guidance, which allows a sexting incident to be reported and recorded, without the young person ending up with a criminal record. In order to provide a middle ground between the incident going unreported, and the image producer/victim ending up with a criminal record, guidance was issued on something an 'Outcome 21' response:

> Further investigation, resulting from the crime report, which could provide evidence sufficient to support formal action being taken against the suspect is not in the public interest – police decision.

Nevertheless, there is still complexity within this given that all sexting incidents are not the same. While a peer-to-peer exchange might be consensual, other factors, such as exploitation, coercion, or deception, can prompt and influence young people's sexting behaviours. A minor may be coerced into self-generating an image as a result of inter-personal pressure or more malicious activity such as blackmail, which often features threats to redistribute other sexual images of the young person. In cases such as these, there is a public interest in sanctioning the behaviour of the offending party. In these instances, there would be no recording of crime against the producer's name, and no move to prosecute would take place. However, the guidance did make it clear that this recording could only be used in the event that there was no evidence of harmful or abusive intent and/or acts associated with the act of sharing the image:

> Outcome 21 may be considered the most appropriate resolution in youth produced sexual imagery cases where the making and sharing is considered non-abusive and there is **no evidence** of exploitation, grooming, profit motive, malicious intent (e.g. extensive or inappropriate sharing (e.g. uploading onto a pornographic website) or it being persistent behaviour. Where these factors are present, outcome 21 would not apply.

This development was viewed as a progressive step forward in policing, while still being constrained by the limitations of the legislation. However, there are still many concerns that while this recording option was available to police officers, its application was disproportionate and inconsistent across the country. As a result, children and young people engaging in sexting practices are falling victim to a post-code lottery where in some instances they would be arrested for doing something that in another location would be recorded as an Outcome 21 incident.

## 8 The Use of Outcome 21 in the UK

Due to these concerns we conducted a Freedom of Information request to all police forces in the UK, to determine firstly the volume of arrests of minors under Home Office crime code 86/2, and also the number of outcome 21 recordings made against minors related to image offences, since December 2016. The specific wording of the request we submitted was:

a. Please could you provide details of the number of arrests related to the taking, making or distribution of an indecent (or pseudo sexual) image of a child (home office code 86/2) where suspect was under the age of 18 since December 2016.
b. If you hold the information, please could you also provide details of the number of arrests related to the taking, making or distribution of an indecent (or pseudo sexual) image of a child (home office code 86/2) where suspect was under the age of 14 since December 2016.
c. Please could you provide the total number of crimes related to the taking, making or distribution of an indecent (or pseudo sexual) image of a child (home office code 86/2) where suspect was under 18 that have been recorded as Outcome 21, since December 2016.

d. If you hold the information, please could you also provide the total number of crimes related to the taking, making or distribution of an indecent (or pseudo sexual) image of a child (home office code 86/2) where suspect was under the age of 14 that have been recorded as Outcome 21 since December 2016.

We specifically asked for data for those under 14, as well as under 18, to determine whether those who were pre-teen, or barely teenagers, were being arrested under this legislation and whether Outcome 21 was being applied in these cases. We acknowledge that, as with any Freedom of Information request related to crime data held, that responses do not allow us to explore context of activity, for example differentiating between those who might have self-generated, those who might have shared self-generated images, and those who might have accessed indecent images of minors online. Furthermore, as with any crime data, the context of the crime is not known and therefore specific inference to behaviours cannot be made. However, Freedom of Information data is useful to look broadly at practice across different forces to determine consistency of approach and, specifically in this case, whether the arrest of minors and Outcome 21 recoridng is being applied consistently. Given the rationale for the application of Outcome 21 recording was that it would reduce the criminalisation of children, or the recording of crimes against them, for actions with little public interest or criminal intent. This data is important to determine whether intention has transferred into practice.

Data from 30 police forces were analysed (two claimed they had no data and three forces claiming exemption under section 12(1) of the Freedom of Information Act[2]) highlighting considerable differences in both crime recording and processing across different forces in the UK. Due to differences in recording and retrieval, we are mindful that we should not directly compare responses from different forces. Therefore, while we present response data in tabular and graphics forms to illustrate types of response, we would caution readers from making inferences between forces (Table 1).

These results demonstrate that in the UK children and young people are still being arrested under crime code 86/2 and that in ten forces arrests are being made to those under the age of 14. Outcome 21 recording is being applied by most forces, to varying levels and the number of outcome 21 recordings, in more cases, far exceeds the number of arrests, which is a positive thing.

Whilst the data provided suggests that Outcome 21 has impacted across forces and is being used to record crimes without the risk of criminalisation for young people, it also demonstrates that there is inconsistent practice across forces. Comparing the number of arrests per force with number of Outcome 21 recordings, to measure proportionality (whilst being careful not to make direct comparisons between forces) we can see major differences in practice (Table 2).

Although we cannot comment on specific cases because we cannot determine the nature of specific crimes and therefore the rationale for law enforcement use of Outcome 21 recording, we would, given that Outcome 21 recording is viewed as a

---

[2]The processing of the request would be too time consuming or costly to the organisation to fall under the expectations of the act.

**Table 1** Arrest and outcome 21 recording from Home Office crime code 86/2 from 30 police forces

| | Arrests 14–17 | Arrests <14 | OC21 14-17 | OC21 <14 |
|---|---|---|---|---|
| Avon and Somerset Constabulary | 8 | 0 | 85 | 70 |
| Bedfordshire Police | 2 | 0 | 67 | 29 |
| Cambridgeshire Constabulary | 10 | 0 | 17 | 34 |
| Cheshire Constabulary | 4 | 0 | 0 | 10 |
| Cleveland Police | 3 | 0 | 2 | 0 |
| Derbyshire Constabulary | 3 | 7 | 300 | 204 |
| Devon and Cornwall Police | 2 | 0 | 103 | 43 |
| Dorset Police | 2 | 0 | 103 | 43 |
| Durham Constabulary | 3 | 0 | 9 | 1 |
| Gloucestershire Constabulary | 6 | 1 | 78 | 31 |
| Greater Manchester Police | 6 | 3 | 414 | 495 |
| Gwent Police | 4 | 0 | 0 | 0 |
| Hampshire Constabulary | 15 | 1 | 2 | 0 |
| Hertfordshire Constabulary | 5 | 0 | 117 | 67 |
| Kent Police | 15 | 3 | 103 | 31 |
| Leicestershire Police | 8 | 0 | 38 | 90 |
| Lincolnshire Police | 7 | 0 | 171 | 117 |
| Merseyside Police | 6 | 0 | 80 | 42 |
| Metropolitan Police Service | 102 | 10 | 54 | 166 |
| Norfolk Constabulary | 14 | 0 | 75 | 60 |
| North Yorkshire Police | 18 | 2 | 0 | 2 |
| South Yorkshire Police | 0 | 0 | 0 | 2 |
| Staffordshire Police | 5 | 0 | 365 | 294 |
| Suffolk Constabulary | 17 | 1 | 99 | 67 |
| Sussex Police | 8 | 3 | 70 | 49 |
| Thames Valley Police | 16 | 1 | 257 | 227 |
| Warwickshire Police | 1 | 0 | 77 | 30 |
| West Mercia Police | 8 | 0 | 112 | 58 |
| West Midlands Police | 10 | 5 | 153 | 367 |
| Wiltshire Police | 7 | 1 | 0 | 0 |

positive alternative to the criminalisation of minors, expect the proportion of arrests to Outcome 21 recording to be low. Whilst in most forces this is the case, there are some with extremely high percentages, which suggest a minor is far more likely to be arrested for this sort of crime than receive an Outcome 21 recording in some areas evidencing the inconsistencies of the application of the policy across forces in the UK.

**Table 2** Proportion of arrest to outcome 21 recording

| | % arrest/OC21 14–17 | % arrest/OC21 <14 |
|---|---|---|
| Avon and Somerset Constabulary | 9.41 | 0.00 |
| Bedfordshire Police | 2.99 | 0.00 |
| Cambridgeshire Constabulary | 58.82 | 0.00 |
| Cheshire Constabulary | N/A | 0.00 |
| Cleveland Police | 150.00 | N/A |
| Derbyshire Constabulary | 1.00 | 3.43 |
| Devon and Cornwall Police | 1.94 | 0.00 |
| Dorset Police | 1.94 | 0.00 |
| Durham Constabulary | 33.33 | 0.00 |
| Gloucestershire Constabulary | 7.69 | 3.23 |
| Greater Manchester Police | 1.45 | 0.61 |
| Gwent Police | N/A | N/A |
| Hampshire Constabulary | 750.00 | N/A |
| Hertfordshire Constabulary | 4.27 | 0.00 |
| Kent Police | 14.56 | 9.68 |
| Leicestershire Police | 21.05 | 0.00 |
| Lincolnshire Police | 4.09 | 0.00 |
| Merseyside Police | 7.50 | 0.00 |
| Metropolitan Police Service | 188.89 | 6.02 |
| Norfolk Constabulary | 18.67 | 0.00 |
| North Yorkshire Police | N/A | 100.00 |
| South Yorkshire Police | N/A | 0.00 |
| Staffordshire Police | 1.37 | 0.00 |
| Suffolk Constabulary | 17.17 | 1.49 |
| Sussex Police | 11.43 | 6.12 |
| Thames Valley Police | 6.23 | 0.44 |
| Warwickshire Police | 1.30 | 0.00 |
| West Mercia Police | 7.14 | 0.00 |
| West Midlands Police | 6.54 | 1.36 |
| Wiltshire Police | N/A | N/A |

In spite of this, Ministry of Justice crime data would suggest that only small numbers of cases involving minors ever enter the criminal justice system. In the data supplied by police forces, a total of 358 arrests of minors under Home Office code 86/2 were made over the response period. However, data from the Ministry of Justice shows that in 2017 54 minors were proceeded against for these crimes and 38 were convicted and in 2018 these figures were 42 and 40 respectively. This would suggest that the Crime Prosecution Service in the UK is reluctant to proceed against minors for these crimes even after arrest. Furthermore, looking at the Ministry of Justice data (see Fig. 1) prior to 2017, the charge and proceeding numbers are also small. Given that there are extremely high outcome 21 figures in some forces this implies (although not establishing causation), that since the advent of Outcome 21, it is far more likely that a recording will be made. This is we would argue a worrying trend because an Outcome 21 recording against a young person can still be recalled in an advanced DBS check, at the discretion of the then chief constable of a given region (with no clear or transparent national guidance or policy on how this discretion should be applied).

## 9 Concluding Thoughts

In conclusion, this data presents a mixed picture. It is positive that Outcome 21 recording is, in a lot of cases, being applied far more than arrest. However, we still see that arrest of minors does occur and children and young people criminalised. Perhaps what is even more concerning, however, is that the practices seem highly inconsistent across forces in the UK and that young people are subject to a postcode lottery should they be discovered engaging in the exchange of intimate images. Further research is undoubtedly needed to unpick the reasons behind the data, particularly with police, youth offending and probation services how youth sexting cases are being processed in the criminal justice system is needed yet research with young people on sexting behaviours is in itself problematic due to the (il)legality of these activities and the ethical complexities associated with research in this field.

Responses to sexting are, however, not just a matter for police as the College of Policing guidance (pg 2) states: 'Police need to work with schools to educate children on the risks of exchanging imagery, to engage as appropriate during investigations, and understand schools' powers to delete images'. There are strong arguments developing among academics, educators, and policy makers that the focus of sexting interventions and educational programs for young people should be deterring the distribution of sexts without the consent of the producer/sender/subject of the image and that such an 'approach would treat breeches of consent, rather than sexual expression itself, as the problem in need of remedy' [35]. As we have also argued many young people are being prosecuted by laws actually designed to protect children from sexual exploitation that do not adequately accommodate consensual sexting by young people [50]. Yet whilst there is increasing evidence that 'the focus of both legal, educational and policy responses should not be on the original consensual creation of the image, but on the non-consensual creation and distribution of the mage' [22], 'young people's narratives illustrate uncertainty about who were the most appropriate adults, with duties of care, to handle incidents of aggravated sexting and/or leaked nudes' [27].

Previously hidden from adult gaze, young people's explorations of each other's bodies and indeed their own sexuality and sexual activity were previously confined to a close and private geographic space [8]. This space has become virtual and multiple and in doing so very public, and it is this publicity that is fuelling the public anxiety in relation to sexting. Rather than shaming young people for sexting, we propose that it is important to recognize that sexting can be an expression of intimacy and 'framing sexual expression only as risk does little to alleviate anxieties or feelings of shame that young people may experience in relation to their sexualities' [3]. A more measured, informed, and realistic response is needed, one that respects young people's rights to self- identity and to agency but also to participation as well as protection. This may not be an easy debate to begin to challenge legal frameworks and current policy, but we argue it is one that needs to start as [50] also observe:

> The context in which the activity occurs should guide the [legal] response. A distinction must be made between adults enticing juveniles and youth voluntarily sending images. Incidents of coercion or exploitation should be treated more seriously than incidents of voluntary and consensual activity. The harassment a youth might experience from peers cannot be equated with the harm that a child experiences as a victim of sexual abuse. In both situations, the youth is subject to negative emotions and effects, but the distinct contexts encourage different responses.

There is a growing awareness and discussion around sexting, with a focus on the deficiencies of current legislative frameworks that serve to criminalize young people's consensual sexual exploration using technology, and the gendered effects of educational campaigns surrounding them. It is apparent that, as argued throughout, differences need to be drawn across the term sexting to more helpfully differentiate between consensual and non-consensual sexting practices, the latter of which encompass the sharing of images between an adult and a child as sexual exploitation or grooming behaviours and those images produced under control or coercion.

> Youth production of sexual images, or what has come to be called sexting, is a di- verse phenomenon. Some episodes involve serious criminal dynamics, such as adults interacting sexually with underage youth or young people engaging in blackmail or other criminal or malicious behavio[u]r, or recklessly circulating images. However, sexting also involves episodes, an estimated 33%, with no malicious elements, that were better characterized as experimental romantic and sexual attention seeking among adolescents [64].

Our research undertaken with police forces in the UK based on concerns that a procedural sticking plaster developed to tackle the failings in a piece of legislation is now being used in ways it was never intended to is now being applied with little regard for how this might impact on young people's future lives. We should stress here that in our over 30 years collective experience in researching this social phenomenon we have always felt (and we were told regularly by young people) that the technical illegality of teen sexting was and is no deterrent. Section 1 of the Protection of Children Act 1978, which relates to the production, manufacture and distribution of indecent images of children, was developed (if one explores the parliamentary debates of the time, as we have) to ensure children and young people were protected from exploitation in the production of indecent child abuse materials produced by adults.

While Outcome 21 was welcomed by many (ourselves included) at the time, its application since inception is a cause for concern. This chapter highlights the high number of outcome 21 recordings being made, and those particularly applied to younger minors. One force in our analysis had recorded Outcome 21s for over 400 young people under the age of 14 since the end of 2015 and as we have seen Outcome 21 is being used in far greater numbers than arrests or charges. At the same time the Ministry of Justice crime statistics show less than 100 minors nationally have been convicted under section 1 of the Protection of Children Act. Therefore, from one perspective, we might argue that this is a good thing—we do not want young people entering the criminal justice system for a consensual exchange on images, albeit those considered illegal under the PCA 1978. But we should also be mindful that while it is viewed as a 'non-conviction', the wording of the police guidance states:

> The discretion on whether to disclose non-conviction information rests with each chief constable managing the process.

In other words, should a minor with an outcome 21 recording be in a position in later life that a DBS check (or whatever the future criminal record check might be) is needed, there is still a chance that this will still be disclosed. We are already seeing, with both pieces of research, major force discrepancies which show Outcome 21 being applied differently across forces. Without published policy on how this discretion by chief constables is applied, we really are at risk of a postcode lottery in terms of whether a minor engaged in sexting might end up with a record that could follow them for the rest of their lives. Furthermore, but importantly is should be questioned 'to what degree children and young people can be expected to understand and accept the law and current narratives about 'sexting', including when and how to seek help, when concepts like suspect and victim status can apparently be so ambiguous' [18]. Given that the often-held mantra from law enforcement and education professionals is "its illegal, that's what they need to learn", we are of the view that a victim of the further distribution of a self-produced indecent image needs understanding and support, not a threat of criminalisation and that a focus on consent is more effective. Before we judge the foolhardiness of the young person's act, we might the parallel acts in the adult world (for example, behaviour on dating apps such as Tinder). However, while adult victims of revenge pornography are now protected by law, young people who become victims still risk ending up with some form of criminal record. This hardly seems proportionate, empathetic or ethical to us.

## References

1. Ahern NR, Mechling B (2013) Sexting: serious problems for youth. J Psychosoc Nurs Ment Health Serv 51(7):22–30
2. Albury K, Crawford K (2012) Sexting, consent and young people's ethics: beyond Megan's story. Cont J Media Cult Studies 26(3):463, 473
3. Albury K, Crawford K, Bryon P, Mathews B (2013) Young people and sexting in Australia: ethics, representation and the law. University of New South Wales, Sydney, Australia
4. Beck U (1992) Risk society towards a new modernity. Sage, London
5. Bond E (2010) The mobile phone = bike shed? Children, sex and mobile phones. New Media Soc 13(4):587–604

6. Bond E (2010b) Managing mobile relationships—children's perceptions of the impact of the mobile phone on relationships in their everyday lives. Childhood 17(4):514–529
7. Bond E (2013) Mobile phones, risk and responsibility: understanding children's perceptions. CyberPsychol J Psychosoc Res Cyberspace 7(1)
8. Bond E (2014) Mobile technologies, everyday experiences and children's everyday lives. Palgrave, Basingstoke
9. Bond E (2016) Sexting. In: Brown M, Rafter N (eds) Oxford encyclopaedia of crime, media, and popular culture. https://doi.org/10.1093/acrefore/9780190264079.013.142
10. Bond E, Phippen A (2019) Police response to youth offending around the generation and distribution of indecent images of children and its implications. https://www.uos.ac.uk/sites/default/files/FOI-Report-Final-Outcome-21.pdf
11. Bond E, Tyrrell K (2018) Understanding revenge pornography: a national study of police officers and staff in England and Wales. J Interpers Violence. https://journals.sagepub.com/doi/full/10.1177/0886260518760011
12. Cohen S (1972) Folk devils and moral panics. MacGibbon and Kee, London
13. College of Policing (2016) Police action in response to youth produced sexual imagery ('Sexting'). https://www.college.police.uk/News/College-news/Documents/Police_actioninresponsetosexting-briefing_(003).pdf
14. Crown Prosecution Service (2015) Revenge Pornography - Guidelines on prosecuting the offence of disclosing private sexual photographs and films available from https://www.cps.gov.uk/legal-guidance/revenge-pornography-guidelines-prosecuting-offence-disclosing-private-sexual
15. Gidden A (1990) The consequences of modernity. Cambridge: Polity Press
16. Giddens A (1991) Modernity and self-identity self and society in the late modern age. Polity Press, Cambridge
17. Gotis T (2015) Revenge pornography, privacy and the law. https://www.parliament.nsw.gov.au/researchpapers/Documents/revenge-pornography-pri-vacy-and-the-law/revenge%20pornography%20privacy%20and%20the%20law.pdf
18. Hales G (2018) 'Sexting' Surge or a conceptual muddle? The challenges of analogue Law and Ambiguous Crime Recording. Police Foundation, Washington, DC
19. Harden J (2000) There's no place like home: the public/private distinction in children's theorizing of risk and safety. Childhood 7(1):43–59
20. Hasinoff AA (2012) Sexting as media production: rethinking social media and sexuality. New Media Soc 14(4):449–465
21. Heins M (2001) Criminalizing online speech to "protect" the young: what are the benefits and costs? In: Wall DS (ed) Crime and the Internet. Routledge, London, pp 100–112
22. Henry N, Powell A (2015) Beyond the "sext": technology-facilitated sexual violence and harassment against adult women. Australian New Zealand J Criminol 48(1):104–118
23. Hutchby I (2001) Technologies, texts and affordances. Sociology 35(2):441–456
24. James A, Jenks C, Prout A (2010) Theorizing childhood. Polity Press, Cambridge
25. Jenks C (1996) Childhood. Routledge, London
26. Jorge, A. (2014) Sexual content and communication. In: Smahel D, Wright MF (eds) Meaning of online problematic situations for children: results of qualitative cross-cultural investigation in nine European countries. EU Kids Online, London
27. Jørgensen CR, Weckesser A, Turner J, Wade Alex (2019) Young people's views on sexting education and support needs: findings and recommendations from a UK-based study. Sex Educ 19(1):25–40. https://doi.org/10.1080/14681811.2018.1475283
28. Karaian L (2014) Policing "sexting": responsibilization, respectability and sexual subjectivity in child protection/crime prevention responses to teenagers' digital sexual expression. Theoret Criminol 18(3):282–299
29. Karaian L, Van Meyl K (2015) Reframing risqué/risky: queer temporalities, teenage sexting, and freedom of expression. Laws 4(1):18–36
30. Kim E, Lee JA, Sung Y, Choi SM (2016) Predicting selfie-posting behaviour on social networking sites: an extension of theory of planned behaviour. Comput Hum Behav 62:116–123

31. Klettke B, Hallford DJ, Mellor DJ (2014) Sexting prevalence and correlates: a systematic literature review. Clin Psychol Rev 34(1):44–53
32. Lee M, Crofts T (2015) Gender, pressure, coercion and pleasure: untangling motivations for sexting between young people. Br J Criminol 55:454–473
33. Lenhart A (2009) Teens and sexting. Pew Internet and American Life Project, Washington, DC
34. Ling R (2012) Taken for grantedness: the embedding of mobile communication in society. MIT Press, Cambridge, MA
35. Lippman JR, Campbell SW (2014) Damned if you do, damned if you don't if you're a girl: relational and normative contexts of adolescent sexting in the United States. J Child. Media 8(4):371–386
36. Livingstone S, Haddon L, Görzig A, Ólafsson K (2011) Risks and safety on the Internet: the perspective of European children. Full findings. London, UK: EU Kids Online, LSE
37. Maus M (2002) The gift. Routledge, Abingdon
38. McGovern A, Crofts T, Lee M, Milivojevic S (2016) Media, legal and young people's discourses around sexting. Glob Studies Child 6(4):428–441
39. Mulholland M (2013) Young people and pornography: negotiating pornification. Palgrave Macmillan, New York
40. O'Connell R (2003) A typology of child cybersexploitation and online grooming practices. Cyberspace Research Unit, Preston
41. Phippen A, Phippen (2018) The UK government internet safety strategy—time to listen to the youth voice? Entertain Law Rev (6)
42. Phippen A (2009) Sharing personal images and videos among young people. South west grid for learning available from http://www.swg.org.uk/staying-safesexting-survey
43. Phippen A, Bond E (2019) The online harms spearmint paper—just more doing more?' Entertain Law Rev (6)
44. Phippen A (2016) Children's online behaviour and safety: policy and rights challenges. Palgrave, Basingstoke
45. Ramiro LS, Martinez AB, Tan JRD, Mariano K, Miranda GMJ, Bautista G (2019) Online child sexual exploitation and abuse: a community diagnosis using the social norms theory. Child Abuse Negl 96. https://doi.org/10.1016/j.chiabu.2019.104080
46. Renold E, Egan RD, Ringrose J (2015) Introduction. In: Renold E, Ringrose J, Egan RD (eds) Children, sexuality and sexualization. Basingstoke, Palgrave, pp 1–22
47. Ringrose J, Gill R, Livingstone S, Harvey L (2012) A qualitative study of children, young people and "sexting": a report prepared for the NSPCC
48. Roche J (1999) Children: rights, participation and citizenship. Childhood 6(4):475–493
49. Scott S, Jackson S, Backett-Milburn K (1998) Swings and roundabouts: risk anxiety and the everyday world of children. Sociology 32(4):689–705
50. Spooner K, Vaughn M (2014) Youth sexting: a legislative and constitutional analysis. J School Violence 15(2):213–233
51. Stroud SR (2014) The dark side of the online self: a pragmatist critique of the growing plague of revenge porn. J. Mass Media Ethics 29(3):168–183
52. Temple JR, Choi H (2014) Longitudinal association between teen sexting and sexual behaviour. Pediatr Off J Am Acad Pediatr 134(5):1–6
53. UKCISS (2016) Sexting in schools and colleges: responding to incidents and safeguarding young people https://assets.publishing.service.gov.uk/government/uploads/system/uploads/attachment_data/file/759007/6_2939_SP_NCA_Sexting_In_Schools_FINAL_Update_Jan17.pdf
54. UK Government (1978) Protection of Children Act 1978 available online from https://www.legislation.gov.uk/ukpga/1978/37
55. UK Government (2019) Offence classification index. https://assets.publishing.service.gov.uk/government/uploads/system/uploads/attachment_data/file/796318/count-offence-classification-index-apr-2019.pdf
56. UK Government (2000) Freedom of Information Act 2000. http://www.legislation.gov.uk/ukpga/2000/36/contents

57. UK Government (2003) Section 45, Sexual Offences Act 2003. https://www.legislation.gov.uk/ukpga/2003/42/section/45
58. UK Government (2015) Section 67, Serious Crime Act 2015. https://www.legislation.gov.uk/ukpga/2015/9/section/67
59. UK Safer Internet Centre, Netsafe New Zealand, Office of the Australian eSafety Commissioner (2017) Young people and sexting—attitudes and behaviours. https://www.esafety.gov.au/-/media/cesc/documents/corporate-office/young_people_and_sexting_attitudes_and_behaviours_pdf.pdf
60. Ward V (2015) Teenage boy added to police database for sexting. https://www.telegraph.co.uk/news/uknews/crime/11840985/Teenage-boy-added-to-police-database-for-sexting.html
61. Weisskirch RS, Delevi R (2011) "Sexting" and adult romantic attachment. Comput Hum Behav 27(5):1697–1701
62. Willard NE (2010) Sexting and youth: achieving a rational response. J Soc Sci 6(4):542–562
63. Winter K, Connolly P (1996) "Keeping it in the family": Thatcherism and the Children Act 1989. In: Pilcher J, Wagg S (eds) Thatcher's children? Politics, childhood and society in the 1980s and 1990s. Falmer Press, London, pp 29–42
64. Wolak J, Finkelhor D, Mitchell K (2012) How often are teens arrested for sexting? Data from a national sample of police cases. Pediatrics 129(1):4–12
65. Yar M (2006) Cybercrime and society. Sage, London

# Image Recognition in Child Sexual Exploitation Material—Capabilities, Ethics and Rights

**Andy Phippen and Emma Bond**

**Abstract** Image recognition—the use of software to identify images for a specific task—has long been proposed as a solution to addressing some of the more laborious and technical complex tasks such as the triaging of child abuse and exploitation imagery. However, a lack of knowledge and understanding of the capabilities, and limits, of image recognition sometimes results in high levels of expectation that cannot be delivered technically. In tackling key challenges in the policing child abuse material in areas such as victim identification, image categorisation and the prevention of replication and communication of images, image recognition algorithms have been proposed as potential solutions. However, a case study approach highlights concerns around issues such as data bias, lack of training data, and data ethics, which highlight that the complexity of image recognition in this domain might not be as effective as one might wish.

**Keywords** Image recognition · Images child abuse · Data bias · Data ethics · Victim identification · Algorithms

## 1 Introduction

Image recognition by computers is, as we will explore in this chapter, often viewed as the solution to tackling the proliferation of child sexual abuse and exploitation material online. We know that both the proliferation of images,[1] and the increased volume of self-generated imagery[2] means that law enforcement and other child protection stakeholders struggle to identify new images, support victims in those images, and prevent the flow of images across. However, while leading edge image recognition techniques have been shown to have success in some domains such as healthcare[3] and

A. Phippen (✉)
Bournemouth University, Bournemouth, UK
e-mail: aphippen1@bournemouth.ac.uk

E. Bond
University of Suffolk, Suffolk, UK
e-mail: e.bond@uos.ac.uk

 
H. Jahankhani et al. (eds.), *Policing in the Era of AI and Smart Societies*,
Advanced Sciences and Technologies for Security Applications,
https://doi.org/10.1007/978-3-030-50613-1_8

IT security,[4] we argue that the complexity of the child abuse images space means that the application of the same techniques will not garner similar results and, equally, present some fundamental rights and ethical challenges. In this chapter we explore why image recognition is being proposed as *the* solution for tackling child abuse material online and why there is a need for those proposing these approaches to understand them in more detail before concluding that they will be a great success.

## 2 Racist Algorithms?

In late February 2020, a tweet[1] went viral with accusation of evidence of a racist algorithm. It was a fantastic, and concerning, example of the flaws in image recognition. In the tweet a person of colour posted a screen shot of her attempt to upload an image of herself as part of a passport application. The system rejected the image claiming that the subject in the picture had their mouth open (she clearly did not). It went on, further compounding the insult, to suggest the image recognition algorithm might have mistakenly identified their mouth as being open because "something this is caused by facial hair of shadows near your mouth" or "try different lighting". By way of even further insult, it went on to state "you can still submit your photo if you believe it should be accepted (for example there's a medical reason why your mouth appears to be open)".

Those responding to the post spoke of similar experiences—one person saying they were told the background was black, and therefore unacceptable, when the "background" was actually her hair, and another said they were told the image was too dark. And in this simple example, we have very useful anecdote that shows the issues with relying on image recognition algorithms in the processing of image data. Clearly the algorithm was not racist, an algorithm is a piece of computer code with instructions on how to execute some form of data processing or problem solving, in this case deciding whether an image was appropriate for use as a passport photograph, based upon some clearly defined policy on what makes an acceptable picture.[2] Algorithms are incapable of feeling, opinion or prejudice, they merely act upon the instructions, and data, with which they are provided.

Image recognition algorithms (at a fundamental level) work by being "shown" many images from their problem domain as *training data*. These images will be processed alongside meta-data which will tell the algorithm the features of the image. In the case of the passport system, with its image validation function, one might

[1]https://twitter.com/elainebabey/status/1232333491607625728.

[2]In the case of the UK Passport system (https://www.gov.uk/photos-for-passports/), these rules are detailed as: contain no other objects or people, be taken against a plain light-coloured background, be in clear contrast to the background, not have 'red eye'. And the subject should: be facing forwards and looking straight at the camera; have a plain expression and your mouth closed; have your eyes open and visible; not have hair in front of your eyes; not have a head covering (unless it's for religious or medical reasons); not have anything covering your face; not have any shadows on your face or behind you.

image the training data contained images of individuals with their mouths open (unacceptable), and those with mouths closed (acceptable). In this way the algorithm is trained to "recognise" the difference between an acceptable and unacceptable image. However, it does not actually recognise the image, it is merely making an approximation regarding whether the data composition for the new image matches characteristics of images from the training set that have been defined as unacceptable. However, how the algorithm comes to that decision is not necessarily going to be exactly as the developers might imagine.

By way of illustration, there is an apocryphal tale often told about an image detection system developed for the military that tried to detect tanks hidden in cover such as trees. While it has been debunked,[5] it is a worthwhile illustration of the issues between believing an algorithm achieves one's aims (an unconscious bias in user acceptance wishing to believe the software is fulfilling its requirements) and actually understanding the function of the algorithm in a logical, transparent and informed manner. The story, which has many variations, purports that an image detection algorithm was developed to correctly identify the different between a tree, and a tank hiding behind a tree, on the battlefield. The algorithm was trained with 100 test images, half of which were trees, the other half being trees with tanks hidden behind them. For each image the metadata alongside stated whether it was a hidden tank or a tree. In a test environment the algorithm would successfully identify an image with near perfect precision—that is, it would be able to tell the difference between a tree and a tank hiding behind a tree with a new image, and was regarded as a great success. However, when deployed in a live system the detection went down to the equivalence of a random match. While at first the reason for this could not be explained, when it was explored in detail it was discovered that all of the training images of trees without tanks were taken on sunny days, and all of those with tanks in the image were taken on cloudy days. When the algorithm was shown a new image, it was accurately matching the image to weather conditions, rather than the object in the image.

While this story has become something of an urban myth, image recognition scholars have acknowledged its viability. Given that most image recognition algorithms "recognise" based upon the data properties of the image, rather than what the image represents in semantic terms, and largely rely on training sets to accurately identify comparable images, the identification of unknown images, or features in an unknown image, is far more complex.

What was clearly at fault with the passport photograph system was the training data used by the image recognition algorithm was not sufficiently diverse. In essence, the algorithm would have needed to be fed images of unacceptable and acceptable images. With a small, non-diverse data set, the algorithm made a false positive match of someone without their mouth open, although, in its interpretation of the data presented, was a correct match given what it knew about the data composition of an image of someone with their mouth open. The lack of diversity in the training data ultimately lead to much negative publicity and, reasonable, accusations of racism. While the algorithm, of itself, could not be racist, the training set selection could, at best, be accused of lacking diversity or, at worst, be accused of deliberately excluding BAME people.

## 3 Image Recognition in Tackling Child Abuse and Exploitation Materials Online

In this chapter, we explore the policy demands, technical capabilities and ethical dimensions in the use of image recognition related to Child Sexual Abuse and/or Exploitation Material (CASM/CSEM). This is an important area in policing, given claims by some senior law enforcement professionals[6] and NGOs[7] about the prevalence of this sort of material online and how difficult it is to manage, catalogue and move toward victim identification, location and recovery. Given the volumes of material law enforcement face, and the claims regarding the use of image recognition technology, it is no surprise that this an area of great interest for the application of this branch of artificial intelligence. However, if such technologies are to be applied effectively and successfully, it is important to understand the capabilities and limits of such approaches, and the potential ethical pitfalls that might arise as a result. In this chapter we explore what works, what is more problematic, and how the role of policy makers might not contribute intelligently to the debate around the use of these technologies. The chapter also explores different technical approaches and their viability, and reflects on debates around the ethics of the approaches chosen.

By way of illustration, a recent political debate in the UK shows how poorly informed rhetoric can result in unreasonable expectations on the technology itself and also service providers in the general, and clearly shows how a failure in understanding of how technology works can result in some outlandish claims. It also raises some ethical challenges should such an approach actually be viable.

In 2017, the House of Commons Health Select Committee conducted an investigation into suicide prevention.[8] As part of this inquiry, the then Secretary of State for Health, Jeremy Hunt, gave oral evidence to the committee, with a focus on young people's mental health and suicide prevention. During the evidence session, among many other things discussed, Mr. Hunt raised the issue of the self-generation and distribution of indecent images by minors—sometimes referred to as teen sexting—and how this can have a negative impact on young people's mental health. He was asked about social media regulation and stated[9]:

> There is a lot of evidence that the technology industry, if they put their mind to it, can do really smart things.

The implication being that technology companies should be "doing more" to make sure the practice of self-producing an indecent image on a mobile device, and subsequently sending the image to one or more recipients, was difficult to achieve if one is a minor. Mr. Hunt continued:

> I just ask myself the simple question as to why it is that you can't prevent the texting of sexually explicit images by people under the age of 18, if that's a lock that parents choose

> to put on a mobile phone contract. Because there is technology that can identify sexually explicit pictures and prevent it being transmitted.

Within this simple paragraph, we have much to unpack when considering whether this proposed technological solution exists in the realms of reality.

Firstly, there is an assumption that any child's device will be easily identified as belonging to a minor. Mr. Hunt seems to be under the impression that any child will own a device set up on contract by their parent. There are a wealth of reasons this might not be the case, such as phones passed between different family members, devices inherited from friends, some form of handset that does not run a sim, but instead, will just use WiFi connectivity and 'pay as you go' phones where there are less precise checks on the age of the end user (particularly if the device is purchased by the parents for a child). There is also the more fundamental issue that even if a parent does add a child's phone onto their contract, this does not necessarily mean that the device will be registered as a device for a minor as it is entirely up to the parent to specify this. Given the challenges in general around age verification,[10] and, at the time of writing, there is no means for the provider to verify age of different users of devices on the same contract, there may be many reasons why the service provider cannot confidently authenticate that the device belongs to a minor in the first place. Therefore, even the first tenant on the argument put forward by Mr. Hunt is inaccurate.

Even if we assume, for the sake of argument, that we can determine the device user is a minor, our next challenge is what does Mr. Hunt actually mean by "transmission" and how one might control it. Any mobile device will have multiple ways in which they might transmit an image to one or many recipients. For example, MMS, WhatsApp, Facebook Messenger, email, Gmail, Bluetooth file exchange, twitter messaging, Instagram messaging, cloud based shared storage, LinkedIn messaging or the device's own proprietary data transfer protocols are all possible on the device of one of the author's of this chapter's device. There are many more apps that would provide the means to communicate images over a data connection. Therefore, at a technical level, Mr. Hunt's suggestion that prevention of transmission is extremely challenging. Is he suggesting each app needs to implement its own image recognition algorithm, and prevent the sending of the image at an application level? Or that there should be processing further into the technology stack such that the device's own operating system, for example, intercepts the image? Again, this is a simple statement that clearly shows there is little understanding of how software actually operates. Would Mr. Hunt's assumption mean that any (global) company that provides the means to share an image now have to implement image recognition?

However, perhaps the more problematic part of his statement is that Mr. Hunt makes the, unfounded, claim that there is technology that exists that can identify a sexually explicit image of a minor. A fundamental concern with this statement is that there is no clear, legally agreed, definition for what *sexually explicit* is. While we do have a clear definition in the UK statute for extreme pornography[11] and an attempt to define pornography in the Digital Economy Act 2017[12] (albeit a definition that would be problematic to try to implement into an algorithm given its reliance of human classification), and definitions for illegal image of children and young people,[13] a *sexually explicit* image is far more ambiguously defined concept. And algorithms are very poor at ambiguity. If there is no hard coded (legislatively speaking) definition of what sexually explicit is, we are immediately challenged regarding how we might implement this consistently in code. If we are to apply a generic machine learning to Mr. Hunt's, apparently established, technology, we need to train the algorithm with data defined as sexually explicit by *someone*. We have already determined that there is no universally accepted definition for sexually explicit so we would have to add another layer of ambiguity by having subjective judgements on an image set by a human, or group of humans, who will determine whether or not an image is suitable for the training data by deeming it sexually explicit. And as we have seen in the example with the passport system, human selected data sets can, of themselves, implement significant bias into the recognition process.

Furthermore, what Mr. Hunt is referring to here is the detection of sexually explicit images of minors—given he is proposing this as a solution to prevent young people from sending these images (because he claims this is one of the reasons young people have poor mental health). Therefore, in order to train an algorithm to identify newly generated sexually explicit images of a minor, the data set needs to comprise of sexually explicit images of children selected by human analysts. This places an unreasonable and potentially illegal burden on the technology provider—even possession of an image outside of a law enforcement arena would mean the company was breaking the law (in the UK—the Protection of Children Act 1978[14]). To expect an organisation to keep a training set of sexually explicit images of minors would be extremely concerning, and goes some way to explaining why such technologies do not exist. Given the complexity in regulating all transmission, as discussed above, are we expecting any company who might provide an app that would allow for the communication of an image to hold their own training data? And, to raise a point to which we will return later in this chapter, how might the subjects of these images consent to their images being used in training data, given the legality of the images and an assumption that they must have had to have been collected by law enforcement agencies. While acceptance of storage of an indecent image of a minor for law enforcement purposes might be forthcoming, if these images were subsequently used for training data, surely consent would have to be granted? Ethically and legally this is a highly problematic proposal that would be virtually impossible for any commercial company to implement.

However, evidence from a Secretary of State carries weight, and will result in other stakeholders believing that this technology is readily available, which will then create greater public dissatisfaction because the sector is not implementing something they have been told is available, even if it is not. Which then leads the technology sector to develop best fit technologies that do not do what is expected, but something that, on the surface, might appear to do what is claimed. Which, of course, does nothing to solve the problems these solutions are supposed to tackle when it turns out to not achieve what is claimed.

However, there is a more fundamental, philosophical issue for us to consider as well—Mr. Hunt appears to be asking the technology sector to create algorithms that would sit on a child's mobile device and make moral decisions on the types of the images the child has taken, and control the communications of these images as a result of the judgements. Surely, this extends the role of the technology provider beyond what is both ethical and socially acceptable? Should we really be expecting private sector organisations to make decisions that impact on the rights of the child, in particular their right to privacy and freedom of expression? The rights of the child being central in any safeguarding decision—and this is certainly a safeguarding judgement that needs to be made.

While there is a case to be made regarding young people engaging in illegal activity, we should also be mindful that there is no *modern* legislation that has tackled the self-generation of indecent images. In the UK, the legislation that is applied is Sect. 1 of the Protection of Children Act 1978.[15] This legislation was developed specifically to protect children from exploitation by adults, and certainly did not consider that the subject of the image was also the taker and distributor of the image. And comparable legislation in other nations (for example the US), struggles to maintain a balance between child protection when exploited by adults compared to the peer on peer sharing of images. The most recent update to US federal law related to teen sexting, the Prosecutorial Remedies and Other Tools to end the Exploitation of Children Today (PROTECT) Act of 2003 makes specific mention in *Title V: Obscenity and Pornography—Subtitle A: Child Obscenity and Pornography Prevention*:

(1) making a visual depiction that is a digital image, computer image, or computer-generated image of, or that is indistinguishable from an image of, a minor engaging in specified sexually explicit conduct;
(2) knowingly advertising, promoting, presenting, distributing, or soliciting through the mails or in commerce, including by computer, any material that is or contains an obscene visual depiction of a minor engaging in sexually explicit conduct or a visual depiction of an actual minor engaging in such conduct;
(3) knowingly distributing, offering, sending, or providing to a minor any such visual depiction using the mails or commerce, including by computer, for purposes of inducing or persuading a minor to participate in an illegal act; and
(4) knowingly producing, distributing, receiving, or possessing with intent to distribute a visual depiction of any kind, including a drawing, cartoon, sculpture, or painting, that, under specified circumstances, depicts a minor engaging in sexually explicit conduct and is obscene, or depicts an image that is or appears to be of a minor engaging in such conduct and such depiction lacks serious literary, artistic, political, or scientific value.

But has no consideration of a differentiation between an image of a child taken by an adult, and an image of a child they have taken themselves. While we consider the criminalisation of children as a result of this legislation in another chapter in this book ("Tackling teen sexting—policing challenges when society and technology outpace legislation"), it is worth acknowledging, when considering the expectations of "algorithmic morality", that the law itself is still struggling to keep pace with modern online behaviour, whether an algorithm should be flagging illegal activity or safeguarding concern, even if code was even capable of making that choice, or even accurately detecting an indecent image of a minor without a potentially illegal training set.

Furthermore, we raise concerns regarding the accuracy of the image recognition when placed in a social or domestic context. While, as we discuss later in this chapter, there may be a place for image recognition in a law enforcement context, this does at least allow human intervention to determine the accuracy of the algorithmic judgements. In a domestic context (for example on a child's mobile phone) there is little opportunity for moderation of the algorithmic choice. Therefore, we have concerns about the accuracy of image recognition algorithms in these situations.

## 4 The Fundamentals of Machine Based Image Recognition

Image recognition in algorithmic form is not really image recognition as we might interpret from a human perspective at all. As discussed above, these algorithmic approaches to "recognition" apply statistical or machine learning techniques to adopt a predictive solution which, for the purposes of detecting unknown images against a training set will apply mathematical techniques to identify common characteristics in a set of images (or increasingly, video). This approach is based upon the data in the image (for example, the proximity of different colour pixels to each other, the frequency of images of different colours, specific colours in specific parts of the image, etc.). More recently[16] artificial intelligence (AI) techniques have been applied and are becoming the de facto approach to identify common characteristics within candidate images entered into a detection system, based upon whatever training data it has been fed. Therefore, these techniques do little to understand the meaning of the image, rather they identify similar characteristics within the data held in the image—in much the same way that a textual processing system would function—the algorithm is loaded with a set of known images and told "find images with a similar data composition to these based upon a set statistical probability there is a match".

With statistical and AI-based image recognition techniques, the identification element still resides in comparing a data artefact with others to identify similarity, using probabilistic methods to make an estimation of similarity and, within thresholds, report on a match. No inference is made by the algorithm concerning the *meaning* of the candidate image, just whether the image is a statistical relative of other images that have had similar techniques applied to them. However, this is an estimate based on similarity, of data in the files, not a similarity of the meaning of the image or a neural interpretation of what is represented in the image. To return to the scenario that forms the core of the discussion in this chapter, two indecent images may appear very different in their composition, and whereas we, as humans, will recognise both as indecent (within our own interpretation of what indecency is), algorithms are unable to make such an inference based on an assessment of the physical properties of an image alone. That is even before we have factored in the additional complexity of considering whether the image is that of a minor. Therefore, while such systems could be trained with a set of indecent images of children such that there might be a likelihood that statistically similar images will be found, this does not mean that such a system would be able to identify *all* indecent images of children, again, just those that have similarity to the training sets will be identified. For example, there is also a risk that indecent images of children might share characteristics with adult pornography, and there might be statistical or inferred matches with this type of content. And as we have demonstrated from the outset of this chapter, training data can have many biases.

Even the most advanced algorithms in this field have acceptance rates that would struggle to be termed reliable without some form in human intervention. Nudity and pornography detection are not significant parts of academic research in image recognition and precision evaluations are scant. In a blog post on Algorithmia[17] in 2016 an advanced "nudity detection" algorithm by the testers returned a maximum positive accuracy of 83.64% and maximum negative accuracy of 87%. Note furthermore that this is an algorithm that detects nudity, rather than indecency, which is similar in most of these studies. Which is unsurprising given the subjective nature of indecency and therefore the challenges for an algorithm to identify it.) Regardless, even in some of the most leading-edge nudity detection techniques, in over 1 in 10 cases, the algorithm would not be able to accurately detect whether an image contained naked skin, let alone whether the image was indecent or a scene of abuse. In order for such techniques to scale to meet the challenge of the identification of indecent images of minors, we require levels of accuracy much greater than many state of the art detection algorithms allow. A more recent study also showed approximately 90%[18] accuracy based upon a very small sample set and the identification of ten selected images (i.e. already classified). If Mr. Hunt's vision of mobile devices that automate the detection and prevention of transmission of sexually explicit images of minors is to come to fruition, getting it wrong in 1 in 10 cases is clearly not ideal and could be commercial suicide from any organisation placing that sort of accuracy of detection into a production environment.

However, with the growing discourse of how technology providers can do "can do really smart things" if they put their minds to it, there is little surprise that these approaches are starting to come to appear in the commercial marketplace. Though the literature does little to demonstrate the effectiveness of image recognition in open social contexts and broad recognition criteria, this does not stop either vendors or politicians from purporting these intelligent algorithms being the next big thing in online safeguarding. Vendor claims that a parent can know "whenever your child takes an indecent selfie" have created a marketplace for "safeguarding" software that aims to reassure parents that their children are prevented from engaging in the exchange of indecent, self-generated, images. While some send a suspect image sent from the child's phone to the parent's own device, others claim "advanced image recognition capabilities", and the ability to reliably identify everything from indecency to self-harm. Several of these products offer a range of functionalities, such as alerting the parent when such an image is generated, forwarding the image to the parent, or posting a warning on the child's phone about a suspect image. There are claims of high degrees of accuracy and very low false positives rates. However, with little scrutiny of these products and their purported functionality, or independent evaluation of their claims in research environments (for the reasons discussed above), we might remain cynical about the precision of these marketing claims.

Given the limitations to the accuracy of image recognition algorithms in published evaluations, we have further concerns about the rights of the child. Should we be happy, even with the rates of sensitivity and specificity maintained by more advanced nudity detection algorithms cited above, that over 1 in 10 children could be falsely implicated in the self-generation of nude images, and that the result of this false detection could be an alert to their parents? A false positive could result in intra-familial distress, conflict and the kinds of sanctions children so often report they fear, for example, a parent demanding access to examine the mobile device, or confiscating it. With software that simply forwards all images onto the parent's phone without the knowledge or consent of the child, this should be considered to be a severe challenge to the child's to privacy. Safeguarding should not replace children's rights, yet there is a view that it is a price worth paying if a child is kept "safe". Even though we struggle to appreciate what safe looks like, or even if these apps do actually safeguard. In a lot of cases of the application of these technologies in safeguarding contexts, a lot of the functionality offered seems to have more to do with control and discipline than safeguarding.

## 5 Image Recognition in a Law Enforcement Context

While we have, until now, used social scenarios to consider the efficacy of image recognition technologies for the processing of unknown indecent images of children (particularly within a self-generation context) we can also see similar techniques being applied in closed, law enforcement systems. There has certainly been significant coverage of the scale of tackling online child abuse images, with the Internet Watch Foundation stating they have identified over 100,000 instances of child abuse in 2018 (their most recently published annual report[19]). This differs as a scenario because, as discussed above, in law enforcement contexts, the image recognition is generally not used to analyse the generation of images in real time, but instead support the law enforcement processes around the triaging of indecent images of children and victim identification based upon previously analysed images.

Within law enforcement this growing reliance upon machine learning systems to tackle the proliferation of child abuse images online that is both worthy and concerning.[20] Such approaches still raise ethical concerns that seem to not meet any moral scrutiny. Given the volumes of imagery that exist online, and the tasks law enforcement face, there is of course a need to have tools to support the role of human analysts in categorising images, initiating take downs and taking out legal proceedings against hosts and identifying victims, or even the more fundamental issue of whether abuse is taking place and the image can be categorised as illegal. There is a need to recognise and categorise images that have not been classified before, and there is a great deal of interest in the use of machine learning approaches to achieve this. Recent announcements with public/private partnerships between law enforcement and commercial identification platforms[21] have shown that these systems can be a significant aid to the complex and challenging task of categorising images of child abuse—usually this approach is conducted by human analysts where, as one might imagine, there can be considerable impact on their mental health as a result of having to categorise and process these images. Therefore, there is clearly a lot of interest in the use of machine learning and training sets to allow an algorithm to do some of this triaging of images. And, as would be the case in any training data, the sets used need to represent the images being processed—therefore such an algorithm would require training data that comprised of previously categorised child abuse images. Through partnership with law enforcement, the training sets used for the image recognition algorithms can be larger and of greater diversity, and they would be protected in law with the use of these images in a way that a commercial company (for example, a mobile telephony provider) would not be able to achieve. In the example given with Griffeye/Taskforce Argos system used by Queensland Police, 300,000 images that had already been categorised by law enforcement professionals were used to train the software, which would, in all probability, improve image recognition capabilities and reduce the load of human analysts to triage images. However, in the rush to address this undoubtedly honourable intention, perhaps we are, again, raising significant ethical concerns which seem to have had no part in the evolution of these systems.

These algorithms work on images with no concern for the content of the image—as far as the algorithm is concerned this is simply a collection of data upon which it needs to apply its defined training or recognition functionality. However, in reality these are images of children being abused. If the image is a mere unit of analysis and the algorithm has no concept of memory, retention or recognition beyond that achieved at a statistical level, should there a consideration of the privacy of the victim in terms of where images are stored, by whom they are accessed, and what meta data exists that might relate to the victims identity? Given the victims in many images will be identified, do they grant consent for these images to be used in databases, or does ownership on the image reside with the law enforcement partner? While there is clearly a law enforcement need for the image, and it is quite rightly stored in an image database, might we be guilty of placing the need of the law enforcement function ahead of the victim in the image and the rights of the child? If the victim has been identified surely they have a right to be aware of where the image is stored and how it is being used?

While we are not aware of any ethical debates that have considered this specific issue in depth, this perhaps reflects the urgency of the situation and the lack of appreciation, at an ethical level, regarding the functionality of the technologies proposed. We might hypothesise that a law enforcement professional or a government minister would have little awareness of the nature of data processing taking place in the algorithm, or the need for significantly sensitive data in order to have it trained. However, we would suggest this is a question that needs to be asked around the rights of the victim when examined through machine based, rather than human, intervention? Does the victim have an equal right to privacy if the image is only analysed by an algorithm rather than a human? We would, surely expect as a minimum, that consent is sought by victims whose images of abuse are being used in these systems.

## 6 So, What Does Works?

We have, in this chapter so far, raised a number of concerns around the use of image recognition technologies for child protection. In the rush for technology companies to "do more" to control the manufacture and distribution of indecent images of minors, we might reflect on the overreliance on technology that has not been proven in the field, something that often befalls the software engineering world. And this should come as no surprise given the pressure that arises from governments needing to be seen to do something to tackle these issues, while perhaps not understanding the technical capabilities of what is called for (aside from claiming technology can do "really smart things").

The responsibility of the service providers to *do more* and to expect technological solutions to what are essentially technological facilitated social problems is rife in the online safeguarding space, and can frequently cause tension between the technology providers and the policy makers (as has been the case with the debate around the UK online harms white paper[22]—which focusses, in the main, on technological intervention to tackle all manner of weakly defined online harms, and the need for a regulator to make sure this happens). We are reminded of the *Politician's Fallacy*,[23] whereby people in public office are looked to to provide solutions to social problems beyond their grasp. Therefore, they fall back onto doing "something", regardless of whether or not that something will be effective. It is the need to be seen to do something, rather than the efficacy of that something, that is important.

Within this text, while argue strongly that technology is not *the* solution to the myriad of online safeguarding issues, even in a specific area such as image processing and recognition. Whoever, we are not saying that technology does not have a role to play, and there are examples of great successes that have arisen as a result of political pressure and applying technology in a way that is effective, because it uses established techniques and approaches that are well proven in terms of data processing.

The policy pressure that were the roots of this approach can be seen in a 2013 speech made by the then UK Prime Minister David Cameron.[24] On the outset of the speech, which is considered landmark in the online harms policy space, there is confusion regarding tackling what Mr. Cameron described as the two challenges in keeping children and young people safe online:

> Now, let me be clear, the 2 challenges are very distinct and very different. In one we're talking about illegal material, the other is legal material that is being viewed by those who are underage. But both the challenges have something in common; they're about how our collective lack of action on the internet has led to harmful and, in some cases, truly dreadful consequences for children.

Initially, Mr. Cameron distinguished between the illegal aspect of child sexual abuse material, and the legal but age inappropriate nature of pornography, but he also said that a lack of action "on the Internet" results in the same impacts on children and young people. While the impact of pornography, and access therein, falls outside of the scope of this analysis, it is addressed in more detail elsewhere.[25] Within the policy area the generalisation and scapegoating of *the Internet*, or *online technology* are both rife and unhelpful. The implication in the speech is that similar routes to tackling these problems are needed, and those routes are technical in nature—a typical example of Politician's Fallacy in action in the technology policy space.

Yet we would argue that the two are very different indeed. In one case, with access to child abuse and exploitation materials, the child is the subject of abuse and exploitation and, in general, the issue is preventing adult access to CSEM images and videos. While there are some concerns around young people accessing CSEM, particularly around peer images,[26] the majority of this material is produced, shared and downloaded by adults. The other issue is trying to prevent young people from accessing pornography. The child in this case is not the subject of abuse, but the citizen wishing to download the content (or, stumbling across it by accident). Prevention for these two scenarios seem to us to be very different tasks, which is why it is concerning that they are linked together in the original speech. We can see, very clearly, that such speeches have a policy impact, and drive industry change. Sometimes this is a good thing, but sometimes it is not. However, in the early roots of this policy, there were clear successes in pressuring industry to change when addressing access to child abuse and exploitation material.

The momentum of the policy pressure was reported to be significant. Mr. Cameron followed up on his initial speech with an "update", at WeProtect in December 2014.[27] In this update he claimed significant progress as a result of dialogue with major players in the technology industry:

> This landmark agreement we're signing amounts to nothing less than a global war against online child abuse. And this is a war we can only win if we fight it together. And we're fighting on 3 main fronts. First, blocking search results that lead to child abuse. Second, identifying the illegal images and taking them down. And third chasing down the perpetrators and enforcing the law....
>
> ...Until recently, it was incredibly easy for people to search the internet for child abuse and get results. And even sometimes have their search terms automatically completed for them. It was appalling. And yet, when we talked about changing it, a lot of people said, 'Can't be done. You can't police the internet. You can't infringe internet freedoms in any way.' But we said you can't have the freedom to search for vile material trumping a child's freedom to have an innocent childhood. So I made very clear the industry would have to find a way to block these search results and if they didn't then we would look at legislation.

A number of successes were drawn from this policy pressure on industry, and showed engagement from the tech industry in dealing with access to child abuse materials. Firstly, in terms of searching for this material and similar, the major search engine providers moved to block a number of search terms, and implement warnings on their search screens[28] if people searched for those terms. According to reporting, up to 100,000 search terms (this list of terms was not made public, but it was claimed they had been "drawn up by child protection experts") that have been used to categorise and index child abuse materials were included, and if an end user searches for these terms they would not yield any search results and would be presented, instead with a warning (or "splash") screen about the legality of trying to access these materials. Should a user try to click through to a site that is known to provide access to indecent images of children, again a splash screen will be used to remind them about the illegal nature of the material they are trying to reach and not provide access to the site.

A further UK Government update on Tackling Child Sexual Exploitation[29] showed further progress, stating that Google has reported an eight-fold decrease in searches of child abuse material on their search platform since the introduction of keyword blocks. The opacity of the search terms was not entirely surprising but does raise concerns. On the one hand, not sharing the list of search terms seems sensible. If people were aware of what terms were being blocked, they would start classifying their content using other terms. However, one issue we return to frequently in this analysis is the lack of transparency in the algorithms purporting to safeguard children online and, therefore, a lack of scrutiny regarding whether claimed functionalities are valid. If there is no way of knowing what these keywords are, or who has ownership over them, it is difficult to monitor feature creep or even authenticate the validity of the search terms.

However, clearly as a part of a larger approach to tackling illegal child abuse material online, these technical interventions were effective. Even with the control of searching for specified terms, we can see that this would be successful because it works with the strengths of data processing. It is very straightforward to a text processing algorithm to match given words against a "watchlist"—in this case the 100,000 search terms used to look for indecent images of children. And given the search engine (as is the case with this text processing) returns the search results, it is within its capability to flag up the legality of searching for these terms. It is straightforward and simple to do from an algorithmic perspective, albeit against a backdrop of significant capacity of search terms being processed at any given time.

In terms of the splash screens that would prevent access to sites that provide access to child abuse materials, again there are clear technical solutions to this approach and key factors in its success. The search engines were making use of the Internet Watch Foundation's *URL* and *hash lists*.

The Internet Watch Foundation (IWF) are a member organisation in the UK, funded by the technology sector, that has legislative powers to determine whether a web address (or Uniform Resource Locator—URL) provides access to child abuse materials. This determination is achieved either reactively as a result of a public report, or proactively (since 2014 when the UK government granted them additional legal powers[30]) searching websites to determine whether they contain this sort of material. If the organisation decides that the material the website provides meets the threshold to be considered CSEM under UK law (specifically therefore mentioned Protection of Children Act 1978, applied effectively in this case[31]) the URL will be added to the IWF list (or, if the web site is hosted in the UK, legal proceedings will be launched against them). Then technology providers who either provide Internet access, or services that might allow access to websites (for example, search engines), can make use of the URL list to block access to these sites It is a simple and effective service and the list is used extensively by internet service providers in the UK. With search engine providers making use of this list, they can very easily incept access to these sites and instead post up warning screens about the nature of the material the end user is trying to access.

The other main service the IWF provide is a *hash list*. We have already touched upon the concept of being able to define a fingerprint of any image (or video) based upon the data of which it comprises. The core principle, referred to as hashing,[32] is to apply a mathematical algorithm to the data in the image to create a unique identifying token (analogous to a fingerprint) such that any time the same process is applied to the same image or an exact copy comprising the same data (which is in essence what an image is—it is a set of data related to pixels of different colours in a grid based layout), the same fingerprint will be created.

In the case of the IWF, images have been identified as child abuse or exploitation material the image will be processed using Microsoft's PhotoDNA algorithms.[33] PhotoDNA differs from more traditional hashing algorithms because, Microsoft claim and have demonstrated, an image can be altered in some ways and the hash value will remain the same. One of the traditional problems with image hashes has been because it was applied on the data in the image (i.e. the image pixels, colour values, image size, etc.) the slightest change to the data (for example, resizing recolouring or cropping the image), the hash value would be different and therefore a match would not be made. PhotoDNA will still produce the same hash, even if the image is changed "a little" and is therefore more robust than most hashing approaches.

For the IWF hash list, once the image has been identified and hashed using the Microsoft service, the hash will be stored. Therefore, a service provider can make use of the hashlist to process images it is accessing. It can then run the same PhotoDNA algorithm on any images it indexes, and if the hash matches, the platform knows, because it is in the IWF hash list, which means its already been analysed by a human moderator and classified as illegal. Again, the "recognition" technology is very straightforward and easy to achieve—if the hash of the candidate image matches one in the hash list, it will be considered illegal and, at the least, blocked.

The IWF makes it very clear on their website that any URL in their list has already been through a judgement against transparent legislation:

> The URLs are assessed according to UK law, specifically the Protection of Children Act 1978, and in accordance with the UK Sentencing Guidelines Council. All URLs added to the list depict indecent images of children, advertisements for or links to such content. This content is likely to be an offence to download, distribute, or possess in the UK. This includes pay-to-view websites as well as sites where child sexual abuse images are swapped, traded or posted.

And similarly, their hashing service has a level of transparency, and can therefore be subject to some scrutiny:

> We turn child sexual abuse images into unique codes (hashes) – think of it as a digital fingerprint. We do this using Microsoft PhotoDNA. With our list, you'll be able to automatically match known images before they appear on your services. You'll also be able to remove illegal images already on your services. You'll receive an updated list every day.

The approach had a very clear technical and legal requirement—to tackle illegal child abuse and exploitation material online. The boundaries of the requirements are defined in law, and as such eliminated ambiguity in the system. Furthermore, by using the IWF URL list, it is a relatively simple (in technical terms) operation to prevent any website on that list appearing in search results.

In all of these elements, there are some key features:

- Clearly defined boundaries defined in legislation and with human analyst intervention (illegal content)
- Unambiguous and effective data processing (does one URL or hash match another?)
- Unambiguous and effective keyword or hash matching.

These approaches work because they are making use of digital technology in ways it is most effective. The IT can work independently and objectively without any need for subjective judgement or outlying interpretation, or probabilistic matching to training data.

However, even within this success we must acknowledge this is not a complete solution. This will only prevent access to child abuse material via search engines and, as reported upon by the IWF itself, the volume of child abuse images accessed via search engines[34] is not large compared to other sources such as image lockers or direct website access. However, there are clear successes to this strategy and we can see a technical solution that has worked in certain scenarios.

We can also see these fingerprinting approaches being extended elsewhere and providing opportunity for service providers to be more proactive in image take downs if they have been identified as illegal. And good example of this can be seen in case legal challenge to Facebook that was settled in 2018.[35] In this case a Belfast teenager took out litigation against Facebook as a result of repeated sharing of indecent images of her, as a 14 year old, on a *shame* page on the platform. While she had repeatedly had these images reported and taken down, the images were reposted several times. Her view was that Facebook's failure to prevent these images being reposted was a misuse of information pertaining to herself, and therefore negligence. While Facebook had resisted the claim, it was eventually admitted as a class action and ended as an out of court settlement.

This case is significant because the logic behind the litigation was sound—if a platform provider has seen a reported image and made a judgement to take down that image because it breaches community standards, presented copyright issues with which the provider not wish to become embroiled or that the image was clearly illegal (as would be the case with an indecent image of a 14 year old) then the use of hashing technology would easily be able to "fingerprint" that image and check any subsequent uploading of images against an internal hashlist if an attempt is made to post it again. Therefore, it could be quite rightly argued once a user has taken the time to report an image and the platform moderators have agreed that the image should be taken down, it is perfectly possible to hash this image and intercept any further attempts to post. Failure to do this, as the litigation argued, would be negligent and an abuse of an individual's personal data. It is interesting to note that while the settlement of the case is private, Facebook has announced a similar approach to tackling revenge pornography posts[36] since the case, although this service was not rolled out across the platform.

## 7 A Need for Greater Understanding and Evaluation

We can see, with this analysis of image recognition in the control of indecent images of children, that there has been a rush to make use of complex approaches that are perhaps still too untested to make effective application in this most sensitive of areas. Policy pressure and poor understanding of the capabilities of recognition approaches, coupled with financial opportunities for vendors, means we are currently in a place where image recognition overpromises and underdelivers. While there are some very successful applications of machine learning based image recognition, such as their application to tumour diagnosis in biomedical systems.[37] This is to be expected if we consider the closed nature of such systems—there is a ready supply of already categorises images that can be used anonymously to build large, robust and unbiased training data, and limited variability in the new images captured to be processed against the machine learning algorithm (i.e. the images capture will be taken with standardised equipment in a medical environment). However, with appreciation of the capabilities, and challenges, in image recognition, we can conclude that to automate the identification of indecent images of minors, either for self-generation or in law enforcement contexts, the challenge is far greater given the diverse nature of the images and the lack of precision in their classification. By contrast with a tumour diagnosis system, one indecent image of a minor may differ, structurally, a great deal from another. Therefore, attempted to build a training set of "typical" images is problematic and, as we have discussed, illegal in most instances. A candidate image may similarly be very different from those in a training set and therefore the chance of a match is very small. With algorithms still struggling to identify images with nudity, let alone nudity within the context of a minor, with the added complication of whether the image is indecent, we would hope that vendors might be responsible in stating the technology is not sufficiently mature, and arguably requires completely different recognition techniques, in order to be successful.

There is a growing need for scrutiny in these algorithms, and there seems to be little evidence of this outside of the academic world. We are placing the ethics of safeguarding into the hands of vendors. One of the key issues with these approaches is the lack of independent evaluation of algorithms or their claimed functionality and functional decomposition—in essence there is a lot of money being invested in these areas, and market share to be gained. Therefore, there is a great deal of commercial sensitivity among service providers. However, with a lack of transparency and shared IP in this area, arguably progress will be hampered and a lack of accountability will result in the potential for algorithm providers claiming functionality that are perhaps not as effective in reality.

Nevertheless, there is clear evidence to suggest that, some approaches that are less exotic are more successful when applied to processing of indecent images of children. By making use of the strengths of computer systems (pattern matching, data processing, repetitive tasks) in tandem with the more subjective needs better served my human moderators (for the classification of images and the detailing of search terms) we can make steps forward in policing indecent images of children online. And they can deliver results while being cognisant of the rights of children, and do not throw up the complex ethical dilemmas unexplored in this very new area of policing.

**Notes**

1. National Crime Agency (2018). "National Strategic Assessment of Serious and Organisation Crime 2018". https://www.nationalcrimeagency.gov.uk/who-we-are/publications/173-national-strategic-assessment-of-serious-and-organised-crime-2018/file.
2. Internet Watch Foundation (2020). "The dark side of the selfie: IWF partners with the Marie Collins Foundation in new campaign to call on young men to report self-generated sexual images of under 18s". https://www.iwf.org.uk/news/dark-side-of-selfie-iwf-partners-marie-collins-foundation-new-campaign-to-call-on-young-men-to.
3. Pesapane, F., Codari, M., & Sardanelli, F. (2018). "Artificial intelligence in medical imaging: threat or opportunity? Radiologists again at the forefront of innovation in medicine". *European radiology experimental*, *2*(1), 35.
4. Xin, Y., Kong, L., Liu, Z., Chen, Y., Li, Y., Zhu, H., ... & Wang, C. (2018). Machine learning and deep learning methods for cybersecurity. *IEEE Access*, *6*, 35365-35381.
5. Branwen, G. (2019). "The Neural Net Tank Urban Legend". https://www.gwern.net/Tanks.
6. ITV News (2019). "Norfolk Police Chief Constable welcomes new tech in fight against child abuse". https://www.itv.com/news/anglia/2019-07-12/norfolk-police-chief-constable-welcomes-new-tech-in-fight-against-child-abuse/.
7. Internet Watch Foundation. "Emerging Patterns and Trends Report #1Online-Produced Sexual Content". https://www.iwf.org.uk/sites/default/files/inline-files/Online-produced_sexual_content_report_100315.pdf.
8. https://www.parliament.uk/business/committees/committees-a-z/commons-select/health-committee/news-parliament-20151/suicide-prevention-inquiry-launch-16-17/.
9. House of Commons Health Select Committee (2016). "Oral evidence: Suicide prevention, HC 300"http://data.parliament.uk/writtenevidence/committeeevidence.svc/evidencedocument/health-committee/suicide-prevention/oral/44159.html.
10. Phippen and Bond (2020). "Fare Thee Well Age Verification, You Will Not Be Missed". Entertainment Law Review 31(2).
11. UK Government (2008). "Criminal Justice and Immigration Act 2008 Part 5". https://www.legislation.gov.uk/ukpga/2008/4/part/5.
12. Uk Government (2017). "Digital Economy Act 2017, Part 3". http://www.legislation.gov.uk/ukpga/2017/30/part/3/enacted.
13. Sentencing Council (2014). "Possession of indecent photograph of child/Indecent photographs of children". https://www.sentencingcouncil.org.uk/offences/magistrates-court/item/possession-of-indecent-photograph-of-child/.

14. UK Government (1978). "Protection of Children Act 1978". http://www.legislation.gov.uk/ukpga/1978/37.
15. Ibid.
16. Bursztein, E., Bright, T., Clarke, E., DeLaune, M., Eliff, D.M., Hsu, N., Olson, L., Shehan, J., Thakur, M. and Thomas, K. (2019). "Rethinking the detection of child sexual abuse imagery on the Internet". https://storage.googleapis.com/pub-tools-public-publication-data/pdf/04788940adb8e0a244a762a90f19c7a94e101b06.pdf.
17. Algorithmia (2016). "Improving Nudity Detection and NSFW Image Recognition". http://blog.algorithmia.com/improving-nudity-detection-nsfw-image-recognition/.
18. Garcia, M. B., Revano, T. F., Habal, B. G. M., Contreras, J. O., & Enriquez, J. B. R. (2018, November). "A pornographic image and video filtering application using optimized nudity recognition and detection algorithm". In *2018 IEEE 10th International Conference on Humanoid, Nanotechnology, Information Technology, Communication and Control, Environment and Management (HNICEM)* (pp. 1–5). IEEE.
19. Internet Watch Foundation (2019). "Internet Watch Foundation Annual Report 2018". https://www.iwf.org.uk/sites/default/files/reports/2019-04/Once%20upon%20a%20year%20-%20IWF%20Annual%20Report%202018.pdf.
20. Bursztein, E., Bright, T., Clarke, E., DeLaune, M., Eliff, D.M., Hsu, N., Olson, L., Shehan, J., Thakur, M. and Thomas, K. (2019). "Rethinking the detection of child sexual abuse imagery on the Internet". https://storage.googleapis.com/pub-tools-public-publication-data/pdf/04788940adb8e0a244a762a90f19c7a94e101b06.pdf.
21. Griffeye (n.d.). "The New Griffeye AI Technology—Trained at Taskforce Argos". https://www.griffeye.com/the-griffeye-ai-technology-trained-at-taskforce-argos/.
22. Martineua, P (2019). "The UK's Tech Backlash Could Change the Internet". https://www.wired.com/story/uk-tech-backlash-could-change-internet/.
23. Chen (2007). "The politician's fallacy and the politician's apology". https://devblogs.microsoft.com/oldnewthing/20070226-01/?p=27853.
24. https://www.gov.uk/government/speeches/the-internet-and-pornography-prime-minister-calls-for-action.
25. Phippen (2016). "Age Verification and Online Pornography—An Effective Safeguarding Approach?" Entertainment Law Review, 2016 (5).
26. Phippen, Bond and Tyrrell (2018). "Peer on Peer Abuse—A national survey of Headteachers and Safeguarding Leads in England and Scotland". https://www.mariecollinsfoundation.org.uk/assets/news_entry_featured_image/MCF-Peer-on-peer-Abuse-Research-Report-Sunday-final-version.pdf.
27. https://www.gov.uk/government/speeches/weprotect-children-online-global-summit-prime-ministers-speech.
28. BBC News (2013). "Google and Microsoft agree steps to block abuse images". https://www.bbc.co.uk/news/uk-24980765.

29. UK Government (2017). "Tackling Child Sexual Exploitation Progress Report". https://assets.publishing.service.gov.uk/government/uploads/system/uploads/attachment_data/file/592588/Tackling_Child_Sexual_Exploitation_-_Progress_Report__web_.pdf.
30. Ross, T (2013). "Internet Watch Foundation given powers to police child porn". https://www.telegraph.co.uk/news/politics/10127862/Internet-Watch-Foundation-given-powers-to-police-child-porn.html.
31. UK Government (1978). "Protection of Children Act 1978". http://www.legislation.gov.uk/ukpga/1978/37/body/1991-02-01?timeline=true.
32. Venkatesan, R., Koon, S. M., Jakubowski, M. H., & Moulin, P. (2000). Robust image hashing. In Proceedings 2000 International Conference on Image Processing (Cat. No. 00CH37101) (Vol. 3, pp. 664-666). IEEE.
33. https://news.microsoft.com/2009/12/15/new-technology-fights-child-porn-by-tracking-its-photodna/#sm.0001mpmupctevct7pjn11vtwrw6xj.
34. Internet Watch Foundation (2015). "Emerging Patterns and Trends Report #1 Online-Produced Sexual Content". https://www.iwf.org.uk/sites/default/files/inline-files/Online-produced_sexual_content_report_100315.pdf.
35. Irwin, A. (2018). "Girl (14) settles landmark action against Facebook over naked images". https://www.irishtimes.com/news/crime-and-law/courts/high-court/girl-14-settles-landmark-action-against-facebook-over-naked-images-1.3349974.
36. Davis, A. (2018) The Facts: Non-Consensual Intimate Image Pilot". https://newsroom.fb.com/news/h/non-consensual-intimate-image-pilot-the-facts/.
37. Komura, D., & Ishikawa, S. (2018). Machine learning methods for histopathological image analysis. *Computational and structural biotechnology journal*, *16*, 34–42.

# Predictive Policing in 2025: A Scenario

**Kevin Macnish, David Wright, and Tilimbe Jiya**

**Abstract** Law enforcement authorities (LEAs) have begun using artificial intelligence and predictive policing applications that are likely to raise ethical, data protection, social, political and economic issues. This paper describes application of a new scenario methodology for identifying issues that emerging technologies are likely to raise in a future six or seven years hence, but that deserve policymakers' attention now. It often takes policymakers that long to develop a new policy, consult with stakeholders and implement the policy. Thus, policymakers need a structured, but concise framework in order to understand the issues and their various implications. At the same time, they also prefer policies that have stakeholder support. These considerations led the University of Twente in the Netherlands and the UK's Trilateral Research to develop the scenario that follows. It is structured with several headings that policymakers need to consider in order to move toward a desired future and avoidance of an undesired future.

**Keywords** Predictive analysis · Policing · Law enforcement authorities · SHERPA project · Predictive policing

---

The original version of this chapter was revised: This chapter has been changed to open access under a CC BY 4.0 license. The correction to this chapter is available at https://doi.org/10.1007/978-3-030-50613-1_13

---

K. Macnish
Department of Philosophy, University of Twente, Enschede, The Netherlands

D. Wright (✉)
Trilateral Research, One Knightsbridge Green, London SW1X 7QA, UK
e-mail: david.wright@trilateralresearch.com

T. Jiya
Business Systems and Operations, University of Northampton, Northampton, UK

 
H. Jahankhani et al. (eds.), *Policing in the Era of AI and Smart Societies*,
Advanced Sciences and Technologies for Security Applications,
https://doi.org/10.1007/978-3-030-50613-1_9

## 1 Introduction

Law enforcement authorities (LEAs) have begun using artificial intelligence and predictive policing applications that are likely to raise ethical, data protection, social, political and economic issues. What issues should policymakers be considering now in relation to such emerging technologies in order to be prepared for a future six or seven years hence, which can be assumed the time policymakers need to develop a policy addressing those issues (or, at least, some of them), to build support for it and to get their political masters to sponsor relevant legislation or regulation? That question impelled the development of the scenario detailed in the following pages.

The University of Twente in the Netherlands and the UK's Trilateral Research led the development of the scenario, which kicked off with a brainstorming workshop of 23 invited stakeholders. The partners drafted a scenario based on that brainstorming session, which they then sent to the workshop participants for comments. With those comments, the partners created a second iteration of the scenario, which they then sent to the SHERPA project[1] stakeholder board (27 experts) for their comments, whose comments, in turn, led to the third iteration of the scenario. The partners then invited the project's contact list of more than 1,000 people to comment on the scenario. The partners then posted the scenario on the project's website and invited visitors to comment on the scenario. In due course, the SHERPA project co-ordinator submitted the scenario to the European Commission. Hence, the scenario was not simply a mechanism to provide structured advice to policymakers, but also a process for engaging increasing numbers of stakeholders, a process intended to lend credibility and legitimacy to the scenario and in particular to its recommendations.

There were several good reasons for involving as many stakeholders as possible in the scenario construction process, which included the following. The involvement of stakeholders facilitated a participatory, deliberative approach to policy-making. It was also important because it helped to uncover issues that might otherwise be overlooked. Further, the involvement of various stakeholders was ideal for exploring possible consequences of current trends in smart information systems (the combination of AI and Big Data), considering desired and undesired futures as a result of such a combination. Furthermore, the stakeholder involvement helped decision-makers in the decision-making process aimed at determining what steps should be taken to reach the desired future and avoid an undesired future.

The partners aimed to develop a plausible scenario six or seven years from the initial brainstorming workshop (held in late 2018) to provide an early warning about how the use of AI and big data is likely to develop and inform policy [12]. The agreed timeframe was seven years up to 2025, as it was sufficiently distant to merit some speculation, but not so distant that the project could indulge in science fiction. The wish was to create a *plausible* scenario that reflected the emergence of advanced technologies yet was sufficiently grounded that it could be justifiably used to tease out the ethical and human rights issues for policymakers and other stakeholders.

[1] See the last section of this chapter for more information about SHERPA, a 42-month, EU-funded project that began in May 2018.

The brainstorming session followed a structured agenda which is reflected in the section headings in the scenario below. The partners structured the scenario to be of optimum use to policymakers, and it addresses the questions policymakers would be expected to ask or be asked by their constituents. The authors describe the scenario as a "policy scenario" because it has been developed for policymakers and addresses the issues they would need to address before submitting a policy proposal to their government ministers. The policy scenario methodology has been described elsewhere.[2]

## 2 The Scenario

In 2025, many police forces across Europe are adopting predictive policing technologies in response to cuts in human resource budgets. Such cuts inevitably led to a rise in crime rates. Many LEAs began experimenting with different predictive policing technologies as a way of cutting crime before it happens. After some false starts, such technologies have evolved as remarkably as facial recognition technologies. Smart information systems, notably artificial intelligence (AI) algorithms, are within the reach of all European LEAs, who now can feed such systems with the vast swathes of data to which they have access. In a manner that is both intelligent and provides useful information in real-time, law enforcement authorities (LEAs) have been experimenting with different applications. Some of these have been developed in-house by the national forces, some have been developed through the European Commission's Horizon Europe research programme, but many are the result of collaborations with private sector players. In some cases, these private initiatives include or result in proprietary data of benefit to the private sector partners.

As one would expect, some approaches and technologies for predictive policing have proven to be better than others. The intelligence-led policing approaches trialled by Pol-Intel in Denmark [1] have served as models of police access to and use of many disparate data sets. The more ambitious applications go beyond accessing data to using those data to make predictions regarding incidents of future crime. Most predictive policing applications have drawn on location-based data to define increasingly localised "hot spots" on which the police should focus attention at particular times, while others draw on personal data to identify likely offenders [6]. Other applications aim to predict likely victims of crime in cases such as domestic violence, or those at risk of becoming offenders in the future. Still other predictive policing applications have turned their attention from visible street crime to the less visible white-collar crimes, including money-laundering, tax evasion, fraud and cybercrime. Some researchers are using these technologies to draw together demographic, census and other social data to determine what factors are most likely to induce someone to

[2]Wright, David, Bernd Stahl and Tally Hatzakis, "Policy scenarios as an instrument for policymakers", *Technological Forecasting & Social Change*, Vol. 154, May 2020. https://www.sciencedirect.com/journal/technological-forecasting-and-social-change/vol/154/suppl/C.

commit a crime. The answers to such questions are expected to make possible early, large-scale interventions where communities and individuals are at risk.

Predictive policing applications must have measurable success factors. Typically, this is a matter of rising or falling reports of crime, but this is an unstable metric. At its heart is a mere correlation and does not prove a causal link between the application and the number of reports. Hence, a decline in reported crime might have come about through using the application, but it might equally be a result of demographic changes. It is possible that reliance on the application has reduced the efficacy of police responses such that many no longer bother reporting crimes as they know that they won't be acted upon. Equally, some applications have been reported as helping the police determine which crimes are worth a response. In some areas, thanks to local press reporting, it is widely known that burglaries will usually not merit a response, and so actual burglaries have increased in number while the number of reports of burglary has declined. On the other hand, the applications may be so successful that police are effectively anticipating crimes and arriving in time to deter the potential criminal from carrying through with their plans. This is plausible given efforts to streamline the online reporting process, itself aided by data analytics and AI, allowing for a smooth and fast process for victims or others to report crimes.

While some of the public feared a move to "Minority Report" policing, in which a computer informs police who is about to commit a crime and then that person is arrested moments before the act, this has not happened [11]. Indeed, the police are adamant that any computer prediction regarding likely crime hot spots or offenders are fed as information to a team of analysts who then combine that with other information before advising patrols. This prevents policing by algorithm from becoming the norm. However, cuts in police funding have reduced the number of available analysts, and the remaining analysts have been noticing that the number of false positives (indications that a crime will occur in an area where no crime takes place) is falling with each year, and worry for the future of their jobs. In 2020, for example, there was only one information analyst working for the whole of the LA Police Department.

Furthermore, budget cuts have pushed many officers with good local knowledge into early retirement. New officers, lacking this knowledge, have come to rely upon the predictive policing system. This has led to fears of automation bias in which officers trust the system despite evidence to the contrary [3, 10], and despite the training, introduced in 2020, to rectify this [4]. Nonetheless, there remains a tension as to how best to act when the system recommends one course of action and the officer disagrees with this recommendation, leading to some complaining that they are being treated like robots.

International comparisons do not end with the numbers of analysts. Many cities in the United States have been aggressive in pursuing predictive policing, particularly after funding to this end was increased shortly after the US 2020 presidential election. Incarcerations have increased, but there is no sign of a change in the demographic composition of the prison population, which is overwhelmingly African-American. China has also been aggressive in developing predictive technologies following the widespread integration of the Social Credit System which incorporates all data on a person, including bank records, medical records and educational attainments [2]. Facial recognition on CCTV is now standard in most Chinese cities, although there is insufficient recognition by the Chinese authorities of the problem of false positives. The general approach is one of "better safe than sorry", leading again to a suspected (albeit unreported) rise in the prison population. Owing to Chinese information-sharing protocols, it is also not certain what the ethnic composition of that population looks like, but there are reports that some communities such as the Uighurs have been all but decimated in recent years as they are arrested on the basis of a likelihood of committing a crime [7]. Finally, efforts at introducing predictive policing in some South American cities, such as Bogota in Colombia, have exacerbated perceived biases as the focus remains on preventing crimes against the wealthy, while police ignore victims from less affluent areas.

Europe has been slower than China and the US in adopting predictive policing technologies, partly owing to the human rights frameworks such as the European Charter for Fundamental Rights and the European Convention on Human Rights, both of which are backed up by laws such as the General Data Protection Regulation, which is seen as an effective means of regulating the use of personal data across society. This regulatory framework has combined with the Horizon Europe research programme, begun in 2020, which continued to focus funding on counter-terrorism efforts, which in turn skewed investment in policing and predictive analytics towards identifying factors in radicalisation and away from more common crimes and even farther away from white-collar crime.

While there has been investment in police use of these technologies, criminals have not been idle. LEA cyber detectives have uncovered applications used by criminal gangs to predict where the police will be at any time of the day or night, often drawing on the same data sets used by the police, made public in the name of transparency and democratic accountability. Others have been found on the dark net offering significant sums to hackers who can reverse-engineer police systems to indicate which parameters are used to predict crimes in order that they can better avoid detection.

The police find themselves caught between a rock and a hard place. The press is critical of any reports of rising crime and cynical of reports to the contrary. The police do not need to be reminded of their duty to do all that is reasonable to prevent crime, but the debate within society as to what is reasonable, including which databases can be routinely accessed, rages on with opinion polls reflecting little more than responses to the latest scandal.

With such a postulated sequence of events on the social and ethical implications of using AI and Big Data in predictive policing, a number of drivers and inhibitors have been identified. These are illustrated in Fig. 1 and explained further in later sections.

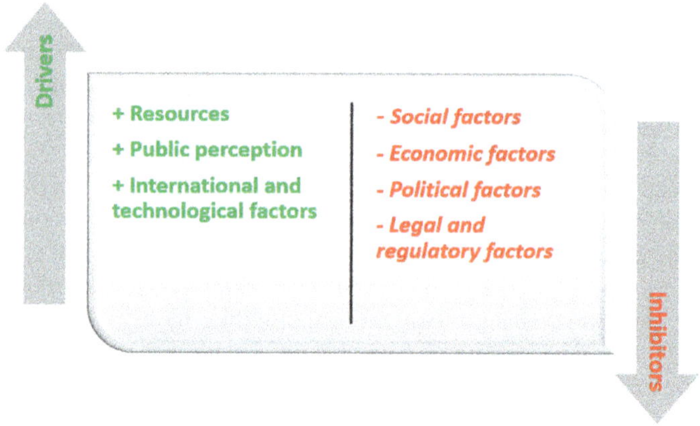


**Fig. 1** Drivers and inhibitors of predictive policing in 2025

## 3 Drivers to 2025

Various drivers have impelled the development of technologies used in predictive policing in 2025, as depicted in Fig. 1 and discussed below.

### *3.1 Resources*

Ever tighter squeezes on funding have led to a decline in the number of officers over the past decade while investment in technology has increased. AI is often treated by politicians as a panacea to limited public funds. There is some dissension in the ranks, as many officers can see that while the police budgets are shrinking, the technology firms developing AI applications seem to be thriving. If police budgets for human resources have been declining, the quantity and quality of data processed by the police have not. In fact, there is now so much data available from so many different sources that the police would be overwhelmed were it not for artificial intelligence.

### *3.2 Public Perception*

Given the increased data available, there is a concern that the police miss intervening in cases where they had the relevant information in advance but did not process it in time. This is widely seen as a dereliction of duty and one that no Chief Constable wants to see on her watch. The public view of the police is ambiguous at best, and there is a high level of expectation on the police and their use of technology. After all, if a member of the public can prove that her stolen phone is in her neighbour's house through using tracking apps like Prey, she wonders what there is to stop the police from entering the home and retrieving the phone? Her reasoning leads her to conclude that the police are either unwilling to help her or that they are hopelessly out of date.

### *3.3 International and Technological Factors*

As noted above, Europe has been less aggressive in employing predictive technologies than other countries, notably the US and China, which have considerable resources and public support to invest in these technologies. Many European data scientists have already migrated to one of these countries to work on systems that European politicians see as being "too weak" to implement. These data scientists opine that we must follow where technology leads and if it can help capture bad guys, then you should use it. This divestment of talent, coupled with the mixed results of the Horizon Europe research projects, has led some European police forces to buy technologies from US and Chinese companies, although they are uncomfortable with the fact that these were likely developed in a manner not consistent with European law. Furthermore, there is the ever-present fear that US or Chinese intelligence agencies will infiltrate these systems through backdoors to spy on their European counterparts.

## 4 Inhibitors to 2025

While there have been several drivers pushing the development of predictive policing technologies towards their current state in 2025, this development has not always been straightforward. There have been barriers that impede progress. These are discussed below.

### *4.1 Social Factors*

Media coverage of increasing use of technology has rarely been positive and, while the intended target was often politicians, it was the police who suffered from adverse coverage. In particular, the press noted the lack of change in the demographics of those arrested and imprisoned. While some have argued that a turn to computerisation in detecting and predicting crime would lead to reduced discrimination, this appears not to have been the case. Instead, data sets have been drawn from non-European countries to ascertain norms, and parameters have been developed by computer scientists unaware of European police priorities. At least one tool was developed in China using a Chinese data set and drawing on factors that were culturally predictive in

China but not Europe. This led to a significant rise in immigrant arrests for the trial period when the application was first tested.

Even where the predictive capacities of the applications have been more effective, these were met by the equal capacities of criminals who were able to emulate the predictive tools and hack into them directly. This has become part of the continuing escalation of methods used by the police and criminals to stay one step ahead of each other. Most applications are in a constant phase of beta-testing as by the time they are sufficiently stable to be rolled out on a wide basis their method has been cracked and they are no longer as effective.

There has also been some marked resistance to change from within the police forces themselves. This has largely been resolved through generational change as the post-millennial generation who grew up on smart phones has come of age and started to enter the workplace, but some resistance remains.

## 4.2 Economic Factors

Resources have been a driving factor in the development of predictive applications but, paradoxically, they have also held back some aspects of development. There has been a chronic shortage of computer scientists developing tools, and a shortage of analysts with the abilities to effectively use those tools. This is largely due to the inability of the public services to compete with private organisations, especially those working in similar areas of technology in other countries. Limited funding has also led to datasets and tools being less reliable than would be ideal, with the result that their accuracy and efficiency sometimes leaves a lot to be desired. Despite this, for some, an 80% conviction rate is good enough, and many are becoming increasingly over-reliant on the systems that have led to a positive (although not a virtuous) feedback loop.

## 4.3 Political Factors

The lack of funding is due to continued attempts to rein in public spending in the post-2008 world. Some politicians worry about the press drubbing them and the police for arresting people for crimes they haven't committed yet. Some sceptics have criticised the lack of effective and convincing metrics demonstrating the success of the technologies.

### 4.4 *Legal and Regulatory Factors*

To ensure accountability in the police use of data analytics and their databases, Parliament adopted laws and regulations that, among other things, made explainability the default mode for algorithms. Politicians had to balance concerns about individual privacy and data protection with the efficacy of police operations. The police were concerned that excessive transparency would give criminals better insight into police methods and, as it turned out, their concerns were justified. Consequently, a committee of the European Parliament has been investigating and debating whether algorithms developed for or used by LEAs should be compelled to have the same standards as others if organised crime benefits from the tiniest scrap of information.

One solution to the stricter regulations imposed by Brussels and national governments on artificial intelligence has been the outsourcing of some technologies to private companies. Google and Facebook have extensive databases of their users and have on occasion helped the police in exchange for access to police databases. Without such incentives, these companies only complied with the minimum requirements of the law, to the chagrin of many LEAs who believed these companies should be doing more to help them in the fight against organised crime. The press saw this outsourcing as having the effect of blurring the borders between policing and the corporate world even more than was already the case in the early 21st century.

## 5 Postulated Impacts of Predictive Policing Technologies

In 2025, the benefits of predictive policing technologies are starting to be felt, even though there is still considerable public discussion as to whether the benefits are strictly attributable to the technologies or other factors. Nonetheless, their use has been part of a marked shift in society and the number of impacts are noted as depicted in Fig. 2.

### 5.1 *Ethical Impacts*

Older police officers resent the tighter constraints on their actions compared to when they started their careers. They feel the so-called "smart" information systems that tell them where to go and what to do, are undermining their own skills, experience and talents in responding to crime. Older policemen don't seem to recognise how organised crime has shifted away from street crime to more high-value crime in money-laundering and cybercrime. At the same time, there is clearly greater accountability and transparency in policing as bodycams record every move of every officer and individual officers are frequently held to account over why they did or did not intervene in a particular situation.

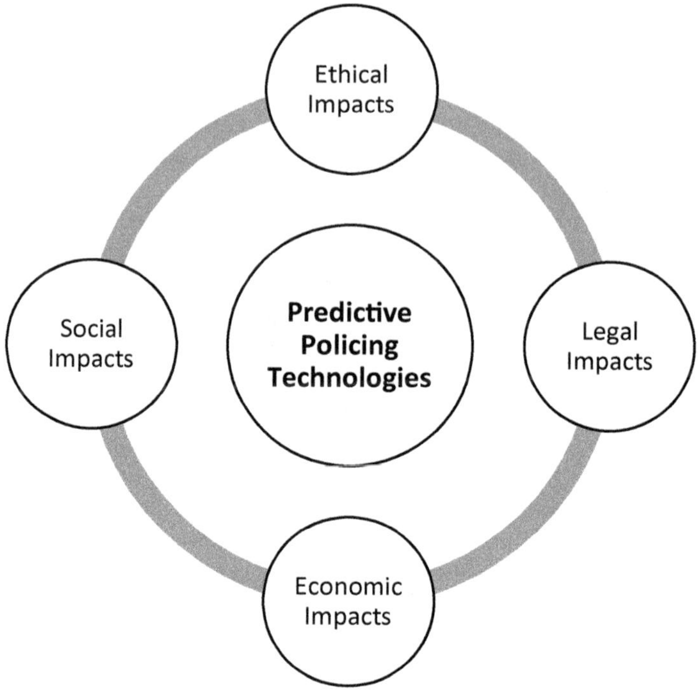


**Fig. 2** Postulated impacts of predictive policing in 2025

Civil society organisations protest that predictive policing technologies are an affront to Europeans' fundamental rights. There is much debate within police ranks and others about whether, when a police officer responds to an algorithm that has 80% predictive capabilities, she is infringing on a person's civil rights by treating him as a suspect on the basis of a statistical calculation rather than his doing anything to warrant suspicion. At the same time, if she fails to act on the prediction, is she thereby failing to uphold the civil rights of potential victims? This debate is ongoing.

More positively, prior to the implementation of predictive technologies, individuals were already being stopped and searched, and arrested, sometimes for spurious reasons. The aforementioned increase in accountability has shed light on discriminatory stop-and-search practices. Overall, predictive policing technologies have reduced some discriminatory practices and embedded others.

The public discussion that accompanied the widespread introduction of these technologies helped ensure that the explainability regulations in Europe were fair, ethical and sensitive to privacy concerns. Public pressures led to the establishment of an independent oversight body to monitor police use of smart information systems.

While media attention has largely focused on the police use of predictive applications, some has focused on corporate responsibility. Since social media giants collect reams of data, they are frequently able to identify child sex offenders or people involved in domestic abuse. However, this information is rarely turned over to the police. Questions are being asked in national legislatures about the social responsibility of these organisations.

## 5.2 Legal Impacts

A key problem with the development of legal and regulatory frameworks in keeping up with technological development is that policy and lawmakers often do not understand the technologies. Technological development is happening faster than the passage of laws and has been impeded by the time lawmakers need to understand recent developments and the subsequent legislative process. The GDPR, which came into effect in 2018, remains generally fit for purpose regarding personal data, but with the aggregation of databases it is increasingly rare to find data that cannot in some context or manner be used to identify a living person. The most applicable legislation for LEAs remains the Police Directive, which has meant that LEAs did not need to seek informed consent when they were investigating persons of interest. With so many AI-powered applications available online, prohibitions against automated decision-making affecting the rights of data subjects have become impossible to enforce except in a few high-profile cases like those against Google and Facebook in 2020–21. That so many enterprises see that it is impossible to enforce some provisions of the GDPR has had the predictable consequence of diminishing respect for the law even from law-abiding companies and citizens.

## 5.3 Social Impacts

Criminals seek advantage over LEAs by taking advantage of new technologies before the police are able to put counter-measures in place. The nature of crime is changing. There is a shifting focus from street crime, which is particularly subject to some of the blunter forms of predictive policing technology, to organised crime and white-collar crimes, including money-laundering, fraud, online scams and hacking.

While organised crime gangs are aware of predictive policing technologies, the public generally has a low understanding of such technologies and their possible negative impacts. The public is bombarded with so much information (and disinformation) about new technologies that it has become jaded. The powers of new technologies have ceased to spark wonder. The majority of the public accept these measures as just part of the cost of living. The public has already learned to cope with substantial levels of surveillance in society—on the streets and in cyberspace. Some people claim that they have altered their behaviour, to appear as conformist as possible, as these days they do not know what will land them in some police database. “Better to play it safe,” they think.

### 5.4 Economic Impacts

We have already noted the savage cuts in police budgets. Also of note is the shift in budgetary priorities from police officers to more data analysts. As the number of officers falls, so the reliance on AI grows, and as the reliance on AI grows, so the same work (or at least similar) is apparently achieved with fewer officers, and funding declines further. One solution has been to outsource certain tasks, such as facial recognition, to the private sector, as the US has done for several years.

## 6 Mitigating the Negative and Accentuating the Positive Influences of These Technologies

For some people, predictive policing was an easy sell. While civil liberty organisations still complain about the bias in algorithms, the public is wary—neither trusting, nor distrusting, but conscious that crime rose several years in a row with cutbacks on police officers. Predictive policing was touted as the artificial intelligence that was going to make huge cuts in crime—which has not happened as organised crime gangs have upped their game too.

Politicians, recognising the need to boost their trust with the public, agreed to adopt a new regulation making algorithms explainable to the public. Each algorithm was to include code saying who created the algorithm, who paid for it, its purpose, website and contact for more information. This dispelled concerns about the police wanting to keep their black boxes black, as it were, but led criminals to a better understanding of police methods and tactics and a spate of hacking attacks on police systems. Meanwhile, some "grey hat" hackers attempted to improve the algorithms to help eliminate bias.

A significant factor in gaining public acceptance was the establishment of trusted independent national bodies to oversee police use of algorithms in predictive technologies. Adequately funded, and staffed with known and respected figures such as Baroness Lawrence in the UK, these independent bodies helped to build trust in the police system. These bodies looked at not only the algorithms themselves but all aspects of police use of data. They considered what data were collected, the purpose of their collection, how the data were processed and storied, and their eventual usage (including secondary use).

The findings of these bodies were, in the early days, significant in developing crucial training programmes for the police about the new technologies and their limitations. Politicians and senior police officials communicated these rules effectively to the public. They hosted regular stakeholder engagement meetings with the public to ascertain their concerns. Local police forces have also been hosting local meetings with residents and community leaders to explain their use of new predictive policing technologies, how these technologies were vital in offsetting the cuts in police staff numbers and, importantly, how accurate these algorithms were in predicting criminal acts.

## 7 Steps Towards a Desired Future and Avoidance of an Undesired Future

Civil society organisations, late-night talk-show hosts and some editorial writers articulated fears that the new predictive policing technologies would yield many false positives, that perfectly innocent citizens could be victimised by the new technologies and placed on a police register without knowing why. There were worries about positive feedback loops in particular locales targeted for attention, leading to a greater number of arrests in these areas, leading in turn to algorithms predicting that these were the areas on which the police should be concentrating. Had there been a blind trust in the efficacy of the algorithms, then this may well have been the case, but fortunately, this concern had been raised so many times that the police and algorithm developers were on guard for such phenomena.

Addressing these concerns directly, by instituting transparency measures and empowering oversight bodies, the police increased public trust and strengthened social cohesion. Predictive policing technologies helped the police focus on previously invisible areas of crime. Data analysts uncovered these areas by training their algorithms with masses of information from disparate sources. This allowed the police to put more effort into tackling white-collar crime and online hate crime. This in turn has had a ripple impact on international crimes such as people trafficking and drug smuggling. In fighting such crimes, the police noticed positive effects in communities that were otherwise subject to the attention of such smugglers. Criminals and their would-be accomplices now recognise that if they commit a crime, the likelihood of getting caught is higher than ever, even though there are lingering worries about the inevitability of at least some false positives that could lead to the harassment of innocent people [5].

The police also appreciated the new technologies as they found that effective intelligence led to their approaching volatile situations with an enhanced awareness of how those situations were likely to play out. These days, it’s rarely the case that a police officer finds himself unexpectedly in the middle of a riot and fearing for his life.

Predictive policing technologies have especially emphasised the prevention of crimes—not only by minutes or hours but also on the factors that lead to criminality. The initial emphasis on street crime led to an outcry by civil society organisations, the media and citizens that such technologies were ignoring corporate crime which has a much bigger impact on society. Always loving a challenge, data scientists recently developed new smart information systems that are expected to enhance the detection of corporate crime and malpractices significantly. These new technologies are bringing ethicists and data scientists together, which is expected to benefit European competitiveness greatly.

## 8 The SHERPA Project

This chapter is informed by the research and work conducted by the EU-funded Horizon 2020 SHERPA project [9]. SHERPA is a collaborative research project that was commissioned for 42 months, beginning in May 2018, by the EU to bring together a range of stakeholders to investigate, analyse and synthesise our understanding, and to make recommendations to policymakers regarding ethical and human rights issues raised by or likely to emerge from smart information systems, notably those embedded with algorithms and artificial intelligence.

The above scenario was one of five developed in the SHERPA project. The others concerned ‘deepfake’ technologies, information warfare, driverless vehicles and robots in education. Each of the five followed the same structure and process of engaging increasingly larger numbers of stakeholders. The five scenarios were submitted to the European Commission in June 2019.

With policy scenarios, we do not aim to predict a specific future. That is impossible. However, we can envisage a plausible future (the scenario) and the many factors—the drivers, barriers, impacts—that policymakers should take into account to enable or avoid a future like that envisaged in the scenario. We do not want a scenario with many variables and possible turns of event. Policymakers prefer a clear, single course of action that has stakeholder support. In addition to the structured approach to its development, our scenario shows the range of factors that policymakers should also take into account in the formulation of policy and recommendations.

One of the objectives of the scenario construction process was to reach a consensus on a plausible future. Participants were challenged to be creative, to leap ahead six or seven years and imagine how the technologies might evolve and what new applications might arise. The present often got in the way of the future in many of the discussions, but mostly the present provided a reality check on a story-telling exercise. We wanted more than the present, as it were, without getting trapped in science fiction. We sought to develop plausible scenarios with recommendations that would be useful for policymakers. The scenario construction process is a way for policymakers to get “ahead of the curve”, to develop policies now that will anticipate or pre-empt an undesired future and promote a desired future. In other words, the policy development process needs to begin now, as it usually takes several years before an identified policy requirement becomes legislation.

The scenarios were instrumental in spelling out ethical and social tensions and their role in the current human rights framework. The scenarios were one of the several methodologies that the SHERPA project used to understand and get to grips with ethics and use of big data and AI. Others included:

- Ten cases studies to explore the ethical and human rights tensions in different AI and big data application domains [8].
- A large-scale online survey of 1,000 European citizens
- A Delphi study with 60 experts.

In these and other project methodologies, the partners sought to engage many stakeholders [12].

## 9 Recommendations

Following the scenario on the social and ethical consideration of using AI and Big Data in predictive policing, several recommendations are put forward. These are;

i. To boost their trust with the public, policymakers should adopt a regulation making algorithms explainable to the public. Each algorithm should include code recording who created the algorithm, who paid for it, its purpose, website and contact for more information.
ii. Law enforcement authorities should ensure that criteria are clear and transparent for personal data to be entered into law enforcement databases.
iii. Policymakers should ensure there are independent regulatory authorities of sufficient size and clout to monitor the data in, and use of, law enforcement databases, and offer commendations or impose penalties where appropriate.
iv. Decision-makers should ensure that measures in preventive policing and community investment supplement developments in predictive policing.
v. Law enforcement authorities should take a balanced approach to local, white-collar and online hate crimes.
vi. Law enforcement authorities should ensure effective training of police officers and database operators regarding the limitations of data analysis, particularly concerning the rates of false positives and automation bias.
vii. The EU should sponsor research on automatically detecting when an attack is being planned and discussed.

## 10 Conclusion

As AI penetrates further into our economies and societies, it is speeding up decision-making such that AI-powered decision-making becomes more needed. Human decision-makers cannot respond fast enough, especially in the instance of attacks on cities and critical infrastructure. AI-powered decision-making raises apprehensions about decisions gone wrong or made without an appreciation of the consequences.

Our scenarios and the methodology we used to create them offer value to policy-makers who wish to engage stakeholders in a structured process considering future developments and their ethical, legal, social and economic impacts. To our knowledge, our structured approach to the scenario construction process is an innovation, yet it flows logically from the development of new technologies and applications to an illustrative vignette to the drivers, the inhibitors, and the ethical, legal, social and economic impacts. The scenarios conclude with some recommended measures to reach a desired future and avoid an undesired future. Our scenario construction methodology is based on engaging with stakeholders from the get-go, from an initial brainstorming workshop through several iterations of the scenario. Part of the reason to invite increasingly greater numbers of stakeholders to review and comment on the scenario is to prompt stakeholders to consider the implications of advanced new AI technologies, the risks and benefits. In other words, construction of a scenario is also an awareness-raising exercise. However, ultimately, a scenario is a policymaking tool, and our scenarios are constructed in a way so that policymakers can readily grasp their import and can use the scenario methodology themselves on other issues.

**Acknowledgements** This chapter is based on research undertaken in the EU-funded SHERPA project which has received funding from the European Union's Horizon 2020 research and innovation programme under grant agreement No. 786641. The authors hereby acknowledge with thanks the comments on the scenario from various stakeholders. The views expressed in this chapter are those of the authors and in no way are intended to reflect those of the European Commission.

## References

1. Bjørnholdt K (2016) New IT should help police catch criminals. Copenhagen
2. Creemers R (2018) China's social credit system: an evolving practice of control (SSRN Scholarly Paper No. ID 3175792). Social Science Research Network, Rochester, NY
3. Cummings ML (2004) Automation bias in intelligent time critical decision support systems. In: AIAA. Presented at the 1st intelligent systems technical conference, pp 557–562
4. Goddard K, Roudsari A, Wyatt JC (2012) Automation bias: a systematic review of frequency, effect mediators, and mitigators. J Am Med Inform Assoc 19:121–127. https://doi.org/10.1136/amiajnl-2011-000089
5. Macnish K (2012) Unblinking eyes: the ethics of automating surveillance. Ethics Inf Technol 14:151–167. https://doi.org/10.1007/s10676-012-9291-0
6. Norwegian Board of Technology (2015) Predictive policing—can data analysis help the police to be in the right place at the right time? Oslo
7. Rollet C (2018) In China's far west, companies cash in on surveillance program that targets Muslims. Foreign Policy. https://foreignpolicy.com/2018/06/13/in-chinas-far-west-companies-cash-in-on-surveillance-program-that-targets-muslims/. Accessed 12 Aug 2019
8. Ryan M, Antoniou J, Brooks L, Jiya T, Macnish K, Stahl B (2019) Technofixing the future: ethical side effects of using AI and Big Data to meet the SDGs. In: Presented at the 5th IEEE smart world congress (SmartWorld 2019), IEEE SmartWorld, Leicester, p 7
9. SHERPA (2018) SHERPA—understanding and analysing smart information systems [WWW document]. https://www.project-sherpa.eu/. Accessed 27 July 2018)
10. Wickens CD, Clegg BA, Vieane AZ, Sebok AL (2015) Complacency and automation bias in the use of imperfect automation. Hum Factors 57:728–739. https://doi.org/10.1177/0018720815581940

11. Wright D (2008) Alternative futures: Am I scenarios and minority report. Futures 40:473–488. https://doi.org/10.1016/j.futures.2007.10.006
12. Wright D, Rodrigues R, Hatzakis T, Pannofino C, Macnish, K, Ryan M, Stahl B, Antoniou J (2019) Smart information scenarios (No. D1.2). Representation and visualization of ethical and human rights issues in SIS. SHERPA-EU Project, UK

# Patterns in Policing

**Peter Cochrane and Mark P. Pfeiffer**

**Abstract** Exactly like the societies they serve; police forces are stressed by tech driven change, a data deluge, and the rise of global connectivity. Major changes in criminal activity, from the everyday, local, simple and solvable, to the globally confounding see a rising number of unsolved crimes. At the same time police budgets and staffing levels are under pressure, whilst criminals enjoy an ever profitable growth. Policing has to turn to technology to address rising complex and render situations understandable. In this context, AI is the 'ace card' with underlying capabilities that eclipse humans. Specifically, AI can digest vast amounts of data, and recognise hidden patterns that escape us! So far AI has excelled in facial, vehicle and movement recognition and is proving its worth in behavioural analysis. Latterly, its ability to detect event precursors has come to the fore, and this may be the first entry into pre-crime prediction.

**Keywords** AI · Pre-cursors · Complexity · Visualization · Prediction · Mapping · Analysis

## 1 A Sudden Transformation

In less than 40 years our world has transited from a slow, disconnected, and largely linear place, to one of frenetic activity engendered by continual global communication, connectivity and networked machines. The scale of data creation and traffic growth has been vast ~1000 fold increase per decade. For Example: In 1980 there were no mobile networks and devices, no internet, PCs, or eMail. Even in 1990, PCs were sparsely distributed and there were no social networks! Today, almost every human on the planet has access to a mobile device, and over 2Bn personal computing

P. Cochrane (✉)
University of Suffolk, Ipswich, UK
e-mail: p.cochrane@uos.ac.uk; peter@ca-global.org

M. P. Pfeiffer
SailLabs Vienna, Vienna, Austria
e-mail: mp@opmiso.com

 
H. Jahankhani et al. (eds.), *Policing in the Era of AI and Smart Societies*, Advanced Sciences and Technologies for Security Applications,
https://doi.org/10.1007/978-3-030-50613-1_10

devices are shipped year-on-year. And at the time of writing; the majority of humanity can connect to the internet to access others, gain information and knowledge, buy and sell goods.

Little wonder people and societies feel a sense of 'future shock'; being out of control, and not understanding the non-linear space of change powered by technology. As individuals, we now carry more computing power in our pockets than was delivered by supercomputers in 1985. Add to this the transformative power of the internet, robotics, social nets, AI and globalisation, plus 24 × 7 global media and, of course our daily data overload, and the picture is all but complete.

The forces of darkness have not slept through these years; they have been quick on the uptake; and they have stolen a March in their ability to adopt and adapt technologies to their criminal, political, subversive and evil purpose. They have also been quick to exploit the slowness of our institutions, companies and peoples by embracing new technologies to attack and exploit relatively defenceless societies.

Virtualised (Cyber) Crime is now >1% of the Global GDP in terms of turnover/economic damage, making it the 35th largest economy on the planet. In contrast, the cost of physical crimes come in at ~4× this figure making it the 18th economy. The two combined eclipse the UK GDP at number 9! The real frightener here is an exponential Cyber Crime growth rate that might see the combined profits rise to the third largest GDP within 5 years.

On another dimension, physical crimes including terrorism are often aided and abetted by the internet, mobile devices, social nets and computing power. We just do not know how big the full picture is, and all our estimates are crude, and probably fall short of reality. So, what can we be certain of? Not a lot it seems! These challenges defy human imagination and ability and we need machine and network help along with far more cooperation between institutions and peoples.

> The Dark Side virtualised very early to network and efficiently share knowledge, tools and resources whilst the Forces of Good tend to be isolated, working in a non-networked and non-sharing manner.
>
> Our only hope is to fight-fire-with-fire by adopting the strategies of the Dark Side. We have better people, networks and computing power, but neglect the power of organisation and sharing

## 2 On the Back Foot

Fundamental human limitations in the way we perceive and analyse threats often sees the domain of Warfare siloed into easily digested activities on land, at sea, in the air, in space; and lately in cyber space. Reality is, the component of information is more generally omitted or ill considered. A more comprehensive and integral view (Fig. 1) accounts for all the domains not only being present but also being connected.

We should also note that no General would wage war without a knowledge of all the conventional forces, but few it seems, fully recognise the threat and power of the Cyber Domain and thereby fail to account for the strategic threat it might pose. And

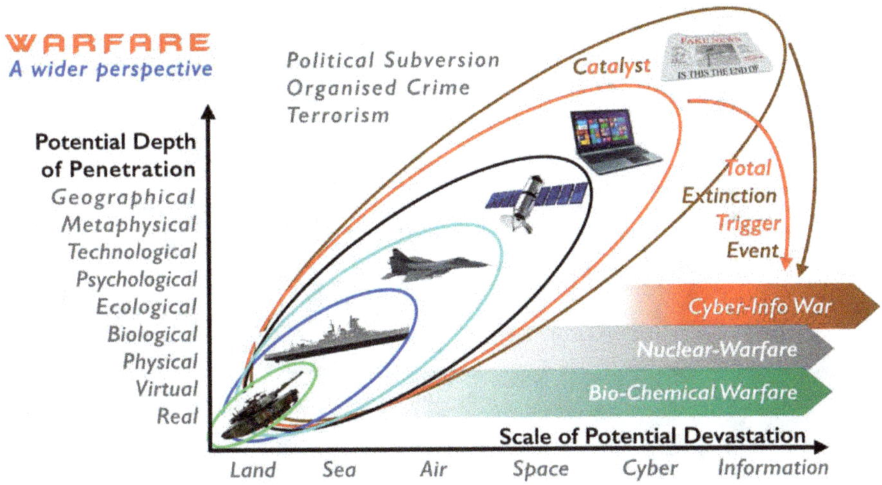


**Fig. 1** The complete sphere of modern warfare

the wider scope and importance of the information space influencing political/public mood and opinion appears wholly neglected, often until it is far too late. In reality; Political Subversion, Organised Crime and Terrorism form an invisible backdrop to this general picture, and that all components are linked and connected in a less than clear manner.

> We have developed technologies to aid and assist humans, and not the other way around
> Peter Cochrane BTLabs 1991

War is no longer a simple, short term game governed by bullets and bombs alone. It is supported by bits, Bytes, data and information, the manipulation of opinion and the massaging of beliefs and perceptions on a global scale. In turn these are the primary components of the longer game of political subversion and battle free takeovers—as epitomised by Mr Putin—Fig. 2.

A further dimension to all this involves those (Rogue States) employing and colluding with organised crime and terrorist organisations in conventional and Cyber/Information Crime/War. In general, their specific objectives and missions are less than clear and their actions often appear illogical, ill judged, and dangerous. This is all amplified by the way they spontaneously weave between politics, war and crime.

> The greatest victory is that which requires no battle
>
> To know your Enemy, you must become your Enemy
>
> Sun Tzu (544-496 BC) The Art of War

And so, we have an enemy with surprise and unspecified/unknown resources on their side; and they decide the target, the time and place, tools, people and mode of

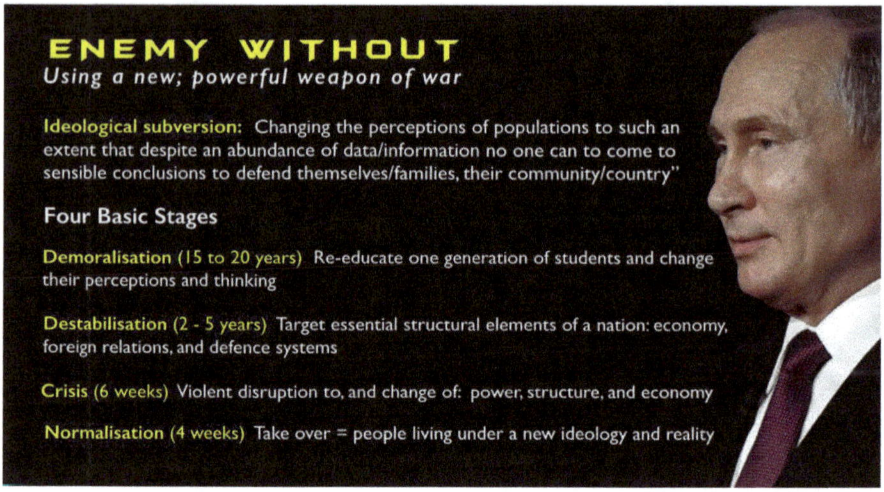


**Fig. 2** The long game of a rogue state?

attack. They enjoy the 'first mover' advantage, and it is impossible for us to be vigilant and on guard 24 × 7. This is a job for our machines. Our task is to try and understand the enemy and their habits and preferences using all the tools and technologies at our disposal so we might present the best possible defence and recovery solutions.

> To be a good defender you have too be a good attacker first Peter Cochrane BTLabs 1992

## 3 Technology to the Rescue

Conventional computing; the storage, sorting, analysis and modelling/war gaming based on vast libraries of static and dynamic data is now well established across industry, police forces and national security agencies globally. Their power and utility is no longer contested and/or doubted as they perform feats way beyond human capacity. But the next phase is now underway with the introduction of AI, facial recognition and biometric evaluation at every level from mobile device up to a national and international concentration. In China for example such technologies adorn their vehicles as well as police officers in the street.

It is reasonably axiomatic as to what facial recognition and biometrics bring to the party, but AI is not quite so clear, and if one phrase defines their primary function, it is 'pattern recognition'. More specifically; AI will recognise patterns in data and behaviours that humans miss.

> AI tends to get the right/new answers by different routes to any human Peter Cochrane BTLabs 1994

In medicine and healthcare the power of AI is now well established in diagnostics, scanned image examination, behavioural analysis and drug design. It also pervades products and industrial plants and warehouses. Law enforcement and the legal system however are on the starting grid whilst the military and national security are have embraced AI to varying degrees and affect.

For the new entries into this world we are at an interesting phase of AI spanning 'dumb and mechanistic' to near 'self-awareness'. At the leading edge AI can observe, analyse, derive the 'rules of the game' and then enter into self learning and war gaming. Table 1 gives a summary of progression by epoch events spanning the past 70 years. It is notable the Crime, Law and Order, National Security, Cyber Security

**Table 1** 70 Years of AI progress in brief

| | |
|---|---|
| 1940 | Digital computer plays game |
| 1950 | Azimov Three Laws of Robotics |
| 1951 | Checkers (Droughts) playing machine |
| 1956 | AI term coined at a Dartmouth conference |
| 1956 | AI becomes an academic discipline |
| 1958 | Programming with common sense |
| 1961 | AI challenges humans on IQ test |
| 1963 | Machine learning demonstrated |
| 1961 | Fuzzy Logic an engineering option |
| 1968 | First chess playing program |
| 1970 | Natural Language Processing |
| 1971 | Language understanding/parallel computing |
| 1956/74 | Golden years of government funding |
| 1974/80 | Hype lead to the first "AI winter" |
| 1980/87 | Knowledge-based expert systems successes |
| 1987/93 | Negative perceptions by governments/industry |
| 1993/20 | Data driven results create high optimism |
| 1997 | IBM's DeepBlue beats Kasparov at chess |
| 2002 | Amazon uses AI purchase recommendations |
| 2011 | Apple releases Siri on the iPhone/iPad |
| 2011 | BM Watson beats human champions at Jeopardy |
| 2012 | Superior medical diagnostics demonstrated |
| 2013 | Machine and Deep learning emerge |
| 2012 | Google driverless cars navigate autonomously |
| 2016 | Google AlphaGo beats a world champion at Go |
| 2017 | Cancer cell identification overtakes human skill |
| 2018 | Contributions to complex Protein Folding analysis |
| 2019 | Amazon widespread ALEXA roll out |
| 2020 | Boston Dynamics Autonomous anthropomorphic robots |

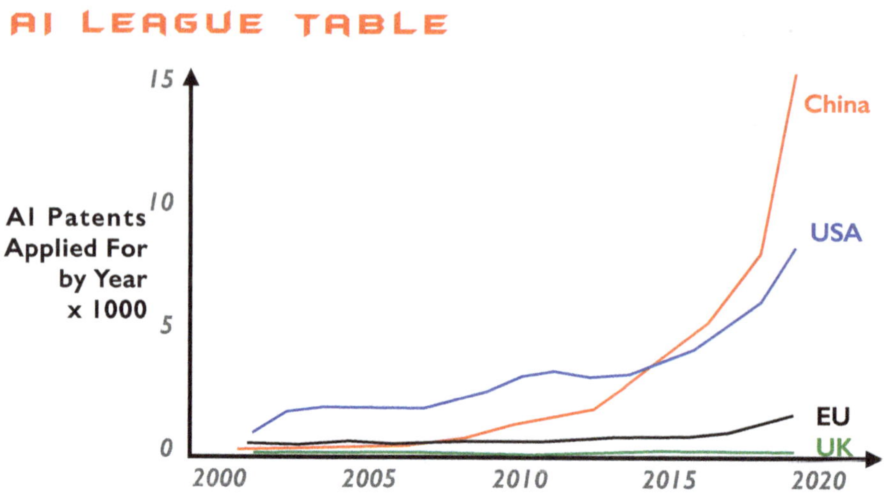


**Fig. 3** The AI Rise and Rise of China and USA

and National Defence are omitted to date. That is not to say AI is not being deployed in these areas, more, it is at an early stage or an advanced and a state secret.

> Whoever masters AI will rule the world
>
> Vladimir Putin 2019

In the race for AI Patents it turns out that China are in the lead with more AI companies and similar (effective) funding levels to the USA. However, it appears that the academic spread of expertise and research is far more distributed across the USA, Canada, EU, and SEA. The Chinese and Russian situations are far less clear! (Fig. 3).

The modern history of AI has followed an exponential growth curve in alignment with Moore's Law and the capability of computing platforms. The computers of the 40–80s were relatively crude and fundamentally incapable of supporting sophisticated AIs of any kind. For example; the Cray 2 Super Computer was the most powerful machine on the planet up to 1990 but is now eclipsed by the Apple iPhone X is now >30 fold more powerful, whilst our super computers exceed 100,000 more powerful.

Possibly at least as important has been the developments in sensory technologies spanning sight, sound, touch, position, movement and orientation. These augment AIs in vehicles, warehouses, factories autonomous civil and military robots of the walking, crawling, climbing, swimming and flying kind. When concatenated with natural language and an understanding of movement and actions; these form the bedrock of an accelerating migration toward self awareness and sentence Fig. 4.

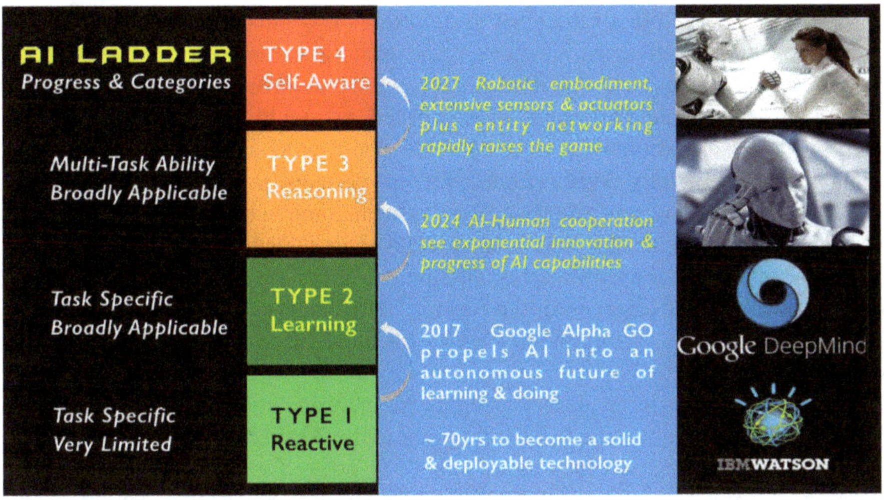


**Fig. 4** A projected AI ladder of progress toward sentience

## 4 People Problem

Whilst the forces of law, order, and national security remain reasonably invariant by people numbers and abilities over decades, the forces of evil have grown in numbers, ability and audacity as they embrace the new technologies to largely avoid being identified and apprehended. In many countries petty crime, theft and burglary go unaddressed whilst serious crimes result in ~10% convictions, ~20% case closures and ~70% detection failure rates. For any society this is extremely corrosive and sees many crimes going unreported.

Funding, resources, recruitment and training are the major stumbling blocks of change. And when 'boom and bust' budgets, dictated by politics define performance targets to continually strain the effectiveness of agencies and throttle adaptation the result is always a degraded effectiveness. Getting the right people and technologies in place, and honing their skills as an organisation in an unstable political climates is all but impossible. And it is not just feet on the ground, but eyes on the screen, imaginative analytics and modelling, that are required in the detection, solution and prosecution of complex crimes.

The many hurdles to realising a just society are growing year-on-year with the courts and barrister workloads seemingly insurmountable as they are limited by 'due process' and overwhelmed by sheer volume. However, the application of AI appears to be the answer. In the UK AI-Barristers are being employed to complete all the document pre-reading and analysis because it is beyond the ability of those employed. And in the USA it has been taken a step further with crime scene analysis, suspect identification, and sentencing, with, at present, a degree of human oversight!

What has emerged in all the USA system trials is ‘human bias’. The AI(s) have been ‘spectators’ to thousands of cases and trials in order to learn the rules and processes. Unlike humans, this does not have to be completed in a serial (one at a time) manner, hundreds/thousands of networked AIs could aggregate their ‘experiences’ to afford an exponentiation of knowledge and understanding across the entire populations. For racially divisive continents this perhaps provides an ideal levelling and assured equity mechanism giving bias free outcome in every case.

However, what we actually see from the USA trials so far (with the limited number of disconnected AIs) is a subsumption of human frailty in respect of race, wealth and societal position that emerges in the form of judgement and sentencing bias. This is mostly in the form of treatment severity for those of colour and/or non-English speaking.

A word of caution here: all technologies are inert and non-malevolent: they only do what we have programmed or taught them to do. At this stage of our technological development our machines have limited, or no, self awareness, and no moral reference, common sense, or societal frame of reference. And so they cannot be held responsible, but we can! And we might expect this situation to obtain for well over a decade, but by degree our machines will become ‘responsible’.

> We cannot blame AI for what it learns from its human teachers Peter Cochrane University of Suffolk 2017

Today, we are asking AI to be our unbiased agents and arbiters of facts, functions and behaviours that we supply. In the first instance they are doing this by learning from us and what we do, our observations, actions and decisions, but later, they can be expected to cut loose on the basis of their own subjective assessments.

> In general Lifeforms and Intelligences are not evil, destructive or malevolent, but they do compete for resources adapt to survive Peter Cochrane University of Suffolk 2017

## 5 Habituality

Curiously; all humans, mobiles, devices, machines have behavioural idiosyncrasies and habitualities. Thus, what we and our machines do almost entirely defines us, and behavioural analysis turns out to be a powerful tool in the prediction, identification, investigation and the prosecution of crime and, or, acts of terrorism.

As the supreme recogniser of patterns and identifier of causality, AI is the ideal tool for searching through mountains of dynamic data in search of relationships, to then filter, identify and map the important and the critical. It also has the ability to predict/project the next most likely actions. No human, or human team is so capable given the scale of the internet, criminality and terrorism.

> Every criminal, terrorist or military action sees pre-cursor indicators/warnings if we only know where to look and how to recognise them Peter Cochrane University of Suffolk 2019

## 6 The Data Deluge

The generators and creators of data and information produce an exponential doubling volume year-on-year. In our domain of interest; people, devices, machines and networks generate vast amounts via PCs, Mobile Devices, Appliances, Vehicles, Purchases, Transactions, ATMs, Searches, Calls, eMail, TXT, IM, Social Nets, Travel, Movements, Relationships, Facial Recognition and more. Whilst it impossible to identify, list and detail ever source and form of data and information within the constraints of this chapter, Table 2 gives an indication of the breadth and depth involved.

The vast majority of data, conversations and actions are irrelevant to the forces of law, order and security, and the big challenge is the identification of the very few that pose a long and near term threat. Most important; are those indicating a clear and present danger!

> Finding a needle in a haystack is easy when you have a magnet, but a bent needle is far harder and demands many tools in parallel, whilst a needle that's thinking about bending is the ultimate analytic challenge Peter Cochrane University of Suffolk 2017

**Table 2** What our technologies (can invisibly) reveal about us

| Mode | PC | Mobile | Wearable | Vehicle | IoT | PoS | ATM |
|---|---|---|---|---|---|---|---|
| Access | | | | | | | |
| Device ID | ✓ | ✓ | ✓ | ✓ | ✓ | | |
| Location | ✓ | ✓ | ✓ | ✓ | ✓ | ✓ | ✓ |
| Carrier | ✓ | ✓ | ✓ | ✓ | ✓ | ✓ | ✓ |
| Line | ✓ | | | | | ✓ | ✓ |
| WiFi | ✓ | ✓ | ✓ | ✓ | ✓ | ✓ | ✓ |
| Blue Tooth | ✓ | ✓ | ✓ | ✓ | ✓ | ✓ | ✓ |
| 3, 4, 5G | | ✓ | | ✓ | ✓ | ✓ | ✓ |
| URL | ✓ | ✓ | ✓ | ✓ | ✓ | | |
| IM | ✓ | ✓ | ✓ | | | | |
| TXT | ✓ | ✓ | ✓ | | | | |
| eMail | ✓ | ✓ | ✓ | | | | |
| Diary | ✓ | ✓ | ✓ | | | | |
| History | ✓ | ✓ | ✓ | ✓ | ✓ | ✓ | ✓ |
| Contacts | ✓ | ✓ | ✓ | | | | |
| Social nets | ✓ | ✓ | | | | | |
| Microphone | ✓ | ✓ | ✓ | ✓ | ✓ | ✓ | ✓ |
| Sensors | ✓ | ✓ | ✓ | ✓ | ✓ | ✓ | ✓ |
| Camera | ✓ | ✓ | | ✓ | ✓ | | |
| Browser | ✓ | ✓ | | | | | |

**Table 3** What our Mobiles (can invisibly) reveal

| Url | Associated devices | IM |
|---|---|---|
| IMI | Connection history | TXT |
| SIM | BlueTooth history | GPS |
| DNS | Browsing history | Diary |
| VPNs | Favourite sites | eMail |
| Apps | Travel history | Notes |
| Carrier | News feeds | Music |
| Camera | Connections | Books |
| Storage | Documents | Health |
| Settings | Recordings | Games |
| Software | Encryption | Movies |
| Passwords | Purchases | Photos |
| Microphone | Location | Groups |
| Serial number | Activity | Contacts |
| MAC address | Vehicle | PodCasts |
| Accelerometers | Routes | Social nets |
| Device type/model | +++++ | ++++++ |

Beyond the raw data collected it is the historical relationships, associations, behaviours, opinions and actions leading up to the present day that provide the vital clues (and cues) to the future. For the mobile phone alone the data available per device may be categorised as shown in Table 3. This also gives some insight of the combinatorial complexity to be expected as the number and varieties of devices and contacts grow. It also indicates the fact that is way beyond the simple analytical abilities of any human or group of humans. It is however in the sweet spot for AI, digital computing, statistical analysis, computer modelling and war-gaming.

## 7 Recent Results

There are many modern machine analysis and prediction methodologies providing results of varying degrees of proven and yet to be tested utility. However, in the interests of brevity, we contain our consideration here to two primary (and recent) examples that indicate what is possible, and what might develop in the future. The first involves the expansion of an established mapping technique used to locate the 'centre of gravity' of criminal activity and the likelihood of the next target/s.

In Fig. 5 a cluster of criminal activity is mapped so the 'centre of gravity' might be determined along with similar likely targets. The modern version of this (Fig. 6) employs the simultaneous analysis of mobile phone locations with time and specific

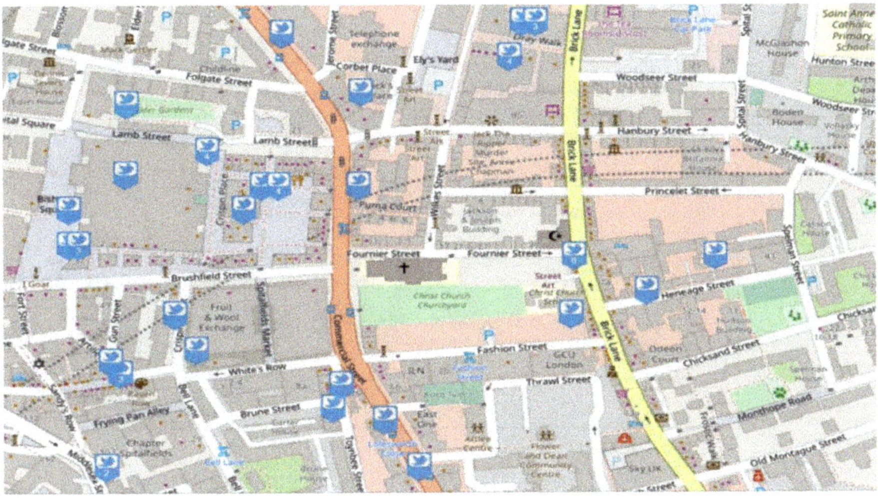


**Fig. 5** Manual visual analysis of clustered burglaries of a similar style and target type

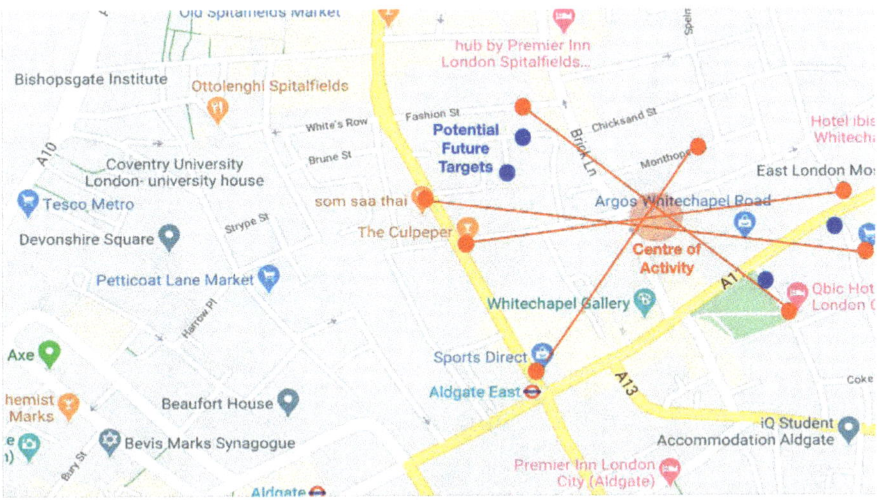


**Fig. 6** Today Automated Data Gathering adds more over time by tracking cell phone movement and clustering

content of calls, TXT, social nets and other apps along with the temporal clustering of related devices (Figs. 7 and 8).

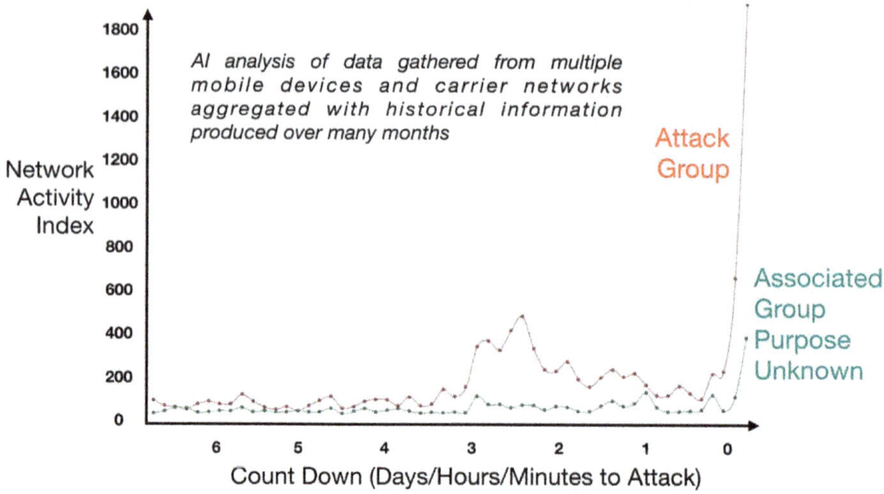


**Fig. 7** AI can then extract additional data from each device to refine the inferencing and modelling process

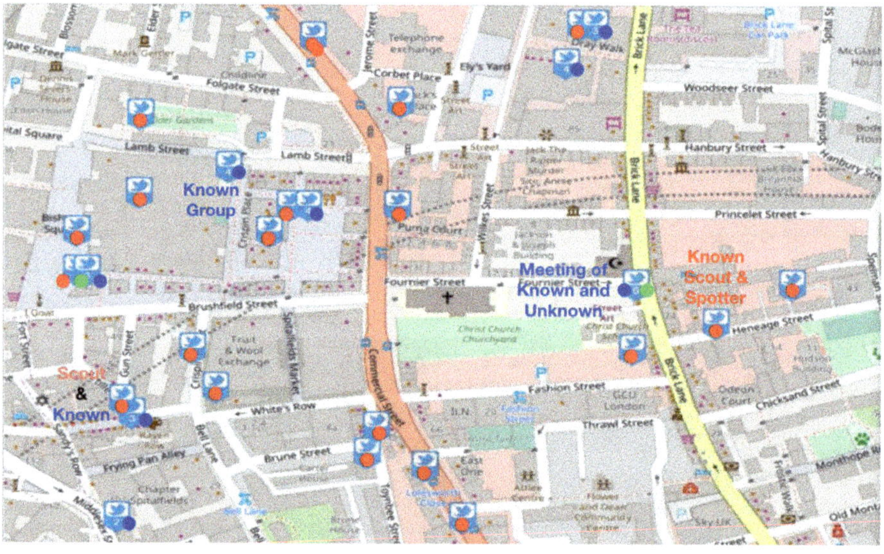


**Fig. 8** Continual 'N-Dimensional Data Analysis' by AI to extract the attack precursor and build up to the attack

## 8 A Cat and Mouse Game

The forces of peace, law and order, are not pitched against enemies that are slow to change and or react, quite the reverse! Their tactics of change are generally purposeful and well timed to confound any attempt to anticipate their intended actions. To overcome such a foe we need a considerable catalogue of prior incidents, interactions, communications, and attack strategies in order for our AI's to 'learn their mindsets'.

> All warfare is based on deception. Hence, when we are able to attack, we must seem unable; when active, we must appear inactive; when near, we must make the enemy believe we are far away; when far away, we must make him believe we are near
>
> Sun Tzu (544-496 BC) The Art of War

Our enemies are cunning to a greater or lesser degree and they use our own technologies and facilities against us in a never ending game of crime and warfare spanning continents, the planet, and technologies. To defeat them, we have to devote more investment and resources than they do, and we have to solve the problem(s) by employing different methods than those of the path and today.

We have prototypes and 'existence theorems' for all the elements of AI, Analysis and Predictions to with this battle, but we do not have the mind sets and investments to make it happen. So there is no doubt that the situation will continue to worsen year on year until the forces for good band together defend themselves, and better still, attack the Dark Side.

There are very few cases in history where the attacked passively accept their fate and fail to respond, and there has never been a war of any kind on the scale of this Cyber and Information War. Sooner or later we are going to have to fight back, and in our arsenal will most likely be analytic and weaponised AI Engines.

> We can't solve problems by using the same kind of thinking we used when we created them
>
> Albert Einstein

## 9 Seeing Through the Fog of Complexity

We close this chapter with one crucial observation on the biggest challenge we face as a species, and that is our innate inability to cope with complexity. By its very nature, war is complex and 'N-dimensional,' and this particular war is the most complex ever. And so, for us to grasp the core of what is happening and what we might do it is essential that we embrace the new technologies of animation and visualisation. These are also available and perfectly aligned with AI, machine learning, computer modelling and war gaming.

> If a picture is worth a thousand words, a moving picture is with a million, whilst an immersive interactive environment is worth a billion Peter Cochrane BTLabs 1993

## Further Reading


1. Cyber Statistical Trends: https://bit.ly/2Qkr2D4
2. Cyber Crime Cost Projections: https://bit.ly/2Uffr9C
3. Cyber War Crippling Cost: https://bit.ly/33kO8Px
4. The Information war: https://bit.ly/33mEqMt
5. A New AI Dawn: https://bit.ly/3b28wHO
6. People The Biggest Risk: https://bit.ly/2TTZV3Z
7. Data Overload: https://bit.ly/2wdoWOz
8. What Dies My Phone Know: https://nyti.ms/2TU7xDF
9. Crime Mapping: https://bit.ly/2UeIvyb
10. Terrorist Precursor Crimes: https://bit.ly/2WiALOk
11. Tracking The Hackers: https://bit.ly/2TVuGWw

# Proposed Forensic Guidelines for the Investigation of Fake News

**Natasha Omezi and Hamid Jahankhani**

**Abstract** The old adage, "seeing is believing", no longer holds true in modern society. Digital media has paved the way for anyone to doctor images and for videos to misrepresent truth. The lines between fact, entertainment, advertising, fabrication and fiction are becoming increasingly blurred as what is termed 'fake news' increases in modern day society. A natural consequence of the increase in fake news is the outcry for investigations into misinformation (think Cambridge Analytica). Investigations need to be forensically sound in order for any evidence to hold up in court. This research aims to propose forensic guidelines for the investigation of fake news by researching current fact checking methodologies and determining whether what is currently in place can be aligned to the current ACPO Forensic Guidelines. In order to do this, it first attempts to establish how easily a non-professional fact checker can detect fake news by carrying out a rudimentary fake news quiz. This was then followed by a review of 41 fact checkers to understand their fact checking methodologies and concluded with a basic fact checking experiment to test the veracity of a subset of the reviewed tools. In concluding, fake news investigations can be aligned to the current ACPO forensic guidelines, however, they will need to be specifically adapted to the three main categories of fake news: images, text and video.

**Keywords** Fake news · Cambridge analytica · Forensics investigation · Deepfakes · Fact checking misinformation · Disinformation · NPCC · ACPO · Cyber propaganda

## 1 Introduction

Digital media has paved the way for anyone to doctor images and for videos to misrepresent truth. Additionally, for instance, once breaking news begins to trend on social media such as Twitter, a barrage of false-claims and content misuse follow suit ranging from half-truths to outright lies. The consequences are a misinformed public,

N. Omezi · H. Jahankhani (✉)
Northumbria University, London, UK
e-mail: Hamid.jahankhani@northumbria.ac.uk

 
H. Jahankhani et al. (eds.), *Policing in the Era of AI and Smart Societies*, Advanced Sciences and Technologies for Security Applications,
https://doi.org/10.1007/978-3-030-50613-1_11

misrepresented people, organisations and events. There are an increasing number of examples of the consequences of misinformation, for instance, Cambridge Analytica, Pizzagate in the 2016 US Elections.

- Cambridge Analytica: a data analytics firm which claimed a major role in the Leave Campaign for the UK's EU membership referendum, was also a key figure in US elections in 2016 that saw Donald Trump become president. Data was harvested from c. 50 million individual Facebook profiles to determine personality traits linked to voting behaviour. The combination of the algorithm and database allowed a campaign to identify possible swing voters and craft messages more likely to resonate with such individuals using psyops (psychological operations), in which people's minds are changed not through persuasion but through "information dominance"—a set of techniques that include rumours, disinformation and fake news. This tool had been used by SL Elections in more than 200 elections around the world, mainly in countries with underdeveloped democracies as they were ill-equipped to defend themselves.
- "Pizzagate" is an infamous example of the impact of fake news on individuals. In December 2016, a man took it upon himself to self-investigate the conspiracy theory that the Hilary Clinton campaign team was running a paedophile ring from a pizzeria. Being influenced by this 'piece of news', the individual turned up at the pizzeria, firing shots. No one was killed and he was arrested and charged with assault and related offences.

In 2016, TalkTalk was issued a record £400,000 fine for security failings that allowed a cyber-attacker to access personal data of c.156,959 customers (Information Commissioner's Office, 2016. The consequences of a data breach however, go beyond potential fines mandated by regulators and the financial strain that is put on the organisation. They include reputational damage resulting in loss of shareholder confidence as well of loss of assets, as can be seen with Facebook's worst ever privacy scandal in the Cambridge Analytica case where c. 50 million US user accounts were compromised and subsequently used to allegedly influence individuals in political choices. Facebook shares fell more than 24%, losing roughly $134 billion in market value in the process, as well as facing massive damages in the Cambridge Analytica suit. However, there is one area that there is not, as yet, robust 'direct' legislation in place and this is the area of 'Fake News'. There are currently a plethora of fact checkers, with various methodologies. However, standardised forensic guidelines will establish uniformity in the industry, possibly globally and ensure that the right steps or the same steps are followed in an investigation. The researcher is of the opinion that this could also help in cross-border jurisdictional disputes.

The scope of this project will cover the methodologies currently used to investigate fake news by using a comprehensive fake news dataset.

Due to the current interest in fake news and all forms of misinformation almost as a global concern, there is no shortage of literature on this subject. The available articles cover a wide variety of perspectives depending on the concern of the researcher or author. An attempt has been made in this paper to narrow the research and review to literature which is directly concerned with the researcher's particular angle of interest—the development of forensic guidelines for investigating fake news.

In attempting to define what digital forensics is, Mark Politt posits that there is no single answer to this question, but that it is a series of tasks and processes in investigation [37]. However, Ricci Ieong describes Digital Forensics Investigation as "a process to determine and relate extracted information and digital evidence to establish factual information for judicial review" [26]. Kruse and Heizer set out the three A's of computer forensics as described as: (1) **Acquire** the evidence without altering or damaging the original data; (2) **Authenticate** that your recorded evidence is the same as the original seized data; (3) **Analyse** the data without modifying the recovered data [30].

The Association of Chief Police Officers (ACPO), now called The National Police Chiefs' Council (NPCC) developed guidelines for Computer Investigations and Electronic Evidence, which are still currently in use.

The current ACPO forensic guidelines for the investigation of computer-based evidence, are as stated below:

> **ACPO Principle 1**: No action taken should change data held on a digital device including a computer or mobile device that may subsequently be relied upon as evidence in court.
>
> **ACPO Principle 2**: Where a person finds it necessary to access original data held on a digital device, the person must be competent to do so and able to explain their actions and the consequent implications on the digital evidence to the Court.
>
> **ACPO Principle 3**: A record of all actions that have been applied to the digital evidence should be created and preserved in such a way that an independent third party forensic expert should be able to follow or examine those processes and reach the same conclusion.
>
> **ACPO Principle 4**: The individual in charge of the investigation has the overall responsibility to ensure that these principles are followed.

In order to cover crimes involving websites, forums and blogs, the ACPO guidelines recommend the proposed method for copying a website is to visit the site and record the relevant pages using video capture software in order to ensure visible representation of how they looked originally. The guidelines also recommend that where there is difficulty in capturing evidence by visiting the site, a request can be made to the internet hosting service provider in order to recover evidence of who has created the web page or posting [1]. This could be the first step in ensuring the forensic investigation of fake news, which is usually posted on web forums, blogs, social media etc.

## 2 Fake News

With the evolution of technology and the explosion of the digital age, the way we use, digest and interact with information has changed. Our sources of information have also changed over time. One aspect of information which has undergone considerable change is news.

News is generally understood to be information about current events and can be provided through different media. The Merriam-Webster dictionary gives the following two definitions of news: "*(a) a report of recent events and (b) previously unknown information* [34]". Other scholars have provided various definitions, ranging from Kershner's definition: "*an account of a recent, interesting and significant event* [29]" to Richardson's definition which describe news as: "*an account of events that significantly affect people*" [39] and Jamieson's and Campbell's definition of: "*a dramatic account of something novel or deviant*" [28]. What is accepted as news, the current method of news consumption and the corresponding sources of news, have all undergone radical change in tandem with the ubiquity of information technology which has increased the consumption of digital information. Within a society, news is crucial, and is mainly for informing the public about current affairs and how it may affect them. News can be international, national or local and all serve to inform the general public about ongoing events. Consuming news has always been the traditional method of informing the public. News consumption has rapidly increased both in the volume of news proliferated and consumed, as well as the speed of dispersion and the reach. The increase in consumption of digital information, has led to the increase in proliferation of news: good, bad and fake.

The impact of fake news has been observed most notably in the 2016 United States elections that saw Donald Trump sworn in as the President of the United States. Even though politics and elections are not the only areas that have been impacted by fake news, the US elections caught everyone's attention, as well as the Cambridge Analytica scandal.

In studying the impact of fake news, Berinsky points out that repetition of rumours can augment their 'fluency', and therefore increase the likelihood of individuals accepting misinformation as truth [7]. However, Bartels' research on The Political Impact of Media Exposure concluded that media exposure only had a minimal impact on political opinion and that the resulting change was negligible. This he posits, is not because media is not persuasive, but because, most individuals would have already had strong political leanings or views prior to being exposed to any media. He points out that media-effects analysts should focus on individuals with "new" or "uncrystallised" opinions [6]. The researcher agrees with this as this was evidenced in the Cambridge Analytica scandal where the target audience were those that had no strong political leanings or were 'sitting on the fence', as it were.

In 2017, Collins Dictionaries declared "Fake News" Word of the Year. The use of the term increased by 365% from 2016 to 2017. As the issue of fake news has become increasingly pressing, calls have been made by various stakeholders e.g. the media, government, and the public, for it to be stopped [27].

## 2.1 Defining Fake News, Misinformation and Disinformation

Tandoc et al. posit that 'fake news' is an oxymoron as "*news is supposedly—and normatively—based on truth*" [46]. The researcher accepts that this is a logical inference as 'fake news' would effectively translate to 'fake truth'. The issue of 'fake news' is not new as the world has always experienced propaganda and politically-aligned bias, purporting to be news. It has been around for as long as there have been writing mechanisms. Propaganda, shock headlines, fearmongering or smokescreens, for instance, have always existed [14]. However, this activity has taken on new forms, hugely magnified by the ubiquity of social media. Current understanding of fake news ranges from political satire to deliberate misinformation, the motives for which vary considerably, including financial and ideological. The common thread is that it serves to influence the reader through the use of inaccurate information or as Gu et al. put it: "*the manipulation of public opinion to affect the real world*" [24]. Allcott and Gentzkow define fake news as "*news articles that are intentionally and verifiably false and could mislead readers* [4]". However, according to the UK Parliamentary report on Disinformation and 'fake news', there is no agreed definition of the term 'fake news' as it is applied to various types of false information including fabricated content, manipulated content, impostor content, misleading content, false context of connection and satire/parody [59].

Other known synonyms include disinformation campaigns, cyber propaganda, information warfare etc. Disinformation and Misinformation are two other terms which have all been used in the attempt to define fake news. The Oxford dictionary defines them as: Misinformation—"*false or inaccurate information, especially that which is deliberately intended to deceive.*" Disinformation—"*false information that is intended to mislead, especially propaganda issued by a government organisation to a rival power or the media.*"

Shu et al. described fake news as "*news with intentionally false information*" [42]. The Digital, Culture, Media and Sports (DCMS) published a report "Disinformation and 'fake news' in July 2018, in which it was proposed that 'disinformation' should be used instead of 'fake news'. This, they purported is because, 'fake news' had been used to describe content that a user might dislike or disagree with and consequently dismiss. They further proposed the definition of disinformation as "*the deliberate creation and sharing of false and/or manipulated information that is intended to deceive and mislead audiences, either for the purposes of causing harm, or for political, personal or financial gain*". This was subsequently accepted by the UK Government [59].

There is an additional category of 'fake news' called 'Mal-information'. This has been described by the United Nations Educational, Scientific and Cultural Organisation as "*information that is based on reality, used to inflict harm on a person, social group, organisation or country.*" [52, 53].

Here, for the purposes of this research, the definition of fake news as accepted by the UK government will be usedl: "*the deliberate creation and sharing of false and/or manipulated information that is intended to deceive and mislead audiences, either for the purposes of causing harm, or for political, personal or financial gain*".

For the purposes of this research the following are ruled out as 'fake news': (a) unintentional reporting mistakes e.g. the report that Donald Trump had removed the bust of Martin Luther King Jr. from the Presidential White House; (b) conspiracy theories (difficult to verify and already strongly believed by the perpetrators of such theories); (c) rumours not originating from a news article (d) incorrect statements by politicians; (e) misleading reports that are not outrightly false [in other circumstances, this could be considered fake news. (f) satire. (However, taken out of context, some satirical comments have been perpetrated as news and could also be defined as fake news).

For instance, in 2016 the now-defunct website, wtoe5news.com, reported that Pope Francis had endorsed Donald Trump's presidential candidacy. This story was shared more than a million times on Facebook, but what was not included, was the disclaimer on its 'About' page which stated that it was a "*a fantasy news website. Most articles on wtoe5news.com are satire or pure fantasy*" [4]. The researcher is of the opinion that of all the different types of misleading content, satire, can be the most unintentionally misleading as disclaimers can be intentionally or unintentionally ignored.

The term 'fake news' will be used interchangeably with 'disinformation' and 'misinformation' in this chapter.

## 2.2 *Types of False or Misleading Content*

According to UNESCO's handbook on Journalism Education and Training, Fake news can generally be categorised at a high-level into the following common types [52, 53]: (a) Wrong time/Wrong Place—this is the most common type of misleading visual where old visuals are re-shared with new claims about what they depict. These can be easily debunked, but not easily pulled back once in circulation. (b) Manipulated Content—This is content that has been digitally manipulated using photo or video editing software. (c) Staged Content—This is original content that has been created or shared with the intent to mislead, such as deepfakes and just outrightly false information.

### 2.2.1 Deepfakes

Deepfakes were originally employed in the pornography industry where it referred to the process of inserting celebrities' faces into pornographic scenes, usually without their knowledge. It is now much more widespread across all spectra of society including the political arena. Chesney and Citron define deep fakes as "*highly realistic and difficult-to-detect digital manipulations of audio or video*" [9].

### 2.2.2 Proliferation of Fake News

Digital platforms, connectivity, the ubiquity of technology, the increase of information and the prevalence of Online Social Networks (OSN), on the one hand have overcome traditional challenges and roadblocks such as physical borders and the constraints of time and distance, making the distribution and sharing of information a lot easier. On the other hand, it means public perception of reality can be more easily influenced and distorted by a small number of individuals through the dispersion of misinformation and disinformation. The growing use of social media to the point that it is considered normative and is ingrained in almost every sphere of modern life including social, business, personal etc. means that the proliferation of any news, particularly fake news is highly likely. McGonagle, in his article, "Fake news": False fears or real concerns?", is of the position that fake news has always existed but that the "game-changing factors" are: "*the sophistication with which fake news is being produced; the scale on which it is being produced, and the speed and effectiveness with which it is being disseminated*" [32]. Despite the fact that the term 'fake news' has been made a lot popular in recent times it has actually been covered extensively by other academic literatures in political science, computer science, psychology etc. Adam Berinsky, in his study on Healthcare Reforms, carried out experiments on political misinformation and posits that rumours acquire power through familiarity and that attempting to quash rumours through direct refutation could actually facilitate their diffusion, as merely repeating a rumour increases its strength, even in the "*context of debunking misinformation with a strong correction*" [7].

The changing habits of news consumption means that there is a higher tendency for people to assimilate news as seen on social media which, also enables the wide dissemination of fake news. Fake news is a unique problem because it exists in so many parts. Its roots and the reasons for which it spreads are myriad and complex. Consequently, one of the reasons it has been able to proliferate so easily is due to the fact that the onus of responsibility does not clearly fall in one place [27].

### 2.2.3 Impact of Misinformation (Fake News)

In assessing the impact of misinformation e.g. fake news, Flynn et al. discuss how political misconceptions can undermine people's ability to form meaningful opinions by distorting public debate, thereby impacting democracy [20]. Kuklinski et al. seemingly well ahead of their time, as far back as 2003, unwittingly predicted events leading up to the 2016 US elections, highlighted the issue of misinformation in the political arena amongst American citizens, inferring that widespread information could lead to collective preferences far different from what it would have been if people were correctly informed [31]. The misinformation of the general public, though not a new phenomenon, appears to be on the increase due to the ubiquity of technology.

## 3 Prevention, Detection and Investigation

The misinformation of the general public is attracting increasing attraction by all facets of society seeking to combat this proliferation of misinformation and disinformation. Researchers, journalists and some members of the general public alike, have taken on this feat with different focuses and in different ways, all with one aim in mind, to combat fake news due to the myriad of negative effects, including, as cited by Shu et al. the fact that "fake news can disturb the authenticity balance of the news ecosystem" [42]. Checking the facts of various news articles, images, memes, videos etc. is now on the increase in modern day society.

### *3.1 Fact Checking Fake News*

To date, there are varying methods that have developed for detecting fake news, ranging from online fact checkers such as factcheck.org, Snopes and Politifact, to other detection tools such as FakeBox. The Massachusetts Institute of Technology (MIT) has carried out research which aims to detect fake news at its source by using machine learning (ML) [12]. It decided to take a different approach from Snopes and Politifact, where the focus is on investigating specific claims, the downside of which is that the time it takes for them to review and debunk the news, is the time that it would have probably gone viral round the world. Fake news has high proliferation rates and therefore the time used to debunk a story is usually time used for it to travel. Other researchers such as Sander van Linden are working on pre-empting fake news by working on stopping misinformation before it starts to spread [35]. As Fake News becomes more and more ingrained in modern society, it is imperative that there is a mindset shift with the general public learning to be a bit more sceptical in their assimilation and 'sharing' of information, i.e. members of the general public should now be at a point where a brief fact-check, based on instinct, is carried out before sharing any information. The researcher is of the opinion, that, on a high level, it is easy for anyone to detect certain types of fake news such as manipulated images, exaggerated facts and will be carrying out a fake news quiz to prove or disprove this.

### *3.2 Fact Checking Tools and Techniques*

The IEEE Computer Society has compiled a list of datasets, fact checking sites, workshops and projects for researchers interested in verification of social media and news-related content. This is comprised of a variety of fact checking tools developed by researchers, journalists, academicians etc. that have an interest in combatting misinformation in its variety of forms.

Figure 1 shows a compilation of datasets for the verification of social media and news-related content, as collated by the IEEE Computer Society.

The types of manipulation that can be done on images and videos are: content manipulation; location spoofing; metadata manipulation; rebroadcasting; repurposing existing images; AI-generated images e.g. deepfakes. In order to establish or verify facts, there are various basic and advanced source and content verification techniques used such as Social Media Account Analysis, Reverse Image Search, YouTube Data Viewer etc. [52, 53] which can be employed.

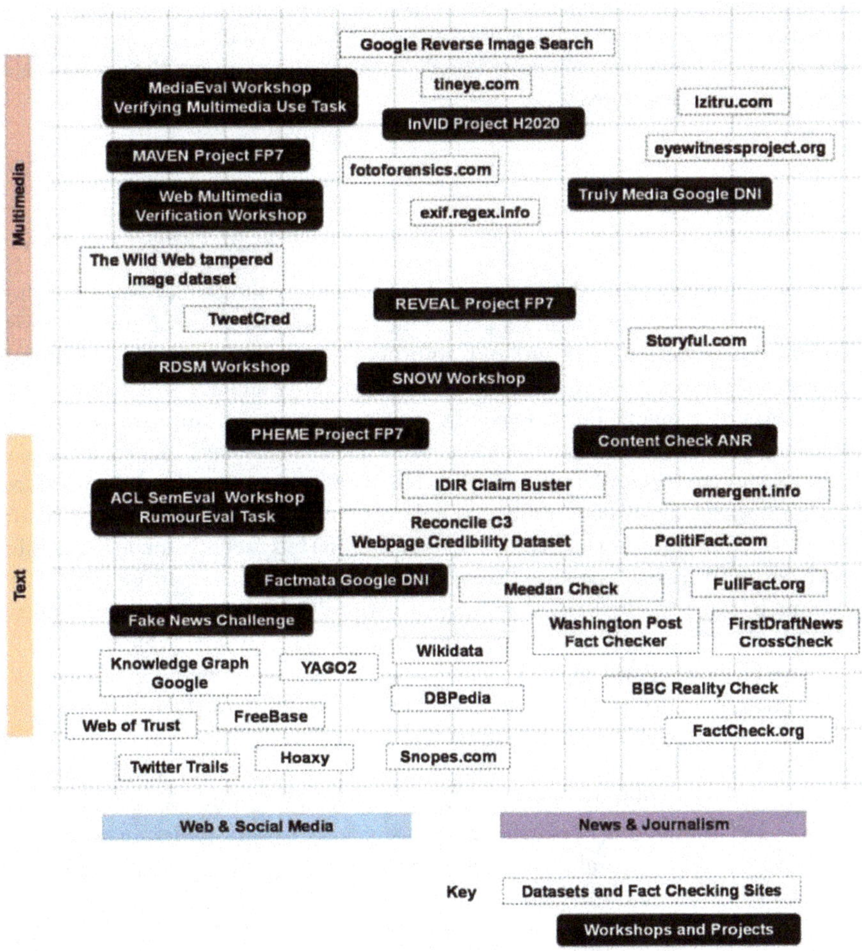


**Fig. 1** Research and dataset landscape for the verification of social media and news-related content [25]

### 3.3 Forensic Investigation of Fake News

Many forensic methods can easily detect changes when pictures and videos have been tampered with, by examining the metadata attached by editing software to these files. However, most of this metadata is stripped away when uploaded to social media platforms such as Facebook and Twitter [25]. REVEAL, A European Commission co-sponsored project, attempts to address this issue by generating tampering probability heat maps based on a number of complementary forensic-analysis algorithms. It involves the inclusion of multiple image-forensics algorithms and side-by-side comparisons, allowing analysts understand where possible digital tampering may have occurred. Additionally, REVEAL discuss a software program called TUNGSTÈNE, used to analyse digital images and photographs for anomalies using filters and algorithms.

### 3.4 Legislation

A natural consequence of the increase in fake news is the outcry for legislation. With legislation comes prosecution and an increased dependency on investigations. Following the successful exposure of Cambridge Analytica, it is possible that more litigation will arise regarding fake news, misinformation and disinformation.

The UK Government has no specific policies for addressing fake news, filter bubbles or echo-chambers. Attempts to address these issues have mainly focused on fake news and have been largely industry-led. The Independent High-Level Group of the European Commission produced a report which recommends not regulating against misinformation [11]. On the other hand, China has recently made it a criminal offence to publish deepfakes or fake news without disclosure. In October 2019, California became the first US state to criminalise the use of deepfakes in political campaign promotion and advertising, in a law called, AB 730 which makes it a crime to publish audio, imagery or video that gives "*a false, damaging impression of a politician's words or actions.*" [47]. Legislation naturally leads to investigations, because where there is law, there will be breaches.

In considering the implementation of legislation for "Fake News", there are concerns over the stifling of free speech. Pew Research Centre carried out a study and found that although the general consensus is that misinformation in all its forms will get worse, there was also a general concern that open exchange of ideas and privacy would be compromised if legislation is introduced [38].

Poynter carried out a review of 50 countries that have taken action against misinformation in some form. The study shows that only 14 out of 50 countries have actually passed laws regarding misinformation. This appears to be due to the challenge of inhibiting free speech. Freedom House rates countries according to how 'free' their legislation is in allowing reporters the ability to report freely.

With more countries looking at legislating against misinformation, it has become more imperative to ensure that investigations are carried out accurately.

### *3.5 Existence of Forensic Guidelines for the Investigation of Fake News*

The researcher did not come across any digital forensic guidelines for the investigation of fake news—that is not to say that they do not exist. It could be that the researchers review scope could have been broader. Nevertheless, the researcher is of the opinion that the current ACPO guidelines could be adapted to the investigation of fake news, thereby leading to proposed forensic guidelines for the investigation of fake news. To this end, the researcher will seek to review and understand current fake checking methodologies in order to determine whether or not they can be converted into some type of forensic guidelines.

## 4 Review of Fact Checking Methodologies

Further to the general techniques employed by most fact checkers, the fact checking methodologies were reviewed in detail, in order to get an insight into the steps taken to carry out these techniques. 41 fact checkers were reviewed by reviewing their methodologies usually found in the 'About' section of their websites. These were collated and compiled.

### *4.1 Fact Check Sites, Workshops and Projects with Their Descriptions*

1. exif.regex.info—Also called Jeffrey's Image MetaData Viewer. This is a photo-info web tool that helps photographers understand camera settings used to take a particular image [22].
2. eyewitnessproject.org—A registered UK charity which runs an app used to capture images (they deal mainly with atrocities). The chief goal of the eyeWitness app is as a tool to aid in holding to account culprits of 'unspeakable' crimes [15].
3. fotoforensics.com—FotoForensics provides tools that help identify alterations to images using various tools for digital photo forensics [21].
4. Google Reverse Image Search—Used to detect visually similar images from around the web.

5. Truepic—A photo and video verification platform aiming to fight against disinformation. Truepic has a patented technology called Controlled Capture which establishes trust in digital photos and videos by verifying their origin, pixel contents and metadata, from the instant the capture button is pressed [49].
6. The Wild Web Tampered Image Dataset—Developed as part of the REVEAL project while working on Image Forensics, Zampolgou et al. investigated the potential for applying image splicing detection in a bid to prevent the spreading of misinformation due to altered images. This led to the creation of this dataset which is a collection of forgeries from various web and social media sources. It also includes, where possible, the image sources that were used to perform the forgeries [58].
7. tineye.com—This is an image search and recognition company. It uses MatchEngine to find duplicated, resized and modified images.
8. TweetCred—This is a real-time system that assigns a credibility score to tweets on a user's timeline.
9. JPEGsnoop—A tiny computer forensic tool that provides information about JPEG images [57].
10. Pic2Map—Pic2Map is an online EXIF data viewer with GPS support that enables the location and viewing of images on Google Maps. Even without GPS data, it can be used as an EXIF data viewer.
11. Pixsy—Online image protection platform which is used to discover where and how images are being used online. Predominantly used by creatives and image owners.
12. WeVerify—Is an online verification plugin that aims to address the complete content verification workflow by verifying textual claims, images and videos (including AI-generated fakes).

#### Multimedia Fact Check Workshops and Projects

13. InVid—InVid Horizon 2020 (H2020) was an innovation action funded by the European Union. InVid is a browser plugin which combines many tools in one place with a view to debunking fake news and verifying videos and images. The tools include: keyframe extractor for videos, metadata extractor for photos and videos, a reverse image search on keyframes, a magnifying tool for photographs and an interface for Twitter Advanced Search.
14. MAVEN Project FP7—The MAVEN Project is a European FP7 Project whose main objective is to develop a suite of tools for multimedia data management and security [40].
15. MediaEval Workshop Verifying Multimedia Use Task—Workshop set up to address the problem of misleading multimedia content (images and videos) by establishing automated ways of classifying viral social media content propagating fake images or misrepresenting images (i.e. presenting real images in a fake context).

16. REVEAL Project FP7—Set up to determine the trust and credibility of images and videos through analysis by extracting attributed verification and debunking reports from social media.
17. Truly Media Google DNI—Web based content collaboration platform for the verification of digital (user-generated) content residing on social networks and elsewhere. Available as a standalone product or as an addon to a news asset platform.
18. FaceForensics ++—*A* dataset of facial forgeries containing manipulations created with Face2Face, FaceSwap, DeepFakes and NeuralTextures [41].
19. Pheme—Builds technology for finding how true claims made online are. Pheme focuses on the veracity of information from social media.
20. Africa Check—Non-Profit Fact Checking Organisation that aims to promote accuracy in public debate and the media in Africa by raising the quality of information available to society across the continent.
21. Chequeado—Non-Partisan, non-profit fact checking website which aims to improve public debate in Argentina through open data and fact checking in order to strengthen democratic discourse, promote the value of truth, and increase the cost of lying.
22. Vishvas News—Multilingual fact checking website based in India.
23. Altnews—Fact-checking website committed to debunking misinformation, disinformation and mal-information encountered daily on social media and mainstream media.
24. VoxCheck—Independent non-profit organisation that aims to promote high quality economic discussions in Ukraine by reviewing statements of politicians and dismantling economic myths.
25. stopfake.org—Ukraine based journalist organisation which aims to verify information, strengthening media literacy of the audience and the struggle for a clear demarcation between journalism of facts and propaganda.
26. Full Fact—UK's independent factchecking charity whose aim is to find, expose and counter the harm that bad information does.
27. Ferret Fact Service—Northern Ireland's first dedicated fact-checking service. Publishes nonpartisan articles on the accuracy of statements by public figures, major institutions, and other attributable claims of interest to society.
28. Media Bias/Fact Check—US based independent online media outlet. Dedicated to educating the public on media bias and deceptive news practices. Aims to inspire action and a rejection of overtly biased media.
29. politifact.com—Non-profit project operated by Poynter Institute in St Petersburg, Florida whose objective is to give citizens the information they need to govern themselves in a democracy.
30. snopes.com—An Independent US publication owned by Snopes Media Group which aims to aims to debunk or confirm widely spread urban legends.
31. factcheck.org—A nonpartisan, non-profit "consumer advocate" for voters. (A project of the Annenberg Public Policy Centre of the University of Pennsylvania) which aims to reduce the level of deception and confusion in U.S politics.

32. Climate Feedback—a worldwide network of scientists sorting fact from fiction in climate change media coverage which aims to help readers know which news to trust [10].
33. factmata.com—An Artificial Intelligence company whose mission is "*to give everyone a better understanding of content*" by using a scoring system, communities and expert knowledge to identify and classify content. Specialises in automated fact checking [18].
34. Emergent—A real time rumour verification tracker. Part of a research project with the Tow Centre for Digital Journalism at Columbia University that aims to fight disinformation by identifying, exploring and correcting false information. It is a web-based tool that tracks, verifies or debunks rumours and conspiracies online. It is content-focused and directly evaluates information, such as the authenticity of a photo [13].
35. fakespot.com—A Chrome plugin that analyses consumer reviews to aid in making better purchasing decisions.
36. Hoaxy—a platform for tracking online misinformation.
37. Twitter Trails—An interactive web-based tool that "allows *users to investigate the origin and propagation characteristics of a rumour and its refutation, if any, on Twitter*" [19].
38. Truth or Fiction—A non-partisan website created for users to investigate e-rumours, fake news, hoaxes, virus warnings etc. The websites' focus tends to be on stories that are most widely circulated on social media. Propaganda, misinformation and disinformation is debunked and context and nuance is offered. Where possible, the source is always mentioned [50, 51].
39. storyful.com—Social media intelligence and news agency that specialise in social media contextualisation and verification. Storyful traces the origins and sources of mis- and disinformation across fringe and mainstream platforms [45].
40. Content check ANR—A content checking project that brings together academic labs with expertise in data management, natural language processing, automated reasoning, data mining and a fact-checking team of French media journalists. Working on developing automated fact checking alongside journalists for verification [2].

## *4.2 Fact Check Techniques*

1. Facebook Account Analysis—used to find out more about a source by analysing their Facebook account.
2. Twitter Account Analysis—Used to Find out more about a source and determine whether or not it is a bot by analysing their social history and tweeting habits.
3. Reverse Image Search—To check if an image was in existence previously, but recaptioned. Can also be used to determine when an image first appeared. Reverse image search also lets you see whether or not earlier versions of the image appear

in other image databases. If it does, it is a red flag. If it does not, this does not prove that it is an original image and additional checks need to be carried out.
4. YouTube Data Viewer—Used to extract hidden data from videos hosted on YouTube. Variables that can be extracted are: exact upload time (useful to determine original video when confronted with multiple copies of the same video and to determine the actual upload date (which can be different from the public timestamp); and all image thumbnails which can be used to conduct a reverse image search in order to find older versions of the same video.
5. Digital Image Forensics Analysis—A set of free tools for digital image forensics including clone detection, error level analysis, meta data extraction, etc. which are able to detect inconsistencies in image metadata that suggest manipulation. Clone detection and error level analysis provide useful insights. The validity of these techniques is highly subject to the context and application.
6. Metadata viewer—Digital and phone cameras create a wide range of data points at the point of capture. EXIF is metadata that is attached to these data points and can include exact date and time, location metadata, device data and light setting information. A major limitation, however, is that social networks strip the metadata from visual content and images shared on Twitter and Facebook will not display EXIF data. However, if the original uploader can be contacted and the original image file acquired, then EXIF can be used to verify the content. Please note that EXIF data can be modified, so further verification is required.
7. Geolocation—Geolocation is the estimation of the real-world geographical location of an object and can be used to determine where a video or image was captured. Where adequate metadata is available, this process can be straightforward. EXIF data from mobile phones often reveal coordinates and a lot of social content (e.g. on Instagram, Twitter and Facebook) is geotagged. However, such metadata is editable and can be misleading. This often, requires cross-referencing visual characteristics and landmarks from satellite imagery from other sources.
8. Weather corroboration—Can reveal historical weather data, allowing checkers to corroborate the weather depicted in the visual with actual historic data.
9. Shadow Analysis—Technique where the internal consistency of any visible shadows is examined on photos and videos. i.e. are the shadows in the expected places, considering the source of light.

## 4.3 *List of Fact Checking Methodologies by Tool*

1. exif.regex.info

   **Fact Checking Methodology**
   Reveals data that may be in an image file such as:

   - Camera shutter speed;
   - Time of capture;
   - Details of information from uploaded image;

- Date picture was taken;
- File type (jpeg, gif etc.);
- File size in megapixels;
- Colour encoding;
- Modify Date;
- Exif Version;
- Date/Time Original;
- Creation Date;
- Components Configuration;
- Exif Image Size;
- Resolution (dpi);
- Sub Sec Time Original;
- Sub Sec Time Digitized;
- Flashpix Version;
- ColorSpace;
- Scene Capture Type.

**URL**: http://exif.regex.info/exif.cgi

2. eyewitnessproject.org

   i. The eyeWitness to Atrocities mobile camera app allows the capture of photos and videos. These are embedded with metadata at the moment the footage was captured.
   ii. The footage is then sent to the eyeWitness server and a chain of custody is created. This is key to allowing photos and videos to be used as evidence in court.
   iii. eyeWitness ensures that the captured information is processed for justice by tagging, cataloguing and processing the visual evidence to meet the requirements of the investigators. This is done by lawyers.
   iv. eyeWitness then works with their client to identify the international, regional and/or national bodies best placed to act on the information.

   **Limitations**: Images need to be taken via their own app and this is only available on Google Play (at the time of writing).
3. fotoforensics.com
   Image is either uploaded on to site or url copied into and image analysis carried out. The features that are analysed are:

   - Digest Process
   - Meta Properties
   - Timestamps
   - Cryptographic Checksums. [A single file will always generate the same hash value. Any minor change to the file will significantly alter the result. Even if the files have the same appearance and size, a single byte change will alter the digest. The cryptographic complexity means that it is virtually impossible for

someone to fiddle with the bytes in order to match the original checksum]. These digests can therefore be used to detect tampering.
- ELA—Error Level Analysis
- Hidden Pixels—which may identify applications
- JPEG %—identifies the last JPEG quality level.
- Metadata—JPEGs contain the most information including: camera's make and model; focal. Metadata also provides information as to how the file was generated and handled and is analogous to the chain of custody for evidence handling, as it can identify how a picture was generated, processed and last saved.

**Limitations**—Hash Collisions are possible. This happens when two different files have the same checksum.

4. Google Reverse Image Search
   Image is uploaded or the url pasted into the search bar.
   - Search carried out over a number of sites.
   - Used to find the original source of an image or the approximate date an image was first publicised;
   - Shows other websites that are using the same image.
5. Truepic
   i. Capture—Creates a trusted chain of custody for photos and videos, right from the source: Once the capture button is pressed, the Controlled Capture pipeline receives data directly from the image sensor, and other sensors such as GPS. It then computes a cryptographic signature (digital footprint) for the image and encrypts all this information for transmission to Truepic's servers. The creation of this unique identifier for the image, initiates the images chain of custody.
   ii. Verification—The image next undergoes a series of over 20 verification tests which include: capture device integrity; date, time, location of capture; that the image is not a recapture of an existing one. Only images and videos that pass these tests are designated as authentic originals.
   iii. Store—The metadata, cryptographic signature and the results of the verification tests of the original image are stored in the Truepic vault.
   iv. Record—An immutable record with the image's cryptographic signature is written to a public distributed ledger which is neither controlled by Truepic nor hosted on their servers. This step closes the chain of custody.
6. The Wild Web tampered image dataset—Methodology unavailable.
7. tineye.com

   Upload image or paste in url.
   Image uses image recognition to search images.

Image is automatically fingerprinted using image recognition and indexed for searching. It does not use metadata to do this (which is a positive as FaceBook and Twitter strip metadata from images).
Images are distinguished one from another using the unique fingerprint generated for each image. These unique digital fingerprints describe the patterns found in the pixels of the images and MatchEngine is able to identify even partial matches of these fingerprints [48].

8. TweetCred—This is a real-time system that assigns a credibility score to tweets on a user's timeline. No further information available.
9. JPEGsnoop

   Displays EXIF data that may have been embedded in a camera e.g. date image was captured; location, camera model, use of flash etc.
   Also includes a database of EXIF markers and compression signatures used by many cameras and photo editors. Provides information on whether it thinks image has been edited or if it is in its original form [57].

10. Pic2Map
    Reveals EXIF information such as:

    Image Information: Brand, Model, Lens, Shutter, F Number, ISO Speed, Flash, Focal Length, Colour Space
    File Information: Image Size, Photo Pixels, File Size, MIME Type, x-Resolution, y-Resolution.
    Date and Time: Date of image creation, Time of image creation, Time Zone.
    GPS Information: Latitude, Longitude, Lat. Ref (indicates whether the latitude is north or south); Long. Ref; Coordinates, Altitude, Direction Ref, Direction, Pointing.
    Location Information: Town/City, City/State, Country.

11. Pixsy
    Uses reverse image search and artificial intelligence to find images.
12. WeVerify

    (a) Verify content and source
    (b) Find rumours and disinformation
    (c) Analyse images and videos
    (d) Discover deep fakes
    (e) Cross-Modal verification.

**Multimedia Fact Check Workshops and Projects**

13. InVid

    (a) Video Context using the Analysis Feature—this is an enhanced metadata viewer for YouTube, Twitter and Facebook public videos and allows the retrieval of contextual information, location (if detected) and apply reverse image search for tweets on the video.

(b) Keyframes Tool—allows the user to copy a video url from YouTube, Twitter etc. or to upload a local video file. Once this is done, the video can be segmented into (real) keyframes and each of them reverse image searched on Google, Yandex, Tineye etc. These are real keyframes and not the thumbnails served by YouTube or Facebook.

(c) Twitter—The Twitter advanced search is used to search for keywords or hashtags using the 'since' and 'until' operators in order to query a time interval, up to the minute. It automatically translates the calendar date, hours and minutes into a UNIX timestamp which facilitates the query e.g. a query to search for the first eyewitness account of an event, just after a 'breaking news' alert. Additional features for the Twitter Advanced Search are: geocode, language, near, from and various other filter operators.

(d) Magnifier Lens—allows users to zoom or apply a magnifying lens to an uploaded image or through the image's url. It is enhanced through a bicubic algorithm to help discover written words, signs, banners etc.

(e) Metadata—The EXIF metadata of an image in jpeg format or metadata of a video in mp4/m4v format can be checked either through a link or a locally uploaded file. Where geocoordinates are available in the picture metadata, a geolocalise button emerges, automatically pointing to the location on Google maps.

(f) Forensic Filters—Eight different forensic filters are used to detect digital image tampering: Dougle Quantization; Error Level Analysis; WAVELET, BLOCK, CAGI, CAGI-Inversed, Median Noise and GHOST. The more filters that display anomalies, the higher the likelihood that the image has been tampered with digitally.

14. MAVEN Project FP7

The MAVEN framework has a suite of tools:

Image source identification—Link a digital image to its corresponding camera to identify image origin.

Image Identification Verification—Verify if a digital image has been globally or locally edited or manipulated (with original image available/not available).

Video Integrity Verification—Assess if a digital video has undergone double encoding and insertion/removal of frames.

Text Localisation and Extraction—Detect and recognise text within unconstrained scene imagery.

Spoken Keyword Detection—Spot previously known keywords in audio tracks.

Face Detection and Recognition—Automatically detect and recognise faces in image and video galleries.

Object and Scene Recognition—Detect company logos and categorise scenes.

15. MediaEval Workshop Verifying Multimedia Use Task

    Multi-media indexing and search (e.g. Near-duplicate detection);
    Forensics—manipulation/tampering detection. Features extracted: probability map
    Web mining and information extraction—trust-oriented feature extraction;
    Machine learning—fake classification;
    Information retrieval and crowdsourcing—trust assessment and labelling.

16. REVEAL Project FP7

    Check content/provenance: original post, location, timestamp, similar posts, website.
    Check author/source: attributed or author; known reliable; known unreliable; popular; reputation; post history;
    Check content credibility: image metadata, location, people, weather;
    Contact author: triangulate facts, quiz author, get authorisation to publish.

17. Truly Media Google DNI
    Find content from a variety of sources;
    Verify using a toolkit of internal and third-party verification tools.
18. FaceForensics++

    - Forgery detection of human observers
    - Automatic forgery detection methods
    - Detection based on Steganalysis features
    - Detection based on Learned features
    - Detection of facial expression manipulation and facial identity manipulation
    - Detection of face swapping.

19. Pheme
    Uses three factors to analyse veracity:

    - the information inherent in the document itself—lexical, semantic and syntactic information;
    - cross-reference with data sources that are deemed trustworthy;
    - analyse information diffusion: who received information, how was it received, when was it transmitted and by whom.

20. Africa Check

    i. Identify the exact claim that is to be verified.
    ii. Contact the person who makes the claim to verify the source or proof of their claim.
    iii. Fact checkers then turn to experts in the field to add nuance and context.
    iv. Authors write their reports, setting out the evidence step by step and indicating the sources used.
    v. Manuscript is passed on to an editor for review.

vi. Article published only once verdict is agreed [3].

21. Chequeado
Uses AI tool called chequeabot that pulls quotes from 30 news outlets across the country and from every speech by the president and in Congress.

    i. Select statement from politicians, economists etc. without discrimination on the basis of their partisan or ideological orientation.
    ii. Confirm that the object of the check has been expressed in documents, media or public areas.
    iii. Confirm relevance to the public agenda due to prominence of person that issued them, public agenda etc.
    iv. Analyse degree of relevance.
    v. Main Buenos Aires newspapers are followed.
    vi. Chequeabot monitors more than 30 national and provincial media, Congress transcripts and presidential speeches.
    vii. Additionally, checks and run on readers suggestions from social media, WhatsApp etc.
    viii. Once data verification is complete, context is added, where relevant.
    ix. Phrases are not checked when there are no data or experts that allow verification.
    x. Anonymous sources are not used. All sources used are cited, and whenever possible, the link to the document and the original data is included in order to aid accessibility [8].

**Additional Information**: *Opinions, comments or statements of commitments are not subject to verification, except when they are based on data or facts whose veracity can be weighted. No opinion is issued.

22. Vishvas News

    i. Select news stories to verify based on nature of the viral post, how viral it has gone and, the source of the viral post.
    ii. Probe the News by attempting to contact the ‘poster’. If unsuccessful, verify using technology including Google Reverse Image search, InVid, tweetb eaver.com etc.
    iii. Publishes its finding in the form of a story in the public domain with screenshots and links [55].

23. Altnews
Select Claim to Debunk based on the following criteria:

    i. Virality of claim (extent, reach and spread); [Virality is considered the most important criterion as Alt News prefers not to write about insufficiently viral misinformation, as this could then trigger virality.]
    ii. Source of the claim (who shared it? A prominent politician? A verified account?);

iii. Nature of the claim (Is it provocative? can it lead to violence or physical harm to individuals?).

Researching the Claim:

- Fact checking is also done by various software and by contacting authorities e.g. police for information and/or clarification.
- Google reverse image search is used for images.
- Contact the person to whom a seemingly fake claim is attributed.
- InVid is used to break videos into individual frames which are then scrutinised.

Evaluating the claim

- Uses a variety of tools and methods to evaluate the veracity of a claim and arrives at a conclusion. Where relevant, more than one tool is used to conclusively debunk the fake claim.

Writing the Fact-Check

- Once above steps are concluded, Alt News puts this in the public domain. If the information is inadequate or out of bounds, Alt News refrains from passing conclusive judgement.

Updating the Articles

- Articles are updated in the event of any errors on Alt News' part.
- Virality is considered the most important criterion as Alt News prefers not to write about insufficiently viral misinformation, as this could then trigger virality [5].

24. VoxCheck
Politician's speech monitored (regardless of governmental affiliation or political party membership) from news releases, TV shows, media and social media;

  i. Statements are collated.
  ii. Adjusted to formatting standards.
  iii. Verification is based only on open data with the relevant links.
  iv. Only the actual statements within the specific context are analysed.
  v. Fact-check writing and editing.
  vi. Peer reviewed by two editors.
  vii. Published [56].

25. stopfake.org

- Refutation of individual fakes,
- Creation of a propaganda archive,
- Information analysis,
- Training on information verification for various interested groups,
- Participation in conferences and seminars [44].

26. Full Fact
    Fact checking process involves a three-stage review.
    Full fact is building scalable, robust, automated factchecking tools to be used in newsrooms and by factcheckers all over the world.
    Live—one of the tools intended to immediately check statements against a database of verified facts.
    Trends—tracks and displays the spread of false information [23].
27. Ferret Fact Service
    Manually scour media and social media outlets for press releases and trending news. Scottish Parliament and Westminster.
    Social media analysis tools are also employed, and the comment sections analysed.
    Initially, once a claim has been selected for verifying, the alleged source is contacted.
    Statement is assessed alongside other available material for veracity purposes.
    Experts are also contacted, where necessary.
    Interpret and evaluate.
    Rate claim. Claims are rated on a scale from True to Unsupported over 7 levels.
28. FactCheckNI
    Researches claims only with publicly available sources. Claim must be:
    a publicly made statement attributable to a specific person (e.g. politician) or an organisation (e.g. report). An assertion or allegation that can be validated or refuted (to a degree) based on past or present actions (i.e. not speculative about the future).
    Contact is made with the person/organisation that made the claim to verify the accuracy of the original statement. Sources provided by the claimant are investigated.
    Due to the varying standards of quality, methodology is verified. Therefore, for instance, information provided by a statutory statistical agency may take less time to validate a dial-in telephone survey.
    Sources of evidence that could contradict the developed conclusion are sought out and all links are provided (those that support as well as refute claims).
    A fact-checked claim is double-checked with at least two people before publishing [16].
29. Media Bias/Fact Check
    Calculates bias by how factual the information is; Not just political bias;

    - In each category, the source is rated on a 0–10 number, with 0 meaning without bias and 10 being the maximum bias (worst).
    - These 4 numbers are then added up and divided by 4.
    - The categories are as follows:
        i. Biased Wording/Headlines
        ii. Factual/Sourcing
        iii. Story Choices
        iv. Political Affiliation [33].

30. politifact.com
    Transcripts, speeches, news stories, press releases and campaign brochures are read to find statements to fact-check. Including TV and social media.
    Selection criteria:

    Check that statement is rooted in a verifiable fact.
    Does statement sound misleading or wrong?
    Is the statement significant?
    Likely to be passed on and repeated by others.
    Would a typical person hear or read the statement and wonder if it is true?
    Statements about topics in the news are selected.

    On the record sourcing:

    Uses on-the-record interviews.
    Publishes a list of sources with every fact-check.
    Attempts always made to contact person, website or organisation.

    Reporting process:

    review what other fact-checkers have found previously;
    a thorough Google search;
    a search of online databases;
    consultation with a variety of experts;
    a review of publications and a final overall review of available evidence;
    Emphasise primary sources and original documentation which are then independently verified except, where PolitiFact must cite news reports from other media that rely on unnamed or unattributed sources [36].

31. snopes.com
    No single method for fact checking due to varying types of material.
    In general, each entry is assigned to one of the members of the editorial staff.
    Undertakes preliminary research.
    First draft of fact-check is written.
    Possible contact with source of claim for elaboration and supporting information. Also knowledgeable individuals and organisations.
    Search out printed information.
    Final product passes through the hands of at least one editor.
    Not focused solely on politics.
    Sources—attempt to use non-partisan information and data sources e.g. peer reviewed journals as much as possible.
    Operate a corrections policy [43].
32. factcheck.org
    Monitors the factual accuracy of what is said by major U.S. political players in the form of TV ads, debates, speeches, interviews and news releases.
    Systematically, go through transcripts and videos looking for statements based on facts.

Engage—or attempt to engage—with the person or organisation that is being fact-checked.
The burden is on the person or organisation making the claim to provide the evidence to support it.
If accurate, drop.
Focus is only on claims that are false or misleading.
Conduct own research if supporting material does not support the claim.
Reliance on primary sources of information e.g. the Library of Congress, the IRS for tax data etc.
Reliance on nonpartisan government agencies for expertise, analyses and reports.
Reliance also on a few respected and trustworthy outside experts [17].

33. Climate Feedback

    - Select an article for assessment, according to subject matter, relevance in current climate change discussion, and potential digital influence.
    - Call on scientists with relevant expertise to participate in article analysis.
    - Analyse selected article, with a focus on assessing (claimed) fact-based assertions and scientific reasoning.—Reviewers are asked to comment on the article to indicate whether the facts underlying the reasoning are consistent with up-to-date scientific knowledge. Reviewers should represent the state of knowledge in the scientific literature, using strongly supported scientific theories and observations as references, and refrain from pointing to partial/isolated/weakly supported findings.
    - The primary objective of scientists is to check the scientific accuracy of the facts and assumptions on which the article is based.
    - Evaluate the article's overall credibility against current state-of-the-art knowledge and thinking in climate science using the following credibility criteria: Factual Accuracy, scientific understanding, context and limitations, logic/reasoning, precision/clarity, sources quality, fairness/objectivity.
    - Summary and Feedback.

34. Emergent
    Rumours are suggested by site users. Staff then review and determine whether the claim is true or false. No further description on the methodology found.
35. factmata.com
    Algorithms find highly-targeted stories and use AI to detect claims, arguments and stance.
    Detect trends;
    Identify people leading public opinion;
    Monitor content and conversation across all digital platforms; 300,000 sites from mainstream news to niche websites; 30 million blogs; Social Media, Police reports; Intranets etc.
    Advanced NLP learns what different types of deceptive content look like and is then able to detect across the digital platforms.

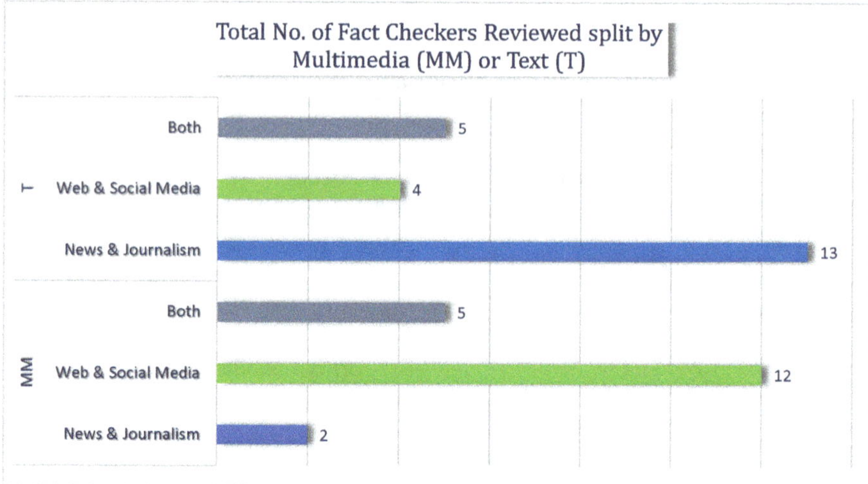


**Fig. 2** No. of multimedia and text based fact checkers reviewed

36. fakespot.com
    Filters out fake reviews.
    No further description.
37. Hoaxy—Methodology unavailable.
38. Twitter Trails—Methodology unavailable.
39. Truth or Fiction
    Various approaches for different fact checking tasks.
    Google text search.
    Contact primary sources.
    Work with experts.
    Review historical documents, video and radio interviews,
    Cross-referencing
    Books.
40. storyful.com—Methodology unavailable. None shared.
41. Content check ANR—Working on developing automated fact checking alongside journalists for verification [2]. Methodology unavailable (Fig. 2).

## 4.4 *Fact Checking Methodology for Text*

Reviewing fact checking methodologies was considered by the researcher to be the most effective way of understanding how various organisations/bodies, carried out fact checking, in order to assess the forensic soundness of the methodologies. It also served to highlight steps that were common to most fact checkers and showed the similarities based on the type of information being checked: image, text or video.

41 fact checkers were reviewed in order to get acquainted with their methodologies and to observe the common stages/steps across all of them. 49 unique methodology steps were identified which have been synthesised and clustered thematically by text, video or image, in the sections below. The methodologies varied in detail from an extreme overview to extremely detailed and technical, particularly for the multimedia fact checkers. Five of the fact checkers did not have methodologies available as they did not give access for their methodologies to be accessed or simply did not put them online. Attempts to contact them to request insight into their methodologies for academic research purposes met with a non-response.

The 41 fact checkers were classified initially, according to whether they are multimedia or text focused. The classification of either multimedia or text does not exclude one from fact checking the other.

Of the 29 Text-Based fact checkers, 13 focused on News and Journalism, four on Web and Social Media and five focused on a mixture of both. Text-based fact checkers are those whose main techniques focus on fact checking textual information such as news, memes, quotes etc. The methodology described below is based on steps that are common to all fact checking sites or tools for text.

1. Selecting a Claim—Not all claims are reviewed. Different fact checkers have different selection criteria. For instance, Chequeado is concerned with political statements and in Argentina and therefore, will not fact check a video with a man eating live mice, for instance. Most fact checkers manually select claims by scouring the internet, using Twitter hashtag analysis to see what is trending, watching the news etc. this can be either automated or manual. Only one fact checking tool carries out automated claim selection, all the rest do this manually, although there appears to be more of an intent for this to be done in an automated fashion. Chequeado, an Argentinian fact checking service, has developed the chequeabot that pulls quotes from 30 news outlets across the country and from every speech by the president and in Congress, using artificial intelligence and Natural Language Processing. Further details of the actual process were inaccessible at this time.

   In considering the development of forensic guidelines, this process of claim selection, though common to all fact checkers, deals with 'how' (the data) was acquired and could have a bearing on chain of custody. This will be further discussed in the Critical Discussion Section.
2. Contact source/originator—All fact checkers incorporate this as one of their main steps, particularly for text fact checking such as political statements, newspaper quotes, celebrity quotes etc. The source is contacted to confirm whether or not the quote, news item etc. had been correctly attributed to them. However, for images and videos, it is not always possible to find or contact the source (due to their viral nature). This is discussed further discussed further in the chapter. There are ways, in some cases, particularly where the EXIF information is still intact to find out some information, such as location where the image was taken; location where the video was uploaded (for YouTube videos); date created etc.

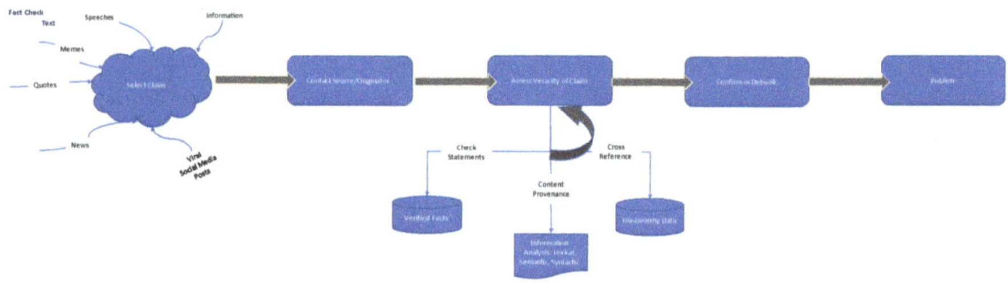


**Fig. 3** Overview of text based fact checking methodology

In a forensic investigation, contacting the source is a step that adds credibility. However, the source needs to be plausible (particularly, where a person needs to confirm or refute a statement), and this needs to be factored in, when assessing the veracity of the response.

3. Verify/Assess Veracity—by liaising with subject matter experts. Additionally,
    - check statements against database of verified facts;
    - cross-reference with trustworthy data sources;
    - carry out content provenance—lexical, semantic and syntactic information analysis to assess context, as one of the forms of misinformation is correct information taken out of context.

    For forensic purposes, this should all be documented as this translates to the equivalent of the chain of custody.
4. Confirm or Debunk—This is the ultimate aim of fact checking: to confirm or debunk. In a forensic investigation, this would also be an important step as the outcome at this stage would definitely influence the investigation.
5. Publish—All fact checkers publish the results of their fact checking on their websites. Some others have linked with various news channels (who actually have their own fact checking teams) to further increase their fact checking capabilities (Fig. 3).

## *4.5 Methodology for Fact Checking Videos*

Based on the datasets reviewed for this research, there was only one unique video fact checker—InVid. All other multimedia fact checkers that offer video fact checking use InVid to do this. This analysis is therefore based on InVid's fact checking methodology.

To verify videos, upload video into InVid tool or paste url into search bar.

i. Run the keyframe tool for videos. This extracts keyframes on which the user can carry out a reverse image search to confirm whether or not there are other instances of the image that can be found on the web.

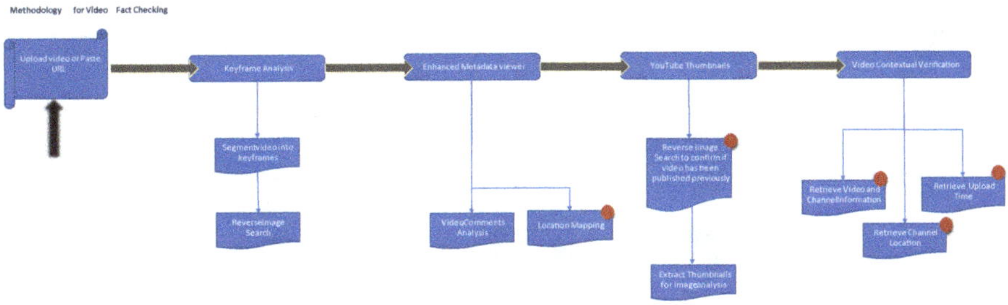


**Fig. 4** Overview of video fact checking methodology

ii. Video Contextual Verification is an enhanced metadata viewer for YouTube, Twitter and Facebook public videos and allows the retrieval of contextual information including location, where available. Please note Twitter and Facebook strip out metadata, so this may not be available if the video was downloaded from any of these platforms. The location will show where the video was uploaded. This can be a step in the forensic investigation of fake news.

iii. The magnifying tool for photographs of the extracted key frames can detect any image manipulation (Fig. 4).

## *4.6 Methodology for Fact Checking Images*

All of the 19 multimedia factcheckers reviewed process images in their fact checking. Additionally, some text-based fact checkers process images, particularly those that review web and social media (9 in number). As with the text fact checkers, the number of methodology steps have been synthesised and combined to give a streamlined overview. The common steps for fact checking images include, but are not limited to:

- Reverse Image Search: This is one of the most common fact checking methodologies used for images and is almost the first port of call. It can be carried out using Google Images or TinEye etc. It serves to find similar images on the world wide web. It is also used to detect the first appearance of an image, what it looked like etc. For forensic investigation purposes, it is a good first step in trying to find the source image. TinEye particularly, shows the date when the image that the search yields was first uploaded onto the internet.
- Metadata Viewer: This reveals a lot about the image such as creation date, geolocation, in some cases, the make of the camera that captured the image etc. Data from this process is important to the forensic investigation process. However, saving and resaving an image can cause some metadata to change or be removed. Timestamps can also be edited within the image at this level, it is therefore not a fool proof method of identifying an image or ensuring that it is the original.

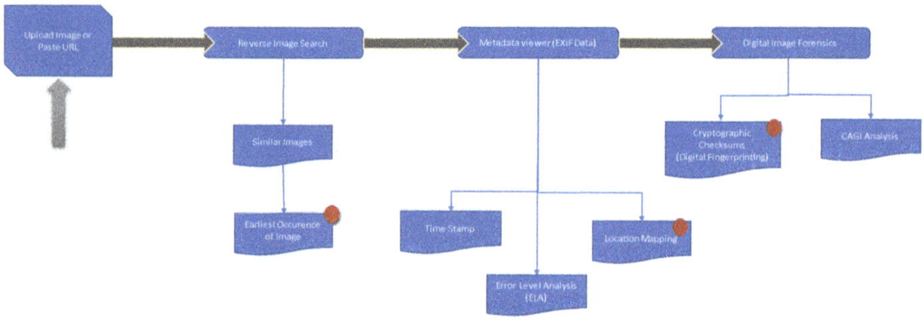


**Fig. 5** Overview of image fact checking methodology

However, it is a useful piece of information as it can indicate the last time a file was saved. Additionally, social media sites, tend to strip off metadata.

- Error Level Analysis (ELA): ELA aids in identifying areas on an image that are at different JPEG compression levels. It therefore helps in identifying whether or not an image has been tampered with. ELA has its limitations if an image has been saved multiple times. The error levels come up minimal due to loss of quality. Therefore, the fact that the ELA of an image is not high, does not mean it has not been digitally manipulated. However, combined with the analysis of additional metadata, ELA can prove useful in forensic investigations of images.
- Digital Image Forensic Analysis: This is a generic term for the various analyses that are performed on an image in a bid to understand whether or not an image has been tampered with. Used together, it can prove very effective. The most common methods are based on meta properties and cryptographic checksums.
- Cryptographic checksums: (also called hashes or checksums) act like digital fingerprints. It is highly unlikely that two different files will have the same cryptographic checksum values. A single file will always generate the same hash value and any minor change will cause a significantly different result—even a single byte change. This can therefore be used to detect tampering.
- Geolocation: This shows, where present, where the image was captured. It displays co-ordinates and some tools actually pinpoint this using Google Maps. Again, this is useful in forensic investigations (Fig. 5).

## 5 Critical Discussion

This research began with the question “can forensic guidelines be developed for the investigation of fake news?”. The journey to answering that question has led to an investigation into what the current forensic guidelines are; what fake news is and isn’t; how fake news is investigated right now and attempting to determine whether or not a chain of custody can be established in its investigation, in order to make it forensically sound and able to be used as evidence in court. The issue of fake news is neither straightforward nor simple and as mentioned, is a unique problem because it exists in so many parts. Additionally, the onus of responsibility does not clearly fall in one place [27]. Also, the fact that the journalism community have reiterated that the onus should not just be on professionals but also on every day users to prevent the dissemination and proliferation of fake news, if there is going to be any headway in combatting fake news [54].

41 fact checkers in total were reviewed. The researcher is aware that this is just a subset of the fact checkers available. From the review, it was observed that fact checking is different for text, image and video, with video and image (multimedia) fact checking being a bit more similar, due to their nature. They also differed in the way news is investigated compared to social media posts, for instance. For instance, TweetCred and Twitter Trails focus on analysing the proliferation of hashtags and how quickly a post is spreading, while TweetBeaver offers a whole suite of analytic tools, where you can look up a user, see who they are connected to, find common friends between two users etc. This was not investigated practically here, however, it could prove a very useful tool in forensic investigations. Investigating news (text-based fact checking) was the most straightforward as the steps were fairly uniform across fact checker, i.e. select claim, contact source, verify, debunk or confirm, publish.

In considering the viability of forensically investigating text-based news, traditional forensic steps cannot be followed in its pure form. For instance, contacting the source may seem like a legitimate step. However, there is the issue of the credibility of the source and all other psychological ramifications. How does the investigator know they are telling the truth? Maybe they normally tell the truth, but there are hidden situations pressuring them into lying. How is that verified?

Videos—Having only one video fact checker in the dataset meant a review may not have been as robust as it could have been. However, certain features such as the keyframe analysis appeared to be helpful as the sequence of the keyframes can be analysed to see if any editing had been done to the video. Also, the ability to create still images out of these keyframes means the still images can be investigated further for image tampering evidence.

Images—there are a plethora of tools dedicated to fact checking images and various pieces of information that can be gleaned from their investigation. Fact checking images lends itself to the most forensically aligned type of 'fake news'. Even though a few fact checkers describe their tools as 'forensic image tools', only two actually align with proper digital forensics in that the chain of custody is of paramount importance: TruePic and eyewitness.org. Both have their own apps which have to be used to capture the image or video. Once this has been captured, it is uploaded directly to their servers and a chain of custody is created. Truepic is also a photo and video verification platform which computes a cryptographic signature, encrypting all the information for transmission to its servers, thereby initiating the images chain of custody.

From the methodology review, certain aspects lend themselves to contributing to the forensic soundness of investigations e.g. for videos: location mapping, channel location, upload time, reverse image search on thumbnails. For images: cryptographic checksums (digital fingerprinting), location mapping and reverse image search to find the earliest occurrence of the image, will all aid in building up a strong forensically sound profile.

Fact Checking Veracity Test—An experimental test was designed to test the veracity of the fact checking tools thereby using a subset of the methodologies reviewed. As expected, testing the news was easier, as it involved mainly google searches, including Google News Archives. Images were a bit more difficult. However, it is the researcher's opinion, that it is with the images and videos that it is possible, to develop forensic guidelines for the investigation of fake news. Therefore, an attempt has been made below to develop and align the process of investigating fake news to the current ACPO guidelines.

| ACPO guidelines | Applicability to fake news investigations |
|---|---|
| **Principle 1**: No action taken should change data held on a digital device including a computer or mobile device that may subsequently be relied upon as evidence in court | This can be applied to the digital investigation of fake news. However, just copying over an image can change the metadata. This may be slightly different for videos. Also, difficult to apply to text-based news (news statements, headlines etc.) |
| **Principle 2**: Where a person finds it necessary to access original data held on a digital device, the person must be competent to do so and able to explain their actions and the consequent implications on the digital evidence to the Court | [a]This can be applied across images and videos and even text |
| **Principle 3**: A record of all actions that have been applied to the digital evidence should be created and preserved in such a way that an independent third party forensic expert should be able to follow or examine those processes and reach the same conclusion | This can be applied to all three. Even in investigating text based fake news, if a record is kept of all steps taken (including who was contacted, keyword searches etc.), this principle can be adhered to |
| **ACPO Principle 4**: The individual in charge of the investigation has the overall responsibility to ensure that these principles are followed | Accountability—Should be possible |

[a]Caveats to the above: Principle 2 concerning original data could be a challenge as it is difficult to determine what is original data where fake news is concerned. Finding the source is the real challenge. The researcher would suggest that the data acquired at the starting point of the investigation should be considered the 'original data'

## 6 Conclusions

The outcome of this research is that, it is possible to develop guidelines for the forensic investigation of fake news, but not in its pure form as the current ACPO guidelines stand. However, the guidelines will be subject to caveats as they will have to be adapted according to type: i.e. fake news (text); fake news (images); fake news (videos). Social media, as well, will have to have its own guidelines although having said that, possibly with the use of cloud computing, it may be possible to trace a post using artificial intelligence.

There is currently a race to improve fact checking capabilities and many are moving on to artificial intelligence, this could improve and overcome the current challenges. This research is positioned for further work to take place in order to develop these guidelines and to implement them in the near future. Such guidelines could aid in standardisation across cross-border jurisdictions, ensuring that the investigation of fake news, is handled in the same way.

It is recommended that a more thorough investigation is made of fact checking methodologies, in order to develop concrete guidelines and that the actual guidelines should be developed. Further research is suggested into the idea of using a forensic suite which will be a collaboration of different tools that can enforce the chain of custody possibly using blockchain to preserve this chain of custody.

## References


1. ACPO (2012) ACPO good practice guide for digital evidence. Metropolitan Police Service, London
2. ANR (2018) Content management techniques content management techniques for fact-checking: models, algorithms, and tools–ContentCheck. ANR, Paris
3. Africa Check (2019) Services. https://africacheck.org/services/. Accessed 21 Nov 2019
4. Allcott H, Gentzkow M (2017) Social media and fake news in the 2016 election. J Econ Perspect 31(2):211–236
5. Alt News (2019) Methodology for fact checking. https://www.altnews.in/. Accessed 23 Nov 2019
6. Bartels LM (1993) Messages received: the political impact of media exposure. Am Polit Sci Rev 87(2):267–285
7. Berinsky AJ (2015) Rumours and health care reform: experiments in political misinformation. Br J Polit Sci, 1–22
8. Chequeado (2019) Method of Verification of Public Debate. https://chequeado.com/metodo/. Accessed 23 Nov 2019
9. Chesney R, Citron D (2019) Deepfakes and the new disinformation war-the coming age of post-truth geopolitics. https://www.foreignaffairs.com/articles/world/2018-12-11/deepfakes-and-new-disinformation-war. Accessed 28 Nov 2019
10. Climate Feedback (2019) Process-how climate feedback works. https://climatefeedback.org/process/#tit3. Accessed 19 Jan 2020
11. Commission European (2018) *A multi-dimensional approach to disinformation: Repor of the High Level Group on Fake News and Online Disinformation.* Publications Office of the European Union, Luxembourg
12. Conner-Simons A (2018) Detecting fake news at its source. https://news.mit.edu/2018/mit-csail-machine-learning-system-detects-fake-news-from-source-1004. Accessed 13 Apr 2019
13. Emergent, 2019. Home. http://www.emergent.info/. Accessed 19 Jan 2020
14. European Broadcasting Union (2018) *'Fake News' and the Information Disorder.* EBU, Brussels
15. eyeWitness, 2019. Welcome to eyeWitness. eyewitnessproject.org. Accessed 15 Jan 2020
16. FactCheckNI, 2019. Methods. https://factcheckni.org/about/methods/. Accessed 25 Nov 2019
17. factcheck.org, 2019. Our Process. https://www.factcheck.org/our-process/. Accessed 26 Nov 2019

18. Factmata, 2019. Technology. https://factmata.com/technology.html. Accessed 16 Jan 2020
19. Finn S, Metatax P, Mustafaraj E (2014) Investigating rumour propagation with twitter trails, s.l.: arXiv.org
20. Flynn D, Nyhan B, Reifler J (2017) The nature and origins of misperceptions: understanding false and unsupported beliefs about politics. Adv Polit Psychol 38(S1):127–150
21. FotoForensics (2020) FotoForensics tutorials. https://fotoforensics.com/. Accessed 16 Jan 2020
22. Friedl J (2019) Jeffrey's image metadata viewer. http://exif.regex.info/exif.cgi. Accessed 20 Jan 2020
23. Full Fact (2019) Full Fact fights bad information. https://fullfact.org/. Accessed 23 Nov 2019
24. Gu L, Kropotov V, Yarochkin F (2017) The fake news machine: how propagandists abuse the internet and manipulate the public. s.l.: Trend Micro
25. IEEE Computer Society, 2019. Digital Forensics Meets Social Media: When Breaking News Hits Your Feed, a "Media Verification Assistant" Can Help Separate Fact from Fiction. https://www.computer.org/publications/tech-news/research/social-media-verification-assistant. Accessed 8 Jan 2020
26. Ieong RS (2006) FORZA–digital forensics investigation framework that incorporate legal issues. Digit Investig 3S:S29–S36
27. Jain L (2018) The technologies that are tackling fake news. https://www.itproportal.com/features/the-technologies-that-are-tackling-fake-news/. Accessed 14 Apr 2019
28. Jamieson KH, Campbell KK (2005) The interplay of influence: news, advertising, politics, and the internet, 6th edn. Wadsworth Publishing, Belmont, CA
29. Kershner JW (2011) The elements of news writing, 3rd edn. Pearson Allyn and Bacon, Boston, MA
30. Kruse WG, Heiser JG (2002) Computer forensics: incident response essentials. Indiana: Pearson Education
31. Kuklinski JH et al (2003) Misinformation and the currency of democratic citizenship. J Polit 62(3):790–816
32. McGonagle T (2017) "Fake news": false fears or real concerns? Neth Q Human Rights 35(4):203–209
33. Media Bias/Fact Check (2019) Methodology. https://mediabiasfactcheck.com/methodology/. Accessed 26 Nov 2019
34. Merriam-Webster (2019) Definition of news. https://www.merriam-webster.com/dictionary/news?utm_campaign=sd&utm_medium=serp&utm_source=jsonld. Accessed 02 Nov 2019
35. Ortiz DA (2018) Could this be the cure for fake news? http://www.bbc.com/future/story/20181114-could-this-game-be-a-vaccine-against-fake-news. Accessed 14 Apr 2019
36. Politifact (2018) The principles of the Truth-O-Meter: PolitiFact's methodology for independent fact-checking. https://www.politifact.com/. Accessed 29 Nov 2019
37. Politt M (2004) Six Blind Men from Indostan, s.l.: Digital Forensic Research Workshop
38. Rainie L, Anderson J, Albright J (2017) The future of free speech, trolls, anonymity, and fake news online. http://www.elon.edu/docs/e-web/imagining/surveys/2016_survey/Pew%20and%20Elon%20University%20Trolls%20Fake%20News%20Report%20Future%20of%20Internet%203.29.17.pdf. Accessed 11 Jan 2020
39. Richardson B (2006) The process of writing news: from information to story, 1st edn. Pearson, Boston
40. Ruiz C et al (2015) The maven project: management and authenticity verification of multimedia contents. IEEE, Turin
41. Rössler A et al (2019) FaceForensics++: learning to detect manipulated facial images. https://arxiv.org/abs/1901.08971. Accessed 19 Jan 2020
42. Shu K, Mahudeswaran D, Wang S, Liu DLAH (2018) FakeNewsNet: a data repository with news content, social context and dynamic information for studying fake news on social media. s.l.: Research Gate
43. Snopes (2019) snopes.com follows all industry guidelines for transparency in reporting. https://www.snopes.com/transparency/. Accessed 25 Nov 2019
44. stopFake.org (2019) About us. https://www.stopfake.org/en/about-us/. Accessed 29 Nov 2019

45. Storyful (2019) Investigations by Storyful. https://storyful.com/news-investigations/. Accessed 20 Jan 2020
46. Tandoc EC, Lim ZW, Ling R (2018) Defining "Fake News". Digit Journal 6(2):137–153
47. The Verge (2019) China makes it a criminal offense to publish deepfakes or fake news without disclosure. https://www.theverge.com/2019/11/29/20988363/china-deepfakes-ban-internet-rules-fake-news-disclosure-virtual-reality. Accessed 30 Nov 2019
48. TinEye (2020) MatchEngine finds duplicate, modified and derivative images. https://services.tineye.com/MatchEngine. Accessed 16 Jan 2020
49. Truepic (2019) A holistic approach to a complex problem. https://truepic.com/technology/. Accessed 16 Jan 2020
50. Truth or Fiction (2019) Our methodology and process. https://www.truthorfiction.com/our-methodology-and-process/. Accessed 24 Jan 2020
51. Truth or Fiction (2019) What we do. https://www.truthorfiction.com/about/. Accessed 20 Jan 2020
52. UNESCO (2018) Journalism, 'Fake News' & disinformation. United Nations Educational, Scientific and Cultural Organization, Paris
53. UNESCO (2018) Journalism, fake news & disinformation: handbook for journalism education and training. UNESCO, Paris
54. Victoria Rubin YCNC (2016) Deception detection for news: three types of fakes. In: Ontario, Proceedings of the association for information science and technology
55. Vishvas News (2019) 'Vishvas' news verification methodology. https://www.vishvasnews.com/methodology/. Accessed 21 Nov 2019
56. Vox Ukraine (2019) How-Check. https://voxukraine.org/en/voxcheck-f-a-q-2/#how-check. Accessed 23 Nov 2019
57. Williams M (2017) JPEGSnoop 1.8.0. https://www.downloadcrew.com/article/19770-jpegsnoop. Accessed 16 Jan 2020
58. Zampoglou M, Papadopoulos S, Kompatsiaris Y (2015) The Wild Web tampered image dataset. IEEE, Turin
59. www.parliament.uk (2019) Parliamentary Business. https://publications.parliament.uk/pa/cm201719/cmselect/cmcumeds/1791/179104.htm#_idTextAnchor001. Accessed 14 Apr 2019

# Current Challenges of Modern-Day Domestic Abuse

**Joe Mayhew and Hamid Jahankhani**

**Abstract** This chapter centres on the emergence of technology in cases of Domestic Abuse using two adjunct parts; (1) how digital coercive control using smart home devices is now an attack vector for abusers and (2) it sets out to highlight the use of a governance model incorporating a risk-based approach following the principles of the Cyber Security Maturity Model (CSMM). Recent reports in the media have identified cases of Domestic Abuse where attackers are using smart home devices to exert coercive control over their partners or former partners. Research importantly highlights a lack of awareness of technology facilitated Domestic Abuse by victims, support workers and law enforcement. This has resulted in the development of a new proposed framework titled SHADA—a Smart Home Anti Domestic Abuse framework, practical challenges and areas of e-policing to better engage stakeholders. The chapter concludes with additional areas of further research and provides an outlook on the use of newer technologies such as AI and considerations for the privacy of citizens in smart societies.

## 1 Introduction

The evolution of the Internet in the past three decades has restructured the way people communicate in business and private life. Together with the evolution of the Internet of Things (IoT), devices are connecting to the Internet more than ever before. From sensors generating temperature data, asking Alexa to check the weather, controlling light bulbs through a phone application or using a ride sharing app such as Uber to work are only few day to day examples where choices, actions and activities are

J. Mayhew
Ernst & Young LLP, London, UK
e-mail: Joe.Mayhew@uk.ey.com

H. Jahankhani (✉)
Northumbria University, London, UK
e-mail: Hamid.jahankhani@northumbria.ac



H. Jahankhani et al. (eds.), *Policing in the Era of AI and Smart Societies*,
Advanced Sciences and Technologies for Security Applications,
https://doi.org/10.1007/978-3-030-50613-1_12

being recorded, transmitted and stored, hopefully securely, by the seemingly free technology-driven conveniences [15].

With these innovations, technology and telecommunications companies developing digital and networked solutions have started integrating three technological systems into urban cites: Internet of Things (IoT), cloud computing and big data analytics. With this system integration, the term "smart city" has been defined. As smart cities are driven on the data input of the citizens, this poses challenges to the security and expectations of privacy. According to [11], "capturing Personally Identifiable Information (PII) as well as data about citizens households and linking this data together to create profiles of people, places citizens in order to make decisions about them" [11]. From the legal point of view, privacy breaches are usually covered under the General Data Protection Regulation (GDPR) in Europe and set of privacy laws in the United States (US) [11]. Except privacy issues, there are other security concerns in smart cities. Smart cities are prone to cyberattacks and another issue is the protection of sensitive data after being collected. It has also become evident that manufacturers of "smart city systems" have little or no experience securing their systems.

Cloud data security Authentication and access control are the main security challenges. Data and resources are stored in various services across the internet which can be accessible by any unauthorized person. Therefore, could services should have identity management system to authenticating users and services. Access control is key component of data security which authenticate and authorize the users to data and resources which they are allowed to see and use [12, 13]. Access control process is to ensure that users are actually valid users and they have access to the company recourses they are trying to access. Authentication is a method which is used to validate the user who is claiming to be and authentication itself is not enough to protect data. It needed another additional layer of security which is authorization which control if user is allowed to access the resources or make any transaction which is being attempted.

Artificial Intelligence (AI) has been a concept that has been part of public discourse for decades, often depicted within science fiction films or debates on how intelligent machines will take over the world relegating the human race to a mundane servile existence in supporting the new AI order [7]. Therefore, the growing use of AI and the speed of its technological advancements may also lead to a lack of understanding regarding security and vulnerabilities that may affect Artificial Intelligence engines.

With the rapid development and deployment of a new generation of artificial intelligence (AI) algorithms and products, AI is playing an increasingly important role in everyday life and is having a significant impact on the very fabric of the modern society. In particular, AI models and algorithms have been widely adopted in a variety of decision-making scenarios, such as criminal justice, traffic control, financial loans, and medical diagnosis [21, 25]. However, a severe security threat to the existing DL algorithms has been discovered by the research community: Adversaries can easily fool DL models by perturbing benign samples without being discovered by humans [19].

The drive to develop smarter cities and smarter societies, will ultimately increase demand for pervasive network access intensifying the necessity for 4G and 5G technology as smart technology relies heavily on access to the Internet. However, this eagerness for further 4G and 5G coverage could have far reaching implications such as making access to the Internet easier for abusers to exert control over their victims from afar.

The term cyber-violence is increasingly working its way into society and refers to repeated abuse committed by one person (the abuser) against a current or former intimate partner through the use of digital technology. The most common methods of harassment and stalking use easily obtainable digital technologies such as phones, tablets, computers and social networking web-sites. With the emergence of smart technologies changing our everyday lives and assisting us to try and live in a more secure and convenient environment, it is being used in reverse as an instrument of psychological warfare on a victim by a perpetrator without any geographical boundaries, [5]. These devices with a connection to the internet, sometimes referred to as 'IoT' devices can be remotely controlled and activated using voice commands or smartphone applications such as smart speakers, wearables etc.

Whilst domestic abuse is not a new subject, it has transcended through the years. Although an outdated patriarchal belief, where men were the head of the family and were encouraged to chastise their wives albeit without losing their temper, this was not always the case. Anna Clark, a professor of history at the University of Minnesota discusses domestic violence in a historical sense [2]. In Clark's paper, she cites work produced by Pomeroy [14], specifically a book titled "*The Murder of Regilla*" which documents the murder of *Appia Annia Regilla Atilia Caucidia Tertulla*, born around A.D. 125 and subsequent trial of her husband following the accusation of him killing his wife over a trivial matter.

During the 1950–80s, Domestic Abuse was satirised in comic strips such as those by the twentieth Century cartoonist Reg Smythe, creator of Andy Capp. Smythe styled his character on an English northern wife beater [22].

Modern understanding and acceptance of domestic abuse has changed over the years, the following timeline from the Guardian [20], provides a brief overview of changes in English law since the late nineteenth Century.

The following is a timeline of Domestic Violence Legislation across England and Wales:

- 1860—Law of Coverture
  - At the point of marriage, a husband became legally responsible for the actions of both his wife and children. This meant he was entitled to use physical or verbal abuse to control their behaviour.
- 1870—Married Woman's Property Act
  - Before 1870, when a woman married, her property automatically became her husband's. After this act, any money she earned or inherited while married stayed hers.

- 1895—Curfew on wife beating
  - This city of London byelaw made hitting your wife between the hours of 10 pm and 7 am illegal—because the noise was keeping people awake.
- 1923—Matrimonial Causes Act
  - This act marked a big change in divorce law. Before, a wife had to prove her husband had been unfaithful and show evidence of other faults. After 1923, adultery could be a sole reason for divorce for women as well as men.
- 1956—Sexual Offences Act
  - This was the first-time rape was defined under specific criteria, such as incest, sex with a girl under 16, no consent, use of drugs, anal sex and impersonation.
- 1961—Contraceptive Pill
  - Contraception was made available on the NHS irrespective of marital status or husband's permission.
- 1971—The first safe house
  - The charity Refuge opens the first safe house in Chiswick, west London, for women and children fleeing domestic abuse.
- 1975—First select committee
  - A government select committee on violence in marriage is created and recommends a minimum of one family place in a refuge per 10,000 people.
- 1976—Domestic Violence and Matrimonial Proceedings Act
  - This was the first legislation dedicated to combating domestic violence. It gave survivors new rights by offering civil protection orders (injunctions) for those at risk of abuse.
- 1977—Housing Act (Homeless Persons)
  - Women and children at risk of violence were acknowledged as homeless. This meant they gained the right to state-funded temporary accommodation.
- 1988—Housing Act
  - Rents became deregulated making it harder for survivors of domestic violence who tried to escape and find private accommodation. Though some argue it helped by developing more supported housing and refuge services.
- 1989—Children Act
  - The law improved levels of child protection and parental responsibility but mostly ignored domestic violence.

- 1991—Criminal Rape Act
  - Before 1991 it was a husband's legal right to rape his wife—marriage implied consent for sexual intercourse. This was the first time a woman had legal protection from marital rape.
- 1996—Family Law Act
  - Important changes to this law gave law enforcement automatic powers of arrest where violence had been used or threatened.
- 2003—Inter-ministerial group on domestic violence is established
  - This group received crucial evidence on the scale of domestic violence and use of refuges. Women's Aid (a charity dedicated to ending domestic violence) played a significant role in providing testimony.
- 2004—Domestic Violence, Crime and Victims Act
  - This made common assault an arrestable offence. This meant that law enforcement could arrest a suspect immediately, rather than leaving them with someone vulnerable while they applied for a warrant.
- 2005—Home Office publishes Domestic Violence: A national report
  - This report was seen as government's first public commitment to taking responsibility for tackling the issue through policy.
- 2010—Government strategy is set out to end violence against women and girls
  - The strategy developed a 2011 plan which included financial commitments to support rape crisis centres and specialist training for health workers in the treatment of survivors.
- 2014—Clare's Law
  - A law is implemented across England and Wales giving people the right to ask law enforcement about a partner's history of domestic abuse.

Based on this timeline developed by the Guardian and prior to 2014, the previous 2000 years have focused solely on the physical aspect of abuse in intimate partner relationships. Aside from the obvious fact that mainstream electronic computing has only been around since the later part of the twentieth Century, recent abuse has taken a more intangible path. Exerting abuse through non-physical means, such as mental, verbal or coercive control. This not a new thing, although the medium to inflict this abuse has moved to a more modern, digital attack vector such as through social media, tracking applications or mobile devices or reading personal emails and text messages.

## 2 Societal Examples

Woman's Aid, a non-profit organisation devoted to supporting victims of domestic abuse in the UK, describes coercive control as a method for controlling a person in order to make them dependent upon their attacker, through isolation, exploitation and deprivation of the victim's independence in their normal day to day activities [24].

Woman's Aid provides a non-exhaustive set of examples of coercive control:

- Isolating you from friends and family
- Depriving you of basic needs, such as food
- Monitoring your time
- Monitoring you via online communication tools or spyware
- Taking control over aspects of your everyday life, such as where you can go, who you can see, what you can wear and when you can sleep
- Depriving you access to support services, such as medical services
- Repeatedly putting you down, such as saying you're worthless
- Humiliating, degrading or dehumanising you
- Controlling your finances
- Making threats or intimidating you [24].

The CPS (Crown Prosecution Service), admits that signs of coercive control may not be immediately obvious to victims [3, 4]. Dating of this information has provided difficult, although an initial assessment dates it around 2015 or onwards (due to a 2015 case being referenced). The CPS states that domestic abuse takes many forms, typically person to person. However, their advice recognises the use of technology and specifically refers to mobile communications, internet communications (such as email and social media) but also mentions "other web-enabled methods" [4]. There is little more information other than this, but at least there is some mention of it. As this space (and the law) matures, there could be further examples provided along with existing, more well-known methods such as email, texts and social media.

Domestic Abuse, Intimate Partner Violence or Coercive Control can take many discreet forms in a digital setting, the following non-exhaustive list outlines some of the key examples of attack vectors:

- Social Stalking—befriending friends of friends on social media
- Reading emails or text
- Leveraging gifts to children such as mobile phones, laptops or tablets with cameras
- Home surveillance such as Internet connected CCTV
- Smart heating controls
- Smart door entry systems
- Personal Assistants—Amazon Alexa, Google
- Smart lighting controls
- Internet connected home audio systems.

Some of these examples can take place whilst both the abuser and victim are still in the same property.

A high proportion of the other examples can take place once an abuser has left the family home. These could take the form of a victim's heating being repeatedly disabled during winter and there is no clear reason why. It could take the form of a smart door entry system constantly ringing. Personal Assistants such as Amazon's Alexa being used to record conversations in the home.

These examples can range from incredibly frustrating, frightening to terrifying for a victim. This is especially so if the victim does not know how to reduce access to these devices remotely, or if the devices were bought and configured by their former partner-come-abuser and removal presents further challenges such as how to remove these devices. In some cases, it may not be possible to remove them and then the challenge of removing access and securing the devices can become an even more difficult situation.

## 3 Current Challenges and Modern-Day Domestic Abuse

More recently, advanced methods for exerting control in a domestic household has been highlighted through smart home or IoT devices. IoT is primarily a marketing term used for everyday devices connected to the internet so that they can be configured, controlled and/or viewed through a web client (e.g. Internet Explorer, Edge, Chrome or Safari) or application, typically through a smart phone or tablet (another IoT device), [23]. Examples of IoT devices include digital assistants such as Amazon's Alexa, Google's Assist, Apple's Siri or Microsoft's Cortana; heating controls such as Hive, Nest, or Honeywell; doorbells or digital locks such as those from Ring or Yale and even home audio systems plus many more examples of IoT (fridges, cookers, toasters, coffee machines), the list is becoming endless. With this explosion of connected devices, it is becoming increasingly difficult to keep up to date.

**It should be noted that there is an argument that the recent abusive actions—digital coercive control, could be considered advanced, yet they could also be considered a simpler abuse method without the feeling of consequence to the abuser**.

Why the argument? Consider the following, the attacks are performed using highly technologically advanced devices that connect to home networks, across the Internet and finally to mobile devices (typically). In between the home automation device and the abuser is a vast amount of silicone, electronics and miles of cabling transmitting and receiving millions of binary ones and zeros orchestrated by millions of lines of software code (culminative). A highly complex mesh of electronics, with the ability to deliver an abuser's threat payload, inflicting misery on their targets. Conversely, with all of this technology in place, designed, manufactured and maintained by nearly a million IT professionals in the UK alone [18], attackers don't need to know how to wire a network, how to setup servers, how to code software. It's already been done. The delivery medium has already been created for reasons other than for someone to use the technology to inflict abuse towards a victim. The attack could be from any location where there is connectivity to the Internet. Providing there is access, it can be instigated without geographic boundary, without the fear of being caught, or without seeing the misery inflicted and therefore without feeling there are consequences for their actions.

It is in this respect, that it is a simpler method for abusers to cause harm, as technology is that advanced where it creates convenience of actions that previously took a moderate degree of thought and physical presence.

Mobile technologies such as 4G provide an integral medium for abusers with mobile devices and their victims. The pervasive access to the Internet through mobile technology provides a "from anywhere and at anytime" capability for abusers. The additional explosion of media-rich supplying connectivity such as 5G adds a new dimension—the ability to launch attacks in greater frequencies, at faster speeds and in higher volumes.

Consider the ability to exert coercive control through the delivery of larger payloads, such as those to smart TVs, smart home power networks or even electric vehicles. The faster network access and edge computing benefits that 5G provides, could be very well utilised by savvier abusers—or even "abusers for hire" in future smart societies and cities, [5, 6].

Work conducted by the Home Office on domestic abuse and the economic and social costs as a direct result state that in England and Wales in 2016/2017, this cost was c.£66billion [9]. This figure comprises costs to health services, policing, victim services and lost output among many other components. Based on details from the Office for National Statistics, the individual cost per victim equates to £34,015, however this is an average and depending on the exact crime, costs can be significantly more according to the Home Office.

The Home Office states the figure is under-estimated as it does not fully reflect the physical harm that victims sustain.

During the COVID-19 pandemic, reported figures on UK Domestic Abuse resulting in the murder of women by men were approximately double the average for the same periods in previous years [16]. The stress associated with financial concerns, living in close quarters for a prolonged period and uncertainty for the future were all quoted reasons for femicide (and some cases child homicide). The inability to access support services for women during the lockdown were possible reasons for this, although the lockdown presented the unescapable abusive environment, behind closed doors whilst isolated in the home.

In addition, charities reported calls about domestic abuse during the lockdown increased by 120% resulting in nearly 100 arrests per day by the Met police [10]. This highlights two key issues: firstly, abuse in intimate partner relationships can be concentrated during a time where there is no escape for victims when they are stuck in doors for 24 h per day and secondly access to critical support services can be impeded should an abuser withhold access to a telephone or the Internet from a victim.

## 4 SHADA—A Proposed Framework

There is no straightforward solution to the issue of digital coercive control. Abusers are finding more intuitive ways to excerpt control and abuse their victims. Technology companies inadvertently make it easier to access our homes and a by-product of this is abusers are taking advantage of this. Furthermore, trying to prove any of this is extremely difficult without the adequate awareness, training or guidance.

Analysis of prior research into digital coercive control and interviews with UK domestic abuse charities three solutions can be proposed. When combined, they provide a theoretical framework to support the reduction of Domestic Abuse, specifically in cases of digital coercive control.

The following outlines a theoretical framework based on initial investigations called **SHADA**: a **S**mart **H**ome **A**nti **D**omestic **A**buse framework.

The SHADA framework highlights three key areas based on previous research:

- **Legislative Amendments**
  - Following research into the UK Domestic Abuse bill, it lacked substance around critical elements such as digital coercive control. As part of SHADA, amendments to the Domestic Abuse bill should include provisions for digital coercive control and protection mechanisms as well as further training and support for law enforcement and support services.
  - There was insufficient information within the Crown Prosecution Services literature that would provide guidance for law enforcement and legal parties. A further legislative amendment would be for the CPS to update their guidance to provide examples of digital coercive control.
- **The role of Technology Developers**
  - Define a functional standard to provide the ability to easily obtain evidence in the event a smart home device is used in cases of Domestic Abuse.
  - Provide a mechanism for dual management of smart home devices to ensure that no single resident is in control.
  - Consider using a standards-based approach (RFC or ISO) for the SHADA framework that gives confidence to consumers.
- **Awareness**
  - Campaigns via TV advertisements, posters in social premises and social media aimed to raise public awareness of digital coercive control.
  - Training for law enforcement on how to recognise instances of digital coercive control and methods to collect evidence.
  - Training for Domestic Abuse support staff to help victims identify examples of digital coercive control.

The aims of this framework are:

1. Ensure there is a legal policy is in place to prosecute abusers and protect victims of Domestic Abuse in cases of digital coercive control.
2. Ensure that technology can instil confidence to buyers of consumer electronics for the smart home and that it is difficult to be used in cases of Domestic Abuse without leaving evidence of activity. Potentially using a Kitemark quality standard as provided by the British Standards Institute [1].
3. Raise awareness for

    a. the public to increase prevention,
    b. law enforcement to recognise digital coercive control & collect evidence and
    c. Domestic Abuse support staff to be able and provide appropriate advice.

## 5 Practical Use and Challenges

The success of implementing a framework such as SHADA relies on an appropriate level of governance and stakeholder engagement across Government, Law Enforcement, Social Services, Public awareness and Original Equipment Manufacturers (OEMs). Applying Cyber Security Maturity Modelling (CSMM) to the framework aligned with stakeholders, can aid in demonstrating the key steps to increasing maturity in society as this drives a risk-based approach highlighting the key controls.

The first stage is to develop a charter and identify the stakeholders and the key outcomes the framework aims to provide. The charter must articulate the who, what and when in the following stages. The charter should provide a clear indication of the stakeholders, their roles and the commitment required within the overall program. The charter should also include the guiding principles of how the program will be governed. First and foremost being the reason why this is here in the first place—to improve the lives of domestic abuse victims and potential victims in the future.

Examples of stakeholders include:

- Government

    - Policing: raising awareness on how to support victims and identify and capture abusers
    - Crown Prosecution Services: examples of abuse activities using digital coercive control to better aid convictions
    - Social Services: at the forefront of supporting victims, developing consistent guidance to provide to victims

- OEMs

    - The designers and manufacturers of technology can play a crucial part by introducing features that are safer and can increase consumer confidence

- GCHQ
  - Increasing public awareness of digital coercive control, raising concerns of privacy and cyber risk
- Academia
  - Working towards increased research and collaboration, academic stakeholders can provide much needed focus among key questions including.

The second stage would be to perform a risk assessment and identify controls as part of the maturity model. Identifying gaps between current and future knowledge requirements/solutions. Engaging with the stakeholders as part of the process will be fundamental to the long-term success. Support from stakeholders will also aid in the weighting and prioritization of gaps leading to value-driven outcomes that will ultimately improve the situation for victims or potentially reduce the likelihood of domestic abuse in a digital setting.

The third stage requires the development of a roadmap to correct the gaps. Grouped on a per-stakeholder basis, the roadmap should provide a clear set of programs that drive the key outcomes across the framework. Supported by the collaborative work with the stakeholders and the wider public including domestic abuse victim's and industry support workers. The roadmap should have clear milestones, check-in points and key measurements of success to ensure this meets the desired outcomes.

Finally, the fourth stage is about providing an executable plan that can be delivered back to stakeholders demonstrating how and where to remediate the issues and improve the lives of domestic victims. This plan, developed with the stakeholders, should show the milestones and costs to achieve the outcomes set out in the charter at the beginning of the process. The plan will enable the stakeholders to conduct their own due diligence and have adequate time to review and where required, request funding.

## 6 E-Policing

The following looks to highlight the lack of awareness and training for the purposes of law enforcement and evidence gathering in e-policing. This is to aid the pursuit of a criminal conviction and protect victims from further harm by deterring abusers.

### *6.1 Training Requirements*

Additional training had been cited as a main area to improve the response from law enforcement and aid them in the identification and prosecution of suspected domestic abusers using technology to excerpt digital coercive control.

The following table provides some examples of the training required:

| Awareness | Identification | Digital forensics considerations |
|---|---|---|
| *Examples highlighting changes in abuser's behaviour* | *How to identify digital coercive control* | *What evidence could be gathered* |
| Abusers using CCTV to monitor their victim | Victim reports that they receive text messages from their abuser when they immediately return home or leave the home although the abuser is not in the vicinity | Subject to appropriate legal documentation, obtain Geo location information of the abuser's mobile phone<br>Check the local logs of the CCTV system<br>With permission of the victim, check their mobile to correlate the time of the messages with Geo location and the CCTV system logs |
| Abuser's changing smart heating controls of their victim's home | Victim reports that heating controls are reset unexpectedly, or dramatically change for no apparent reason | Check the heating system logs, some (but not all) provide the ability to track changes<br>Check ISP logs for incoming connections to the smart heating system<br>Check that the victim's controller has not been locked out |
| Abuser's controlling behaviour of smart assistants | Victim reports that smart home assistants begin acting strangely such as the default language has changed, there are inappropriate messages being played or alerts sounding at unsociable times | Check the application log of the smart assistant |

## 7 Future Research

Working with support organisations and victims can further increase awareness for law enforcement where feedback on examples of the abuse victims have been experiencing will be invaluable in identifying and pursuing abusers. However, this must be done in a manner sensitive to victims and therefore may not be practical in all circumstances.

One of the key challenges is collecting evidence to pursue a criminal conviction. Evidence could take multiple forms although this could be subject to ambiguity that could be detrimental to securing a prosecution. An example of this is where there are unsuitable examples provided by the CPS as a guide and as such, additional guidance may need to be sought such as the non-exhaustive examples listed previously that could support law enforcement in these cases.

The SHADA framework in principal, is a hybrid approach that attempts to bridge the gap between the social sciences aspect and the cyber security conflicts of digital coercive control. The SHADA framework could benefit from applying governance controls more familiar to Cyber Security Modelling, a risk-based approach to managing controls in future research.

The following table illustrates an example of this early investigation into the model with specific focus on technical controls to reduce the risk of domestic abuse through digital coercive control:

Former partner leaves the home but still has access to smart devices in the home:

| Risk | SHADA component | Example | Risk level |
|---|---|---|---|
| *Domestic abuse scenario* | *Relation to the SHADA component* | *Example control* | *Risk level* |
| Unable to access log data on smart home devices | Legislative protection | Mandatory logging of access data held in the vendors secure cloud environment, accessible only with court order abiding to local laws | Medium |
| Smart home devices are still accessible by a former partner | Consumer confidence | Simpler ability to remove access to devices, authorising only those that are permitted | High |
| The administrative access controls are still in the sole position of the former partner/abuser | Consumer confidence | Dual administrative access to devices by default—e.g. using a two-person rule with potential vendor remote lockout | Medium |
| Disbelief of the victim's complaint of digital coercive control by social or law enforcement services | Raise awareness | Creation of training material and mandatory awareness training for social services and law enforcement at a national level to ensure consistency of knowledge transfer | High |

All of this is fine providing the appropriate level of governance can be applied. This means implementing best practices that can be conveyed to all of society in terms how to detect and protect. The list could become exhaustive, not only because technology moves at unprecedented rates, but because the ability to capture and mitigate all the ways in which technology can be used to exert digital coercive control is a mammoth endeavour.

Further considerations for future research include the fields of Artificial Intelligence, Predictive Analytics and Machine Learning. The application of these newer technologies to devices used in cases of domestic abusive could yeild greater results for smart societies. Imagine analytics from the applications used to control smart devices with the geo-location data and combining it with Artificial Intelligence could expose abusers using technology for digital coercive control in cases of domestic abuse. This will undoubtedly raise concerns of privacy and the potential for misuse either in a commercial or societal setting. Who owns the data, how could this be used in more nefarious ways, how could we ensure privacy concerns are met—are all these crucial in building public confidence or destroying it?

## 8 Conclusion

Adapting to the fast-changing landscape of digital coercive control is exacerbated by even faster changing smart home technology in smart societies. Trying to stay up to date with technology is a futile effort as new vendors bring newer products to market and even newer features out quicker and quicker. Part of problem is first recognising that abusers are using smart home technology to coercively control their victims. Recognition that these types of attacks are taking place will provide some comfort to victims, but not much. Secondly, how can this be proven? All things leave some form of digital fingerprint, a log entry or other forms of evidence that can be collected and submitted into evidence.

The SHADA framework provides a multi approach methodology to recognising the issues, creating awareness and proposing amendments to legislation where appropriate. It incorporates a mixed approach as there is no single answer. There is a justification for technology manufacturers to do more and the SHADA framework could give the opportunity to build in features that could provide consumers with increased confidence such as shared administrative responsibilities of smart home devices. There is however, a counter argument that this could mean less security in smart home devices.

This is why the introduction of risk based controls will be the key to driving change, introducing a charter to outline the key milestones, identifying gaps and working with stakeholders such as government, original equipment manufacturers and law enforcement to develop an executable plan with specific outcomes help drive the much needed change which will be a necessity for smart cities and smart societies of the future.

## References

1. BSI (2019) BSI Kitemark™. https://www.bsigroup.com/en-GB/kitemark/product-testing/. Accessed 1 Sept 2019
2. Clark A (2011) Domestic violence, past and present. J Women's Hist 23(3):193–202
3. Conseil De L'Europe (2011) Council of Europe convention on preventing and combating violence against women and domestic violence, 12 April 2011. https://rm.coe.int/168046031c. Accessed 27 Aug 2019

4. Crown Prosecution Service (2015) Domestic abuse guidelines for prosecutors. https://www.cps.gov.uk/legal-guidance/domestic-abuse-guidelines-prosecutors. Accessed 20 July 2019
5. cybersmartcities.com (2018) The overwhelming world of smart cities—cyber-kinetic and privacy threats in smart cities, 11 March 2018. https://cybersmartcities.com/privacy/smart-city-cyber-kinetic-privacy-risks/. Accessed 10 Mar 2020
6. digitalpulse.pwc.com.au (2017) Why we need smart cities, 11 March 2017. digitalpulse.pwc.com.au, https://www.digitalpulse.pwc.com.au/why-we-need-smart-cities/. Accessed 11 Mar 2020
7. Dwivedi Y, Hughes L, Ismagilova E, Aarts G, Crispin Tom, .... Michael D (2019) Artificial Intelligence (AI): multidisciplinary perspectives on emerging challenges, opportunities, and agenda for research, practice and policy. Int J Inform Manag 101
8. Gillray J (1782) Sir Francis Buller, 1st Bt ('Judge Thumb'). National Portrait Gallery, London, England
9. Home Office—econ (2019) The economic and social costs of domestic abuse, January 2019. https://assets.publishing.service.gov.uk/government/uploads/system/uploads/attachment_data/file/772180/horr107.pdf. Accessed 29 Aug 2019
10. Hymas C (2020) More than 4,000 domestic abusers arrested as victims calls to police increase by 30 per cent in lockdown, 24 April 2020. Accessed Telegraph https://www.telegraph.co.uk/politics/2020/04/24/4000-domestic-abusers-arrested-victims-calls-police-increase/
11. Kitchin R (2016) Getting smarter about smart cities. Department of the Taoiseach on behalf of the Government Data Forum, Dublin, Ireland
12. Martin G (2019a) The meaning and origin of the expression: rule of thumb. https://www.phrases.org.uk/meanings/rule-of-thumb.html. Accessed 27 May 2019
13. Martin JA (2019b) What is access control? A key component of data security. https://www.csoonline.com/article/3251714/what-is-access-control-a-key-component-of-data-security.html. Accessed 16 Mar 2020
14. Pomeroy SB (2007) The murder of Regilla: a case of domestic violence in antiquity. Hardvard University Press, Cambridge, MA
15. Sharma S (2020) Data privacy and GDPR handbook. Wiley, Hoboken, NJ, USA
16. Smith KI (2020). Coronavirus doesn't cause men's violence against women, 15 April 2020. Accessed Counting Dead Women https://kareningalasmith.com/2020/04/15/coronavirus-doesnt-cause-mens-violence-against-women/
17. Sommers CH (n.d.) The "Rule of Thumb for Wife-Beating" hoax. https://www.infotextmanuscripts.org/djetc/other_hoff_thumb.html. Accessed 1 July 2019
18. Statistica (2018). Number of employed information technology professionals in the United Kingdom (UK) in 2018, by occupation (1,000 s), 17 September 2018. https://www.statista.com/statistics/778333/information-technology-professionals-employed-uk/. Accessed 22 June 2019
19. Szegedy C, Zaremba W, Sutskever I, Bruna J (2013) Intriguing properties of neural networks. arXiv preprint arXiv 61(99):1312. https://arxiv.org/abs/1312.6199. Accessed 29 June 2020
20. The Guardian Newspaper (2014) Domestic violence legislation in England and Wales: timeline. https://www.theguardian.com/society-professionals/ng-interactive/2014/nov/28/domestic-violence-legislation-timeline. Accessed 27 May 2019
21. un.org (2017) World population projected to reach 9.8 billion in 2050, and 11.2 billion in 2100, 10 March 2017. https://www.un.org/development/desa/en/news/population/world-population-prospects-2017.html. Accessed 11 Mar 2020
22. University of Kent—British Cartoon Archive (2016) Reg Smythe [Andy Capp]. https://www.cartoons.ac.uk/cartoonist-biographies/c-d/RegSmythe_AndyCapp.html. Accessed 27 May 2019
23. weforum.org (2018) 5 big challenges facing big cities of the future, 11 March 2018. https://www.weforum.org/agenda/2018/10/the-5-biggest-challenges-cities-will-face-in-the-future/. Accessed 11 Mar 2020

24. Women's Aid (2015) What is coercive control? https://www.womensaid.org.uk/information-support/what-is-domestic-abuse/coercive-control/. Accessed 19 July 2019
25. Wu W, Gong K, Huang T (2020) Ethical principles and governance technology development of AI in China. Engineering

# Correction to: Predictive Policing in 2025: A Scenario

**Kevin Macnish, David Wright, and Tilimbe Jiya**

## Correction to: Chapter "Predictive Policing in 2025: A Scenario" in: H. Jahankhani et al. (eds.), *Policing in the Era of AI and Smart Societies*, Advanced Sciences and Technologies for Security Applications, https://doi.org/10.1007/978-3-030-50613-1_9

Chapter (9), "Predictive Policing in 2025: A Scenario" was previously published non-open access. It has now been changed to open access under a CC BY 4.0 license and the copyright holder updated to 'The Author(s)'. The book has also been updated with this change.

The updated version of this chapter can be found at https://doi.org/10.1007/978-3-030-50613-1_9



H. Jahankhani et al. (eds.), *Policing in the Era of AI and Smart Soceties*,
Advanced Sciences and Technologies for Security Applications,
https://doi.org/10.1007/978-3-030-50613-1_13

Printed in the USA
CPSIA information can be obtained
at www.ICGtesting.com
LVHW010804280224
773030LV00003B/146

9 783030 506124